Psychology of Learning and Instruction

Psychology of Learning and Instruction

A Performance-Based Course

Robert G. Packard

University of Missouri

Charles E. Merrill Publishing Company
A Bell & Howell Company
Columbus, Ohio

Published by
Charles E. Merrill Publishing Company
A Bell & Howell Company
Columbus, Ohio 43216

International Standard Book Number: 0-675-08761-9

Library of Congress Catalog Card Number: 74-12593

Cover photo: Courtesy of the National Education Association.

4 5 6—80 79 78

Printed in the United States of America.

To   Jack Michael
        Wells Hively
        Marv Daley

Contents

Section II: Instruction

Section III: Evaluation

33   Preparing Traditional Achievement Tests   403

34   Evaluation of Instruction   429

35   Individualizing Instruction   445

36   Design Your Own Instructional System   457

37   Design Your Own Management System   459

38   Presentation and Evaluation Project   461

39   You-Name-It Project   463

40   Review and Application II   465

      For Further Study: An Annotated Bibliography   *471*

      Index   *475*

To The Student

Many texts simply *present information.* This text is designed to help you *develop skills.* If you work through each unit as suggested, not only will you become able to talk intelligently about the basic processes of learning and instruction but you will also acquire skills that are basic to teaching at any level and in any subject matter area.

Few topics are as intriguing and critical as the question of how a dependent and relatively incompetent infant becomes an independent, flexible adult with an amazing variety of complex skills. Once a person's genetic pool is determined at conception, very little occurs to change the developmental process. But what that person learns after birth is tremendously dependent on the people and events in his environment.

To the teacher, this implies not only a frightening responsibility but also the exciting opportunity to treat learning and instruction as a science. It means that a teacher can learn to analyze the conditions under which learning occurs, measure relationships between these conditions, and define the critical methodologies.

It is possible to predict and control learning in the classroom. The skill of teaching can indeed be taught.

Most educational psychology courses are justly rated rather low in interest and usefulness. One important reason is that most educational psychology textbooks simply present a mass of research data on the factors that may affect learning. Teachers, however, want and need to know how to organize the important data into a complete instructional system that will actually help them be effective teachers.

This text attempts to teach you basic knowledge and skills that are directly related to successful teaching. The first section will teach you the basic principles of human behavior and give you some skills in applying them to classroom situations. The second section teaches you the basic skills of analyzing instructional tasks and integrating the principles of learning with this analysis into an effective technology of teaching. The third section gives you skills in testing and evaluating the progress of your students and the effectiveness of your instruction; it also guides you in putting everything together into an effective instructional system. Each section also offers a variety of application projects and enrichment readings so that you can extend your knowledge base and practice your teaching skills.

The approach here is not eclectic. The learning focus is primarily that of operant conditioning. The instructional focus is primarily that of behavioral task analysis, functional presentation methods, and criterion-referenced evaluation for mastery learning.

The approach is not intended to be exhaustive. There are many other areas of educational psychology which are often interesting and sometimes useful in instructional settings. The choices of what to include and which approach to emphasize were primarily functional choices. On the basis of applied research and project data and the author's personal experiences, these chosen approaches appear not merely to be compatible but more importantly to be impressively effective, applied methodologies. They seem to achieve what they were deliberately designed to achieve—success in the classroom.

In working with each successive unit, you will find the following suggestions helpful:

1. Before studying, skim through the unit to get an overview. Focus on the paragraph headings, the objectives, the diagrams, the italicized words, and particularly the study-guide questions interspersed throughout the unit. These questions reflect precisely what you are expected to be able to do or say when you have finished the unit.
2. Begin studying the unit until you come to the first set of study-guide questions. Test yourself on these questions, check your answers against the preceding page(s) to see if your answers are exact and complete and your examples appropriate.
3. Continue through the unit in this way. If you have any doubts or problems with any point, be sure to check with your instructor soon. It is very important that you master all the objectives before proceeding to the next unit.

Several thousands of students have worked through these units in a self-paced, individualized way, with short mastery quizzes after each unit. The successes and problems, comments and critiques of each student, incorporated in three previous revisions of this text, have contributed immensely to the clarity and effectiveness of the units.

I am also indebted to many others who, like the students who helped develop these units, have been careful and patient teachers and generous friends, particularly Bill Franzen and Hans Olsen, Doris Knight and Sandy Laham, and my wife Sally.

R.G.P.
November, 1974

Psychology of Learning and Instruction

Section I

An arrow indicates that prior units are prerequisites for the next unit. A △ identifies a key application/synthesis unit for purposes of summative evaluation.

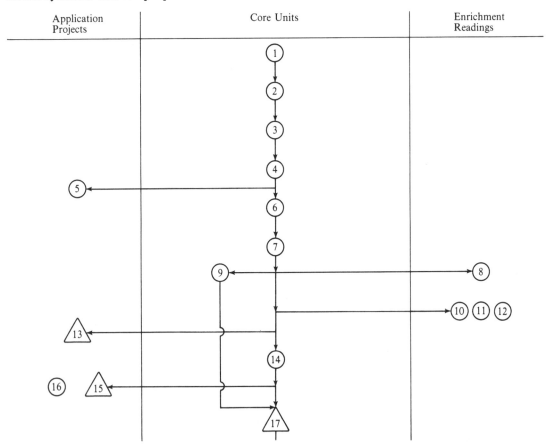

| Application Projects | Core Units | Enrichment Readings |

Learning

If you want to understand the process of learning and instruction, and especially if you want to learn how to teach well, you will need more than a knowledge of learning theories or lots of experience with good teachers. You will need to be able to analyze behavior (that is, the observable actions of people—like students and teachers). You also will need to be able to arrange things and events and your behaviors so that a student's behavior changes. Learning is, after all, a change in behavior. When a student learns to read or add or create or experiment, his behavior changes—he begins to do and say things that he did not do or say before. Perhaps, in addition to behavior changes, there are other things that change in his mind or soul. But you as a teacher won't be able to observe those "inner" changes, so they can't be of much use to you in determining whether a student has learned something, what you should teach next, how to handle interfering discipline problems, etc. By focusing carefully on the observable events, you will have the information you need to make good instructional decisions.

Units 1–3 introduce you to the science of learning and instruction. In these units you will learn some general terms and procedures related to analyzing the teaching-learning process and the specific factors that determine when and whether learning takes place, and to predicting and controlling this process.

The next two units introduce you to some basic skills in observing and recording behavior patterns and relationships. Of course you can already observe behavior patterns and make judgments about the important functional relationships among these events—you do it everyday in your relationships with other people. Many times your judgments are correct, but often they are not. Where the futures of many minds are riding on your decisions, it's

3

important that you be as sure as you can about every important decision you make. In the classroom there is simply no just substitute for thorough and carefully collected data as a base for your decision making.

In future units, you will learn to integrate these skills with others in carrying out an actual behavior change project of your own.

The principles and procedures that you will have learned in the first few units are only general. Your knowledge of them will enable you to handle many of the typical classroom learning and discipline situations, but not all of them. The experimental analysis of behavior has produced a large body of specific detail and refinement regarding these basic principles. The next several units will teach you some of these details, and your knowledge of them will equip you to handle some of the less typical instructional problems so that you can be effective with each of your students. In addition, you will see how the principles of behavior analysis are applicable to a wide variety of human settings, especially educational.

Units 9–13 focus primarily on practical application of the principles of behavior analysis. You will read a behavioral analysis of how schools have traditionally controlled student behavior and of current alternatives. You will study examples of the efforts of other elementary and secondary teachers to apply behavior analysis principles to their classroom learning and discipline problems, and you will use their successes and failures as a basis for designing your own hypothetical classroom management system. Finally, you will get a chance to synthesize the principles, procedures, and examples of these and previous units in a live behavior-change project of your own.

It is very important to remember that behavior change is a two-way street. A teacher's behavior in the classroom is determined largely by what the students do as a result of her actions (this is especially clear in a very disruptive class). Where there's control, there's countercontrol. When a teacher is apparently "in control" of a class, the students are also reinforcing and thus controlling the behavior of the teacher.[1] When the class is "out of control" and apparently being run by the students, the teacher is usually reinforcing or allowing access to reinforcement for behaviors that interfere with instruction.

Usually most of the control of behavior is unintentional or, as we say, left to chance. A major part of the teacher's job is to arrange these controlling and countercontrolling contingencies deliberately, intelligently, and humanely. Mistakes will be made, of course, but not as many as if this job is left to chance.

You, as a teacher, must be able to change your own behavior; if you cannot, the behavior of your students will probably not change much either. The general principles and procedures of behavior analysis apply to this task also;

---

[1] For some interesting examples of how "powerless" junior high students shaped certain behaviors (e.g., praising, keeping things orderly, and being friendly) of their teachers, parents, and peers, see the article "Little Brother is Changing You," *Psychology Today* (March 1974):42.

your behavior is a function of its consequences in the same way as is everyone else's.

Units 14–16 deal directly with behavioral methods for changing your own behavior.

Unit 17 consists of review and application exercises.

Analysis of Teaching and Learning: Introduction

OBJECTIVES

When you complete unit 1, you should be able to:

* state the basic elements of a scientific approach to teaching and apply this approach to hypothetical classroom situations;
* state the steps involved in developing an empirical explanation of a functional relationship, contrast this with the development of a pseudo-explanation, and apply these explanatory procedures to original examples.

Experimental Analysis of Learning

The art of teaching is becoming a science.

In the past, widely publicized efforts to improve education have rarely been directed toward analysis and improvement of teaching and learning as such. Instead, large sums of money have been spent for more and better schools, more and better teachers, more and better students going to school and to college, and more and better curriculum and audio-visual materials. Rarely has it been asked *how* those "better" teachers are to teach those "better" students in those "better" schools and how the new materials are to be made effective.

There are, of course, truly artful teachers and brilliant students. Perhaps some day we will understand their skills and talents and how they acquired them, so that we can systematically produce more of them. At present, however, they are true exceptions that defy specification. We simply do not know what makes an artful teacher.

Most teachers must make do with information, routines, and rules of thumb passed on to them by other teachers and rely primarily on their own experiences. Unfortunately it is very difficult for teachers to learn from their experiences; they rarely see any of their long-term successes or failures, and they have neither the time nor the skills to trace any short-term effects to their specific causes.

And most students spend most of their school days doing or avoiding things they don't want to do. Though we've abandoned the cane, education is still based largely on punishment (scolding, ridicule, loss of privileges, embarrassment, extra work, fines, expulsion).

This intuitive and compulsory approach to teaching is no longer necessary. A more effective technology of teaching is becoming available. Based on laws and principles derived from an experimental analysis of human behavior, teaching can be viewed not simply as the dispensing of information in entertaining ways, but also as the careful arrangement of relationships between a student's behaviors and the events that precede and follow these behaviors so that each student learns. The resulting methods are especially useful for the 90 percent or so of the teachers who are not truly artful and of the students who are not already brilliant.[1]

Careful observation is the basis of any science. Of course, people are always observing things. Scientific observation is different from everyday observation because it includes observation of a behavior or event in great detail, accompanied by precise recording and measurement of these details. When many such observations have been made of the same event in the same situation, the scientist can use this precise information to define relationships between this event and others, as well as to predict new occurrences of this event.

An example: Hilary Rottenkid is a student in a school near you. Everyday observation of Hilary has been done by teachers, parents, social workers, probation officers, and others. They describe Hilary as hyperactive, unpopular, fat, emotionally disturbed, mentally retarded, and having a learning disability. Notice that none of these terms describe Hilary's behavior (what he *does*). If you sat in on his class in order to observe and record hyperactive events or unpopular behavior or the details of his learning disability, you would have

---

[1] See B. F. Skinner, *The Technology of Teaching* (New York: Appleton-Century-Crofts, 1968), especially chapters 2, 4, and 5.

trouble being specific. And if a friend of yours did the same thing during the same class period, chances are your two records wouldn't agree at all. Of course you could observe and measure his fatness by putting him on a scale. But how do you measure hyperactivity? When Hilary trips another student in the aisle or gets out of his seat, are these always instances of hyper-activity?

1. Why can't we train teachers to be artful teachers?

2. How does the experimental analysis of behavior define teaching?

3. Can you identify the basic elements of any science (observe, record, measure, relate, predict)? What's the difference between everyday observation and scientific observation?

4. How would you define "emotionally disturbed?" Is your definition precise—based on observable behaviors—so that other people could use only your definition to agree on exactly which students are or are not "emotionally disturbed?" Try it—if you have difficulty, join the club.

Science requires that objects of study be events or behaviors that are clearly observable and measurable, and that the descriptions of these events be in *behavioral terms*—terms that identify behaviors clearly enough for several people to agree on the occurrence or nonoccurrence of the behavior. In the case of Hilary Rottenkid, this means observing and measuring what Hilary does, when, how often, after what other events, and before what other events. We might find for example, that Hilary got out of his seat twenty times during the period, and each time the teacher yelled "sit down" or "get back in your seat, kid" (kid was one of his nicknames). On five of these occasions the teacher didn't notice Hilary out of his seat for about a minute, until he had bumped, punched, or thrown something at another student. The other student responded with "Get lost, kid," or a counterblow, which of course attracted the teacher's attention and another "Sit down." After each such command, Hilary sat down.

These behavioral records are useful because they represent real behaviors. We can begin to predict some of Hilary's behaviors (when he will sit down) and those of the teacher and other students (when they will say "Get lost" or "Sit down"). And we begin to see some relationships between behavioral events. Whenever the teacher says "Sit down," Hilary sits down (which is probably why the teacher keeps saying it). Why does Hilary keep getting up and occasionally disturbing others? One possibility is that whenever he does, he gets attention—the teacher looks at him and talks to him (even if it is critically), and at times other students do too. But this is not an empirical statement—just a guess. Hilary might have a nervous system that won't allow him to sit still for more than a few minutes at a time. An empirical statement about these behavioral relationships must, by definition, be *based on data* carefully collected and precisely measured.

If there is a relationship between Hilary's getting-out-of-seat behavior and the teacher's yelling at him, then one behavior should change when the other does. We could investigate this by changing the variable we guess is controlling the behavior. In this example, we could make sure that the teacher yelled at Hilary within five seconds *every time* he got out of his seat. If after several days we counted Hilary's getting-out-of-seat behavior and found that it had increased from twenty to thirty-five times, we would have some empirical evidence for stating that there was a *functional* or controlling relationship between these two behaviors.

It's still possible, however, that some other event "caused" the increase. So we might try another change. Say we arranged it so that the teacher *never* paid attention to Hilary when he was *out* of his seat but *always* gave him some kind of attention whenever he had been *in* his seat for more than two minutes. If after several days we counted only five out-of-seat behaviors by Hilary during a class period, we would have convincing evidence that these forms of teacher attention were controlling out-of-seat behavior. Furthermore, we would know that teacher attention also could control the opposite behavior (in-seat) and probably several other behaviors besides.

This was a hypothetical example. Hilary's behavior might just as well have been controlled by the attention of other students, his math workbook, or a hemorrhoid. The point is we can't be sure until we observe and record specific behaviors, describe them in measurable terms, and look for empirical relationships between them.

5. Construct your own hypothetical behavior-problem example. Specify observable behaviors, frequency records (how often the behavior

occurs per unit of time), several "guess relationships" between the behavior and other temporally related events, and a procedure for changing a related event in order to verify your "guess."

Notice in the example that once we had decided on *specific behaviors* to observe, we were able to obtain some useful information. In practice we might refer to Hilary's behaviors as "hyperactive" behaviors. And as long as that name refers to those observable and measurable behaviors, it is simply a shorthand label for those behaviors. But frequently these labels also imply an explanation, and thus become *pseudoexplanations*—that is, they imply a deceiving explanation for the behaviors, when they were originally meant only to indicate the occurrence of a certain type of behavior.

The label "hyperactive" is often used not only to describe a class of physical activity behaviors by a student but also to explain *why* the student does all these things; emotional immaturity might be used to describe a student who does not study by himself for more than a few minutes at a time, who throws temper tantrums, or who demands his way with other students, but the label frequently implies that the reason he does these things is because there is some part of his body or mind which has not developed beyond the infant stage. The same is true for such labels as slow learner, intelligent, popular, aggressive, good attitude, paranoia, learning disability, and bright. Rarely do we have any empirical justification for claiming a causal connection between the behaviors we observe and their implied internal cause, because nowhere do we make contact with anything except the behaviors themselves.

It is easy to fall into this pseudoexplanation trap. If you observe one of your students reading books at every opportunity, taking them home with him, working hard to finish other assignments so that he can read a few minutes extra, and talking a lot about the books he has read, you would report to his parents that this student has a good attitude towards reading, or that he likes to read. If they ask you how you know that, you can describe the set of behaviors that you referred to when you said he likes to read. If they ask you why he reads so much, you might say it's because he likes to read or because he loves reading for its own sake. This answer is not really an answer at all; it doesn't explain the behaviors nor add any new information. To say that he likes to read means that he reads a lot; "he reads a lot because he likes to read" is the same as "he reads a lot because he reads a lot."

A pseudoexplanation is born when we take an everyday label that we use to summarize a class of behaviors and begin to imply that the label actually is a cause of these behaviors. Of course this is circular; we start with several behaviors, put them together with a shorthand label (rather than describing each behavior every time we want to refer to it), then presume that because these behaviors all have the same label they are therefore caused by the same thing, and finally we imply that this cause for these behaviors is in fact the label, which originally was no more than a communications convenience.

But this circularity is usually subtle. We don't usually come right out and say that Johnny is unable to read because he has a disability; we frequently leave it as an unspoken implication. The danger, of course, is that when we have a pseudoexplanation for a problem, we stop looking for the real explanation and choose ineffective methods for changing the behaviors.

If that's not bad enough, pseudoexplanations often lead to *expectancy effects* sometimes called the Pygmalion effect (recall the plot in Shaw's play or in *My Fair Lady*). Labels, as well as many other aspects of the educational environment, can and do establish expectations of what a student will achieve in school, and these expectations come true—a sort of self-fulfilling prophecy. Though a teacher may wish or hope that a student will do well, her realistic expectations for him can be affected by the student's past IQ score, notes and labels given him by past teachers, and his race and social class. The teacher's expectations alter the teaching behaviors and ultimately the achievement results of the student. This effect is predictable in certain settings, particularly urban, where the overall expectations are low.[2]

A science of learning must go beyond pseudoexplanations. *Empirical explanation* begins with careful and systematic observation of specific behaviors that are really observable and measurable. Then by careful and controlled manipulation of one factor or variable in the situation, and then another and another, relationships between the behavior and other (preceding or following) events can be measured and defined.

The general procedure is:

1. Specify the behavior precisely enough so that independent observers would all agree when it occurs and when it does not occur.
2. Record the repeated occurrence of this behavior—its frequency during a set period of time, its duration for each occurrence, or its intensity; record events that are antecedent or consequent to the behavior; also record any changes in the situation or time or place in which the behavior occurs.
3. When the data show that a certain event reliably precedes or follows the behavior whenever it occurs, then test the relationship between these two events. For example, see what happens to the behavior when the preceding or consequent event is arranged so as not to occur with the behavior.
4. If the behavior ceases or drops dramatically in frequency, then you can say empirically that these two events are lawfully related.

---

[2] For an interesting review of related studies, see J. D. Finn, "Expectations and the Educational Environment," *Review of Educational Research* 42 (1972): 387–410.

Such relationships are also called *functional relationships*. As in math, one thing is a function of another when its occurrence is in some way or degree dependent on the occurrence of the other. Two behavioral events are related functionally when one event's frequency or duration is dependent on the other's frequency or duration, as in the case of Hilary Rottenkid's out-of-seat behavior and his teacher's attention to it.

6. What is a pseudoexplanation? Give an original example and show how it might develop. (Be sure your example distinguishes between the description stage and the explanation stage.)

7. Explain how a pseudoexplanation can lead to a harmful expectancy effect.

8. What does "empirical" mean? What is a "functional relationship"? What are the specific steps in developing an empirical explanation of a functional relationship?

Once a teacher has identified a functional relationship between some behavioral events in the learning situation, she has acquired scientific knowledge about that learning, which can be put to use in two powerful ways. First, if the occurrence and characteristics of Event B depend on the occurrence and characteristics of Event A, then your knowledge of Event A gives you the ability to *predict* the occurrence and characteristics of Event B. In Hilary's case, we can use the identified functional relationship between Hilary's out-of-seat behavior and the teacher's yelling at him to predict several things: about how many times Hilary will get out of his seat tomorrow, how often the teacher will yell at him tomorrow, what would happen if the teacher stopped yelling at him, etc.

In addition, functional relationships give you the ability to *control* Event B, by arranging that Event A does or does not occur, by changing some characteristics (such as the frequency or duration) of Event A, or by inserting another controlling event between A and B. In Hilary's case, we can use the identified functional relationship to control either Hilary's behavior or the teacher's behavior. Hilary is already controlling the teacher's behavior, whether they know it or not. Hilary can get the teacher to yell or stop yelling just by varying his out-of-seat behavior. And the teacher can control Hilary's out-of-seat behavior by varying her response to him. This hypothetical case is symptomatic of most social-interaction situations. What we do depends largely on how people have in the past reacted (and can be expected to react) to similar behaviors of ours, but their responses also are controlled in turn by our reactions. Control of human behavior is always a two-way process.

Behaviors or events, when under scientific observation, often are called variables. The term *dependent variable* refers to the specific behavior whose occurrence or frequency or value is dependent on the occurrence (or frequency or value) of another behavior or event. This other event is then called the *independent variable* since its occurrence or characteristics are independent—not dependent on the occurrence of the first behavior. In the above description, the antecedent event (Event A) is the independent variable and Event B is the dependent variable. In Hilary's case, his out-of-seat behavior is the dependent variable since its occurrence and frequency varied with (was dependent on) the teacher's attention behavior (the independent variable).

Notice that in Hilary's case (and in many other cases) the dependent variable might just as well have been the independent variable. If our immediate focus of interest had been on the teacher's yelling behavior, we would have observed and measured its occurrences and its antecedent and consequent events. We would have found, of course, that the teacher's yelling behavior (which we have now made our dependent variable) was indeed functionally dependent on the antecedent event of Hilary's getting out of his seat (our new independent variable). This interchangeableness is to be expected, however, when we realize that every behavior is controlled by some other event(s) and every behavior, in turn, controls some other event(s) at least in some way or to some degree. In practice, then, the dependent variable is the behavior we want to be able to predict and control, and the independent variable is the behavior we hope will provide the tools to do so.

9. Construct original examples of the two main uses (to predict, to control) of identified functional relationships.

10. Can you distinguish between independent and dependent variables? Construct original examples.

Analysis of Teaching and Learning: Part A

OBJECTIVES

Upon completing unit 2, you should be able to:

* describe how the probability of a behavioral event can be determined by analyzing the antecedent events and conditions, the consequent events, and the contingencies which functionally relate the behavior to its consequences, and apply this analytic procedure to events in your own experience;
* analyze consequent events in terms of their effect (reinforcing, punishing, neutral) on behavior patterns and their originating process (learned, unlearned) and construct original examples of each;
* describe, with original examples, how neutral events can become reinforcing or punishing events through pairing or chaining.

Let's consider now some of the general terms, principles, and procedures of the analysis of human learning. In general, the probability that a specific kind of behavior will occur (or will not occur) depends on three kinds of variables: (1) the antecedent events and conditions which precede and accompany the behavior; (2) the contingencies which functionally relate the behavior to its immediate and historical consequences; (3) the consequent events themselves. We'll look at these three sets of variables in some detail, though not necessarily in the above order.

Consequent Events

Most behavior is functionally related to its *consequences.* Such behavior is called operant behavior. When we flick a light switch, we get light; when we work, we get a paycheck; when Hilary got out of his seat, he got a response from his teacher. The probability of just about every kind of behavior depends on its consequences. If you didn't get light after flicking the switch, you'd soon stop flicking the switch; if the paycheck stopped coming, you'd stop working (unless there were some other consequences for working); when Hilary no longer got the teacher's attention, his disruptive behavior decreased; and when Hilary started getting attention when he was in his seat, he stayed in his seat more.

Naturally, a behavior which is already completed can't then be changed. What changes is the probability that *that kind of behavior* will occur again. So when we speak of "behavior" being affected by its consequences, we mean "behavior of a certain kind."

This is a basic law of behavior: *a behavior's probability depends on its consequences.* And like the law of gravity and other laws of nature, this law of behavior applies to all humans, twenty-four hours a day, at home, work, and in the classroom, and to elementary, secondary, and college students as well as their teachers. Furthermore, this functional relationship between behavior and its consequences is true whether this relationship is purely accidental or deliberately arranged. The art of teaching starts to become a science when the teacher starts to arrange these relationships carefully in order to facilitate each student's learning.

Contingency

The usual name for behavior-consequence relations is *contingency.* A contingency is a specific relationship between a certain behavior and a certain consequence; the relationship specifies that *if and only if* the behavior occurs will this consequence occur. Contingencies can be purely natural (if a person steps out of this thirteenth floor window, he will be mopped up off the street), or carefully arranged ("if you practice your piano lesson for 30 minutes, you can watch the next TV show"), or completely unintended (a child hates to see his father come home from work because he frequently punishes the boy for the day's misbehaviors identified by the mother).

> 1. Identify the three kinds of variables which together determine the probability of a behavior occurring.

2. The consequences of a specific behavioral event don't change that event. What do they change?

3. Give an example of a behavior of your own and show how it is controlled by its consequences. Identify the measurable behavior, the reinforcing or punishing event, and the contingency relating the two.

4. Give an example of another person's behavior that is controlled by the consequences you give or don't give. Identify the measurable behavior, the reinforcing or punishing event you control, and the contingency relating the two.

5. Define contingency. Construct original examples of natural (imposed by laws of nature), accidental (imposed unintentionally by a person), and arranged (imposed intentionally by a person) contingencies.

Since there are innumerable kinds of events that occur as a consequence of behavior, the best way to talk about consequent events is in terms of their *effect* on the behavior they follow. If a consequent event maintains or increases the frequency of a behavior, it is called a *reinforcer*. If a consequent event decreases the frequency of a behavior, it is called a *punisher*. If a consequent event has no effect, it is called *neutral event*. For example, if you criticize a friend whenever he brags to you about his accomplishments, your criticism is a reinforcing consequence if his bragging to you continues or increases; your criticism is a punisher if his bragging to you decreases; and your criticism is neutral if his bragging continues whether you criticize it or not.

Notice that there is no such thing as a reinforcer or punisher *un*related to an actual behavior. We can't say that food is always a reinforcer; people who are very sick to their stomachs do not come to the dinner table because the consequences (smell, sight, and eating of food) are punishing to them. As we have seen, criticism can reinforce some behavior and punish other behavior. Before we decide whether a certain consequent event will act as a punisher or a reinforcer for a given behavior, we have to look at its *actual effect* on the behavior. In other words, reinforcers and punishers must be defined behaviorally.

The temptation is to decide beforehand what is reinforcing and what is not. The problem with this is that the *real effects* of consequent events are not at all influenced by the names we give them. This is the danger in thinking of a reinforcement as "the giving of a reward." Some consequences that we call "rewards" strengthen behaviors; some don't. Some "punishers" also strengthen behavior. Remember in grade school when the teacher loudly and publicly ridiculed Tommy Largemouth for being the only bad boy in her class? Remember seeing Tommy grinning from ear to ear after receiving this individual attention? What was the effect on his behavior? Often a child will figure that any attention is better than none.

Moreover, the same "thing" can act as both a punisher and a reinforcer, depending on whether it is presented or withdrawn. Giving someone a kiss can reinforce a lot of preceding behaviors; withholding a kiss can punish the same behaviors. If you find the loud, constant talking of your friend punishing, then any behaviors that remove you from that noise (or the noise from you) will probably be strengthened. For this reason, the total consequent *event* is more important than the "thing." A consequent event can be the presentation of a thing, the occurrence of a behavior by someone else, an opportunity to do something, the withdrawal of a thing, the nonoccurrence of a usual behavioral response, the elimination of an opportunity to do something, etc. For example, money is a *thing,* but it cannot be a reinforcing *event* for you unless you are given the opportunity to receive it; *receiving* money or spending it is a reinforcing event. Whatever the event is, if it follows a behavior and strengthens it, then it is a reinforcer, and the process of following the behavior with this event is called reinforcement. If the event follows a behavior and weakens it, then that event is called punishment. Consider the following:

1. You tell your date, "Sorry, no necking tonight because you got angry with several other drivers. You know I think that's dangerous and childish. Goodnight!" Is this an example of reinforcement? Punishment? If so, what is the reinforcer or punisher?
2. During the next several dates, your friend restrains himself from acting dangerously to other drivers. Now can you say what has happened?
3. After these dates, you thank him for his improved driving and give him a kiss, etc. The improved driving continues. What is the reinforcer?
4. Whenever the child whines or cries to get her way, her mother calmly puts her in a chair (or empty playpen or crib) and says "When you are done, you can get down and play again." After several days of this contingency, the whining has almost disappeared. Is this reinforcement? Punishment? If so, what is the reinforcer or punisher?

5. The coach says "five extra laps for anyone missing a signal." The players are more attentive to the signals. Is this reinforcement or punishment? Careful!

Answers:

1. Reinforcement and punishment are defined behaviorally—that is, in terms of the actual effect on subsequent behavior. In this example, you don't know the effect so you can't tell.
2. Now the change in driving behavior appears to indicate that you have punished the behavior of getting back at other drivers.
3. And you (presumably) are reinforcing his restraint with your acts of affection. Notice that the reinforcer is an event, or at least the expected opportunity for that event.
4. The whining behavior is being punished by requiring the child to stay in his chair and perhaps also by withdrawing the opportunity to play.
5. This is reinforcement because the attentive behavior increases. But the reinforcing event is the absence of a punisher.

Notice that we can reinforce and punish by *not giving* something as well as by *giving* something. We can reinforce by delivering a reinforcer (a kiss) or by withdrawing a punisher (less running). We can punish by delivering a punisher (sit in your chair) or by withdrawing a reinforcer (not tonight, Henry). The critical question is: What is the effect on behavior?

Sometimes you will hear people using the term "negative reinforcement" to refer to punishment. This, of course, is a contradiction in terms and makes for confusing communication. By definition, reinforcement strengthens behavior, so it can't weaken behavior, even if it is "negative." Negative reinforcement refers to the process of strengthening a behavior by withdrawing a consequent punishing event.

6. Be able to define reinforcer, punisher, and neutral consequence, with original examples involving *you* as either the behaver or the consequator. Identify the contingency in each example.

7. Is praise a reinforcer? Is spanking or scolding a punisher? (Remember that reinforcers and punishers must be defined behaviorally.

8. Why is a reinforcer an event rather than a thing?

If some events act as reinforcers for some people and as punishers for others, and in some situations but not in others, we have a real problem in identifying how an event will function without having to try it out first. There are several ways to be fairly certain beforehand.

Some events are reinforcers or punishers because of their dependence on our biological makeup. From birth we all seem to come equipped with the capacity to be reinforced by food when we are food-deprived (and the more deprived we are, the less difference it makes what kind of food it is), by water when we have been deprived of water, by many kinds of sensory stimulation (visual, tactile, auditory, movement in space, etc.), and by a variety of other bodily conditions which are related to the survival of the individual or the species. Similarly, there are biologically dependent events which are punishers for us all, such as blows and cuts on the body, organic malfunctions, extremes of heat and cold, or loud noise. We can usually rely on such events having pretty much the same effect on most humans. Such events which are biologically related are called *unconditioned* or *unlearned* or primary reinforcers and punishers. They make up only a small proportion of the important consequent events that influence human behavior.

A far larger proportion of reinforcing and punishing events is related to the specific culture and the individual experiences of each person. These events are called *conditioned* or *learned* or secondary reinforcers and punishers. At birth these events were neutral events for each of us. But as each of us began growing and experiencing, some of these neutral consequent events were frequently paired (presented at the same time) with unconditioned reinforcing (or punishing) events. The gradual effect of this frequent *pairing* was to give the neutral event the effect of a reinforcing event. In our culture, such events as approving or disapproving, smiling or frowning, and giving money become conditioned reinforcers because of their frequent relation to other unconditioned consequent events.

Pairing

Consider the following example from a study of smiling behavior in infants. Every time the four-month-old infant smiled, the mother picked up the infant, smiled in return, spoke softly to the child, jostled, patted, and stroked him for one-half minute. After a series of such events, the smiling behavior of the infant increased from two to over five times per five minutes. Some of these consequent events, such as the jostling, were functioning as unconditional reinforcers (reinforcing the infant's smiling), but other events, such as the return smile and the talking, were probably neutral events that were being paired with the unconditioned reinforcers. Later on, these events will come to act as conditioned reinforcers for this child because of this pairing. However, the effect of this type of pairing is not permanent; the pairing of a conditioned reinforcer with some unconditioned reinforcer must be repeated at least occasionally or the conditioned reinforcer will lose its reinforcing properties.

As another example, consider praise. At birth, praise was not a reinforcer, but now it is for most of us because very early in life praise accompanied a variety of other consequences that were already reinforcing. And if a student is not turned on by a teacher's praise, she can usually change that by giving him a lot of actual reinforcers for small tasks done well and pairing them each time with praise for the work.

In pairing, the neutral consequent event does not have to be paired with an unconditioned event; it can be paired with an event that was itself previously conditioned. In general, to make a neutral consequent event into a reinforcing (or punishing) consequence, arrange so that when the reinforcing event is given, the neutral event also occurs at the same time or just before it.

Conditioned reinforcers can develop in another way—by being made means to a reinforcing end. If a chain of successive responses and consequent events is related in such a way that each member of the chain is a necessary condition for obtaining the next member but only the final event was a reinforcer before the chain began, then the intermediate events become conditioned reinforcers because they are conditions to the final reinforcing condition. This process is called *chaining*. Money becomes a conditioned reinforcer by chaining; we work, then we get money, then we pay money and get other learned reinforcers or unlearned reinforcers like food. For a hungry man, food is an unlearned reinforcer, but a city map which helps him locate a restaurant, the starting of the car after he gets in and turns the key, the appearance of the restaurant after he turns the corner, the arrival of the waitress after he sits down at a table, the descriptions on the menu after he opens it, etc., are all conditioned reinforcers for him, presuming he has had previous experience with these events.

Pairing:

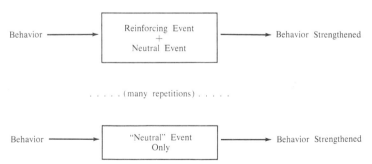

By following a behavior with *both* a reinforcer (which by itself would strengthen the behavior) *and* at the same time a neutral event (which by itself would have no effect), the neutral event will gradually take on the reinforcing properties of the reinforcing event and will no longer be "neutral."

Chaining:

$$\text{Behavior}_1 \xrightarrow{} \text{Neutral}_1 \xrightarrow{} \text{Behavior}_2 \xrightarrow{} \text{Neutral}_2 \xrightarrow{} \text{Behavior}_3 \xrightarrow{} \text{Rfer}$$

. . . . . (repetitions of this chain)

$$\text{Behavior}_1 \xrightarrow{} \text{"Neutral"}_1 \xrightarrow{} \text{Behavior}_2 \xrightarrow{} \text{"Neutral"}_2 \xrightarrow{} \text{Behavior}_3 \xrightarrow{} \text{Rfer}$$

$$\text{or Behavior}_1 \xrightarrow{} \text{"Neutral"}_1 \xrightarrow{} \text{Behavior}_1 \text{ Strengthened}$$

In this situation, the formerly neutral events become conditioned reinforcers by being frequent links to an event that is already reinforcing. Then, like money, such "neutral" consequences can stand by themselves as reinforcing events.

There is one important difference between pairing and chaining. In pairing there is no time lag between the neutral event and the reinforcing event, but in chaining the neutral event(s) leads to (is a means toward) and occurs some time before the terminal reinforcing event.

9. Be able to define unconditioned (unlearned) and conditioned (learned) reinforcers and punishers, with original examples of each as they affect you.

10. Define pairing and chaining. Construct an original example of each and describe how the neutral consequence came to be reinforcing or punishing for you. (Remember that pairing refers to pairing two consequent events, not a behavior and a consequence.)

unit 3

Analysis of Teaching and Learning: Part B

OBJECTIVES

When you finish this unit, you should be able to:

* define the Premack principle, describe with original examples two ways in which the effect of a reinforcing or punishing event is relative to other alternative events and to other situational factors, and construct original examples of the facilitative use of the Premack principle in the classroom;
* define and contrast the procedures of extinction and time out and construct original examples of situations in which each would be appropriate;
* define and contrast stimulus discrimination and generalization, construct original examples of each, and describe with an original example how one preceding stimulus can be used to get a response under the control of another preceding stimulus;
* use the seven "rules for managing consequences" to analyze original or hypothetical learning situations and to predict behavioral outcomes.

Premack Principle

Although unconditioned (unlearned) events affect most humans in generally the same way, we can't be as certain about the effectiveness of conditioned (learned) events before we actually see their effect on behavior because we often cannot know enough about the history of an individual to be sure the event is actually a reinforcing event for this individual, at this time, and in this situation. There is, however, a quick way to assess the relative effectiveness of a great many such events, and it doesn't require detailed knowledge of the individual's conditioning history. It is based on a general rule called the Premack principle (first analyzed and stated by a psychologist, David Premack, in 1959) which states that of any two events or behaviors, the more probable one will function as a reinforcer for the less probable one. A very loose way of saying this is "Do what I want you to do, then you can do what you want to do." But "want" is hard to specify behaviorally. A more precise and helpful statement of the principle is this: *If any higher frequency behavior is made contingent on a lower frequency behavior, the lower frequency behavior will be strengthened* (will increase in frequency).

The use of this principle makes it much easier to identify beforehand some effective reinforcing events for a given individual, especially in the classroom. Consider this situation. In a classroom, we arrange materials for a variety of activities, including some reading materials, some math workbooks and games, some materials for physics and electricity experiments, and a phonograph with records and a headset. We allow the students *free access* to any of these activities for one-half hour, and we record the amount of time each student spends in each activity. We find that Wenda Whoopy spends 15 minutes grooming herself, 5 minutes talking with Gladys, and 10 minutes promenading among the boys. The Premack principle tells us that if we restrict Wenda's access to the comb and mirror and make such access contingent on a specified period of time talking to Gladys (that is, talk to Gladys in order to groom), we can increase the amount of time she spends talking to Gladys. Of course, we could make any of the other activities in which she didn't spend any time contingent on the opportunity to groom and strut (for example, a small math or reading assignment), and any of those would increase also. Say we also observe that Timothy Titmouse spends all his time reading and seldom talks to anyone. If we observe that these preferences remain fairly stable over several observation periods, we might decide to make Tim's opportunity to read contingent on a little social activity, such as five minutes of talking with a classmate or playing a game with several others. In this way we would be reinforcing a less preferred activity with a more preferred activity.

The educational importance of this principle is that it gives the teacher an easy-to-use motivational system. All she has to do is observe her students, measure their preferences among the available activities, and make access to one activity dependent on prior engagement in a less preferred activity. She can use the activities already available, without having to use elaborate activities from elsewhere. And she can be pretty sure, in advance, that her choice of reinforcing events is accurate because it is based on student preferences in a free-access situation.

The Premack principle illustrates another important fact about reinforcement: the actual effectiveness of reinforcing or punishing events is *relative*—relative to other possible consequent events and relative to other circumstances or situational variables. In Wenda's case, for example (review it if necessary), promenading could be used as a reinforcer for Wenda, *depending* on what other options are available to her. Watching a football game regularly on Saturday may be a reinforcing event for you, unless on a given Saturday you are given tickets to a game; the chance to actually go to the game might decrease the reinforcing effectiveness of watching TV. So reinforcement is relative to the *other available options,* and the effectiveness of a specific consequent event depends on whether it is a higher or lower probability event than these other options.

In addition, reinforcement is relative to other *situational* factors—present or past. There are a variety of ways in which this relativity takes effect. For example, the relative probabilities of several consequent events can easily *change* over time. If a student prefers reading to math and reading is made contingent on math for a period of time, doing math right might eventually become the preferred activity of the two, especially if the contingencies are carefully arranged. Current situational factors can also modify the reinforcing effectiveness of a consequent event. Watching a certain weekly TV show may be a regular reinforcing event for you, but if on a given day the show is a rerun, the event might lose some of its reinforcing value.

As we have seen, food is a reinforcer in one situation (hunger) and a punisher in another situation (nausea) for the same person, and it is probably a neutral event just after a satisfying meal. To move to a room that has a temperature of thirty degrees is a reinforcing or a punishing event, depending on whether the room you left was zero degrees or sixty degrees. If someone smiles at you and says "good work," this consequent event is reinforcing or punishing, depending on whether you had just completed a good piece of work or just tripped over your feet and landed in the mud.

These examples of the various ways in which reinforcement is relative illustrate the need for careful and continuing consideration of the past and present circumstances surrounding the consequent events and their relationship to behaviors.

1. Can you define the Premack principle *precisely,* with an original illustration of how you have used or experienced it?

2. Think of several specific ways you could use the Premack principle to improve your teaching. (Each illustration should include all the components of the principle: higher and lower probability events, contingency, result.)

3. Construct an original example illustrating each of the two ways in which consequent events are relative in their effect on you. (Specify a situation in which the effect of one consequence is increased or decreased by the introduction of (a) an alternative consequence or (b) a situational factor or change.)

Extinction

As we saw before, the effects of most reinforcing and punishing events are somewhat temporary. When a reinforcing event no longer follows a certain kind of behavior and the behavior is not otherwise reinforced, the frequency of that behavior will eventually decrease. This process of withholding *all* reinforcing consequences for a *certain* behavior is called extinction. We saw an example of extinction when the teacher ignored Hilary's out-of-seat behavior.

Extinction works if the reinforcer(s) for the behavior is completely withdrawn. But the "if" is critical and sometimes difficult to pull off for two reasons:

1. Withdrawing one reinforcing consequence for the behavior may not be enough; there may be *other reinforcing events* which we overlook or over which we have no control, and these may continue to operate to maintain the behavior. In Hilary's case, the attention from other students for his antics might maintain (reinforce) his behavior, even though his teacher was attempting to extinguish that behavior by withholding her attention to it. (Notice that extinction, like reinforcement and punishment, is defined by its effect on behavior, not simply by the procedure that is used.)

2. Another reason why extinction is sometimes difficult is because its effectiveness requires complete *consistency.* It's tough to consistently withhold attention from someone who keeps whapping you on the back. When a child puts up a fuss at not being able to have or do something, you might be able to ignore his fussing consistently for a while, but it becomes louder and more disruptive. Then, when you

give in with attention, one of the things you have reinforced is the increased intensity of his fussing and, by definition, the chances are greater that he will yell louder the next time he wants his way. Once you decide to ignore a bit of behavior, you can't allow any exception to occur.

Time Out

A stronger type of the extinction procedure called *time out* sometimes helps to overcome both these difficulties. Time out means the loss of *all* reinforcers for *all* responses for a certain period of time following a certain kind of behavior. A child who throws a tantrum can be put in a room until a minute or two after he stops fussing. If the procedure is carried out calmly, quickly, and with as little attention as possible, if the room is devoid of potential reinforcing activities, and if subsequent good behavior is immediately reinforced, the tantrum behavior will quickly decrease in frequency after several such experiences.

Children and adolescents sometimes use a form of time out with their peers by excluding one member from all activities of the group because of some behavior, though the exclusion is not usually permanent unless the behavior reoccurs. Adults are reported to do the same thing on occasion. Teachers used to combine time out and ridicule (punishment) by using a dunce cap and a chair facing the wall for misbehaving students. Many teachers today think of ways to use time out (without ridicule) for an especially disruptive student, but it generally is not necessary for very long. Remember that in using time out it is important to reinforce desired behavior immediately and frequently whenever the student is not in a time-out period.

Preceding Events

So far we've looked at behaviors, consequences, and the contingencies relating one to the other. The third variable that influences the probability of human behavior is the preceding stimulus conditions which set the occasion for the response or behavior to occur. A preceding stimulus is an event that precedes a kind of behavior and influences when or how the behavior will occur. The clock has a great deal of this kind of "stimulus control" over our daily behaviors because our past experience has taught us that at such-and-such a time we had better get moving or we will miss the bus or ride to school, that another time is the period for eating, etc. When a teacher says "Look at this" or when he starts writing on the board, this is a preceding stimulus for the student's response of looking. The consequence is the information conveyed.

In most cases the degree of control that a preceding stimulus event has will depend on the *consequences* for responding to that event. If the information the teacher offers is seen as worthless and of no personal consequence to the student, the student is apt to stop looking in response to future such stimulus events.

Preceding stimuli are important in education in various ways. Much school work, such as reading printed symbols, adding numbers on a page, following printed diagrams, or interpreting formulas, requires certain kinds of responses to certain kinds of preceding stimuli. We can get such responses going in the first place by using heavy prompts, which are one kind of preceding stimulus. We might say to a student: "What is this letter" (a preceding stimulus), to which he replies: "I don't know." (his response to the question and to the written letter *M*). We could then introduce another kind of preceding stimulus, a prompt, by saying "Say Mmmmmmm," while also showing him the letter *M*. Since the child already can produce imitative responses, he says "mmmmm," and we can consequate that response by saying "good."

By itself this bit of chaining is not enough to teach the child to say "Mmmmmm" whenever he sees the letter *M*. By *pairing* one preceding stimulus (the prompt) that already gets the desired response with the preceding stimulus that we want to control the response (the letter *M*) and by reinforcing the response in the presence of both stimuli, we have increased the probability of that stimulus-response relationship.

In this form of pairing preceding stimuli, several elements are necessary:

1. a preceding stimulus which does elicit the desired response;
2. a preceding stimulus which does not elicit the desired response (but you wish it to do so eventually);
3. pairing these two preceding stimuli;
4. reinforcing the correct response when it occurs in the presence of these preceding events.

The result of this pairing will be that eventually the response will occur to the desired preceding stimulus when presented by itself.

In sports and music, we learn by making responses to several types of preceding stimuli. Some of these preceding events strongly affect the response (e.g., instructions, sample response by another for our imitation), while others have little or no effect at first (e.g., what we are thinking or saying to ourselves, the kinesthetic feedback or "feel" of the previous response, the sound of the previous chord, the notes on a page). But these "neutral" preceding stimuli soon gain more and more control because of their regular pairing with the stimulus that already elicited the response. When a checkout person, for example, first learns to punch the cash register keys, the controlling preceding stimulus is the symbol on each key, but gradually the control shifts to kinesthetic feedback cues (the *feel* of where the fingers are in relation to parts of the machine), and the checkout person no longer needs to look at the keys. These feedback cues were there all along, but only by consistent pairing with the controlling preceding stimulus (sight of the key symbols) did they gain effectiveness as controlling preceding stimuli.

In addition, we want to make sure the student attends to and responds only to those characteristics of the preceding stimulus that are *essential.* To do this, we vary the nonessential characteristics of the stimulus (the size of the letter *M,* its position on a page, its shape, etc.), by presenting stimuli that have none of the essential characteristics of our target stimulus (such as the letter *n,* or *e,* or *p*), and consequating each response accordingly.

When a person consistently responds one way to one stimulus and another way to a different stimulus (e.g., to the letters *M* and *N*), we say he has learned a *discrimination.* In chemistry, a student learns to discriminate between (respond differently to) the symbols NaCl and HCl or he's in big trouble. Notice that the learning of a discrimination is defined by the discrimination *performance* of the learner, not by what he or his teacher says he has been taught or by what lesson he has been submitted to.

There is another, perhaps competitive, process called *generalization,* which means that a person responds the same way to two different stimuli which have much in common. A student may respond the same way to the letters *M* and *N* or to *b* and *d* because each member of the pair has several characteristics in common with the other. We usually don't discriminate between such comments as "good work," "beautiful job," "well done," "fine job," or "right on"; they are all seen as social reinforcers for something we have just said or done. If we teach a child that the color of a fire engine is called "red," then he is likely (but less so) to call burgundy-red or light-red "red." And there is the story of a college student who regularly slept from the beginning of a certain class straight through to the bell. During one class, he abruptly sat up, closed his notebook and headed for the door because an alarm clock had been set off beneath his chair. He generalized when he should have discriminated.

Later units will analyze more thoroughly these and other aspects of the preceding stimulus variable in human learning and teaching.

4. Can you illustrate two problems to be careful about in using extinction?

5. In what kind of situation would you use time out rather than extinction?

6. Think of an original example in which one kind of preceding stimulus is used to get a response under the control of another preceding stimulus. (Remember, you pair two preceding stimuli, not a preceding stimulus and a behavior.)

7. Check to see if you can define discrimination and generalization and construct original examples. (Remember to define them in terms of observable events.)

Rules for Managing Consequences[1]

By way of both review and application, let's look at several rules for using the above principles effectively in the classroom. Keep in mind, however, that although we use labels like "teacher" and "student," the rules apply also to other relationships such as parent-child, friend-friend, husband-wife, and counselor-counselee. And even in the classroom, the rules of teacher and student are often reversed in the dynamic interplay, especially since the good teacher learns something every time he interacts with a student.

Rule 1: Consequence Identification—Describe consequent events (reinforcers or punishers) *only* in terms of their effect on the student. To put it negatively, don't call a consequent event a reinforcer for a certain student because you think it will maintain or increase his behavior or because it has worked that way for other students. It's perfectly reasonable for you to use these reasons for making your initial choice of consequent events for a student, but you can't be sure they will work that way for this student until you try them or until you assess his preferences in a free-access situation. Most students will work for praise and attention, but some will not; other students will work for the attention of their peers, but not for a teacher's. Even though having students compete for a set number of A's and B's seems to be reinforcing to many teachers and administrators, it may not be so for some students, particularly those who rarely got such a mark in the past. Nor is what a student says about his own motivation the critical factor; students who say they are trying as hard as they can and really want to learn a particular subject can still show considerable improvement when contingencies for academic improvement are carefully arranged.

---

[1] The following section is based partly on an excellent monograph by Jack Michael, *Management of Behavioral Consequences in Education* (Inglewood, Calif.: Southwest Regional Laboratory for Educational Research and Development, 1967).

This rule applies also to punishers. A teacher frequently uses "punishing consequences" such as scolding, criticizing, or embarrassing because she is immediately reinforced for doing so—the student stops his misbehavior or freezes in his tracks or blushes or stares in rapt attention. But is her consequence a punisher for the student? Careful observation frequently shows that the behavior the teacher criticizes continues to occur at least as often, even though it stopped momentarily when she yelled at him. If a behavior is being maintained or increased, it is being reinforced. In this case the teacher's attention to the student is a reinforcing event for his misbehavior.

Rule 2: Relevant Criteria—"What you reinforce is what you get." In establishing your contingences for reinforcement, be sure your *criteria are precisely related to your goals.* If you reinforce spending time on a task ("work on your math for twenty minutes and then you can . . ."), all you may get is time spent. Or if your criteria is speed ("as soon as you can finish ten problems, you can . . ."), you may not get the accuracy you want.

What a teacher really wants is academic *improvement* in each of the students. So you must make your criteria for each contingency conform precisely to the goals of each particular task. Violation of this rule is responsible for much of the failure in our schools since it is possible for students to participate in public education without learning. We punish a student for being disruptive, truant, or uncooperative, but if he is generally cooperative he can avoid much of the punishment, interact considerably with the teacher and other students (which is probably reinforcing), and still learn very little.

Rule 3: Consistency—Pay close attention to the consequences of a student's behavior *at all times and in all situations.* If you are sure that your criteria are reasonable and fairly easy to achieve for this student, then be consistent. Don't make exceptions, don't relax your attention or forget about it during some periods. Of course, perfect consistency is impossible, but the principles of behavior and its consequences are still working when the teacher is tired, angry, preoccupied, or otherwise unobservant. Consequences affect behavior, whether the contingencies are in the lesson plan or not.

Rule 4: Immediacy—Consequences should come *as close in time after the behavior* as possible. If you delay the reinforcer or punisher, the effect will be weaker, and the consequences might very well affect some other completely irrelevant behavior. If a student comes to you for help on his math and you scold him for something he did earlier during recess, you may decrease the likelihood that he will again ask for help from you or that he will work as hard on his math or that he will like math as much. If you want a student to pay attention to his work or to hang in there when he has some trouble with a task, then reinforce him at the time he is doing that; waiting till later will weaken the effect.

Of course, there are ways to mediate reinforcement or punishment, and these ways often seem to be violations of this rule. Verbal promises and threats,

grades, points, and tokens are frequently used to delay the backup consequences. But when they work it is because these mediators have become
conditioned reinforcers or punishers themselves. When we carefully examine
such long-range activities as getting a grade or a degree or doing research, we
can usually find many consequent events along the way that maintain the
behavior.

Rule 5: Frequency—Don't underestimate how often you should reinforce
for optimal behavior change. Most teachers do. They want to get the most
educational activity with the least reinforcement. The problem is that the
longer the period of educational activity without reinforcement, the more
likely it is that the appropriate response will extinguish and some interfering
behavior will occur, such as daydreaming, doodling, or other irrelevant activity. Notice the difference between this rule about frequency and the rule
regarding immediacy. If a student's response (or task) is to "do this assignment," you may be requiring dozens of individual responses before reinforcement. Even though you reinforce him immediately after this total "response,"
this may not be frequent enough, depending on his past experience with
consequences for this type of work. Even a task of working one simple addition
problem involves a series of responses (sitting down, gathering materials,
looking at the problem, adding mentally, writing, etc.). This may require too
many responses before reinforcement and may violate the rule of frequency if
the student has not been reinforced for any of these behaviors. Optimum
frequency depends on the student and how he responds.

Furthermore, long periods of responding without reinforcement usually
imply long periods without feedback about the accuracy of the student's work,
and this can make large amounts of his current and future work worthless or
even a hindrance. In general, if you want a certain kind of behavior to dominate over all others, give as much reinforcement *as often as possible* for this
kind of behavior.

Sometimes this is difficult. Some reinforcers are in limited supply, others are
subject to rapid satiation, and some (like certain activities) take a lot of time.
In such cases, give the reinforcers frequently but in *small amounts*—just large
enough to still function as reinforcers, and allow frequent periods of preferred
activity, keeping each period as short as possible without losing its reinforcing
value. In general, however, whenever an error is made in this regard, it is
usually in the direction of stinginess.

Rule 6: Small Steps—Sequence your student's work so that the *steps you
reinforce are small and frequent.* This rule is related to the previous rule in
that large steps do not allow for frequent reinforcement, evaluation, and
feedback. To avoid this, most units (such as chapters, assignments, sets of
problems) must be broken down into a series of small steps.

Again, the usual error in determining step size is overestimation; teachers
who already know the material tend to underestimate the difficulty students

will have in learning it. Think of some courses you have taken in which most of the material was new to you and you had little opportunity for feedback until after the mid-semester exam. A few students do very well in these (and all) courses, but if you are unfortunate enough to have made a few key misinterpretations early in the semester, they may have snowballed into massive problems by mid-semester time—or you have become discouraged by the "difficulty" of the course. Small steps with frequent feedback and reinforcement make this problem unnecessary.

Now think of primary students just beginning to learn to read and handle numbers. Here the snowballing effect is much more likely because the skills being taught are almost always prerequisites for the next skills—that is, unless you master the first (addition, subtraction, or letter sounds), there's no way you can hope to master the next (multiplication or word sounds).

The size of each step should be determined on the basis of the difficulty of the responses for a given student. This will of course vary from student to student. A useful rule of thumb is this: If a given student can be expected to get at least 75 percent of his responses correct following the step, then the step is probably small enough (though the student who gets 75 percent still needs some remediation to master the objectives). When in doubt, however, choose the smaller step size.

Rule 7: Be Careful with Punishment—Punishment works, and it's simple and efficient, which is why it is the favorite and even the dominant technique of many teachers. Punishment is also painful, and schools should offer as little pain as possible. In some cases punishment is a reasonable choice because a few brief painful experiences are preferable to the unending pain of a lifetime maladjustment, but *punishment should only be used when it will eliminate a behavior that produces even greater punishment.*

Furthermore, there is the problem of conditioning. Any stimulus event that is frequently associated with punishment tends to take on a punishing effect itself. Even threats of removing a privilege must occasionally be backed up by the punishment to be effective. When a large proportion of a student's contacts with his teacher are followed by punishment or threat, you can expect all the typical reactions of avoidance, escape, aggression, etc. Even if the student doesn't break windows, attack the teacher, or become a truancy problem, he is apt to initiate fewer contacts with the teacher, show less interest in school and in school activities, and badmouth the teacher and educational affairs in general.

Any teacher, whether or not she has a native gift for the art of teaching, can teach effectively by carefully arranging and managing the events surrounding behaviors of each student. In this sense, *teaching is the careful arrangement of contingencies of reinforcement under which a student's behavior changes.*

8. Be able to describe each rule, when given its title, and for each rule describe a typical classroom situation in which a teacher might be tempted to violate the rule.

9. Describe a real-life situation in which an event intended to be punishing is really reinforcing.

10. Explain why a mediating consequent event need not violate the rule regarding immediacy.

11. How can you give reinforcement frequently and avoid satiation or excessive time off task?

12. State the rule of thumb regarding step size. Give an example from your own experience in which this rule was followed or violated.

13. Give an example from your own experience of where a frequent punishing event affected more than just the behavior being punished.

14. We often hear people saying things like "I never did like math" or "I never was very good in music—I guess music-lovers are born, not made." Cite three or more of the rules which, if followed, might have made things different for such a person, and explain how.

15. State and defend or criticize the concluding definition of "teaching."

Observing and
Recording Behavior

OBJECTIVES

When you complete unit 4, you should be able to:

* describe several ways in which careful and complete data recording in the classroom can be of considerable value to you as a teacher, as well as several dangers and mistakes you can avoid by using an objective observation and analysis procedure;
* interpret a graph and present data of your own in graph form;
* describe and differentiate between baseline and experimental phases, and describe the "envelope" method for predicting what a "significant difference" in the experimental phase data will look like;
* specify three procedures (reversal, control, multiple baseline) for determining whether a change that you introduced into a classroom situation was really what made the difference in student performance.

Why Measure?

You already have rather well-developed skills in observing the behavior of others. You have already learned how to be sensitive to important cues and how to respond appropriately to these cues. But these skills of selection and interpretation may be a hindrance as well as a help. Since you have learned to select or pay attention to certain aspects of another's behavior and not other aspects and since no one can attend to every detail, you run the risk of overlooking some details which may be functionally related to future events. Furthermore, your perception and your interpretation of behavior can easily be swayed by your expectations—perceptive selection habits you have developed, details you have frequently noticed before in similar situations, what others expect you to see and report, and what would be most advantageous for you to see and report.

The reports of witnesses to accidents, criminal acts, and ordinary conversations supply many examples of the human observer's tendency to observe selectively and to insert subjective interpretations as if they were really observed. The same kind of tendency occurs daily in classrooms. In her end-of-the-year report on students, a teacher might describe one student as hyperactive. What the teacher observed was something like this: the student sat in his seat for three minutes and drew with his crayons, then got up and went to another student's seat and took a different colored crayon, went back to his seat and drew for thirty seconds, got up and returned the crayon, went to another student's seat and took another crayon, punched him in the arm when the other student objected, etc., etc. Many rapid series of behavior units like this might disturb the teacher, and as a result the teacher would be more apt to pay attention to and even exaggerate all of this student's behaviors, though she might not notice similar behaviors of another student who was less disturbing to her. The student's teacher next year, after reading the report, will tend to expect the "hyperactivity" to continue in the next grade. At the end of the next year, the student's report might contain words like "maybe some brain damage or a learning disability." Such labels may not represent careful observational data, and they surely represent subjective interpretation.

The teacher who wants to be an objective observer must stick as closely as possible to the actual behavior data and be careful of interpretive remarks that are based on inferences. It is not easy to do this, partly because pure behavioral data sounds so dull and unnatural. To observe and record only the behavior that occurs demands a great degree of self-discipline both in continued concentration on a series of behavioral details and in recording only what was observed, without subjective interpretations.

Once you have observed and recorded a stream of behavioral events, you can then begin to analyze these data by looking for *patterns* between similar behaviors and their consequences or their preceding events, patterns of interaction between the student and peers or teacher, and the particular *effects* of certain procedures (new or old) on specific behaviors. You will probably not find what you are looking for with certainty, but you will probably find *suggestive evidence* that certain events usually followed certain behaviors, that other events usually preceded other behaviors, and that the frequency of certain behaviors changed or did not change when new procedures were introduced. On the basis of these suggestive data, you may have a *hunch* that a certain consequent event, if made contingent on a certain kind of behavior, might increase that behavior. But this would have to be tested out by implementing the contingency and then carefully observing the specific behavior, the consequence, and the frequency. Of course, analysis of behavioral sequences must be tailored to fit the kind of problem one is investigating.

When you are doing purely exploratory observation, you want to keep a running account of as many behaviors as you can, as well as when they occurred, how long they lasted, and what behaviors by others preceded, concurred with, or followed them. From this running narrative, you can find evidence to suggest one or a few specific behaviors to look at closely. Then you gather more detailed information on these behaviors and analyze these data very carefully.

"I can just picture myself as a teacher trying to record all the behaviors and their times for thirty students for seven hours a day." The picture is ridiculous, of course. Seldom does a teacher need to be concerned about all the behaviors of all the students all the time, but whenever there is some question of concern, there is need for precise and accurate data.

To make the task of data recording less overwhelming, a beginning teacher might choose to focus at first on just one problem student for a sample period of time each day. Later on, several behaviors of several students can be recorded without much trouble.

The academic progress of each student is of prime importance; here the need for continuous measurement is critical. The good teacher cannot risk guessing in this area. She must have at least daily records of what each student did, what tasks each attempted, where each had trouble, how long it took each, the reinforcing event preferences of each, and so forth. Without these accurate records, the teacher has no reliable basis for making daily decisions about the best next step for each student.

Furthermore, as we will see in later units, if the teacher has a truly individualized academic program for the students and manages the consequences well, there is seldom any cause to worry about disciplining the students. The consequences for good work *can be* made strong enough to override rather quickly the temptation of students to engage in counterproductive activities. But it's impossible to manage instruction and its consequent events well without precise data.

It is also helpful and convincing to have solid evidence when you try to enlist cooperation of parents ("Johnny always finishes his work at home"), or explain results to other teachers ("It can't work"), or sell the principal ("The students don't need that").

So extensive data recording has many important values for a teacher who wants to teach well. Precise descriptions of behavior allow the teacher to:

1. verify whether or not preconceptions about a student are true;
2. discover behavior patterns which might suggest a solution to a problem;
3. make instructional decisions which increase each student's achievement and satisfaction;
4. evaluate the effectiveness of each part of each student's program;
5. document a situation, a result, or a need in communicating with other educators and interested parties.

1. List several kinds of errors a teacher could make in observing students.

2. What do you look for in a recorded stream of behavioral events? And if you find it, what do you do with it?

3. Describe several values in data recording for a teacher.

Baseline

Let's say you wanted to increase the amount of time Johnny spends actually working on his assignment because your impression is that he wastes a lot of time daydreaming. Before you try to change it, however, you should first verify your impressions; just how much time does Johnny spend working? First you *define* what you will accept as "working" behavior. Since you can't get inside his head and discover whether he is actually reading or thinking, you might decide that whenever he is using the appropriate materials and has his eyes directed towards them, you will count that as "working."

Then you begin to *record* how much time he spends working. You might choose a fifteen minute independent work period to use as a sample period. A stop watch would make the job much easier; simply start the watch whenever he is working, stop it when he stops working, start it up again when he starts. At the end you have a total number of minutes he spent working, out of the possible total fifteen minutes. You would want to repeat this data recording for at least several days because his behavior during a short period on a given day may not be typical of what he usually does.

These preliminary data, collected before you make any change in your procedures, are called *baseline* data. One reason you need these baseline data is so that after you have introduced some modification you can compare the results empirically with the behavior rate before the change and tell whether what you did made any difference.

How long the baseline period should run depends on the behavior, the observation sessions, and the data you get. What you want is reasonable assurance that if you continued collecting baseline data they would look very much like what you already have. You can't have this assurance if the behavior you are concerned with occurs throughout the day and you have observed and recorded it only five minutes each day for three days and always at the same time and in the same environment. Furthermore, if the data show a possible downward or upward tendency, you will have to continue collecting baseline data until the tendency is confirmed or until the data level off within a predictable range.

In most cases, you should probably observe and record unobtrusively—i.e., in such a way that the person does not know you are closely observing his behavior. If a person knows he is being observed, he may change his behavior from what it typically is because, based on his past experience, he expects you to deliver some good or bad consequences contingent on what he does. But in certain situations you may judge, for example, that the person might lose confidence in you if he discovered your recording activities.

If the person does know you are observing him, his change in behavior might be just temporary, and he might soon revert back to his usual behavior when he learns that there is in fact no new consequence contingent on his behavior. Prolonging the baseline phase of data recording will show you when and to what degree this happens. You can't rely on this temporary change; sometimes the behavior never reverts back, especially when the observer is an important reinforcing agent to the person being observed. In self-management, for example, there are many reported studies in which fingernail biting, hair pulling, and even cigarette smoking decreased steadily to a zero rate when the person began simply to record the baseline frequency of his own behaviors. In these cases the new procedure of carefully recording the frequency of such behaviors was enough to accomplish the objective, perhaps simply by helping the person discriminate his own behavior.

Graphing

Now back to our example of Johnny's working behavior. Say your record for one week looked like this:

Day	Minutes
Monday	8
Tuesday	6
Wednesday	12
Thursday	7
Friday	8

A column of numbers is not a good way to display measures, especially as the column gets longer (as yours will), but you can easily transform it into a graph that will give you a quick and easy picture of the information.

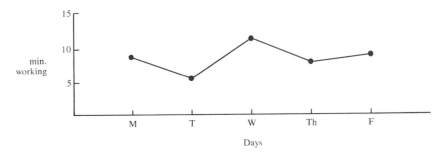

Figure 4–1

As you can see in figure 4–1, the units of time are plotted along the x- (horizontal) axis and the behavior frequency (in this case minutes of working) is plotted along the y- (vertical) axis. Each data point is plotted by lining up the point with the scales on both the vertical and the horizontal axes.

Instead of recording the rate of behavior (that is, its frequency per unit of time) as was done above, you might sometimes want to record the ratio of behavior to opportunity. This is an especially useful method when the time period for observing does not stay the same from day to day. For example, say that when you were observing Johnny's working behavior, Wednesday's independent study period lasted twenty-five minutes instead of the usual fifteen minutes for some unforeseen reason. Looking at figure 4–1 you might think that Johnny did much better on Wednesday than on the other days, but the longer period on Wednesday simply means that he had more opportunity on Wednesday to add up the minutes of working time. You can correct for this misleading impression by graphing the ratio of behavior to opportunity. Change each data point into a percentage by solving a fraction whose numerator is the actual behavior frequency and whose denominator is the total possible behavior frequency. For example, on Wednesday Johnny worked 12 minutes out of a possible 25 minutes, so the ratio is 12/25 or close to 50 percent, which means that about half the time he was working. A ratio graph for this baseline period would look like figure 4–2.

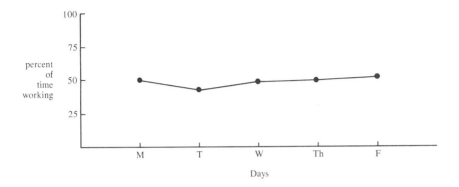

Figure 4–2

Now it is clear that Johnny's rate of working behavior stays pretty constantly at about 50 percent. Whenever the opportunity for exhibiting the behavior varies significantly from one observation period to another, you must make some adjustment such as the ratio method to make your behavioral picture accurate.

Experimental Phase

Once you have a baseline of data that seems stable and reliable, you can proceed to implement the change in contingencies that you suspect will change the behavior in some way. This change marks a new phase in your graph and in your observational study called an *experimental phase.* But you continue to record data on the same behavior and in the same way as you did before so that you can justifiably compare the data in the baseline and new phase.

But now you need a way to tell whether what you are doing is having any effect or enough effect to make your efforts worthwhile. There are statistical calculations you could make with your data, and in some cases they may be the most appropriate way to tell. Statistics are not always necessary to make quick on-line judgments about the effectiveness of your changes. Wells Hively has suggested a very useful way to eyeball a graph to make these judgments. He calls it the *envelope method.*[1]

Suppose you want to see whether giving a student time to read comic books in math class will increase the number of problems he answers correctly. For your baseline you give him a thirty-minute period each day to work problems, without saying anything about comic books, and count the number of problems he answers correctly each day. Notice that with this behavior there's no need for a stop watch; you can simply make slashes or mark numbers on a piece of paper. Your graph at the end of two weeks looks like figure 4–3.

---

[1] Wells Hively, unpublished notes, University of Minnesota, 1970.

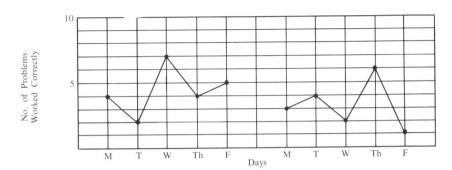

Figure 4-3

You can see from figure 4-3 that he's doing a little work every day, but not a lot, and as time goes on he doesn't seem to be getting any faster or slower. You might be willing to predict what the third week's data would look like. You can do this by eye; imagine you are fitting an envelope over the record so that the envelope covers about 80 percent of the points and extend it into the next week (see figure 4-4).

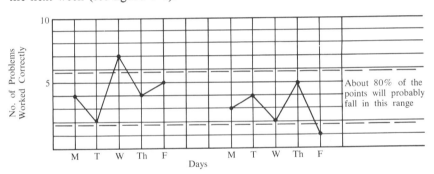

Figure 4-4

It is very important that you make this prediction before you make a change in the conditions or procedures. If you make an arrangement for the student to work for comic books and then try to look back and see whether it makes a difference, your prediction will be so cluttered up by what you know really happened that you will never be able to trust it. We usually want our experiments to be successful because the consequences for success or failure are frequently strong. Unless we predict in advance and commit ourselves to a preset criterion for "success," we are apt to interpret chance or minor changes as signs of success.

Your prediction should include not only what the baseline would look like if it were continued, but also a quantitative statement of how much change you will require in order to label your procedure successful. If after you change a contingency 70 percent of the data points still fall within the extended baseline envelope, the 10 percent change could easily be due to chance. However, if 70 percent of the data points fall outside the envelope, then the change in behavior is clear and substantial. In any case, be sure you decide on your own standards before you change a variable.

After you've made a prediction, you can do something different and compare the results to that prediction. Suppose you arrange to let the student spend five minutes reading a comic book for each ten problems that he completes correctly. If the results look like those in figure 4–5, you could be fairly certain that the comic book contingency was effective.

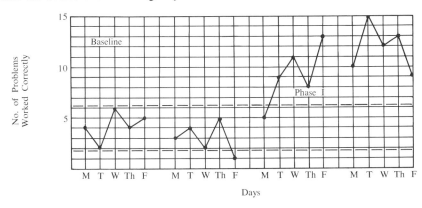

Figure 4–5

Any method of prediction is very risky if you only have a few data points in the baseline. For that reason you will usually need at least a week of baseline data.

If the baseline is not as stable as Johnny's, then prediction is more risky. But again this risk can be reduced by extending the baseline period. In general, the more variable the baseline record is, the longer the baseline should be continued. There are no hard rules telling you how long to collect baseline data before introducing a change. In general, before you make a change, you should be convinced that if you continued baseline, 80 percent of the data points would continue to fall within the 80 percent envelope range.

4. Why is a graph useful?

5. Try drawing a graph of imaginary data. Be sure each axis is clearly identified, the behavior is an observable one, and the baseline phase and at least one experimental phase are clearly marked.

6. What is a baseline? Why is it necessary?

7. Why is it important to make a prediction based on your baseline before introducing a change? Describe the "envelope" method.

8. On what basis should you decide whether or not your baseline phase has lasted long enough? Describe how baseline observation can, by itself, produce behavioral change.

Evaluating the Change

What if the baseline record looked like figure 4–6?

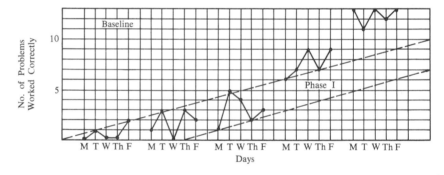

Figure 4–6

Even before you've made any change (baseline), you can see that his baseline rate is increasing. You can still make a prediction, but since the baseline is not "stable," the prediction is much chancier. A "straight-line" prediction as illustrated in figure 4–6 may or may not make sense. Some sort of curve line might be just as reasonable. In figure 4–6, it looks like there was a clear effect because of the contingency. But how can we be sure?

There is also the danger, no matter how stable the baseline appears, that the effect is real but due to some *other change,* not the one you made. You might have been inadvertently giving the student more attention and praise at the same time that you offered him the comic book contingency, or his parents might have imposed some contingency on the student at the same time. It is often difficult to separate and pinpoint the cause-effect relationships.

There are procedures you can use to convince yourself that the change you make is critical and has important effects of its own. You could get some other students, keep the same records on them, and introduce the comic book contingency at different times. If most of their records showed a rather sudden change shortly after this arrangement, you may begin to feel confident that the effect is "real." The idea of exposing several people or groups to systematically different conditions and comparing their performance has in it the basic statistical notion of *"control group."* The control-group method requires you to take several groups, which are in approximately identical situations during baseline, and change one variable for one group while keeping the other group in baseline conditions or introduce the change to both groups but at different times, and then compare the performance of the two groups under these different conditions. See figure 4–7.

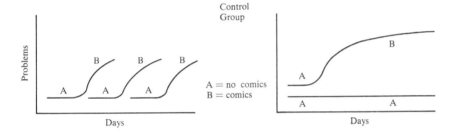

Figure 4–7

Or you might use a *reversal* procedure. Remove the comic book contingency in a second experimental phase and return to baseline conditions to see if the behavior rate returns eventually to baseline rate. In this method, the one person is serving as his own control. Many teachers don't like to use the reversal method because they don't want to lose the good results they have achieved, even for a few days. See figure 4–8.

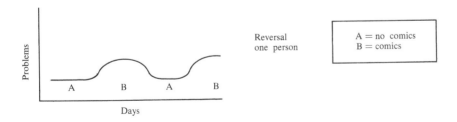

Figure 4–8

Still another way called the *multiple baseline* method is to record several behaviors (of the same general type) of *one* person and then apply the contingency to each behavior at a different time. For example, you could record the rate of a student's work in math, spelling, and reading and in your experimental phase apply the contingency to math only (while continuing to record the baseline rate in the other subjects), then later apply the contingency to both math and spelling, and finally to all three. See figure 4–9. If you find a clear increase in each rate when (and only when) the change is applied to each subject, your confidence in the procedure is justified. If you find that when you apply the change to only one subject the rate for all subjects increase, it's probable that some other change besides the one you made helped produce the increase.

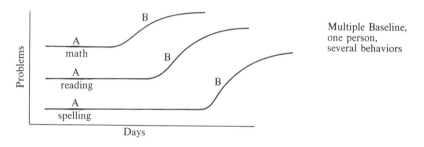

Figure 4–9

The trick in making up your plan of procedures is to arrange a sequence of conditions for one or more persons and behaviors in such a way that you will learn as much as possible as quickly as possible.

9. Describe three ways (reversal, multiple baseline, control group) to be sure that the experimental change you made really made the observed difference in the data.

unit 5

Classroom
Observation Project

OBJECTIVES

In unit 5 you are to:

* carry out a classroom observation and analysis project of your own, in which you define a specific set of classroom behaviors, identify some "guess relationships" among these behavioral events, collect precise data on these events, and present the data in graph form to illustrate your guess relationships.

If you have the opportunity to visit a real classroom and observe its operation, the experience can be very useful and instructive, providing you have prepared yourself to take full advantage of the situation. You will want to do much more than just get a general "feel" for what happens in the classroom. A more thorough analysis of the classroom activity will give you practice at precise recording and measurement of classroom behavior and also give you very specific ideas about what you might do or not do in your own classroom.

Whether your opportunity to observe is for one hour or several hours, on one day or spread over several days, the following notes will help you prepare yourself to use the time well.

1. Use the first part of the observation period to get a general global feel for what is going in the classroom. Take notes on the physical ar-

rangement of the classroom, the materials and procedure the teacher is using, the availability of other resources, the amount of verbal interaction between the teacher and the students and among the students themselves, and the amount and general purpose of physical movement in the classroom. Complete this overall description as quickly as possible; remember that your overall impressions will continue to be formed through the rest of your observation period as well.

To prepare for this initial stage, construct a form to record your general impressions; list each of the general aspects of the classroom and its procedure that you want to note, with several blank lines after each, and include space at the end for additional notes. This kind of form, prepared in advance, not only saves you some time during the actual observation, but it also forces you to think about and define the specific aspects of the classroom you wish to note.

2. As soon as possible, you should begin to record the sequence of behaviors, the action and reactions of teachers and students. Unless you plan for this in advance, you will spend most of your time writing, with very little left for looking, and your notes will probably be somewhat confusing and useless. To avoid this, you need to pre- pare a recording schedule or form and spend some time practicing using it. At the end of this unit, there is a suggested Behavior Interac- tion Recording Schedule (see figure 5–1) which you could use for this second stage of your observation. You can also use your own revised version of this schedule or another one of your own making.

   Whatever form you use, it should contain a set of categories of possible teacher or student behaviors, inclusive enough so that you can record most of the potentially significant events that occur, and simple enough so that it can be used to record behaviors quickly. The temporal relationships between the events should also be recorded. The results of your recordings can thus be analyzed to give an overall yet detailed statement of the behaviors and their time sequence, fre- quency measures for specific types of behaviors, and analytical state- ments about possible functional relationships existing between several types of student/teacher behavior.

3. From such an analysis, you then have some data-based reasons for focusing in more detail on specific behaviors and/or specific persons. Your data might suggest that the behavioral interaction between the teacher and one particular student was especially interesting or trou- blesome for one reason or another; a special recording form for these specific behaviors would then be appropriate. Or you might want to focus on the types of verbal interaction between teacher and students; the Flanders Verbal Interaction Analysis Schedule or one of its many

variations[1] would be appropriate here. You might want to focus simply on the type of questions and questioning methods the teacher uses; using unit 29 you could devise a recording form to collect this information. Similarly, you might chose to concentrate on collecting data regarding the types and frequency of teacher feedback, teacher praise or disapproval, request for attention by a particular student, off-task responses by a particular student, etc.

Whichever special focus you choose, it must be defined precisely and in measurable terms beforehand, and your recording system must include the temporal relationships between one behavior and another.

---

[1]See Ned A. Flanders, *Analyzing Teacher Behavior* (Reading, Mass.: Addison-Wesley Publishing Co., 1970), or check the references to other systems in Volume 4, Number 1 (Fall 1970) issue of *Journal of Research and Development in Education.*

Behavior Interaction Recording Schedule

Teacher Behaviors

Direct:	give directions, rules, assignments.
Inform:	present material, explain.
Prompt:	demonstrate a response, give a student hints or supply part of a response.
Question:	present a question to the students, open or closed.
Feedback:	evaluate a student response, identify correct or wrong features.
Praise:	for a response or part of a response by a student or students.
Ignore:	give no response to a noticed student response.
Disapprove:	express disapproval for a student response or lack of one.
Other:	any other teacher response or lack of one that might be significant.

Student Behaviors

Task Response:	a nonverbal behavior that is appropriate to teacher directions; e.g., working in a workbook, reading text, working on a project.
Verbal Response:	requested by teacher or uncued, but appropriate to teacher directions.
Attending Response:	appropriately looking at the teacher, a display, or another student.
Request for Information:	ask question about content, or for materials, directions, or privilege.
Request for Attention:	raise hand, call teacher's name; other direct means.
Off-Task Response:	a nonverbal behavior that is not appropriate to teacher directions; e.g., disruptive noise, aggression, clear inattention to current task.
Passive:	no apparent response (appropriate or inappropriate) at all.
Other:	any other student response that might be significant.

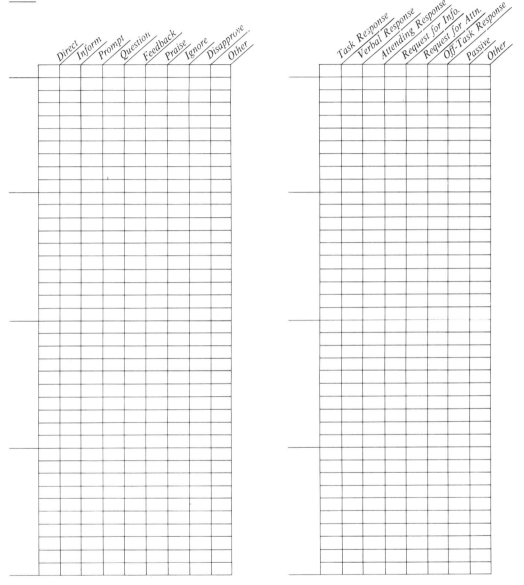

Figure 5–1

Behavior Interaction Recording Schedule

51

Figure 5–2 is an example of a filled-in Behavior Interaction Recording Schedule.

Notes on the Use of the B.I.R.S.

1. When the behaviors of a *class* of students are being observed and recorded, it is useful to indicate how many students performed the behavior you checked. A quick way to indicate this is to make a check mark and an M,S.,F., or 1 to indicate that the behavior was performed by *m*ost, *s*ome, *f*ew, or only one of the students. In a class of thirty students, M could indicate 20 or more, S, 10–20, and F, 2–10.

2. The use of this or any recording schedule requires you to make quick decisions about the categories into which each behavior fits. The first time you use a schedule you will undoubtedly misplace some behaviors and not see others. For this reason it is necessary to practice using the instrument *before* you have to depend on the accuracy of your recordings. *Videotapes* of a classroom scene are especially useful for this practice, especially if you and several other students can view the same scene and later compare notes to check your accuracy. *TV talk shows* offer another opportunity to practice; here you would substitute host for teacher and guests for students. Not all the behavior categories will always apply, but the number of people being observed is small and this is an advantage when first learning the schedule.

3. If a specific behavior continues for an extended period of time (e.g., thirty seconds or longer), you can use a dash after the check to indicate this extension of the same behavior.

4. There are a variety of ways to analyze the data after you have finished observing and recording. You can simply total the various columns to give an overall indication of frequency of certain kinds of behaviors by the teacher or students. It might be more helpful to look for interaction patterns. You might find a pattern in which most teacher behaviors are directing and informing behaviors, while the students are either attending or passive; or you might find that both teacher and student behaviors are well distributed among many categories; or you might find that many of the student behaviors fall into the off-task category, followed usually by disapproval or direction behaviors by the teacher. These are three distinctly different interaction patterns. Each would suggest a different focus for your third observation stage.

Teacher Behaviors

Student Behaviors

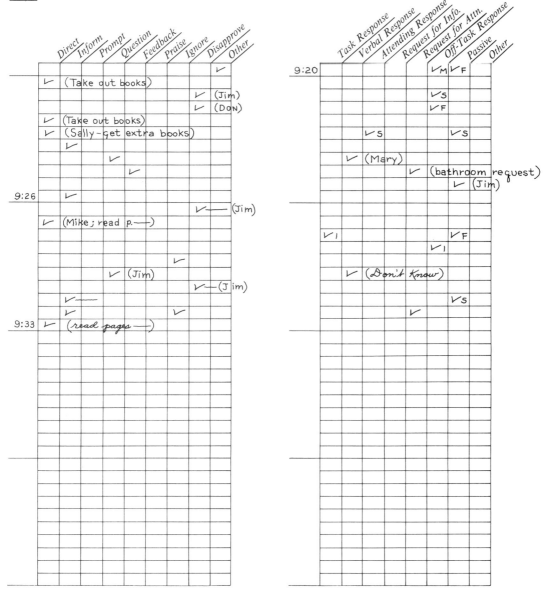

Figure 5–2

Behavior Interaction Recording Schedule

53

Be sure that you check your own school's policy regarding procedures for school visits before you contact the principal of the school you wish to visit. When you meet with the principal to ask his permission, be sure to note the procedural details that he suggests. He is responsible for the day-to-day operation of the school, and he will want your visit to be unobtrusive so that the students are not distracted from their instruction.

If you have the opportunity to visit a classroom several times (say for an hour or so each time), then you can use the time between visits to decide on the specific behaviors you will record and the forms you will use. This will also give you time to have your behavior definitions and forms reviewed by your instructor before you use them.

Your final report on your observation project should include all your records, as well as your analysis of the data in one or more of the ways suggested in this unit and/or by your instructor.

Analysis of Human Learning: Part A

OBJECTIVES

When you finish this unit, you should be able to:

* list a large variety of real-life reinforcing and punishing events, including verbal and social consequences, and describe how each becomes reinforcing or punishing for an individual;
* analyze and explain classroom behavior patterns in terms of the Premack principle and describe several methods for determining a student's hierarchy of preferred activities;
* define five schedules of reinforcement, differentiate them on the basis of procedure, uses, and patterns of responding during reinforcement and extinction, and cite real-life examples of behavior patterns maintained under each schedule;
* describe how neutral consequences can accidentally become reinforcers or punishers, and construct original examples of such unintentional teaching.

Early Applications

The science of behavior began in the laboratory, where the behavior of lower organisms was subjected to detailed investigation. Gradually this analysis produced laws and procedures for strengthening and decreasing a specific type of behavior, molding (shaping) entirely new forms of behavior, predicting when and under what circumstances a behavior would occur, building long and complex chains of responses and, in short, constructing virtually any pattern of behavior that could be defined clearly enough to specify when the reinforcer should be delivered. These laws and procedures were the important products of this new science.

There were also the more spectacular showpieces, of course, like pigeons who played ping-pong or tunes on the piano or who guided bombs to their target with incredible accuracy or who served as quality inspectors on assembly lines (with better results than their human counterparts). In the realm of "higher mental processes" there were the chimps who were trained to discuss psychology with their trainers or to count objects and use the binary number system to report how many there were or to discriminate concepts and form rules.

The application of these principles from animal to human behavior has been surprisingly straightforward. There are quantitative differences, of course, in the number and complexity of things a human can learn. The main qualitative difference seems to be in what a person already has learned when he begins to learn something else. For example, his ability to communicate to himself and others and his resulting ability to think and reason complicate his reaction to somewhat different future events.

Perhaps the first practical human application of these principles occurred in 1943 when Dr. Fred Keller designed a program to teach Army Signal Corps recruits to receive Morse Code. The fact that he arranged to reinforce every correct response immediately (as opposed to the delivery of an overall performance score the next day) made a big difference in the efficiency and effectiveness of the training program. This same technique of "immediate feedback" after a student responds to the stimulus material is an essential feature of what is now called programmed instruction, a technique now in use at all levels of education.

In the 1940s and early '50s, concerted attempts were made to apply these principles to some "way out" groups of humans, such as psychotics, retardates, and delinquents. Autistic children, who show little more than simple repetitive motor behaviors like rocking or hitting themselves, have been trained to care for themselves, talk, play with others, read, write, and compute. At first the reinforcers were food items; later praise and attention were paired regularly and then occasionally with food, toys, or privileges; in this way these more "natural" events were made into reinforcing events. Long-term institutionalized schizophrenics were taught normal speech and behavior patterns and other skills enabling them to function effectively in the "normal" world.

Even individuals who thought they were blind and were considered blind by their associates were taught to perform tasks which required them to discriminate various visual stimuli. Of course, these people were functionally blind but not completely so in a physical sense. It is interesting to note that after this training they used visual cues only when reinforcement depended on their use; when depending on the assistance of others was reinforced, they acted as if they were completely blind. In the last decade, the application of contingencies of reinforcement to educational settings has begun to be investigated, and we will consider many examples later in this unit as well as in succeeding units.

Unlimited Reinforcers

The list of potential reinforcers and punishers is as extensive as the list of behaviors they can change. At birth, there are only a few biologically dependent events that reinforce or punish a behavior they follow—unlearned reinforcing events such as food, water, bodily stimulation, and unlearned punishing events such as loud noise, a blow to the body, extreme heat or cold. This means that most consequent events are neutral events for an infant. But not for long. A person immediately begins to learn that these neutral events frequently come tied closely with other events that are not neutral. An infant cries when he is hungry or uncomfortable, and as a consequence he gets food, but he also gets the sight of his mother, a lot of fondling, cooing, and smiles. Through repeated pairings of food (the unconditioned reinforcing event) and the neutral events which accompany food, the child "learns" to cry (or later on, to smile, to make sounds, to walk) for these consequent events by themselves. They become reinforcing events in their own right, though they will still need to be paired at least occasionally with unlearned reinforcers to maintain their effectiveness.

The general *rule,* then, is this: to make any neutral consequent event into a reinforcing event, closely and frequently follow its occurrence with an event that is already reinforcing. A neutral event can become a punishing event by a similar pairing process. Words like "stop that," "No, don't," become punishers if they are closely followed by a slap or spanking or loss of privileges. After frequent pairings of this type, the word itself acts not only as a signal that more severe punishment might now be given but also as a learned punisher by itself.

Other neutral things like coins, paper money, tokens, gold stars, points, grades, trading stamps can be "conditioned" in the same way by arranging for other already reinforcing events to be available as backup reinforcers. These token reinforcers then become *mediating* events to the attainment of other reinforcers and acquire some reinforcing properties of their own. Because these mediating reinforcers can be given frequently in small amounts, collected, and later exchanged for events that can be dispensed only at certain times, they are very helpful to the teacher who wants to reinforce each student's improvement with reinforcers that are effective for him.

1. Name several important products and applications of the early analysis of behavior.

2. How does a neutral event become a reinforcing or punishing event for a person? Can you think of an original real-life example?

3. Give several examples of mediators for punishing events.

For humans, the *verbal* behavior of others is probably the largest category of learned reinforcers and punishers. Words of praise or interest or criticism and certain tones of voice, smiles, and frowns that frequently accompany this speech become strong "*social*" reinforcing and punishing consequences for most humans because they have in the past frequently preceded a wide variety of other events that are already effective reinforcers or punishers. Most of us will work to get such social consequences—or to avoid getting them.

There are exceptions. You will occasionally find students in your classes who are not turned on by praise—yours or anyone else's. For them, praise and criticism are *neutral* events. In their past experiences, praise and criticism were too infrequently paired with goodies and badies to become learned consequences. You can, of course, still make praise a reinforcer for such a student by using the frequent pairing procedure, but first you must find a consequent event that is already an effective reinforcing event for this student. At the other extreme, you will meet students who are, as we say, overly dependent on what others think. For them social reinforcers are so strong that they override the effect of other potential reinforcing events. You may think it's better (that is, the chances for desired consequences are better) for you to do your own thing in certain situations, despite the risk of criticism from others. But that isn't the way this kind of student learned it. He learned in his past experience that social reinforcers were the only way to fly and that social punishers signaled unbearable consequences. In all of these cases, the future arrangement of contingencies, if done carefully and systematically, could change the behavior patterns of these students and the effectiveness of social events on their behavior. A student who is moderately turned on by social consequences can be made extremely dependent on them. The same student could be taught that social reinforcers are usually empty words and not worth paying them attention.

And now you say, "why would anyone want to do that?" For the same basic reason that a person would "want" to do anything else—because he has *learned* from the consequences of similar behavior in the past that doing this (or anything else) leads to good consequences for the doer (or to the avoidance of bad consequences). That answer is not entirely facetious. We all know of parents who have taught their children to hate them; in general, they accomplish this by making many of the consequences for the children's behavior punishing events, with the result that not only are specific behaviors punished but also those who do the punishing (the parents) and everything connected with the punishment (the home environment) become conditioned punishers. Why do parents do that? Because the results are reinforcing to them; that is, in the past these parents frequently got the results they wanted (quiet, obedience, no hassle, etc.) by punishing, and they don't know any other way to get these results. The children reinforced the parents' punishing behavior. Everyone, including parents and teachers, operates under the same laws of behavior. The usual reason why any of us does anything is because we have *learned* from the consequences of similar past behavior that doing it leads to good consequences for us.

So far this whole examination of human behavior and its functional relationship with surrounding events is *amoral.* You will learn many things about human behavior, how it gets going, why it changes or doesn't change. You will learn rules and procedures for strengthening, weakening, or otherwise modifying the behavior of others and of yourself. When carefully used, they will work to whatever end you choose. And your choice of ends is itself functionally related to your past experiences. How you *should* choose to use this skill is another question—very important—but more appropriate to individual and social ethics than to the analysis of behavior.

But as a teacher (or parent or friend) you don't really have much of a choice *whether* or not to change behavior by arranging consequent events. Since most human behavior is primarily a function of its consequences, you really have three choices:

1. carefully arrange reinforcing consequences for the behavior which, in your best judgment, will be useful and produce overall happiness and satisfaction for the behaver and his society;
2. leave the choice of behaviors, contingencies, and consequences to the person's peers;
3. leave the choice of behaviors, contingencies, and consequences to chance factors.

Whichever you choose, the other person will still learn. If you choose the second or third option, the things he learns may be "bad" from your point of view, but they nevertheless will be learned according to the same laws of human behavior. If you choose the second or third option because you "don't want to play God," you have decided to let other people and chance factors "play God," probably less effectively and carefully than you. Abdicating one's responsibility to teach does not abrogate the laws of learning.

Premack Principle

Rather than think of behavior as one kind of thing and reinforcers as another kind of thing, it is better to think of both as *events* (or nonevents), as happenings or activities (or the absence of them). After all, the behavior of one person can be a consequent or preceding event for another person's behavior. Your word of praise to a student for his persistence at working out a problem is a behavior (yours) and a reinforcing consequent event for his hanging in there, and his continuing to work until he succeeds is a behavior (his) and a reinforcing event for you for encouraging him. Furthermore, reinforcers are technically not things but events or activities. Food is not the reinforcer; the eating of food by a hungry person is the reinforcer, and that makes it an activity or event. Money as a thing is not reinforcing, but the events of receiving it and getting to use it are reinforcing.

Viewing both behaviors and consequences as events makes it easier to analyze situations in terms of the Premack principle. You can increase the frequency of any of a student's activities by making his access to another more preferred activity dependent on first engaging in this target activity. All behavior change involves a contingency between a less preferred event and a more preferred event.

To find out what a student's preferred activities are, you might simply ask him. But in some difficult cases, the student's verbal response may be inaccurate, unhelpful, or even nonexistent. Or you could simply observe his choices in a normal classroom situation for several days. Again in some difficult cases you may not learn much because a student may have learned that if he wants to avoid trouble his only choice is to shut up, do the minimum work, and no more.

The free-access method is often the best way to measure a student's activity preferences. A teacher might give the students an hour of free time during which each student can choose whatever he wants from a set list of activities, some related directly to the subject matter and some only indirectly or not at all. The teacher can limit the possible activities to those that are tolerable to her and others. By observing the choices of each student and the length of time taken by a student in each activity, the teacher has a reliable index of each student's preferences. She can then arrange a contingency (lower probability to higher probability) and get the academic results she wants without requiring anything other than what's available in the classroom. The teacher is not limited to just "things" as reinforcers. Sometimes, as in Wenda's case (above), the teacher does not need a free-access period to determine some preferences. At other times, just asking the student will produce useful information about his preferences. Use of this method in high school classes has shown that doing homework in another subject or getting the opportunity to engage in a variety of enrichment activities, experiments, creating drama, etc. can be high probability events for many students.

4. Name several "social" consequences and describe how they come to be reinforcing or punishing events.

5. Why are some students indifferent to social consequences while others are excessively dependent on them?

6. Why would a teacher teach a student to hate school? (Remember, a teacher's behavior is influenced, knowingly or not, by consequences just like everyone else's.)

7. Explain the Premack principle in terms of events and preferences. What are three methods you could use to determine a student's preferences?

To this point, what you have learned about human behavior can be called a very general overview. The analysis of human learning has a great deal more detail and precision to it, far more than can be taught here. But the more you know about these details, the more confidently you as a teacher can arrange contingencies for each of your students and the more successful you and they will be. The following sections and units look more closely at some details of human behavior.

Schedules of Reinforcement

The quickest way to increase a behavior is to reinforce it every time it occurs (*continuous* reinforcement). But this is not the most economical way. A teacher would go bananas if she tried to praise each student after he had read and understood each paragraph, and the students might never finish an algebra course if after each problem they were given ten minutes in a more preferred activity. Besides, continuous reinforcement may result in satiation at which point the reinforcer loses some of its effectiveness. There are other schedules we might use, and each schedule has its own characteristic effects on behavior.

We might choose an intermittent schedule of reinforcement—that is, reinforce *some* of the behaviors of a certain type, but *not every one.* There are several types of intermittent schedules. An intermittent contingency might specify the *number of responses* (after you've worked these ten problems correctly, you can finish reading your story), or it might specify an *interval of time* (if you stay in your seat for the next five minutes, you can go to recess). And the interval of time or the number of responses can be *predictable* (every ten problems or every five minutes) *or unpredictable* (every ten problems on the average, but in fact after 7, then 12, then 3, then 18 problems).

Each of these schedules of reinforcement is effective, though there are some limits. For example, reinforcing a student's reading after every twentieth book is not a reliable procedure to start with because he has to experience too many unreinforced events before reaching criterion and he probably would never get to the reinforcer. The same problem exists in the marking system for many students. If the final grade is the only or one of the few reinforcers he gets for several months of school work and homework, he's on the train to dropout city—unless in the beginning of his school experience he received nearly continuous reinforcement for each little bit of accomplishment, and only gradually was that schedule faded to an intermittent schedule of larger and larger amounts of work for reinforcement.

The general rule is: "When you are *beginning* to teach a new task or new kind of behavior, reinforce (or punish) *continuously;* as the behavior becomes fairly *stable* and proficient, *gradually shift to intermittent* reinforcement and *gradually require more and more* correct responses prior to reinforcement.

There is another critical rule (which we will see more of later); always reinforce little bits of *improvement* or steps in the right direction. If you want Harry Holyterror to become a turned-on student, perhaps the first thing you will have to reinforce is just sitting in his seat for a few minutes, then sitting and paying attention, then doing at least something in his workbook, then doing something correctly in his workbook, etc. If you start out by waiting until Harry has done one page of his workbook problems correctly, you may still be waiting when they bury both of you.

8. Define: continuous reinforcement, intermittent reinforcement, predictable and unpredictable, satiation.

9. Can you explain the two rules about when and what to reinforce—to a friend who hasn't studied this unit?

There are important reasons, other than saving yourself time and effort, for gradually moving to a thin intermittent schedule of reinforcement. These reasons have to do with the different ways in which behavior responds to the different kinds of schedules. First you have to learn to read a cumulative graph (see notes on reading graphs in unit 4).

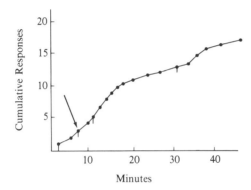

Figure 6–1

Figure 6–1 is a stylized graph, just for illustration. On the vertical axis is marked off the dependent variable (here we'll presume just any response) and on the horizontal axis we mark off the elapsed time (minutes here, but it could be hours, days, weeks, or just trials or sessions if each session was of equal length). Each *dot* represents a *response,* and it is made just above the time when it occurred and just beside the total number of responses made so far. For illustration, an arrow points to the dot which represents the third response which happened after about eight minutes had passed. Finally, the little *hatch mark* under the dot (and under several other dots in the graph) means that after that response, *reinforcement* occurred.

Connecting each dot with a continuous line gives you a quick picture of how the frequency of the behavior is increasing or decreasing. As the *slope* of this line (i.e., the degree to which the line slants or is tilted upward) increases we see that the behavior is increasing in frequency per minute or in rate. In this illustration, the first, third, and fifth responses were reinforced, and we can see that the slope of the line increases (it starts tilting more and more vertically), which means that the responses are occurring more and more frequently. Of course we could tell the same thing by counting how many responses occurred in the first ten minutes (four) and in the second ten minutes (seven), but it's easier to just look at how the slope of the line is changing.

For the first five responses, the reinforcement schedule was a predictable intermittent one (every other response was reinforced). Then things changed. The seventh response was not reinforced, nor the next, and the frequency of responding dropped dramatically. Later on another single response was reinforced, and the rate of responding increased but only briefly.

Now if you're sure you understand the above, let's go on to see what difference the various schedules make on behavior rates. If you're a little hazy about any aspect of a cumulative graph, review the above few paragraphs.

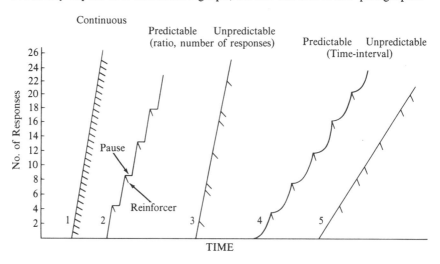

Figure 6–2

Figure 6–2 is a stylized illustration of the relative difference in behavior rate produced by different kinds of schedules. The left-hand line illustrates the general kind of data you might expect from continuous reinforcement (unless satiation occurred); notice it gives the highest rate of responding of all the schedules.

The next two lines depict intermittent reinforcement of some (but not all) of the responses. If the number of responses is the same for each reinforcing event (predictable), the rate is high but not as high as with continuous reinforcement; notice that with this schedule there is a short pause of no responding after each reinforcement before the subject gets back to work at about the same rate as before. You've probably noticed this in your own work habits; when you have several assignments or jobs of similar size, you tend to "take a break" after you finish one, or maybe just sit back for a few seconds, even though the reinforcement in this case is the secondary one of simply finishing the job. But if the reinforcement is unpredictable, the pause after reinforcement is eliminated.

The fourth and fifth lines illustrate performance under schedules where the passage of time is what determines when reinforcement occurs, rather than the number of responses. If the interval of time is regular (predictable) for each reinforcement, then the performance will have the "scalloped" effect seen in line 4; after each reinforcement, there is a period of no responding, then a *gradually* increasing rate of responding until just before reinforcement when it reaches a high rate. A perfect illustration of this is your study behavior for a class that has only a mid-semester and a final exam (and no papers or other presentations). A cumulative graph of your study behavior outside of class will probably look much like this fourth line; no study the first few weeks, then a little, increasing to a final few nights of heavy cramming before the mid-semester exam, and then a long pause and the same process leading to the final. If the amount of time before reinforcement is unpredictable, the rate of responding is very steady. If you reinforce a student whenever you look up and find him studying and you look up at various intervals averaging about every three minutes, this is the kind of steady study behavior you will get (presuming, again, that your reinforcer is a good one for him). Notice, however, that both of these time schedules produce a generally lower rate of responding than do the schedules which reinforce a number of responses. Notice also that making the schedule unpredictable generally eliminates any noticeable pause after reinforcement, whether the unpredictable schedule is for number of responses or for passage of time.

10. Practice drawing a graph of a specific behavior of a hypothetical student under each of the five kinds of schedules of reinforcement. Be able to explain the meaning of all aspects of the graphs (axes, number of responses and reinforcers, slope of line).

11. What is peculiar about the predictable ratio (number responses) schedule as opposed to the unpredictable ratio schedule?

12. What is peculiar about the predictable time-interval schedule as opposed to the unpredictable interval schedule?

13. Which schedule produces a higher rate of responding—ratio or interval?

14. Which schedule produces periods of no responding—predictable or unpredictable?

Schedules and Extinction

Another important difference in the effects of various schedules is seen when you later withdraw the reinforcement altogether (the process called *extinction*) for that particular behavior.

Figure 6-3, a series of data lines, shows the relative rates of responding during extinction after the response has been reinforced under different kinds of schedules. You can tell from the hatch marks where reinforcement was withdrawn (where extinction began). After continuous reinforcement the behavior during extinction drops out very quickly, though a couple of responses will occur occasionally after periods of no responding. After predictable intermittent reinforcement, whether for responses or passage of time (lines 2 and 4), complete extinction takes a little longer than after continuous reinforcement, with bursts of responding occurring occasionally. After unpredictable intermittent reinforcement (lines 3 and 5) total extinction of the response takes quite a long time and is relatively smooth in its decline.

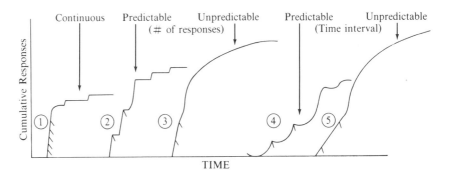

Figure 6-3

The fact that unpredictable intermittent reinforcement takes so long to extinguish is important to the teacher (and anyone else concerned about behavior) for several reasons. First, if the behavior is one that you want to maintain, then if it is now on an unpredictable schedule and you for one reason or another forget to reinforce when you want to, all is not lost; you don't have to start over, the behavior won't weaken very much or very fast, and you can easily make up for it. Second, if the behavior is one you want to eliminate, then a behavior that was on an unpredictable schedule can never be reinforced—not even once—or you may have another big job on your hands in trying to extinguish it. Take for example the case of a child who had thrown a temper tantrum everytime she was put to bed, and as a result one of the parents had to stay with her in her room until she fell asleep. When the parents decided that had to stop, they simply put her to bed, closed the door, and left her to cry by herself. Figure 6-4 is a graph of her crying behavior. This graph is *not* a cumulative graph; each dot represents the number of responses (in this case, the number of minutes spent crying) for one night; in a cumulative graph, the number of minutes for one night would have been added to the number of all the previous nights. Therefore, in this graph you can't use the slope of the line to indicate change in frequency.

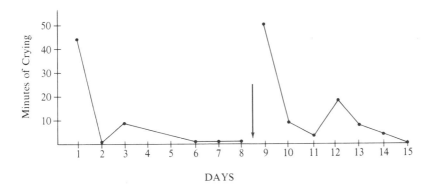

DAYS

Figure 6–4

The first night the screaming lasted forty-five minutes, but the parents gave no attention to it. The second night, nothing (exhausted?). It reappeared on the third night but gradually disappeared after that, until the girl's grandmother babysat one night. The girl cried a little and the grandmother stayed in the girl's room until she fell asleep. The next night (day 9), the response was back again, strong as ever, and the parents had to endure another week of extinction. The moral of the story is: if a lousy behavior has had a long history of intermittent reinforcement, let only the strong of heart attempt to extinguish it. One inconsistency, and you may have had it. But there is also hope. After day 15 the parents reported no further crying tantrums for the next two years. For parents, that's a good reinforcer!

Exceptions

Remember, however, that these are stylized records. In practice, it rarely works out in exactly these ways, especially in human affairs. You already know one important reason for this. Recall the matter of making a neutral event into a reinforcing event by pairing it frequently with an event that is already reinforcing. If you arrange for a reinforcing event to follow a certain behavior that you want increased, no matter what schedule or schedules you use in doing this, chances are high that *other neutral events* will regularly accompany this reinforcing event. Since conditioning, like all the laws of behavior, works whether you advert to it or not, some of these accompanying events will be paired with the reinforcer frequently enough to take on some of the reinforcing properties of the original reinforcer. Now, if later on you decide to extinguish that behavior by withholding the original reinforcer, these other *conditioned reinforcers* will still be reinforcing the behavior for some time. This will delay the process of extinction, and for a time it may appear that "extinction doesn't work."

The longer the history of reinforcement for this behavior, the greater the probability that formerly neutral events have become strongly conditioned reinforcers for the same behavior. Take the case of Felicia Fetchum and Eddie Eager, who have had a long and sometimes torrid friendship. Now Felicia decides to cool it with Eddie. But even though the big reinforcers are consistently withheld, Eddie's approach behaviors (thinking about Felicia, calling her, waiting for her after class) will still be reinforced by such conditioned reinforcing events as the sight of her, the sound of her voice, the smell of her perfume (even on others), and the sight of places where they used to meet. Total extinction may take some time.

15. Which schedule leads to the quickest extinction? Which schedule leads to the slowest extinction?

16. What happens if a teacher forgets once to reinforce a desired behavior that has been on an intermittent schedule? Why?

17. What happens if a teacher gives in once and reinforces an undesired behavior after trying to extinguish it? Why?

18. Can you think of an original example of how unintentional conditioning can delay or prevent extinction?

Analysis of Human Learning: Part B

OBJECTIVES

Upon completing unit 7, you should be able to:

* define superstition and describe how this form of accidental learning takes place, with original examples;
* contrast reinforcement and punishment on the bases of behavioral effect, direction of effect, extinguishability of effect, sensitivity of effect to intensity and quantity, schedule effects, and generalizability of effect;
* define and differentiate between escape and avoidance behavior and construct original school-related examples of each;
* define shaping, describe its procedural steps, and apply these steps to an original teaching situation which calls for shaping;
* define and differentiate stimulus generalization and stimulus discrimination, construct original examples illustrating how each is learned, and show how each is a part of imitative learning;

Superstition

Schedules of reinforcement that depend on passage of time presume of course that during each time interval the behavior occurred at least once. So even with time interval schedules there is a contingency between reinforcement and behavior, but in one sense this contingent relationship is in "the eye of the beholder." If you observe a chain of events and decide that a reinforcing event is indeed contingent on a behavior, then you would say that the change in that behavior was learning. If you decide the relationship between the reinforcing event and the behavior was not dependent but just an *accidental temporal relationship* (they accidentally occurred close in time to each other but no one deliberately designed it to happen that way), then you might call the behavior superstition. Behavior which has no intended influence on the occurrence of the reinforcing event can still be maintained and strengthened by repeated but coincidental pairings.

Skinner's classic experiment on superstition involved giving pigeons a little grain every fifteen seconds, no matter what the bird had been doing. Though the delivery of food was not contingent on any specific behavior, the bird was likely to be doing something each time the food was delivered, and this behavior was therefore more likely to occur at the end of the next time interval.

In this experiment most of the birds developed some regular, identifiable pattern of behavior. One bird "learned" to turn counterclockwise several times during the interval; another regularly stuck his head in an upper corner of the cage just before reinforcement; two birds developed a pendulum swinging of the head and body, first a sharp movement out and then a slower return; and another acquired a dance response consisting of a hopping step from the right to the left foot. Later, when the time interval was increased to one minute, the birds learned a temporal discrimination and delayed their "superstitious" behaviors until 20–30 seconds had elapsed since reinforcement. When the feeder was later disconnected, more than 10,000 superstitious responses were recorded in extinction, even though reinforcement had never been deliberately contingent upon this or any other response.

So it's the *deliberateness* of the contingency that separates magic from science. A basketball player might breathe deeply and relax, or he might make the sign of the cross and bounce the ball three times; either behavior might be followed by a successful free throw. One man might discharge silver iodide crystals into a cloud, another might engage in a rain dance; either behavior might be followed by rainfall. And rituals or charms that ward off disaster are especially easy to learn; they usually "work" since disasters are usually infrequent. The point here is subtle but important: it doesn't matter whether the behavior causes the reinforcing event or not, what is important is that the behavior is regularly followed by the reinforcer. It is the temporal relationship, not the logical connection, that is important in explaining, predicting, and controlling behavior.

1. What is superstition, and how does it develop?

2. What's the difference between superstition and learning?

3. Give an example of a superstitious behavior that you have learned related to education. (Be sure you can identify the unintended contingency.)

Punishment

In many ways reinforcement and punishment are simply the same process but in opposite directions. Their definitions are identical except for the direction of the behavioral effect: reinforcement (punishment) is the increase in (reduction of) the future probability of a specific behavior as the result of the immediate delivery of a consequent event for that behavior. Both reinforcement and punishment work; they produce a real change in behavior. The effects of both will eventually disappear when the consequent event is no longer delivered contingent on the behavior. Both are more effective when the consequent event is more intense or in greater quantity. And if the consequent event is gradually changed to an intermittent schedule, the effects of either reinforcement or punishment are prolonged when the consequent event is no longer contingent on the behavior. All of these effects, which you studied earlier in regard to reinforcement, apply also to punishment. The only difference is in the direction of the future probability of the specific behavior.

Recall also how the Premack principle offered a useful way to look at the relative effects of two different events. Just as the more probable of two events or activities will reinforce the less probable, so the less probable will punish the more probable. If a student's work on successive curriculum assignments is regularly followed by praise, recognition for improvement and persistence, advancement and good marks for each piece of work, chances are the rate and quality of his work will continue to improve because access to the more preferred event (receiving approval) is contingent on a form of behavior which is less preferred than the approval. If on the other hand his work is regularly followed by criticism, embarrassment, and humiliation, his behavior will decrease (be punished) because now the consequent event is probably less preferred than his working behavior.

There is another important similarity between reinforcement and punishment. The effects of both can generalize to other behaviors and consequent events. When approval, recognition, advancement, etc. regularly follow acceptable bits of work, not only will the student's specific assignment work be affected, but also other related behaviors such as coming to class (on time), paying attention to the teacher, speaking highly of the class, the teacher, and the curriculum materials, and generally doing things that give others the impression that he likes the school, the class, and everything about it. Of course, this generalization effect is not always so complete, but there is this tendency for the effects of a reinforcing event for one specific behavior to carry over to a lesser degree to other behaviors which are connected to that reinforced behavior.

Furthermore, other events besides the specific reinforcing event of receiving approval will become reinforcing events by conditioning; the classroom, the teacher's presence, the completion of an assignment begin to be reinforcing events themselves since they regularly accompany the primary reinforcing event.

The same kind of generalization effect is also true for punishment. Not only are the wrong answers punished but also other behaviors like giving any answers at all, participation in class, saying good things about the class and the teacher, coming to school on time or at all, paying attention in class; such behaviors may also be weakened because these behaviors are connected to the specific behavior being punished. And other events besides the specific event of receiving disapproval may become punishing events themselves, such as the classroom, the subject matter itself, the teacher, and even school in general. Anxiety, fear, and conformity are other possible behavioral manifestations of the generalization of punishment.

In home life, for example, some parents punish all forms of "disrespect for adults" by their children. If the punisher is effective and consistently given, the disrespect will decrease, but so will other behaviors of the children toward their parents. Frequently the punishment generalization effect occurs in spite of the fact that "I'm his parent—he will never hate me." Think of your own childhood, whatever it was like, and your reaction when your parents showed approval and pride in what you did, or when they scolded, disapproved, ignored, or punished you.

As another illustration, consider the area of work. A superficial analysis might suggest that on-the-job behavior is maintained primarily by the reinforcer of a periodic paycheck. But for many people the paycheck doesn't increase or decrease contingent on the amount or quality of work they do (within rather wide limits); raises depend greatly on the cost of living or the company-union negotiations. Furthermore, many workers interact with their supervisors only when something has gone wrong that hurts corporate profits (e.g. tardiness, absenteeism, or sloppy work). For these and other reasons, the process for many workers is probably punishment, not reinforcement. The worker performs at a minimally acceptable level in order to *avoid* criticism, embarrassment, or loss of a steady paycheck.

Emery Air Freight reports[1] that it made money by changing this pattern somewhat. Its customer-service department was supposed to respond to cus-

---

[1] *Business Week,* December 18, 1971.

tomer inquiries about shipments within ninety minutes, and most thought this was being done nine times out of ten. A baseline measurement showed that the goal was being met only 30 percent of the time. Its shipping department was supposed to combine packages into large containers whenever possible (saving much money on air shipment costs), and everyone claimed this was being done 90 percent of the time. Baseline data indicated 45 percent. In each case, the workers were given daily checklists (for feedback), and supervisors responded to any degree of improvement by any employee with immediate and personal praise and recognition. When there was no improvement, the employee was told "At least you are recording your performance honestly." Within a few days performance in both departments had jumped to the original goals and remained there for two years.

This was obviously not a very elegant or complicated procedure, but the basic ingredients were there: baseline, target behavior, contingency, reinforcers, continuous measurement. Simple, but it worked—without punishment and with adults.

From your own experience you can see that both reinforcement and punishment work and that both can have very strong generalized side effects. When you choose to use reinforcement or punishment, you choose to cause their side effects; usually that's a bonus for reinforcement but a strong reason for not using punishment.

Escape and Avoidance

Escape and avoidance are two other side effects of punishment. When you escape, you do something that gets you *out of* a punishing situation that you are already in; when you avoid, you do something that *prevents* a punishing event from happening at all.

To put it another way, when a behavior leads to the removal of a punishing consequent event which is already present, that behavior is called escape behavior, as for example when you quickly remove your foot from a tub of scalding water or when you turn off the alarm in the morning, or when a student fakes illness in order to get sent from the classroom to the nurse's office. The events from which the person escapes by making the specific response are called punishing or aversive events.

When a behavior leads to the nonoccurrence or postponement of a punishing event that would otherwise have occurred, that behavior is called avoidance behavior, such as ducking your head when you approach a low beam or blowing on a steaming cup of coffee or skipping a class that's been dull in the past. These avoidance behaviors are of course learned; previous painful experiences were usually preceded by some *warning signal,* which quickly becomes a conditioned punisher by itself as well as a signal to engage in some behavior which will prevent the primary punisher from happening. Think of how "look out" and "stop that" have become conditioned punishers for you, as well as signals for avoidance behavior.

Escape and avoidance behaviors are very common in everyday situations, perhaps as common as reinforced behaviors. And of course a great many of our behaviors probably represent a mixture of both. But think of the many kinds of things you do each day: getting up in the morning, driving carefully, going to classes, studying, being on time for things, doing tasks around the house, making comments or not making them to friends, teachers, parents. It is even possible that most student behaviors are primarily avoidance behaviors. If a student's daily experience in school is very aversive, he will use any way he can find to reduce or eliminate the aversive events, and his efforts will be reinforced to the extent that they are successful. Or he will avoid the situation, just as the person who has been frequently reinforced will eagerly return to the source. The same kind of behavior is predictable on the part of one spouse toward another or on the part of an adolescent toward his parents.

4. Identify one difference and five similarities between reinforcement and punishment?

5. Construct original examples illustrating the effects of one kind of consequence generalizing to other consequent events and also to other behaviors.

6. Can you think of some escape behaviors and some avoidance behaviors that you have learned in regard to school? (Remember: escape is withdrawing from an already punishing situation, while avoidance is staying out of a situation that might be punishing.)

Shaping

When the behavior to be changed already occurs moderately often, then the general procedure is to arrange a contingency for the occurrence of a potentially reinforcing or punishing event to follow the behavior whenever it occurs and later on to fade the schedule of this contingency to some form of intermittent consequation. If the desired behavior rarely if ever occurs exactly as desired, this procedure is obviously unworkable. You can't reinforce a behavior if it never occurs. In this case the behavior can be shaped or *successively approximated*.

The basic idea is to find the closest form of behavior currently occurring in the person's repertoire, design a sequence of small steps from that behavior to the terminal behavior desired, then reinforce each step in succession until it is reliably learned.

Programmed materials are a good example of shaping in that they take a student from some prerequisite skills to a more complex terminal set of skills. A programmed text in introductory statistics, for example, takes a student who already has basic math skills through a sequence of carefully planned steps, each step building on the other, until he is able to manipulate a set of data numbers and determine a variety of basic statistics for those data. In fact all teaching, to the extent that it is successful, is a shaping process of differentially reinforcing successive approximations to the terminal objective. Specifically, the process involves the following steps:

1. decide on the *terminal* behavior you want;
2. find some *current* baseline behaviors on which you can build;
3. identify a *consequent event* that is clearly reinforcing for this person;
4. break the terminal behavior down into *small steps* with some current behavior as the first step;
5. reinforce the behavior that meets the *criterion* for the first step until it is reliable and proficient;
6. move on to the *next step* and reinforce only those behaviors that meet this more demanding criterion;
7. continue in the same way with *each successive step* until the *terminal* objective is proficient;
8. gradually fade from continuous to *intermittent* reinforcement.

If in the process the person does not reach a new criterion after several tries, perhaps the step is too large, and you should lower the criterion for a time to a new intermediate step.

As an example, let's assume you want to shape cooperative play behavior in a student. Baseline observation indicates that this student spends most of his time working by himself or playing by himself in an isolated area of the classroom or playground; the only exception is his eagerness to interact with you, the teacher. Occasionally he comes close to other students when moving from one area to another or when approaching the teacher.

On the basis of this information you decide that your *terminal objective* is that the student spend 50 percent of his free time in cooperative play with other students, that the current behavior on which you can build is the student's approach to other students, and that the reinforcer you will use is teacher attention and praise. Now you can break the terminal objective down into *small steps* with the current behavior as the first step; you first reinforce the student whenever he is within six feet of other students (by your attention and praise for something he has been doing and perhaps a reference to what other students are doing as a source of ideas for his own activity); after the frequency of his coming close to other students has increased noticeably, then reinforce him only when he is close *and* paying attention (however slight) to what other students are doing; then only when he is interacting (however briefly) with other students; then only when he is cooperatively interacting (however briefly) with other students; then only when he has interacted cooperatively with other students for a longer period of time.

In this shaping process you would have to be careful that your attention to the student did not draw him away from the other students. This can be done by including the other children in your comments and praise, by praising the other students for playing with this student, and by supplying items that might make cooperative play easier and more desirable. But if this shaping is done carefully and consistently, you can expect the child in several weeks to be spending at least half his time playing with other children, working on tasks together, even sharing.

Besides steps that are too large (or, for that matter, too small), other extremes must also be avoided in shaping. Requiring only one successful performance of the behavior at each step is not enough to insure that the slightly improved behavior is reliable and proficient at that level. On the other hand, if you reinforce him too many times at a given level it is going to take him longer to master the task at the next level because the heavy reinforcement will establish that intermediate behavior too firmly. Shaping must be managed in such a way that the behavior is established just firmly enough to give the learner a foothold for the next step.

Even among older students, it is often necessary to shape good study behavior by initially reinforcing crude approximations such as sitting at a desk and getting materials ready. If a high school student rarely studies, it may accomplish nothing to describe the complex terminal behavior of good study habits to him and insist that he is old enough and responsible enough to do it on his own. The good teacher takes each of his students *as he is* and *builds* from there.

Verbal behavior offers other examples of sharing. Catatonic schizophrenics who had been mute for close to two decades were taught to answer questions and even initiate conversation in several months, using lip movement as the initial behavior and sticks of gum as the unlikely reinforcer. Shaping also plays an important role in the way normal children learn to talk. There is evidence that an infant makes all the vocal sounds required by the language. At first, new parents are likely to reinforce any sound that is vaguely related to a word. "Wa-wa" might get the child some water as well as praise and fondling. Later on, the parents require the child to repeat and imitate: "Say Wa-ter." As the child speaks to people other than his parents, they will not work as hard at understanding him and so even closer approximations to good speech will be required. And even later, baby talk is ignored or punished.

7. When is shaping called for?

8. Construct an original example of how you would shape a behavior. (Remember the steps: specify target and current behavior, successive small steps; progressive reinforcement at each criterion.)

9. On what basis should you decide how long to stay at each stepwise criterion in shaping? Why not longer? Why not shorter?

Discrimination and Generalization

Up to now we have been concerned primarily with consequent events—when they occur, on what schedule, and what effect they have on the rate of behavior. The *preceding stimulus event* has already been shown to be important as a signal, prompt, or warning cue. As you saw, avoidance behavior is usually signaled ("stop that" is a preceding stimulus for a child to change his behavior in order to avoid a verbal or physical blast). And in superstitious behavior we saw that the simple passage of time can act as a signal or cue that reinforcing events will be available contingent on certain behavior.

Stimulus *discrimination* refers to the situation in which a person responds differently to preceding stimulus events that differ in some way. This differential responding is brought about by *differential reinforcement*—that is, reinforcing a certain response in the presence of a certain preceding stimulus and not in the presence of others. A young child, for example, may say "da-da" when he sees any one of a variety of adults, and initially he will get lots of attention for it; but sooner or later his parents will differentially reinforce "da-da" only when the child's father is present, and the child will learn discrimination. *Differential responding* is the only way we can determine that someone can tell the difference between one thing and another. So you can easily see why knowledge of discrimination learning is important for a teacher.

On the other side of the coin is stimulus *generalization,* the occurrence of the same response to a similar but different preceding stimulus. Reinforcement is also responsible for generalization; the person responds in the same way to this new preceding stimulus because it has some (perhaps many) of the same characteristics as another stimulus to which he responded and was reinforced. The control exercised by the original preceding stimulus is shared by other stimuli, even though the behavior has never been reinforced in their presence, but the shared control depends on the number and kind of *characteristics* the stimuli have in common. The child who says "da-da" to all men does so because they all share many of the same characteristics her father has; the child has yet to learn to discriminate which characteristics are essential to her father and which are irrelevant, but simply common to all men.

Discrimination and generalization enter into almost everything we do. Whenever we move a part of our body (step, lift, reach, push, kick, stop), our action is under the control of a preceding stimulus. Sometimes the speed and accuracy with which we make these discriminations and generalizations are critical, as in driving a vehicle or playing sports. A student learns to watch a teacher's eyes to see if she is paying attention to him, to judge the teacher's mood from her tone of voice, facial expression, and gestures. We do the same with our friends. A teacher trains her students to make certain kinds of responses to certain math symbols, to make certain vocalizations in the presence of certain printed symbols (oral reading), to pluck certain strings in the presence of certain written notes or chords, to turn their eyes toward the teacher when she says "look at this."

In the long run, the probability of a certain behavior depends on the person's history of reinforcement for that behavior, but at any given moment, the behavior also depends on the stimuli that are present. Preceding events serve as a *link* between the past and the present; they bring the efforts of past reinforcement to bear on current behavior.

Imitation

Imitation is a special form of learning which involves both stimulus generalization and discrimination. From infancy children are reinforced for imitative behavior. Parents, for example, name an object and tell the child to repeat the name sound and praise him when he does. Only later is the child expected to name the object without the imitative prompt. Teachers do the same thing when teaching a new word or task; at first they give heavy prompts, then partial prompts, all involving total or partial imitation. After a while, the sight of another person doing or saying something is enough of a preceding stimulus to elicit a similar behavior. The person who imitates already can do or say the component parts of the total behavior he is imitating; what he learns is the putting together of these components in a certain way at a certain time. For example, aggression can be learned through imitation, even if the models are on film. A child who sees a film of children hitting other children and getting good things because of their aggression is more likely to do the same in similar situations. He already knew how to swing his arm, how to aim it at an object, how to discriminate the cues for the reinforcing event of "getting my own way," and how to generalize to similar situations. What he learns through this imitation is to put these behaviors together in the presence of certain preceding stimulus situations in order to get certain desirable consequent events.

Students in their early teens also exhibit considerable imitative learning. They discriminate (sometimes not too accurately) the behaviors that lead to reinforcing consequences when done by a parent, a teacher, a classmate, a sports hero, an entertainment idol, and others. He puts together similar behaviors he can already do in hopes of gaining (or at least fantasizing) the same kind of reinforcing consequences for himself. With experience we also learn to discriminate which behaviors are worth imitating, and we get better at making this imitation less obvious and more "natural" looking in order to increase our chances for good consequences from this imitation.

It is clear that imitation or modeling is an important part of every student's learning. A student's way of working for desirable consequent events or his way of working to avoid punishing events is more likely than not to resemble the behavior patterns of others around him, such as his parents, his brothers and sisters, his friends, his teachers. If he fails repeatedly in these imitative attempts to get certain consequences, he may well change his tactics, but he is apt to try them first because he can generalize from the behavior of others (and its consequences) to his own similar behavior. For this reason, the procedures the teacher uses to control and change the behavior of the students are worthy of careful thought; at least some of the students will imitate at least some aspects of that behavior.

10. Can you define stimulus discrimination and stimulus generalization, with original examples illustrating how each is learned?

11. Construct your own example of imitative learning by students, showing how the discriminations and generalizations are learned.

In this and previous units you have learned some basic principles and methods involved in analyzing how human behavior patterns develop and change. You will find more illustrations of these principles and methods, especially relating to elementary and secondary classroom situations, in units 11 and 12.

If you are skeptical about the usefulness of this analysis, try it yourself. Unit 13 outlines the steps you should take in applying these principles and methods in a real human situation. In any case, this kind of application practice and experience will make you a better teacher in the future. Now is a good time to read through unit 13 and begin thinking about and planning for your behavior change project.

unit 8

Different Strokes for Different Folks—
Individual Preferences and Reinforcing Events

OBJECTIVES

When you complete this unit, you should be able to:

* identify reinforcing event preferences associated with social class and racial background and describe how these differences can develop;
* describe procedures for teaching a child a sense of control over his reinforcers and for helping a child move up the reward scale.

Within a single family, different members are turned on by different kinds of reinforcing events (e.g., what kind of music to listen to, what type of recreational activities to choose). As you already know, this is due to differences in past experiences with reinforcing events and the neutral events that may have been paired with them. These experiences and pairings can be expected to differ even among members of the same family.

For the same reason you can expect even bigger differences in the kinds of events that turn people on when you compare people from different cultural, racial, religious, or ethnic groups. There is very little hard research on the nature of these differences, but the following article suggests several logical approaches. It will also give you practice at translating dynamic and sometimes vague descriptive terminology (e.g., "strong ego") into more measurable and useful statements.

MINORITY SUBCULTURES
AND THE LAW OF EFFECT*

Robert J. Havighurst

Since the 1950s we in the United States have become more and more acutely aware of and concerned about the socially disadvantaged segment of our society. We have joined a "war on poverty." We have declared racial segregation in the public schools to be illegal. We have passed a Civil Rights Act. These things we have done out of our conviction that democracy is morally right and can be made to work better in our society than it has in the past.

We have also defined rather accurately the "socially disadvantaged" group as consisting roughly of the bottom 15% of our population in terms of income and educational achievement. Some people would argue that this is too small a proportion. They would add another 10% to make it a quarter of the population. Others would go as far as to define all manual workers and their families (about 60% of the population) as socially disadvantaged, but this kind of proposition could not be supported with data on inadequacy of income, educational achievement, stability of family, law observance, or any other major index of standard of living. While the stable working class (or upper working class), consisting of 40% of the population, is slightly below the white collar group in average income, educational level, and other socioeconomic indices, this group is not disadvantaged in an absolute sense, does not feel disadvantaged, and has an active interchange of membership with the white collar group between successive generations.

As for the truly disadvantaged group of 15–20% of the population, there is disturbing evidence that this group is in danger of becoming a permanent "underclass" characterized by absence of steady employment, low level of education and work skills, living on welfare payments, and social isolation from the remainder of society.

The presence of this social and human problem cannot be passed off in any of the ways that might have been possible a century ago, or might be possible today in the poor countries. It cannot be ascribed to inherited inferiority of the disadvantaged. It cannot be blamed on the country's poverty, since we are an affluent society. It cannot be passed off with the optimistic prediction that the current group of disadvantaged will soon become assimilated into the general society as most ethnic groups have done in the past—the Irish, Germans, Swedes, Poles, Italians, etc.

The problem is brought to a head by the clearly established fact that the children of this group are *not* doing as well in school or in the world of juvenile work as did the children of poor people 50 and 100 years ago.

*Reprinted and abridged from the *American Psychologist* 25 (1970):313–22. Copyright 1970 by the American Psychological Association. Reprinted by permission.

Furthermore, most Americans believe that true democracy means equality of economic and educational opportunity. There is a growing conviction that the proof of the existence of equality of economic and educational *opportunity* is the achievement of economic and educational *equality* by the previously disadvantaged groups within a reasonable period of time, measured by decades and not by centuries or even by generations.

THE WAR ON POVERTY?

For the past 10 years our principal attack on the problem of social disadvantage has been through the "war on poverty." We have spent much talent and energy and a good deal of money without raising the educational or occupational achievement level of this group appreciably, except in a few unusual situations. These unusual situations, in which disadvantaged children and youth have made normal or even superior progress, do not provide us with any broad program ideas that can be applied widely. They seem to tell us that:

1. No mere quantitative changes in the school program are likely to work. It does not bring a widespread improvement to extend the school day by an hour, or the school year by a month, or to reduce class size, or to revise school attendance boundaries.
2. Close and minute attention to the process of teaching a particular subject at a particular age may be useful.
3. We should look closely at children and their particular learning behavior for clues to action.

A LOOK AT WHAT WE KNOW

Examination of known facts about school achievement of definable social groups in the United States shows that poor school achievement is not primarily a problem of ethnic subcultures, but rather is primarily a problem of the lowest socioeconomic group interacting to a limited degree with minority subcultures.

There are certain ethnic minorities that do very well—as well or better than the national average in school achievement. Outstanding among these are the Japanese, Chinese, and Jews. The adults of these groups have an average occupational status above the national average, and the children of these groups do better than the national average on tests of school achievement.

Other ethnic groups do poorly in these respects, but these groups also have substantial numbers who equal or exceed the national average. There is no single ethnic group of any size that can be said to be disadvantaged educationally and economically *as a whole group.* Negroes might be thought of as a disadvantaged group, and this would be true, historically. But at present there is a large and growing Negro middle class and a large and growing Negro upper working class whose occupational status is average or above and whose children do average or better work in school.

The same statement applies to Puerto Ricans, Mexican Americans, and American Indians. It is the least educated and the least work-trained members of these groups who do least well in American society. These groups all have substantial and growing numbers of people who perform at average or higher levels of occupational status and whose children do well in school.

Thus, when we speak of the group of socially disadvantaged people in America, we are speaking of some 15–20% of the population who are like each other in their poverty, their lack of education and work skills, but unlike each other in ethnic subculture. Crude estimates indicate that this group contains about 20 million English-speaking Caucasians, 8 million Negroes, 2 million Spanish-Americans, 700,000 Puerto Ricans, and 500,000 American Indians.

These people have poverty in common. Insofar as there is a definable "culture of poverty," they share that culture. Still, a small fraction of them, though poor, do not have the characteristics of the "culture of poverty."

It may be that their various ethnic subcultures have something to do with success or failure in school and in the labor market. If so, it must be the combination of poverty with the ethnic subculture that produces these effects. It may also be true that other ethnic subcultures, such as the Japanese and Chinese, serve to prevent poverty.

THE IMPLICIT CONTRACT

It may be useful to examine the educational problem of the socially disadvantaged in terms of the *implicit contract* that a family and a school accept when a child is entrusted by his family to a school. The parents contract to prepare their child for school entrance, both cognitively and affectively. They further contract to keep him in school and to make home conditions appropriate for his success in school. The school contracts to receive the child, teach him as well as it can, taking account of his strengths and weaknesses and the ways in which he can learn most effectively.

Very little of this contract is put into legal codes, but the education of the child is successful only when both parties carry out their obligations fully. Sometimes one or both parties fail to understand the nature of these obligations.

In the case of the socially disadvantaged parents of this country, nearly all of them fail to meet the terms of the contract. But the schools generally fail also by failing to understand how the children of these families can learn most successfully.

The Human Reward–Punishment System

The principal proposition of this article is that the job of educating socially disadvantaged children would be done much better if educators understood the nature of rewards and how they function in human learning, and applied this knowledge to their work with children and with parents of socially disadvantaged children.

Leads to this proposition exist in the literature of research on education, but do not force themselves on the educator. For example, Davis (1965) offered one of these clues in his paper "Cultural Factors in Remediation." He noted that his wife, then working as a substitute teacher in the Chicago public schools, made a discovery about the way disadvantaged children may learn arithmetic. In a second grade in a ghetto school she found several children, including one nine-year-old boy, who could not count beyond two or three. The following day was Valentine's Day, and she brought some candy hearts to school. She told the children they could have as many candy hearts as they could count. The *nine-year-old boy thereupon counted 14 candy hearts.* Davis goes on to say that teachers of "culturally low-status children" should learn how their children live, and then work out new materials and ways of teaching in order to *encourage* and *approve* those students who have experienced little except disapproval, stigma, and failure in the conventional school program.

In the years since 1960 a number of psychologists have studied the nature of rewards in human learning. Among others, the work of Zigler, Rotter, Katz, and Crandall has widened the field of research and has stimulated others to work in this field.

What these people have in common is the following proposition: Human learning is influenced by a variety of rewards, which are themselves arranged in a culturally based *reward–punishment system* which is learned.

This requires us to examine the nature of rewards. We cannot simply assume that "a reward is a reward and that is it," as we might be tempted to do if we were studying the learning behavior of cats, or pigeons, or rats. It was more or less obvious to researchers that reward systems might vary with social class, or with ethnic subculture. It seemed likely that a child learns his reward system mainly in the family, but also in the school, and the peer group, and the wider community.

Analysis of the Reward–Punishment Concept

The reward–punishment concept, and its related reinforcement theory, has been developed rather differently by each of three groups of psychologists.

Learning theorists, starting with E. L. Thorndike, have tended to use the concept to refer to something done *to* the learner by an experimenter or observer that influences the behavior of the learner. On the other hand, social psychologists and personality theorists have included the subjective experience of the learner as a source of reward-punishment. Thus, a person may be rewarded or punished by his own feelings or by the attitudes of other people toward him.

THEORY OF THE EVOLUTION OF REWARD-PUNISHMENT

It appears, then, that we can distinguish four major types of reward-punishments. The earliest, in terms of operation in human learning, is satisfaction or deprivation of physiological appetites—the physiological needs for food and pain avoidance. In this same category belong other material rewards that arise later in physiological development, either through the maturation of the organism or through experience—such rewards as release of sexual tensions, toys and play materials, money, and, perhaps, power over other people.

Next in order of appearance comes approval-disapproval from other persons, beginning with praise and reproof and expressions of affection and esteem from parents, and extending to approval-disapproval from others in the family and adults such as teachers, and from age-mates.

Next comes the self-rewarding and self-punishing action of the child's superego, or conscience. This is extrememly important from the point of view of educational development, because it means that the child who has reached this level can become capable of pushing ahead with his own education without being stimulated and directed by his parents or his teachers or his peers.

Finally comes the rewarding and punishing action of the ego, the executive functions of the personality. This is more difficult to conceptualize as a source of reward or punishment, but it is essential for an adequate theory. It is essential as a means of *anticipation* of future reward or punishment, success or failure, which will result as a consequence of an action performed now, in the present.

There are six major propositions of educational significance that have received some research testing.

1. *Different subcultures carry their children along this evolutionary path at different rates and in different ways.*

    Several researchers have tested this proposition using social class as the subcultural variable. Zigler and de Labry (1962) compared the performance of middle class and lower class six-year-old children on a task of classifying cards on the basis of color and shape, and using intangible reinforcement ("right" and "wrong") and tangible reinforcement (tokens to be cashed in for toys). They found middle class children to be superior with intangible reinforcement, but this superiority vanished when lower class children were given tangible rewards.

Probably there is very little difference between middle class and stable or upper-working-class families in the ways they teach their children to move up the evolutionary reward scale. Probably the big difference is between the stable upper working class and the "underclass" or lower working class. But it appears that most of the experiments reporting on social class differences used working-class samples of the upper-working-class level.

Two studies have clearly differentiated between these working-class levels. Hess and Shipman (1965) differentiated Negro lower class children into a group with stable upper-working-class characteristics and another group whose mothers were receiving Aid for Dependent Children. There was a substantial difference between the two groups in the mother-child relationship in a learning situation. Also, Davidson and Greenberg (1967) studied high achievers and underachievers among Harlem Negro lower class children, and found large differences in the orderliness of the home life between the two working-class groups.

2. *There are differences between ethnic subcultures among disadvantaged groups in the reward systems they teach their children.*

Although all of the severely disadvantaged families share some common characteristics of the "culture of poverty," they may also have different ethnic cultural traits which lead to different reward systems. There is evidence of such differences between Negro, Appalachian white, and some American Indian groups.

American Indians have a wide variety of tribal cultures, and therefore it is dangerous to generalize about "Indians." However, among contemporary Indian groups there appears to be a general virtue of cooperation and mutual support within an extended family and to a lesser degree within a tribal community. It might be inferred that praise–blame from family and from peer group is the most effective form of reward–punishment for Indian children living in Indian communities.

The hypothesis of peer-group rewarding power is supported by observations of school behavior in several different places. Wax (1969) reports that in both the Cherokee group in Eastern Oklahoma and the Sioux of South Dakota the children tend to form a close-knit group with its own system of control that baffles the teacher. An observer in an Oklahoma Cherokee school writes,

Observing the upper-grade classroom, I concluded that the students regard it as their own place, the locus of their own society, in which the teacher is an unwelcome intruder, introducing irrelevant demands. It is rather as though a group of mutinous sailors had agreed to the efficient manning of "their" ship while ignoring the captain and the captain's navigational goals [p. 101].

The children do not tolerate an individual show of superior knowledge. Often a teacher cannot find any pupil who will volunteer an answer to a question that several of them know. In oral reading, the whole class tends to read together in audible whispers, so that the child who is supposed to be reciting can simply wait when he comes to a difficult word until he hears it said by his classmates. Generally, pupils like to work together, and to help each other. Consequently, the weak students are carried along by the stronger ones, and the stronger ones do not exert themselves to excel the weaker ones. This same kind of behavior was noted by Wolcott (1967) in his study of Kwakiutl children in British Columbia.

The peer group may be less effective as a source of reward-punishment for Appalachian disadvantaged children. They seem to get their rewards mainly within the family circle. Conceivably, the teacher may be a more potent source of reward for Appalachian than for Indian children, if the teacher develops a motherly or fatherly relation with them.

The Negro lower-class children may operate much more at the level of approval–disapproval from the teacher than the Indian or Appalachian children. They are less likely to have both parents in the home, and they probably get less parental approval–disapproval. They do not generally fall into the mutual help pattern of the Indian children. The peer group becomes a powerful influence on the Negro children probably after the age of 9 or 10, but its influence operates mainly in out-of-school contexts—on the playground or the street corner.

This proposition needs much more research before it can be pushed very far. But the contrasting school behavior and school success of the various minority groups argue for the existence of different systems of rewards and punishments, as well as different achievement goals to which these systems are directed.

3. *In general, external rewards (material or intangible) have positive values for disadvantaged or failing children.*
This proposition differs from the first in being valid for all social classes, leaving open the question of the relative effectiveness of these kinds of rewards in different social classes. There is a growing amount of solid, practical evidence for this proposition, growing out mainly from the *operant-conditioning* programs and experiments stimulated by Skinner. They all have in common the giving of a reward for every small step in the direction of the desired learning. Work with pre-

school children, such as that done by Bereiter and Engelmann (1966), is being studied widely and their practices repeated at primary grade levels.

It is not established whether material rewards, such as pieces of candy, are more effective than verbal praise. Intermediate between them is some kind of point system, whereby a child gets a point for every correct answer (sometimes a point is subtracted for errors), and the points may be "cashed in" later for material objects, or special favors such as a trip to the zoo.

Several school systems have established a "reinforcement technique" for working with children who have various kinds of school adjustment problems, academic and behavioral. This method seems to work equally well with middle class and lower-working-class children, as long as the child is having a school problem. The procedure is to diagnose the child's problem carefully, to work out a series of small steps from where he is to where he should be, and to reward him for each step. For example, an 11-year-old boy with a third-grade reading level but otherwise average intelligence may refuse to read with his sixth-grade class, and thus make no progress. Rewarding him for reading with his class does no good, because he makes himself ridiculous in the eyes of his classmates. (The punishment is greater than the reward.) But if a counselor studies the boy, discovers his third-grade reading level, and then arranges for individual remedial work with rewards for each advance above the third-grade level, the boy may catch up with his age-mates within a few months.

Validity of a symbolic reinforcement program with underachieving children was indicated with a junior high school group in Chicago, in a situation in which one might expect social reinforcement to have relatively little value. Clark and Walberg (1968) experimented with a system of massive symbolic rewards in classes of sixth- and seventh-grade Negro children in a Chicago ghetto—all the children being in classes for after-school remedial reading, because they were from one to four years below grade level in their school work. The reward system consisted of tallies made by each child on a card containing numbered squares. Whenever a child made a correct response or showed some other sign of learning, the teacher praised him and asked him to circle the next number on his card with a special colored pencil that he was to use only for this purpose. The cards were collected at the end of the class period. No other rewards were given for the points gained.

Teachers of nine remedial classes were instructed to give praise rewards so that even the very slow ones would get several in a session. After six sessions of this sort, five of the nine teachers were selected at random, and confidentially asked to double or triple the number of rewards they gave, while four control group teachers were told to "keep up the good work."

As a result, the experimental groups got many more tally numbers, while the control groups remained at the early levels. After five weeks a reading test was given, and the experimental groups exceeded the controls by a substantially and statistically significant amount.

4. *An effective reward system in a complex, changing society must be based on a strong ego.*

This crucial step in the reward–punishment theory being developed here conceives the ego as a source of reward–punishment, as well as the executive and planning function of the personality. To develop this set of ideas we may turn to a recent article by Bettelheim (1969) entitled "Psychoanalysis and Education." Bettelheim starts with the conventional dynamic personality theory of learning by young children through rewards given first by the id (the physiological appetites) and then by the superego (the internalized praising and blaming voice of the parents). Therefore, learning based on the pleasure principle is supplemented by learning based on the superego, which carries a child from learning for fun to learning even if it is hard work because his superego rewards him for this kind of learning and punishes him for failing to learn. We all recognize that much necessary learning is hard work, and will not take place under the pressure of the id.

Perhaps this last sentence is not quite accurate. There are a number of creative teachers and writers about teaching who in effect take the position that the way to teach children successfully (whether they are socially disadvantaged or socially advantaged) is to get the id behind their learning experience, that is, to give their "natural drive to learn," their "native curiosity," free play, and to count on their learning "creatively" in this way throughout their school experience.

For example, Kohl (1967), in his book *36 Children,* describes how he worked for a year with a class of 36 Negro slum children who were below average in academic skills. He did get results. There is no reason to doubt this. His method of encouraging them to write about their fears, their hates, and their likes, about the bad and good things they experience in their homes and streets, loosened their pens and their tongues, added to their vocabulary, and got them interested in school. It seems that Kohl was helping them marshal the forces of the id on behalf of learning. But how far can this go? How far can a slum child (or a middle class child) go toward mastery of arithmetic, of English sentence style, of knowledge of science and history, if he is motivated only by his drive to express his feelings, or possibly also by his desire to please his friendly and permissive teacher?

We do not know how far this kind of reward will carry a child's learning. We might guess that it would carry children up to about the seventh-grade level. Therefore, we should ask Kohl and others of this school of thought to prove that their methods will carry children to the eighth-grade level. No such claims appear to have been substantiated, except in the case of socially advantaged children, such as those attending A. S. Neill's school at Summerhill, England. And some observers of this school argue that it can only work with children who have a strong British middle class superego, and can profit from teaming their somewhat starved id with the superego in the pursuit of learning.

Bettelheim (1969) argues that the main function of education is to help the ego develop so that with the aid of the superego it controls the id, but at the same time it balances the superego by allowing reasonable satisfaction of the id. "The goal of education ought to be a well-balanced personality where both id and superego are subordinated to reality, to the ego [p. 83]." "Nothing automatically assures ego growth, neither punishment nor reward. The only thing that assures it is having the right experiences to stimulate and foster growth at the right time, in the right sequence, and in the right amount [p. 84]."

Thus, the ego becomes a source of reward and punishment through enabling the child to promise himself realistically a future reward for doing something unpleasant at the moment and through making the child take the blame for the future consequences of his mistakes of judgment or his mistakes of self-indulgence.

5. *A strongly developed ego gives a sense of personal control and personal responsibility for important events in one's life.*
   The ego can only become an effective reward and punishment giver if the social environment is orderly enough to permit the ego to operate on the basis of a rational study of reality. This is substantially the case with the family and the community environment of the middle class and the stable working class in America. But the disadvantaged groups we have been considering do not experience this kind of orderliness in their environment, and do not transmit to their children a sense of confidence in an orderly environment.

   Consider, for example, a child of a stable working-class home in which the family has supper at a regular time, the children have a time to play after supper, and a time to go to bed. A four-year-old child in this family has learned a routine for the evening. He finishes his supper and carries his dishes to the place where they will be washed. He then plays with toys for a while, and then goes to his bedroom, puts on his pajamas, and goes to his mother who has finished the supper dishes. He says, "I'm ready for bed. Now let's read." His mother gets out a picture book, and they "read" together for a while, he nestled against his mother's body. Then she says, "Bedtime," and they go to his bed, where she kisses him goodnight. This is an orderly environment, in which the child's ego is developing so that it can promise him satisfaction if he does his share to bring it about.

Now consider a child of a mother with six children receiving welfare payments to care for them, because she has no husband at home. Rarely is there much order in this home. Hardly can this child count on starting a train of events by doing some household chore which eventually brings him into his mother's lap to read with her. She is just too busy, too preoccupied with a hundred worries and a few desires; she may not be able to read beyond the third-grade level, and she may dislike reading. She is not likely to have learned about the necessity of her children having regular rewards and punishments given consistently by her as a means of teaching them.

A good deal of research has been done on the acquisition by children of a sense of control of rewards. Rotter (Rotter, Seeman, and Liverant, 1962) has studied the "sense of personal control of the environment." Crandall (Crandall, Katkovsky, and Crandall, 1965) studied a child's feelings about whether his own efforts determine the rewards he gets from school and from important people or whether this is a matter of luck or the whims of important people. Battle and Rotter (1963) found that middle class and white skin color tended to be associated with a sense of self-responsibility and control of the outer world's rewards and punishments. Coleman (1966) in the National Survey of Educational Opportunity asked students to agree or disagree with three statements such as "Good luck is more important than hard work for success." Negro students had a greater belief in luck as the disposer. Coleman says, "It appears that children from advantaged groups assume the environment will respond if they are able to affect it; children from disadvantaged groups do not make this assumption, but in many cases assume that nothing they do can affect the environment—it will give benefits or withhold them but not as a consequence of their own action [p. 321]." Negro children who answered "hard work" scored higher on a test of verbal performance than did white pupils who chose the "good luck" response.

Hall (1968) studied a group of young Caucasian and Negro men aged 18–20, all from working-class families in a big city. He divided these young men into three categories according to their work adjustment—one group who had a record of stable employment or went back to school and succeeded there; one group called "rolling stones" who had a recent history of frequent job changes or of going back to school and dropping out again; and a third group whom he called "lookers" who just loafed around, neither working nor going to school. He used with them a questionnaire aimed to measure their sense of control of the environment through their efforts. There was a clear difference in scores between the three groups, the "stable performers" having the most belief in their ability to control their environment.

From these studies it can be inferred that the ego is a less powerful source of reward, and the ego is itself weaker, in the socially disadvantaged groups. The child who can predict the consequences of his behavior can maximize his rewards.

6. *People learn to operate at all of the several levels of reward by the time they reach adolescence, and the level at which they operate varies with the action area.*

It is possible for a person at adolescence and later to operate in terms of physiological appetite rewards in one area of action, in terms of praise–blame from peers in another area, in terms of ego reward or punishment in yet another action area.

For example, a 17-year-old boy may seek id rewards or satisfaction of physiological appetite in his relations with the opposite sex. He also may seek the id rewards of excitement in doing perilous things such as driving a fast car, diving from a high diving board, rock climbing in the mountains, gang fighting, stealing cars. Some of these things he may do alone, thus cutting off rewards from others, and it is hard to see how one can get ego rewards from doing dangerous things for no purpose other than the thrill or from matching one's wits against nature.

This same boy may play a good game of tennis or basketball partly to get the reward of approval from his peers. He may work long hours at night on a high school course in calculus for advanced standing in college, primarily because his ego tells him he will be rewarded in the future by a successful occupational career.

Probably a social class and an ethnic subculture teaches a person to choose certain areas for certain kinds of rewards. For instance, some American Indian cultures may teach their children to rely on praise–blame from peers for much of their school behavior. A big-city, Negro, lower-working-class culture may teach boys to learn to fight, to play basketball, to throw rocks at school windows, and to smoke "pot" through id rewards and peer group rewards, while it teaches them to expect punishment from teachers for their behavior and lack of achievement in school.

But a particular Negro boy may become so accurate at "shooting baskets" on the park playground that he no longer gets much feeling of reward from being the best in his neighborhood. He may happen on an older high school athlete who rewards him by playing with him, or a man in the neighborhood who tells him that he might become a second Cazzie Russell, if he keeps on. At this point his ego may become effective as a promiser of future reward if he stays in school and makes his grades and then makes the school basketball team.

The study by Gross (1967) of "Learning Readiness in Two Jewish Groups" provides a striking illustration of action areas apparently selected by the minority group subculture for differential rewards. Ninety Brooklyn Jewish boys aged about six years and all middle class were given a set of tests of cognitive development. About half of the boys came from Sephardic families (immigrants from Arabic or Oriental countries) and half came from Ashkenazic families (immigrants from Europe). The mothers were all native born, and English was the household language. The boys with European family background were decidedly superior in the cognitive measures to the boys with Arabic-Oriental family backgrounds. There was a 17-point IQ difference on the Peabody Picture Vocabulary Test. Yet the parents were all middle class Jews living in the same big city. Intensive study of the family training and background experience of the two groups of boys revealed little difference except in the mothers' attitudes toward wealth. Twice as many Ashkenazic (European) mothers said that earnings were "unimportant" in their desires for their children, and three times as many Sephardic mothers said they wanted their sons to be "wealthy."

One may infer from this study the reward systems in the two groups of families (which were very similar according to the sophisticated methods used to study them) were directed toward different areas of action.

EDUCATION OF DISADVANTAGED MINORITY GROUPS

What can we say from this partially confirmed theory about the education of disadvantaged minority groups?

First, we can say that teachers would teach better if they had a systematic theory of the working of reward and punishment in the learning of children, and if they put this theory into practice. Their theory should include the concept of a heirarchy of reward levels, and they should understand what levels of reward are operating in their classes.

Second, we can assume that most socially disadvantaged children are lower on the evolutionary reward scale, at a given age, than are the advantaged children. Therefore, the teachers of these children should reward them with a great deal of praise, and perhaps with a point system that produces material rewards.

Third, a major goal of all teachers at all levels should be to help the child strengthen his ego as a controller and rewarder of his behavior. This means that the teacher cannot be content with using praise and other forms of external reward, although these should be used when they are needed. The teacher should help the child move up the reward scale.

Progress toward strengthening the ego can only be made in school by putting order and consistency into the school situation, so that the child can learn how to control his environment on the basis of the reality principle. This can be done for individual children partly by individualized instruction which enables them to learn and to predict their own learning in relation to their effort to learn. This can be done for a school class by an orderly program in which students know what their responsibilities are, participate in making decisions about their work, and get accurate information on their progress.

Since the family of the disadvantaged child so often fails to perform its part of the implicit contract, there is bound to be dissatisfaction by school teachers and administrators with the situation, and critics will sometimes blame the school and other times the family subculture. Probably the educator will have to spend much of his energy working with parents and leaders in the local subculture, helping them and receiving help from them to create an environment in the home and neighborhood that supports the learning experience of the child and directs it along socially desirable lines.

REFERENCES

Battle, E., and Rotter, J. Children's feelings of personal control as related to social class and ethnic group. *Journal of Personality,* 1963, **31,** 482–490.

Bereiter, C., and Engelmann, A. *Teaching Disadvantaged Children.* Englewood Cliffs, N.J.: Prentice-Hall, 1966.

Bettelheim, B. Psychoanalysis and education. *School Review,* 1969, **77,** 73–86.

Clark, C. A., and Walberg, H. J. The influence of massive rewards on reading achievement in potential urban school dropouts. *American Educational Research Journal,* 1968, **5,** 305–310.

Coleman, J. S. *Equality of Educational Opportunity.* Washington, D.C.: United States Government Printing Office, 1966.

Crandall, V. C., Katkovsky, W., and Crandall, V. J. Children's beliefs in their own control of reinforcements in intellectual-academic achievement situations. *Child Development,* 1965, **36,** 91–109.

Davidson, H. H., and Greenberg, J. *Traits of School Achievers from a Deprived Background.* (Cooperative Research Project No. 2805) Washington, D.C.: United States Office of Education, 1967.

Davis, A. Cultural factors in remediation. *Educational Horizons,* 1965, **43,** 231–251.

Fenichel, O. *The Psychoanalytic Theory of Neurosis.* New York: Norton, 1945.

Gross, M. *Learning Readiness in Two Jewish Groups.* New York: Center for Urban Education, 1967.

Hall, W. S. Levels of productive economic and educational involvement in the culture among lower class young men: A comparative study. Unpublished doctoral dissertation, Department of Education, University of Chicago, 1968.

Hartley, E. L., and Hartley, R. E. *Fundamentals of Social Psychology.* New York: Knopf, 1952.

Hess, R. D., and Shipman, V. Early experience and the socialization of cognitive modes in children. *Child Development,* 1965, **36,** 869–886.

Katz, I. Some motivational determinants of racial differences in intellectual achievement. *International Journal of Psychology,* 1967, **2,** 1–12.

Kohl, H. R. *36 Children.* New York: New American Library, 1967.

Marshall, H. H. Learning as a function of task interest, reinforcement, and social class variables. *Journal of Educational Psychology,* 1969, **60,** 133–137.

Rotter, J., Seeman, M., and Liverant, S. Internal versus external control of reinforcement. A major variable in behavior theory. In N. F. Washburne. (Ed.), *Decisions, Values, and Groups.* Vol. 2. London: Pergamon Press, 1962.

Skinner, B. F. *Science and Human Behavior.* New York: Macmillan, 1953.

Thorndike, E. L. *The Elements of Psychology.* New York: Seiler, 1905.

Thorndike, E. L. *The Fundamentals of Learning.* New York: Bureau of Publications, Teachers College, Columbia University, 1932.

Wax, M. L. *Indian Education in Eastern Oklahoma.* (Research Contract Report No. O. E. 6–10–260 and BIA No. 5–0565–2–12–1) Washington, D.C.: United States Office of Education, 1969.

Wolcott, H. F. *A Kwakiutl Village and School.* New York: Holt, Rinehart and Winston, 1967.

Zigler, E., and de Labry, J. Concept-switching in middle-class, lower-class, and retarded children. *Journal of Abnormal and Social Psychology,* 1962, **65,** 267–273.

1. Describe the "underclass" in terms of its characteristics, numbers, and ethnic composition.

2. What is meant by the "implicit contract"?

3. Identify the type of reinforcement Havighurst suggests might be most effective with Indian children; with young lower-class Negro children; with Appalachian children. How might these differences develop?

4. A child can learn "to promise himself realistically a future reward for doing something unpleasant at the moment." From your study of unit 7, explain this learning without resorting to the intervening construct of "a strong ego."

5. Explain the results of the studies cited in section 5 in terms of the "Rules for Managing Consequences" explained in unit 3.

6. Explain, using only measurable terms, what is meant by helping a child "move up the reward scale." In practice, what procedures does this require?

unit 9

Imitation and Aggression

OBJECTIVES

When you finish with unit 9, you should be able to:

* give a behavioral explanation of vicarious reinforcement and imitative learning and construct an example of a classroom application;
* identify the additional explanatory problem associated with a nonbehavioral explanation of imitative learning;
* describe how aggression is learned and how extinction and imitation are involved, illustrating the process with an original example;
* specify the four components of a strategy to eliminate aggressive behavior, with a classroom illustration.

We have all had direct experience with imitation (or modeling) processes. We have imitated, and we have seen others imitating. The objects of imitation can be parents, teachers, peers, media heroes, public figures (famous and notorious), and children.

More important than the question of who, are the questions of what and why. Research and teaching experience both indicate that the most useful and valid way to approach these questions is behaviorally. We imitate *behaviors* that we have seen leading to consequent events we consider *reinforcing*.

It is clear that children have ample opportunity to observe how others behave and what the consequences are for different types of behavior. Imitation, for children, is a very important vehicle by which they learn behavior patterns. Moral development, in fact, is primarily a function of imitative learning. Children observe their parents, friends, and teachers tell the truth or lie, keep their promises or break them, get their way by aggression or persuasion or whatever. They also see the results of such actions. In this sense, imitation is a form of vicarious learning. In these cases, the children can already do the various behaviors of speaking, remembering promises, hitting, etc. What they learn by imitation is exactly what form the behavior should take in specific situations in order to maximize the probability of reinforcement.

Adults display less clearly imitative behavior. In part this is because adults already have well-established patterns of behavior that reliably lead to the kinds and frequencies of reinforcing events they need. Besides, adults have also learned more subtle and sophisticated ways of imitation because imitation that is too blatant and obvious is frequently punished by the adult world.

Bandura's research on imitative learning supports this approach.[1] He has shown, for example, that a child's moral judgments are less age-specific than is implied by Piaget's studies and that exposing the child to a social model whose behavior and its consequences are controlled for can effectively develop or change similar behavior by the child.

Many studies have shown that children, when exposed to films or other controlled samples of children or adults performing certain actions and being reinforced (or punished) for them, will frequently exhibit an increased frequency in the modeled behavior (or decreased frequency, if the behavior was punished).

A similar effect has been shown in regard to instructional training. A child is more or less apt to follow rules and instructions for behavior depending on how many other peers, teachers, or adults the child observes following or disregarding those rules.

Imitation is also used deliberately and effectively in the formal education offered by schools, particularly in speaking, writing, and motor skills. Students copy letters, follow rules, guidelines, and plans, echo pronunciations, and imitate bodily movements in learning to dance or play a sport. Of course, the teacher intends that the student be able to do more than simply imitate a response, but modeling is useful in getting such behaviors going initially, before the dependency on the model is gradually eliminated. Finally, as we have seen, emotional and moral behaviors are also imitated by students in school, with either the teachers or peers serving as the model, though for these behaviors the imitative learning is less often deliberately intended to be modeled.

---

[1] See, for example, the article by A. Bandura, "Influence of Models' Reinforcement Contingencies on the Acquisition of Imitative Responses," *Journal of Personality and Social Psychology* 1 (1965): 589–95.

These modeling phenomena are explainable in terms of what you already know about the way human behavior is learned. When a model is reinforced for a certain type of behavior the observer's behavior can be changed in the same way that it would be if the observer himself had been reinforced. The observer already knows how to do the behavior (or something similar to it), or he at least thinks he does, and the observer has in the past also experienced the same kind of reinforcing event, or something similar to it. In observing the model, what he sees is the connection between a specific behavior and a specific reinforcing event. (We are presuming, here, that the reinforcing event is actually reinforcing for the observer.)

Vicarious vs. Direct Reinforcement

In this sense, then, we can say that modeling is a form of vicarious reinforcement or punishment. Vicarious reinforcement is simply reinforcement that is given directly to a model but it indirectly increases the probability of similar behavior by the observer. As you might expect, however, seeing someone else reinforced for a behavior you can do is not as effective as direct and immediate reinforcement to you. In one of Bandura's studies,[2] children who observed models punished for being aggressive engaged in fewer aggressive responses than did subjects whose models were neither punished nor rewarded for the same behaviors. This was as expected. However, when in the same situation the children were offered direct reinforcers for themselves for being aggressive or nonaggressive, the differences between the two groups were completely eliminated.

If you think about this result, you may think of some interesting implications. It may help to explain, for example, the conflicting reports we get on the effects of television on children. A child may be apt to imitate the behaviors he sees on television, unless he is already being reinforced effectiveiy for incompatible behaviors by his own real environment. Advertising also attempts to elicit imitative behavior from us. A man who receives little social reinforcement from his peers and less enthusiastic receptions from women than a man in a commercial seems to may be very likely to model commercialized samples of behavior and invest in a supercharged machine, a pack of certain small cigars, or a new brand of toothpaste.

There may also be implications regarding capital punishment and incarceration. We jail and sometimes kill criminals partly because we hope that others will, by inverse imitation, avoid or cease criminal activity. Punishment of the model is aimed at inhibiting the would-be criminal observer. But as long as the observer has or expects strong reinforcers for criminal activity, it may not

---

[2] See A. Bandura, "Social Learning through Imitation," in *Nebraska Symposium on Motivation,* ed. N. R. Jones (Lincoln, Nebraska: University of Nebraska Press, 1962).

make much difference whether the model is reinforced or punished for similar behavior.

1. Give a behavioral explanation for the occurrence of imitative learning.

2. What is meant by vicarious reinforcement? For vicarious reinforcement to be effective, why and in what way must direct reinforcement be used?

3. Construct a specific example of your own to illustrate how a teacher might use modeling as an instructional technique.

We all learned very early how to yell, throw, hit, and kick because we were reinforced by the results of these actions. Yelling across the street or down to the basement, hitting a balloon or ball, kicking a ball or stone, and scratching an itch achieved desirable results, sometimes including the praise of others. Most of us were *told* not to use these behaviors to hurt others; some of us were also *taught* the same. People who were not taught this usually have been called aggressive, hostile, or tantrum-throwers. (Remember our behavioral definition of teaching and learning.)

Learning to Be Aggressive

The most useful way to understand the development of such behaviors is in terms of past experiences with the consequences for similar behaviors. If, instead, we try to explain them in terms of weak superego, guilt, or an internal hostile drive, we must work with nonbehaviors which are not directly observable. Freud, for example, postulated an unlearned death instinct as the cause of aggression. That leaves us with the task of explaining both the aggressive behavior and the nonbehavioral "cause."

For example, "frustration" is frequently cited as the cause for temper tantrums. But the term "frustration" can easily become a pseudoexplanation, leaving us with the problem of explaining both the frustration and the aggression. In such cases, frustration usually means not getting a usual or expected reinforcer. A child may have learned from past experience that he can get a snack before supper or stay up past bedtime by pleading, whining, making big promises, etc. When the parents tightened up the rules a little, he found that he had to increase his protest behavior by crying louder, stomping his feet, throwing things, or threatening; and when he did increase the intensity of his protesting, he began to get his way again. Later on his parents decide to call a halt to this contingency by not giving in; they try to outlast the child, but he comes on even stronger and longer, and eventually they give in. And when he meets similar situations in school and with his playmates, he is liable to try the same thing.

One important thing the child learns by these experiences is that protesting frequently leads to a payoff. But he also learns that, when that doesn't work, increasing the intensity or duration of his protest behavior frequently gets him what he wants. He has been taught to throw wild tantrums, not by having them reinforced (they were not that wild in the beginning), but by having the reinforcer withheld *until* the intensity of the protest behavior increases and then giving in.

Forms of aggressive and hostile behavior are developed in much the same way. Minor hostility is at first reinforced, but then reinforcement is withheld for this behavior. This is extinction, and frequently when a response is first put on extinction, the response will temporarily increase in frequency of intensity before decreasing and disappearing. But if, after the initial increase, the behavior is again reinforced, the behavior is now more likely to occur at the increased intensity. Simply withholding reinforcement is not enough to develop aggressive behavior. What is critical is that more intense forms of the behavior are reinforced when they occur.

Aggression and Imitation

There is also ample evidence that aggressive behavior can be prompted through observation of a model. Children exposed to aggressive models (real-life or in filmed or cartoon versions) act more aggressively afterward, and even imitate some behaviors that are probably new to them (e.g., sitting on a doll, hitting a doll with a hammer).

Adults also seem highly susceptible to imitation of aggressive behavior. In experiments by Walters and his associates,[3] one group of adults was shown a knife fight scene from the film *Rebel Without a Cause;* another saw a film showing some adolescents engaged in art work. Then both groups were asked to participate in an experiment to study the effects of punishment on learning. In this experiment, the adults first received several mild shocks, so that they

---

[3] See the article by R. H. Walters et al., in *Science* 136 (1962): 872–73.

would realize what the punishment was like, and then were asked to administer a shock to a student whenever he made an error (as indicated by a flashing red light). The adult could also control the intensity of the shock he gave a student. In actuality the students did not receive the shock, though the adults did not know about an unconnected electrode. In general, the results indicated that adults exposed to aggressive filmed behavior were considerably more aggressive toward erring students, as measured by both the frequency and intensity of the shocks they were willing to give. The implications of studies such as these are sobering, to say the least, but again, it is probably true in these situations that the effects of direct reinforcement override those of vicarious reinforcement.

Similarly, Sears and his associates[4] have shown that mothers who would not tolerate aggressive behavior by their children and yet did not use aggressive means to stop it had the least aggressive children. The converse also seems to be true; if you want your children to be highly aggressive and hostile, let them get away with it frequently, but when you do punish, get hostile yourself.

This analysis of aggression should give you some ideas about handling similar behavior in the classroom. Let's say you have a student who is aggressive toward other students in standard ways such as hitting, kicking, biting, hair pulling (depending partly on the age of the students). How do you handle him?

First of all, do whatever you can to eliminate any payoff for the aggression. If the aggressor has gotten his way because of his aggressive behavior, intervene to prevent that from continuing. Ignore the behavior whenever possible, and perhaps urge and teach other selected students to ignore it also. If the aggressive behavior is dangerous or too disruptive at first, you could probably use a time out period of five minutes or so as a consequent event until the instances are more easily ignored.

In arranging consequences for this behavior, don't get hostile yourself. He may already be imitating the aggression he has observed in others, and you will simply add to his problems if you become another of his models. If you must punish the behavior, use withdrawal of reinforcing opportunities, rather than physical or verbal aggression. Remember also that clear rules and instructions can assist in the behavioral change, unless you or other students frequently disregard them. State the rules and the reasons as coolly, clearly, and briefly as you can; then impose the consequences. A heated scolding is often counterproductive.

Finally—and this is true in just about every case of eliminating an undesirable behavior—be sure you take every opportunity you can to reinforce the opposite (incompatible) behavior. In this case, you will want to be especially

---

[4] See the book by R. R. Sears et. al., *Patterns of Child-Rearing* (New York: Harper and Row, Publishers, 1957).

alert for any instances of cooperative behavior and reinforce them immediately and strongly with praise, attention, and/or privileges. Initially with severe cases, you may have to reinforce crude approximations to cooperation, until the new behavior becomes more reliable and appropriate.

Incidentally, physical or verbal attack on another person is not the only form of aggression. Telling a child he's smarter than the rest or quicker or more considerate or a harder worker than the rest or giving him a grade that tells how he did *relative* to the others in the class—these are ways of reinforcing a student for beating out the rest. On the other hand, we could reinforce a student for improving on his *own* past performance. But many school experiences, especially the usual "curve" marking system, teach a student that achievement and excellence mean coming in on top of others.

4. Why does an attempt to explain aggressive behavior in terms of a person's guilt or hostility simply double the explanation problem?

5. What are the two things a child learns when he learns to be aggressive? How is extinction a part of this learning? How might imitation be involved?

6. Construct an original example, perhaps from your own experience, of a situation in which a child learns aggression from his teacher or parents. Identify the two contingencies that are learned.

7. Construct your own real or imaginary example of aggressive behavior, and describe what you would do as a teacher to eliminate it. Be able to identify the four steps in your example (prevent payoff, reinforce incompatibles, give clear rules, don't model hostility).

Look What They've Done to My School, Ma— Failures in Education

OBJECTIVES

When you complete this unit, you should be able to:

* analyze the traditional uses and results of aversive control in schools, cite several reasons for teachers' reliance on aversive contingencies, and paraphrase Skinner's critique of several current alternatives (natural learning, attention through novelty, and discovery learning).

We fail in significant ways with at least 50 percent of the people who go through our elementary and secondary school systems. Chances are that you would be classified in the upper 50 percent, so you may have difficulty relating with sympathy to "the other half." If you want to teach well, however, you will need to examine very carefully the traditional practices and methods used in schools. Batting .500 is excellent in baseball, but it's a deplorable and unnecessary record for a teacher.

The following article examines some of the practices responsible for this poor success rate. Underlying these practices is a basic principle, all too prevalent in many of our schools, which holds that it's the student's responsibility to learn, while the teacher's responsibility is to present information and punish nonlearning and noncompliance. There is a workable alternative, of course, and that is the subject of the other units in this book.

WHY TEACHERS FAIL

B. F. Skinner

The most widely publicized efforts to improve education show an extraordinary neglect of method. Learning and teaching are not analyzed, and almost no effort is made to improve teaching as such. The aid which education is to receive usually means money, and the proposals for spending it follow a few familiar lines. We should build more and better schools. We should recruit more and better teachers. We should search for better students and make sure that all competent students can go to school or college. We should multiply teacher-student contact with films and television. We should design new curricula. All this can be done without looking at teaching itself. We need not ask how those better teachers are to teach those better students in those better schools, what kinds of contact are to be multiplied through mass media, or how new curricula are to be made effective.

Perhaps we should not expect questions of this sort to be asked in what is essentially a consumer's revolt. Earlier educational reforms were proposed by teachers—a Comenius, a Rousseau, a John Dewey—who were familiar with teaching methods, knew their shortcomings, and thought they saw a chance to improve them. Today the disaffected are the parents, employers, and others who are unhappy about the products of education. When teachers complain, it is as consumers of education at lower levels—graduate school authorities want better college teaching and college teachers work to improve high-school curricula. It is perhaps natural that consumers should turn to the conspicuous shortcomings of plant, personnel, and equipment rather than to method.

It is also true that educational method has not been brought to their attention in a favorable light. Pedagogy is not a prestigious word. Its low estate may be traced in part to the fact that under the blandishments of statistical methods, which promised a new kind of rigor, educational psychologists spent half a century measuring the results of teaching while neglecting teaching itself. They compared different methods of teaching in matched groups and could often say that one method was clearly better than another, but the methods they compared were usually not drawn from their own research or even their own theories, and their results seldom generated new methods. Psychological studies of learning were equally sterile—concentrating on relatively unimportant details of a few typical learning situations such as the memory drum, the maze, the discrimination box, and verbal "problems." The learning and forgetting curves which emerged from these studies were never useful in the classroom and came to occupy a less and less important place in textbooks on educational psychology. Even today many distinguished learning theorists insist that their work has no practical relevance.

For these and doubtless other reasons, what has been taught as pedagogy has not been a true technology of teaching. College teaching, indeed, has not been taught at all. The beginning teacher receives no professional preparation. He usually begins to teach simply as he himself has been taught, and if he improves, it is only in the light of his own unaided experience. High-school and grade-school teaching is taught primarily through apprenticeships, in which students receive the advice and counsel of experienced teachers. Certain trade skills and rules of thumb are passed along, but the young teacher's own experience is to be the major source of improvement. Even this modest venture in teacher training is under attack. It is argued that a good teacher is simply one who knows his subject matter and is interested in it. Any special knowledge of pedagogy as a basic science of teaching is felt to be unnecessary.

The attitude is regrettable. No enterprise can improve itself to the fullest extent without examining its basic processes. A really effective educational system cannot be set up until we understand the processes of learning and teaching. Human behavior is far too complex to be left to casual experience, or even to organized experience in the restricted environment of the classroom. Teachers need help. In particular they need the kind of help offered by a scientific analysis of behavior.

Fortunately such an analysis is now available. Principles derived from it have already contributed to the design of schools, equipment, texts, and classroom practices. Programmed instruction is perhaps its best known achievement. Some acquaintance with its basic formulation is beginning to be regarded as important in the training of teachers and administrators. These positive contributions, however, are no more important than the light which the analysis throws on current practices. There is something wrong with teaching. From the point of view of an experimental analysis of behavior, what is it?

AVERSIVE CONTROL

Corporal punishment has always played an important role in education. As Marrou says,

> ... education and corporal punishment appeared as inseparable to a Hellenistic Greek as they had to a Jewish or an Egyptian scribe in the time of the Pharoahs. Montaigne's well-known description of "punished children yelling and masters mad with rage" is as true of Latin as it is of Greek schools. When the men of antiquity thought back to their schooldays they immediately remembered the beatings. "To hold out the hand for the cane"—*manum ferulae subducere*—was an elegant Latin way of saying "to study" (28).

The cane is still with us, and efforts to abolish it are vigorously opposed. In Great Britain a split leather strap for whipping students called a taws can be obtained from suppliers who advertise in educational journals, one of whom is said to sell 3,000 annually. (The taws has the advantage, shared by the rubber truncheon, of leaving no incriminating marks.)

The brutality of corporal punishment and the viciousness it breeds in both teacher and student have, of course, led to reform. Usually this has meant little more than shifting to noncorporal measures, of which education can boast an astonishing list. Ridicule (now largely verbalized, but once symbolized by the dunce cap or by forcing the student to sit facing a wall), scolding, sarcasm, criticism, incarceration ("being kept after school"), extra school or home work, the withdrawal of privileges, forced labor, ostracism, being put on silence, and fines—these are some of the devices which have permitted the teacher to spare the rod without spoiling the child. In some respects they are less objectionable than corporal punishment, but the pattern remains: the student spends a great part of his day doing things he does not want to do. Education is in more than one sense "compulsory." If a teacher is in any doubt about his own methods, he should ask himself a few questions. Do my students stop work immediately when I dismiss the class? (If so, dismissal is obviously a release from a threat.) Do they welcome rather than regret vacations and unscheduled days of no school? Do I reward them for good behavior by excusing them from other assignments? Do I punish them by giving them additional assignments? Do I frequently say, "Pay attention," "Now remember," or otherwise gently "admonish" them? Do I find it necessary from time to time to "get tough" and threaten some form of punishment?

The teacher can use aversive control because he is either bigger and stronger than his students or able to invoke the authority of parents or police who are. He can, for example, coerce students into reading texts, listening to lectures, taking part in discussions, recalling as much as possible of what they have read or heard, and writing papers. This is perhaps an achievement, but it is offset by an extraordinary list of unwanted by-products traceable to the basic practice.

The student who works mainly to escape aversive stimulation discovers other ways of escaping. He is tardy—"creeping like a snail unwillingly to school." He stays away from school altogether. Education has its own word for this—"truancy"—from an old Celt word meaning wretched. A special policeman, the truant officer, deals with offenders by threatening still more aversive consequences. The dropout is a legal truant. Children who commit suicide are often found to have had trouble in school.

There are subtler forms of escape. Though physically present and looking at teacher or text, the student does not pay attention. He is hysterically deaf. His mind wanders. He daydreams. Incipient forms of escape appear as restlessness. "Mental fatigue" is usually not a state of exhaustion but an uncontrollable disposition to escape, and schools deal with it by permitting escape to other activities which, it is hoped, will also be profitable. The periods into which the school day is broken measure the limits of successful aversive control rather than the capacity for sustained attention. A child will spend hours absorbed in play or in watching movies or television who cannot sit still in school for more than a few minutes before escape becomes too strong to be denied. One of the easiest forms of escape is simply to forget all one has learned, and no one has discovered a form of control to prevent this ultimate break for freedom.

An equally serious result which an experimental analysis of behavior leads us to expect is that students counterattack. If the teacher is weak, the student may attack openly. He may be impertinent, impudent, rude, or defiant. His verbal behavior may be obscene or profane. He may annoy the teacher and escape punishment by doing so surreptitiously—by groaning, shuffling his feet, or snapping his fingers. A "tormentor" is a surreptitious noisemaker especially designed for classroom use. Physical attacks on teachers are now common. Verbal attacks in the teacher's absence are legendary.

Counterattack escalates. Slightly aversive action by the teacher evokes reactions that demand severer measures, to which in turn the student reacts still more violently. Escalation may continue until one party withdraws (the student leaves school or the teacher resigns) or dominates completely (the students establish anarchy or the teacher imposes a despotic discipline).

Vandalism is another form of counterattack which is growing steadily more serious. Many cities maintain special police forces to guard school buildings on weekends. Schools are now being designed so that windows cannot be easily broken from the street. A more sweeping counterattack comes later when, as taxpayers or alumni, former students refuse to support educational institutions. Anti-intellectualism is often a general attack on all that education represents.

A much less obvious but equally serious effect of aversive control is plain inaction. The student is sullen, stubborn, and unresponsive. He "blocks." He refuses to obey. Inaction is sometimes a form of escape (rather than carry out an assignment, the student simply takes punishment as the lesser evil) and sometimes a form of attack, the object of which is to enrage the teacher, but it is also in its own right a predictable effective aversive control.

All these reactions have emotional accompaniments. Fear and anxiety are characteristic of escape and avoidance, anger of counterattack, and resentment of sullen inaction. These are the classical features of juvenile deliquency, of psychosomatic illness, and of other maladjustments familiar to the administrations and health services of educational institutions. There are other serious disadvantages of aversive control. Behavior which satisfies aversive contingencies may have undesirable characteristics. It may be unduly compulsive ("meticulous" once meant fearful); it requires effort; it is work. The student plays a submissive role which is less and less useful as cultural practices move away from totalitarian patterns. Rousseau could complain further that scarcely more than half the pupils of his day lived to enjoy the blessings for which the pleasures of their childhood were sacrificed. Fortunately that is no longer true, but the sacrifice continues.

Aversive methods also have effects on teachers. The young teacher may begin his career with a favorable attitude toward his profession and toward his students, only to find himself playing a consistently unfriendly role as a repertoire of aggressive behavior is repeatedly reinforced. The prospect does not attract or hold good teachers. At times the profession has been tolerable only to weaklings or those who enjoy treating others aversively. Even when moderately used, aversive practices interfere with the kinds of relations with students which make more productive techniques feasible.

In college and graduate schools the aversive pattern survives in the now almost universal system of "assign and test." The teacher does not teach, he simply holds the student responsible for learning. The student must read books, study texts, perform experiments, and attend lectures, and he is responsible for doing so in the sense that, if he does not correctly report what he has seen, heard, or read, he will suffer aversive consequences. Questions and answers are so staple a feature of education that their connection with teaching almost never occasions surprise, yet as a demand for a response which will meet certain specifications, a question is almost always slightly aversive. An examination, as a collection of questions, characteristically generates the anxiety and panic appropriate to avoidance and escape. Reading a student's paper is still likely to be called correcting it. Examinations are designed to show principally what the student does *not* know. A test which proves to be too easy is made harder before being given again, ostensibly because an easy test does not discriminate, but more probably because the teacher is afraid of weakening the threat under which his students are working. A teacher is judged by his employers and colleagues by the severity of the threat he imposes: he is a good teacher if he makes his students work hard, regardless of how he does so or of how much he teaches them by doing so. He eventually evaluates himself in the same way; if he tries to shift to nonaversive methods, he may discover that he resists making things easy as if this necessarily meant teaching less.

Proposals to add requirements and raise standards are usually part of an aversive pattern. A well-known educator (4) has written:

> We must stiffen the work of our schools . . . we have every reason to concentrate on [certain subjects] and be unflagging in our insistence that they be really learned. . . . Senior year [in high school] ought to be the hardest. . . . [We should give] students work that is both difficult and important, and [insist] that it be well done. . . . We should demand more of our students.

These expressions were probably intended to be synonymous with "students should learn more" or possibly "teachers should teach more." There may be good reasons why students should take more mathematics or learn a modern language more thoroughly or be better prepared for college or graduate school, but they are not reasons for intensifying aversive pressures. A standard is a level of achievement; only under a particular philosophy of education is it a criterion upon which some form of punishment is contingent.

It is not difficult to explain the use of aversive control. The teacher can easily arrange aversive contingencies; his culture has already taught him how to do so. In any case, since the immediate effects are clear-cut, effective techniques are easily learned. When the control begins early and is maintained consistently, and particularly when it takes the moderate form of "gentle admonition," by-products are minimized. Systems which are basically aversive have produced well-disciplined, obedient, industrious, and eventually informed and skilled students sometimes to the envy of teachers who cannot skillfully use the same techniques. Even the students themselves may be impressed and may return years later to thank their teachers for having beaten or ridiculed them.

Aversive control can be defended as "nature's way." In learning to turn a hand spring, a child improves by avoiding bumps and bruises. The natural environment teaches a person to act in ways which resolve puzzlement or reduce the threat of not knowing. Why should the teacher not imitate nature and arrange comparable aversive contingencies, such as puzzling the student to induce him to think or make him curious to induce him to explore. But nature is not always an admirable teacher. Its aversive contingencies are not a model to be copied but a standard to be excelled.

Aversive contingencies also provide an opportunity for the student to learn to adjust to the unpleasant and painful, to act effectively when threatened, to submit to pain, but they are usually not well designed for that purpose. As Rousseau pointed out, a child may be taught to cope with aversive stimulation, but the required contingencies are not easily combined with contingencies designed to teach other things.

Aversive control is no doubt sanctioned in part because it is compatible with prevailing philosophies of government and religion. It is not only the teacher who holds the student responsible for doing what he ought to do or punishes him "justly" when he fails. It is not only the failing student who is told that "ignorance is no excuse." Schools and colleges must, of course, share in the ethical and legal control of the societies which support them and of which they are a part, and they have comparable problems of their own to which aversive control has always seemed relevant, but alternative courses of action should be considered. Existing systems with their unfortunate by-products cannot be defended as necessary evils until we are sure that other solutions cannot be found.

Most teachers are humane and well disposed. They do not want to threaten their students yet they find themselves doing so. They want to help but their offers are often declined. Most students are well disposed. They want an education, yet they cannot force themselves to study, and they know they are wasting time. For reasons which they have probably not correctly identified, many are in revolt. Why should education continue to use the aversive techniques to which all this is so obviously due? Evidently because effective alternatives have not been found. It is not enough simply to abandon aversive measures. A Summerhill is therapeutic not educational: by withholding punishment teachers may help students who have been badly treated elsewhere and prepare them to be taught, but something else is needed. Tolstoy soon abandoned the school for the children of his serfs in which no child was obliged to go to school or, when in school, to pay attention, and similar experiments by the anarchists and one by Bertrand Russell also failed.

TELLING AND SHOWING

A child sees things and talks about them accurately afterward. He listens to news and gossip and passes it along. He recounts in great detail the plot of a movie he has seen or a book he has read. He seems to have a "natural curiosity," a "love of knowledge," an "inherent wish to learn." Why not take advantage of these natural endowments and simply bring the student into contact with the world he is to learn about? There are practical problems, of course. Only a small part of the real world can be brought into the classroom even with the aid of films, tape recorders, and television, and only a small part of what remains can be visited outside. Words are easily imported, but the verbal excesses of classical education have shown how easily this fact may lead to dangerous overemphasis. Within reasonable limits, however, is it not possible to teach simply by giving the student an opportunity to learn in a natural way?

Unfortunately, a student does not learn simply when he is shown or told. Something essential to his natural curiosity or wish to learn is missing from the classroom. What is missing, technically speaking, is "positive reinforcement." In daily life the student looks, listens, and remembers because certain consequences then follow. He learns to look and listen in those special ways which encourage remembering because he is reinforced for recalling what he has seen and heard, just as a newspaper reporter notes and remembers things he sees because he is paid for reporting them. Consequences of this sort are lacking when a teacher simply shows a student something or tells him something.

Rousseau was the great advocate of natural learning. Émile was to be taught by the world of things. His teacher was to draw his attention to that world; but otherwise his education was to be negative. There were to be no arranged consequences. But Émile was an imaginary student with imaginary learning processes. When Rousseau's disciple, Pestalozzi, tried the methods on his own flesh-and-blood son, he ran into trouble. His diary is one of the most pathetic documents in the history of education (17). As he walked with his young son beside a stream, Pestalozzi would repeat several times, "Water flows down-hill." He would show the boy that "wood swims in water and . . . stones sink." Whether the child was learning anything or not, he was not unhappy, and Pestalozzi could believe that at least he was using the right method. But when the world of things had to be left behind, failure could no longer be concealed. "I could only get him to read with difficulty; he has a thousand ways of getting out of it, and never loses an opportunity of doing something else." He could make the boy sit still at his lessons by first making him "run and play out of doors in the cold," but Pestalozzi himself was then exhausted. Inevitably, of course, he returned to aversive measures: "He was soon tired of learning to read, but as I had decided that he should work at it regularly every day, whether he liked it or not, I determined to make him feel the necessity of doing so, from the very first, by showing him there was no choice between this work and my displeasure, which I made him feel by keeping him in."[1]

GETTING ATTENTION

The failure of "showing and telling" is sometimes attributed to lack of attention. We are often aware that we ourselves are not listening or looking carefully. If we are not to punish the student for not looking and listening, how can we make him concentrate? One possibility is to make sure that there is nothing else to be seen or heard. The schoolroom is isolated and freed of distractions. Silence is often the rule. Physical constraints are helpful. Ear-phones reassure the teacher that only what is to be heard is going into the student's ears. The TV screen is praised for its isolation and hypnotic effect. A piece of equipment has been proposed which achieves concentration in the following desperate way: the student faces a brightly lighted text, framed by walls which operate on the principle of the blinders once worn by carriage horses. His ears are between earphones. He reads part of the text aloud and then listens to his recorded voice as he reads it again. If he does not learn what he reads, it is certainly not because he has not seen it!

A less coercive practice is to make what is to be seen or heard attractive and attention-compelling. The advertiser faces the same problem as the teacher, and his techniques have been widely copied in the design of textbooks, films, and classroom practices. Bright colors, variety, sudden change, big type, ani-mated sequences—all these have at least a temporary effect in inducing the student to look and listen. They do not, however, *teach* the student to look and listen, because they occur at the wrong time. A similar weakness is seen in making school itself pleasant. Attractive architecture, colorful interiors, comfortable furniture, congenial social arrangements, naturally interesting

---

[1] A contemporary of Pestalozzi's, Thomas Day, author of *Sandford and Morton,* a book for children, "died from a kick by a horse which he was trying to break in on Rousseau's principles, a martyr to Reason and Nature" (37).

subjects—these are all reinforcing, but they reinforce only the behaviors they are contingent upon. An attractive school building reinforces the behavior of coming in sight of it. A colorful and comfortable classroom reinforces the behavior of entering it. Roughly speaking, these things could be said to strengthen a positive attitude toward school. But they provide merely the setting for instruction. They do not teach what students are in school to learn.

In the same way audio-visual aids usually come at the wrong time to strengthen the forms of behavior which are the principal concern of the teacher. An interesting page printed in four colors reinforces the student simply for opening the book and looking at it. It does not reinforce reading the page or even examining it closely; certainly it does not reinforce those activities which result in effective recall of what is seen. An interesting lecturer holds his listeners in the sense that they look at and listen to him just as an interesting demonstration film reinforces the behavior of watching it, but neither the lecture nor the film necessarily reinforces listening or listening in those special ways which further recall. In good instruction interesting things should happen *after* the student has read a page or listened or looked with care. The four-color picture should *become* interesting when the text which accompanies it has been read. One stage in a lecture or film should be interesting only if earlier stages have been carefully examined and remembered. In general, naturally attractive and interesting things further the primary goals of education only when they enter into much more subtle contingencies of reinforcement than are usually represented by audio-visual aids.

MAKING MATERIAL EASY TO REMEMBER

It is possible that students may be induced to learn by making material not only attractive but memorable. An obvious example is making material easy. The child first learns to write in manuscript because it resembles the text he is learning to read; he may learn to read material printed in a phonetic alphabet; he may learn to spell only words he will actually use; if he cannot read he can listen to recorded speech. This sort of simplification shows a lack of confidence in methods of teaching and often merely postpones the teacher's task, but it is sometimes a useful strategy. Material which is well organized is also, of course, easier to learn.

Some current psychological theories suggest that material may be made memorable in another way. Various laws of perception imply that an observer cannot help seeing things in certain ways. The stimulus seems to force itself upon the organism. Optical illusions are often cited as examples. These laws suggest the possibility that material may be presented in a form in which it is irresistibly learned. Material is to be so "structured" that it is readily—and almost necessarily—"grasped." Instructional examples are, however, far less persuasive than the demonstrations offered in support of them. In trying to assign an important function to the material to be learned, it is particularly easy to overlook other conditions under which learning actually occurs.

THE TEACHER AS MIDWIFE

No matter how attractive, interesting, and well structured material may be, the discouraging fact is that it is often not learned. Rather than continue to ask why, many educational theorists have concluded that the teacher cannot really teach at all but can only help the student learn. The dominant metaphor goes back to Plato. As Emile Bréhier puts it, "Socrates . . . possessed no other art but maieutics, his mother Phaenarete's art of delivering; he drew out from souls what they have in them . . ." The student already knows the truth; the teacher simply shows him that he knows. As we have seen, however, there is no evidence that the boy in the scene from the *Meno* learned anything. He could not have reconstructed the theorem by himself when Socrates had finished, and Socrates says as much later in the dialogue: "If someone will keep asking him these same questions often and in various forms, you can be sure that in the end he will know about them as accurately as anybody." (Socrates was a frequency theorist!)[2]

It must be admitted that the assignment was difficult. The boy was starting from scratch. When Polya uses the same technique in presiding at the birth of the formula for the diagonal of a parallelepiped his students make a more positive contribution because they have already had some geometry, but any success due to previous teaching weakens the claim for maieutics. And Polya's promptings and questionings give more help than he wants to admit.

It is only because mathematical proofs seem to arise from the nature of things that they can be said in some sense to be "known by everyone" and simply waiting to be drawn out. Even Socrates could not argue that the soul knows the facts of history or a second language. Impregnation must precede parturition. But is it not possible that a presentation which has not seemed to be learned is the seed from which knowledge grows to be delivered by the teacher? Perhaps the intellectual midwife is to show the student that he remembers what he has already been shown or told. In *The Idea of a University* Cardinal Newman gave an example of the maieutic method applied to acquired knowledge. It will stir painful memories in many teachers. A tutor is talking with a candidate about a bit of history—a bit of history, in fact, in which Plato's Menon lost his life.

---

[2] It is astonishing how seriously the scene from the *Meno* has been taken. Karl Popper has recently written (34): "For Meno's slave is helped by Socrates' judicious questions to remember or recapture the forgotten knowledge which his soul possessed in its ante-natal state of omniscience. It is, I believe, this famous Socratic method, called in the Theaetetus the art of midwifery or maieutic, to which Aristotle alluded when he said that Socrates was the inventor of the method of induction."

T. It is the *Anabasis* you take up? . . . What is the meaning of the word *Anabasis?*
C. is silent.
T. You know very well; take your time, and don't be alarmed. Anabasis means
. . . *C.* An ascent. . . .
T. Who ascended? *C.* The Greeks, Xenophon.
T. Very well: Xenophon and the Greeks; the Greeks ascended. To what did they
ascend? *C.* Against the Persian king: they ascended to fight the Persian king.
T. That is right . . . an ascent; but I thought we called it a descent when a foreign
army carried war into a country? *C. is silent.*
T. Don't we talk of a descent of barbarians? *C.* Yes
T. Why then are the Greeks said to go *up? C.* They went up to fight the Persian
king.
T. Yes; but why *up* . . . why not *down? C.* They came down afterwards when they
retreated back to Greece.
T. Perfectly right; they did . . . but could you give no reason why they are said
to go *up* to Persia, not *down? C.* They went *up* to Persia.
T. Why do you not say they went *down? C. pauses, then,* . . . They went *down* to
Persia.
T. You have misunderstood me.

Newman warned his reader that the Candidate is "deficient to a great extent
. . . not such as it is likely that a respectable school would turn out." He
recognized a poor student, but not a poor method. Thousands of teachers have
wasted years of their lives in exchanges which have been no more profitable
—and all to the greater glory of maieutics and out of a conviction that telling
and showing are not only inadequate but wrong.

Although the soul has perhaps not always known the truth nor ever been
confronted with it in a half-forgotten experience, it may still *seek* it. If the
student can be taught to learn from the world of things, nothing else will ever
have to be taught. This is the method of discovery. It is designed to absolve
the teacher from a sense of failure by making instruction unnecessary. The
teacher arranges the environment in which discovery is to take place, he
suggests lines of inquiry, he keeps the student within bounds. The important
thing is that he should tell him nothing.

The human organism does, of course, learn without being taught. It is a good
thing that this is so, and it would no doubt be a good thing if more could be
learned in that way. Students are naturally interested in what they learn by
themselves because they would not learn if they were not, and for the same
reason they are more likely to remember what they learn in that way. There
are reinforcing elements of surprise and accomplishment in personal discovery
which are welcome alternatives to traditional aversive consequences.[3] But

---

[3] As Pascal pointed out, "Reasons which one has discovered oneself are usually more persuasive than those which have turned up in the thinking of others"—but not because the reasons are
proprietary; one discovers a rule describing contingencies of reinforcement only after having been
exposed to the contingencies. The rule seems to the discoverer particularly apropos because it is
supported by the variables it describes.

discovery is no solution to the problems of education. A culture is no stronger than its capacity to transmit itself. It must impart an accumulation of skills, knowledge, and social and ethical practices to its new members. The institution of education is designed to serve this purpose. It is quite impossible for the student to discover for himself any substantial part of the wisdom of his culture, and no philosophy of education really proposes that he should. Great thinkers build upon the past, they do not waste time in rediscovering it. It is dangerous to suggest to the student that it is beneath his dignity to learn what others already know, that there is something ignoble (and even destructive of "rational powers") in memorizing facts, codes, formulae, or passages from literary works, and that to be admired he must think in original ways. It is equally dangerous to forgo teaching important facts and principles in order to give the student a chance to discover them for himself. Only a teacher who is unaware of his effects on his students can believe that children actually discover mathematics, that (as one teacher has written) in group discussions they "can and do figure out all of the relationships, facts, and procedures that comprise a full program in math."

There are other difficulties. The position of the teacher who encourages discovery is ambiguous. Is he to pretend that he himself does not know? (Socrates said Yes. In Socratic irony those who know enjoy a laugh at the expense of those who do not.) Or, for the sake of encouraging a joint venture in discovery, is the teacher to choose to teach only those things which he himself has not yet learned? Or is he frankly to say, "I know, but you must find out" and accept the consequences for his relations with his students?

Still another difficulty arises when it is necessary to teach a whole class. How are a few good students to be prevented from making all the discoveries? When that happens, other members of the class not only miss the excitement of discovery but are left to learn material presented in a slow and particularly confusing way. Students should, of course, be encouraged to explore, to ask questions, to study by themselves, to be "creative." When properly analyzed, the kinds of behavior referred to in such expressions can be taught. It does not follow, however, that they must be taught by the method of discovery.

The Idols of the School

Effective instructional practices threaten the conception of teaching as a form of maieutics. If we suppose that the student is to "exercise his rational powers," to "develop his mind," or to learn through "intuition or insight," then it may indeed be true that the teacher cannot teach but can only help the student learn. But these goals can be restated in terms of explicit changes in behavior, and effective methods of instruction can then be designed.

In his famous four idols, Francis Bacon formulated some of the reasons why men arrive at false ideas. He might have added two special Idols of the School which affect those who want to improve teaching. The Idol of the Good

Teacher is the belief that what a good teacher can do, any teacher can do. Some teachers are, of course, unusually effective. They are naturally interesting people, who make things interesting to their students. They are skillful in handling students, as they are skillful in handling people in general. They can formulate facts and principles and communicate them to others in effective ways. Possibly their skills and talents will someday be better understood and successfully imparted to new teachers. At the moment, however, they are true exceptions. The fact that a method proves successful in their hands does not mean that it will solve important problems in education.

The Idol of the Good Student is the belief that what a good student can learn, any student can learn. Because they have superior ability or have been exposed to fortunate early environments, some students learn without being taught. It is quite possible that they learn more effectively when they are not taught. Possibly we shall someday produce more of them. At the moment, however, the fact that a method works with good students does not mean that it will work with all. It is possible that we shall progress more rapidly toward effective education by leaving the good teacher and the good student out of account altogether. They will not suffer, because they do not need our help. We may then devote ourselves to the discovery of practices which are appropriate to the remaining—what?—ninety-five percent of teachers and students.

The Idols of the School explain some of the breathless excitement with which educational theorists return again and again to a few standard solutions. Perhaps we should regard them as merely two special cases of a more general source of error, the belief that personal experience in the classroom is the primary source of pedagogical wisdom. It is actually very difficult for teachers to profit from experience. They almost never learn about their long-term successes or failures, and their short-term effects are not easily traced to the practices from which they presumably arose. Few teachers have time to reflect on such matters, and traditional educational research has given them little help. A much more effective kind of research is now becoming possible. Teaching may be defined as an arrangement of contingencies of reinforcement under which behavior changes. Relevant contingencies can be most successfully analyzed in studying the behavior of one student at a time under carefully controlled conditions. Few educators are aware of the extent to which human behavior is being examined in arrangements of this sort, but a true technology of teaching is imminent. It is beginning to suggest effective alternatives to the aversive practices which have caused so much trouble.

1. Cite several "publicized efforts to improve education" which Skinner says have failed. In contrast, what aspect of education should we emphasize, according to Skinner?

2. Cite several examples illustrating Skinner's contention that education is still primarily based on aversive control. Cite several examples of student behavior that are likely to result from this.

3. Give several reasons why, according to Skinner, teachers rely on aversive contingencies.

4. According to Skinner, what is wrong with students learning in school "in a natural way"?

5. Describe several ways schools try to keep the student's attention. Why does Skinner criticize these methods?

6. Cite several reasons Skinner gives for saying that discovery learning is no solution to the problems of education.

unit 11

Examples of Applied Behavior Analysis

OBJECTIVES

When you complete this unit and unit 12, you should be able to:

* identify the procedures, contingencies, and results in several articles describing the application of behavior analysis to elementary and secondary classrooms;
* describe tactics for minimizing problems associated with recording, reinforcer identification, and supervisor cooperation;
* design a contingency management system for a hypothetical classroom in which you are the teacher.

In this unit you will study a variety of examples in which the principles described in the previous units are applied to academic, motivational, and disciplinary behaviors in regular secondary and elementary classrooms. There are nonexamples also—situations in which the techniques did not work and analyses of why they failed. Hopefully, these studies will serve as a bridge between your study of the principles and techniques and your application of them in real teaching-learning situations.

Perhaps the best way for you to handle this unit is to scan the first article rather quickly just to get the general focus and results of the study, then use the study-guide questions as a guide to your study of specific parts of the article. Then do the same for the other articles.

TOKEN REINFORCEMENT SYSTEMS IN THE REGULAR PUBLIC SCHOOL CLASSROOM*

R. J. Karraker

Token reinforcement systems have demonstrated their effectiveness in controlling behavior in a variety of settings, including mental hospitals (Ayllon and Azrin, 1965, Atthowe and Krasner, 1965, Gericke, 1965), hospitals for retarded (Girardeau and Spradlin, 1964; Birnbrauer, et al., 1965), a training school for delinquents, (Cohen, 1967), special education classes in public schools (O'Leary and Becker, 1966; Clark et al., 1967), and a remedial classroom (Wolf et al., 1966).

All of these experiments and demonstrations have in common the fact that the token reinforcement system has very much maintained a "research flavor." Most programs are characterized by (1) observers in addition to the behavioral managers, (2) close supervision and direction by individuals trained in an analysis of behavior, (3) research funds for consequences, (4) complete nonintervention from administrative personnel in their respective institutions, and (5) a relatively high degree of control of the environment.

Although virtually every published report of token reinforcement systems claims unqualified success in modifying behavior, the extent to which token systems can be employed by the regular public school classroom teacher without such supportive services and conditions has not been explored. It has been suggested (Baer, in press) that teachers not undertake behavior modification projects because of the unreliability of observation. However, the position taken by this author is that attempts to assess procedures objectively by systematic data collection, even in the absence of impressive reliability data, is appropriate if these techniques are to be incorporated in the mainstream of education.

The past year part-time graduate students who are also employed full time as teachers have been executing behavior modification projects based on principles of learning from an experimental analysis of behavior. Over the past year ten teachers chose to implement a token reinforcement system in their classrooms. The teachers formulated their plan, and then consulted the author for advice before beginning the project. Each teacher evolved his own adaptation of a token-reinforcement system. The type and number of target behaviors, the length of baseline observations, the contingencies, the consequences presented or withdrawn, and the duration of the project varied in each project.

The students were informed, in order to reduce the probability of falsification of data, that their grade in the course was not contingent upon modifying the behavior. In addition, the author visited each project at least once, and sometimes more than once, during the semester.

Projects in Secondary Schools

Inner-City Study Hall

A thirty-minute study hall in a predominantly black school was reported to be a problem by the supervising teacher. In analyzing the behaviors that were disrupting the class, the pinpointed behaviors of talking without permission and being out of seat without permission were identified. In discussions with the teacher it became apparent that one condition that may have been functionally related to these behaviors was the observation that the students were not bringing to the study hall materials that would permit effective study behaviors. The teacher suggested that if each student brought to the class a pencil, a notebook (or paper), and a book, study behaviors *could* occur.

Premodification data on these three behaviors were collected for 11 successive class days: talking without permission, being out of seat without permission, and bringing study materials (book, pencil, and paper) to study hall.

The recording procedure was that the teacher would record each student who emitted the defined behaviors. It was suggested to the teacher that recording each instance of the talking out and out-of-seat behavior would be more sensitive to the consequence to be implemented, but she preferred to record just whether or not the student emitted the behavior as this would simplify her recording operations.[1]

Figure 1 presents the percent of the class which emitted each of the behaviors. Absentees were not counted in computing the percentages. The median percent of students who brought all three study materials to class was 50. For those who talked without permission the median percent was 64. Finally, the median percent of those who were out of seat without permission was 28.

In selection of a consequence to make contingent upon emission of the desired behaviors, the P-hypothesis (Premack, 1959, 1965) was invoked.[2] Briefly, the P-hypothesis states that any behavior that is higher in probability of occurrence (High Probability Behavior or HPB) than another (Low Probability Behavior or LPB) can be used as a reinforcer to increase the rate of the LPB. In observing the behavior of students in this study hall, talking to one another and reading comic books were HPBs, while emitting study behaviors were LPBs.

Therefore, the following contingency contract was presented to the students by the teacher. If the students displayed pencil, paper, and a book when they entered the study hall, and if during the first 20 minutes they did not talk or

---

[1] This is an example of the compromise that often must be made in getting these techniques implemented by teachers in their classrooms. If the behavior is brought under control, teachers can subsequently be "shaped" into better applications of the procedures.

[2] For elaboration of the P-hypothesis and its application to human behavior, refer to Homme, 1965; Homme and Tosti, 1965.

rise from their seats during the study hall, the last 10 minutes they would be permitted to sit by a peer and converse quietly or read comic books at their desks.

Figure 1 illustrates the effect of this procedure. The median percents during the 15 sessions the contingency contract was in effect were bringing study materials 90, talking out 25, and being out of seat 0. On session 19, some calculators were placed at one end of the study hall. This was to be a temporary arrangement, but the teacher observed that this situation was likely to interrupt her control of the environment, so she added the consequence of five minutes' time on the calculators to the conversation-time and comic-book contingencies.[3]

On session 27 she told the students the contingency contract was no longer in effect. This return to premodification conditions resulted in median percents of 29 (materials), 81 (talking out), and 0 (out of seat) over a 10-day period. During this period the students were unhappy with the teacher for removing the contract, and most of the talking out consisted of questions to her regarding why the contingencies had been removed.

For five sessions the teacher reinstated the contingency contract and there was an immediate change in all three target behaviors. This condition would have been run longer but a school vacation interrupted data collection. The atypical behavior as shown in Figure 1 in session 38 was the result of a fight that had been precipitated prior to the study hall but continued at intervals during the period.

Suburban Biology Class

A secondary biology teacher was concerned about the percent of her class which was earning grades of C or below on quizzes which were administered three times a week. The quizzes contained items that should have been easy for the students if they had read the assignment. There was an effort to keep each quiz reinforcing rather than punishing, and with this effort the label "progress check" (Homme, 1965) was employed to describe them. A major exam every two or three weeks was being administered in addition to the progress checks. Conventional letter grades were being given to the students prior to data collection.

Although the following contingency contract was made with the entire class, the data reported are on only 16 students who had an average grade of C or below before the contract was introduced. Prior to session 1 the students were told that grades would no longer be administered, but points would be awarded depending upon the percent correct on the progress checks: 90% or better = 3 points; 80 through 89% = 2 points; 70 through 79% = 1 point; and, below 70% = –1 point.

---

[3] This is an example of the many events that often terminate these projects.

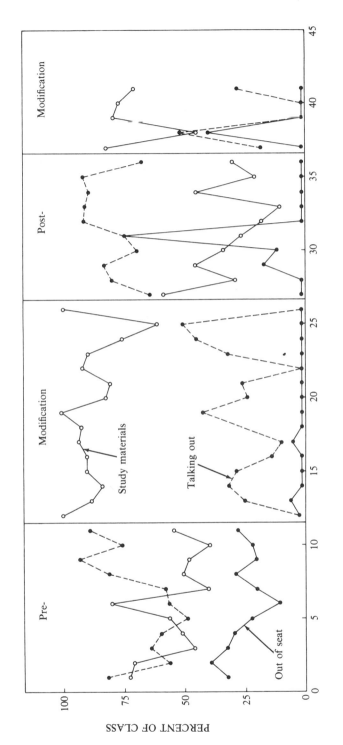

FIGURE 1.

Percent of class bringing study materials, talking without permission, and being out of seat without permission during an inner-city study hall.

Five progress checks were given to the students with no other consequence attached to the points.

Figure 2 indicates that under the point system with no further contingencies, the 16 students had a median of 60% correct on five progress checks. On session 5, the following announcement was made: "We will now have a major exam every other Friday. You can avoid taking this exam by cashing in 10 points. You may use the points you have accumulated during this past two-week period."

The teacher's rationale for selection of this particular consequence was that if the students had 10 points available, they were acquiring the skills on a daily basis (an average of 80% through 89%) and a major exam would not be necessary to assure acquisition of the material. During 11 progress checks of this contract the 16 low-achieving students had a median percent correct of 74.

On session 16 the teacher announced the point system was being abandoned, and the class would return to the conventional grade system on the next progress check. Performance of the 16 pupils decelerated to a median of 46% correct over the next 4 progress checks. This is a lower percent than before the exam contingency was introduced.

One interesting side effect of this project was that several of the students who were maintaining a B or better average prior to the project began comparing their accumulated points, and competition in regard to total points earned was evidenced. Some of these students would not cash in their points to avoid the exam in order to "hoard" their points.

PROJECTS IN ELEMENTARY SCHOOLS

Second-Grade Class

A second-grade teacher was concerned about the rate of her class talking without permission. The teacher recorded each instance of a student talking without permission on a golf counter attached to her wrist (Lindsley, 1968). Data were collected during the 210 minutes daily that the pupils were under the teacher's direct tutorage (minus lunch, recess, and classes taught by other teachers).

Premodification data revealed a median rate of .19 talkings out per minute over an 8-day period (See Figure 3). The consequence the teacher selected was a 15-minute story time at the end of each day. The teacher placed in front of the room a chart with each pupil's name written on one side. The first time a pupil talked without permission, the teacher walked to the chart and placed a cover over his name. She also advanced her golf counter and did so after each succeeding response. This procedure did reduce the talking out initially, but the pupils soon learned that the consequences were attached to the first re-

Median percent correct on biology progress checks of 16 low-achieving students.

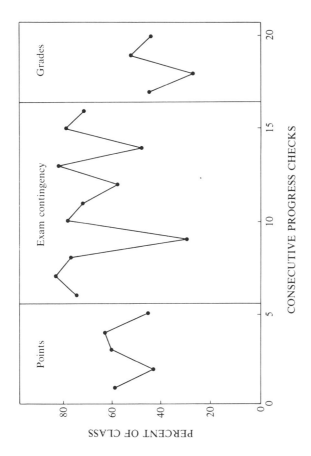

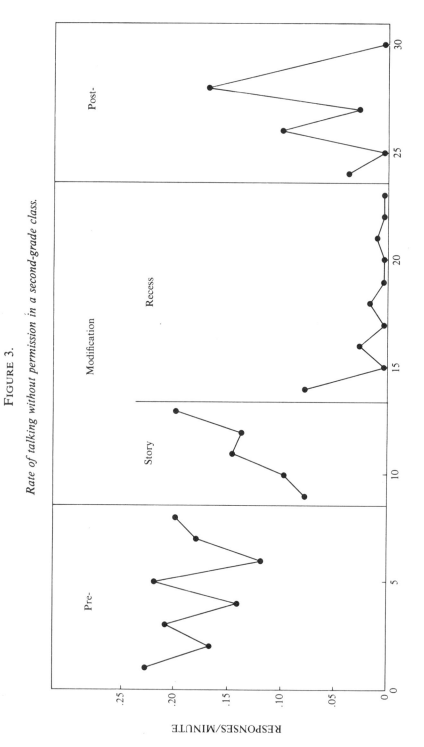

FIGURE 3.

Rate of talking without permission in a second-grade class.

sponse only. The data show an initial decrease the first day of this procedure, but the next four days resulted in a steady increase in the behavior with a median rate of .14.

The teacher observed that it would be necessary to select a consequence that would be responsive to every talking out that occurred, so she began assessing one minute loss of recess time for every response. She kept a cumulative record of the talking out on the chalkboard, and also continued her recording on the wrist counter. The first day of this contingency there were 17 talk-outs in the 210 minutes. Over the next nine days the talking out was reduced drastically, with six days of less than three responses occurring. Removal of the contingency resulted in the behavior returning to within the premodification level with a median rate of .07 talkings out per minute.

Fifth-Grade Spelling

A fifth-grade teacher was concerned that a boy in her class was consistently close to the bottom of his class on spelling tests. This performance was in contrast to his level of achievement in other subject-matter areas. In addition, the pupil's scores on standardized achievement tests led the teacher to state that he was performing well below expectations considering these scores.

The teacher had expressed her intention earlier to acquire permission from her principal to make the majority of recess time contingent upon academic performance. The principal agreed to the arrangement, and the teacher checked her gradebook and figured percent correct on spelling tests for the first five weeks of school. The median percent for the class was 70 and the median percent for the subject was 40. It can be observed from Figure 4 that test premodification data revealed the subject never had the lowest percent correct in the class, but was below the class median on each test.

The consequence implemented was one minute of afternoon recess for each word spelled correctly. During premodification the number of words on each test varied between 12 and 20, but beginning on the sixth week the number of words presented was 20 on each test.

Figure 4 illustrates the effect of this procedure. The subject's percent correct jumped from the premodification median of 40 to 100, while the class median also rose from a median of 70 to 90. The variability of performance of the class also indicates the effectiveness of the procedure.

Prior to the test on week 12 the pupils were informed recess would no longer be contingent, and the behavior decelerated for both the subject and the class. The median for the class during the nine weeks of post-modification was 76, while the subject's median was 39.

The teacher managed this arrangement by controlling when the pupils left the classroom at the time recess was made available. Those students who had spelled all 120 words correctly left the room immediately. Other pupils were

FIGURE 4.

Percent correct spelling performance of a fifth-grade pupil and his class. The pupil's percents are the solid data points, and the class medians are the open circles. The lines through the data points indicate the range of class performance.

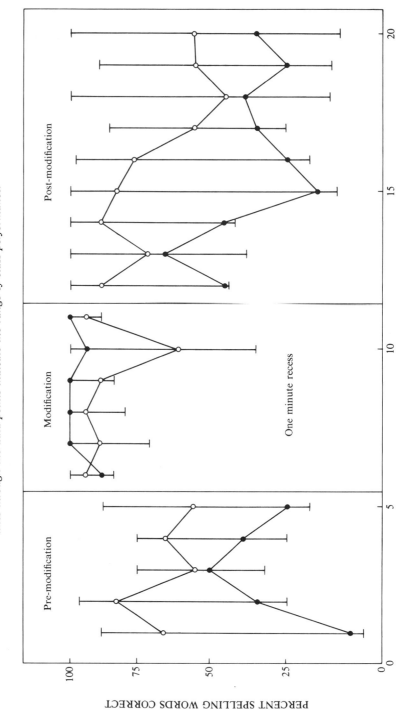

permitted to leave contingent upon the number of corresponding minutes they had earned on their spelling test.

PROBLEMS IN THE APPLICATION OF TOKEN REINFORCEMENT SYSTEMS

Recording the Behavior

Most behaviors in classrooms are of such low frequency that a rate measure in terms of minutes is often meaningless to teachers. For example, reporting a rate of behavior at .07 per minute has quite different effects on teachers than saying a behavior occurred twice in a thirty-minute class. Therefore, rates utilizing behavior over longer units of time (such as class period) communicates more clearly to teachers. Perhaps rates under one per minute could be employed for those persons with experience in looking at data, but for feedback to classroom teachers, frequency or cumulative response measure may be preferable.

A second observation is that recording duration of behavior is difficult for teachers. For some behaviors, it is the fact that the behavior is initiated, rather than the duration of the behavior once initiated, that is significant. For instance, a child who talks out in a study hall interrupts the study behavior of others, and whether the behavior occurs for five seconds or one minute may be less important than the fact that he did talk out. Also, recording on a time-sampling technique is difficult when other teaching behaviors are being emitted simultaneously.

If observers are available, more continuous recording techniques (such as recording the behavior in ten-second intervals) would provide data more sensitive to procedures. However, most classroom teachers simply do not have access to observers.

Finding Consequences

Most teachers who have information about token reinforcement systems and have been exposed to Homme's application of the Premack Principle (Homme, 1965; Addison and Homme, 1966) still have difficulty identifying consequences to employ. Such obvious consequences as recess time, access to library books, magazines, art activities, story time, class monitor, opportunity to tutor others, early lunches, teacher proximity on specified occasions, parties, nonrequired school supplies, trips, films, preferred school subjects and other individualized high-probability behaviors are at times difficult for teachers to identify. Of forty-two graduate students who employed behavior-modification projects last semester, 46% indicated deciding on a consequence was their biggest problem. Deciding on a behavior to modify was mentioned by 19%, recording the behavior by 13%, and deciding on a principle of learning on which to base the modification procedure by 9%. There were miscellaneous problems which accounted for 1%.

Aversive Control

In the beginning it was almost demanded of the students that they arrange their modifications to avoid any form of aversive control. Justification for this demand was easy to document (Skinner, 1961; 1965). However, some teachers began using a point-less component in their systems anyway, and the dire consequences that have been predicted to result from aversive control were not observed.

Specific Failures

Three such systems were classified by either the teacher or the author as failures.

Teacher A. This teacher implemented a token system in a fourth-grade class with four target behaviors. Students earned tokens for scoring 80% or better on exams and turning in assignments on time. Tokens were lost by talking out without permission and not being seated within one minute after each bell sounded. Tokens were backed up with choice of activity in free time, opportunity to tutor other children, and extra recess time. Tokens were exchanged for the consequence at the end of the day, and it was planned to extend gradually the number of days per payoff.

Three problems contributed to the failure of the tokens to modify behavior. (1) The teacher reported the introduction of the system to the pupils went "badly." Her instructions were not taped, so it is impossible to recapture exactly what she said. She attempted to explain verbally how the system would operate instead of just demonstrating the contingencies. This tactic generated many questions and confusion regarding target behaviors, contingencies, etc. (2) All four target behaviors were augmented at once, which contributed to the reported confusion. (3) The consequences, while high-probability behaviors for many individuals, may not have been effective for the class, as the class voted on what consequence would be available at the end of the day. In retrospect, this teacher either did not have a consequence that was reinforcing to the entire class, or she was poorly organized at the beginning and set up too many target behaviors.

Teacher B. This teacher set up a token system to decelerate disruptive behaviors in a fifth-grade class—hitting, pinching, or tripping others. After one week of modification the teacher reported the behaviors were not decelerating. The class was observed, and on one occasion reliability of the teacher's observations was found to be less than 40% agreement.

It was discovered that the teacher did a lot of individualized teaching and was often physically not in a position to accurately record the behavior. She has now implemented a system with such target behaviors as turning in work on time, 80% or better correct on exams, and pages completed in arithmetic workbooks, all of which result in a permanent record on the environment.

Teacher C. This seventh-grade teacher increased the frequency of work turned in on time with a token system backed up by an RE menu (Addison & Homme, 1966), which included availability of comic books for fifteen minutes every Friday. She failed to change the RE menu frequently, and lost control when the students read all of the available comic books.

Repercussions in Schools

When the abstract for this paper was written, two events had occurred that were quite alarming. One elementary principal had told a teacher that "behavior modifications" sounded too Orwellian, and he did not intend to have any "brainwashing" going on in his school. The second incident was a school psychologist's recommendation to a principal that "psychology was in too much of a state of flux" to begin implementing such systems. Apparently some administrators should be desensitized to the term "behavior modification" before teachers announce what they are doing.

This past semester teachers were encouraged just to begin their work and if questioned about it by fellow teachers or administrators to show them the data. Challenges such as these are best met by objective data and observation of the system in operation.

Many pupils who have been exposed to token-reinforcement systems have requested other teachers to implement such systems in their classrooms, and some parents have volunteered feedback to the teacher that their child seemed quite enthusiastic about the new procedure in school.

CONCLUSIONS

The teachers who have implemented token-reinforcement systems have all indicated initial enthusiasm for the projects. Even the teachers whose systems were reported as failures are either currently planning or conducting other token arrangements. In every project the system is being adapted to situations encountered on the initial trial.

The behavior-modification projects have proven to be a very useful teaching technique. Students report their motivation to increase as a result of the project, and part of the class discussion centers around the data class members are collecting. At the end of the course, students consistently report they consider the behavior-modification project the most useful part of the class.

REFERENCES

Addison, R. M., and Homme, L. E. 1966. The reinforcing event (RE) menu. *National Society for Programed Instruction Journal* 4: 8–9.

Atthowe, J. and Krasner, L. 1965. The systematic application of contingent reinforcement procedures (token economy) in a large social setting: A psychiatric ward.
Paper read at American Psychological Association, Chicago, 1965.

Ayllon, T., and Azrin, N. H. 1965. Measurement and reinforcement of behavior of
psychotics. *J. exp. anal. Behav.* 8: 357–83.

Baer, D. M. In press. Recent examples of behavior modification in preschool settings.
In Neuringer, C., and Michael, J. L. *Behavior Modification in Clinical Psychology,*
ed. C. Neuringer and J. L. Michael. New York: Appleton-Century-Crofts.

Birnbrauer, J. S., Wolf, M. M., Kidder, J. D., and Tague, C. E. 1965. Classroom
behavior of retarded pupils with token reinforcement. *J. exp. Child Psych.* 2:
219–35.

Clark, Marilyn, Lackowicz, J., and Wolf, M. M. 1967. A pilot basic education program
for school dropouts incorporating a token reinforcement system. Unpublished
manuscript, Bureau of Child Research, University of Kansas.

Cohen, H. L. 1967. Motivationally oriented designs for an ecology of learning. A paper
presented at the American Educational Research Association, New York, 1967.

Gericke, L. L. 1965. Practical use of operant conditioning procedures in a mental
hospital. *Psychiatric Studies and Projects* 3: June.

Girardeau, F. L., and Spradlin, J. E. 1964. Token rewards in a cottage program. *Ment.
Retard.* 2: 345–51.

Homme, L. E., and Tosti, D. T. 1965. Contingency management and motivation.
National Society for Programed Instruction Journal 4: 14–16.

Homme, L. E. 1966. Human motivation and environment. In *The learning environment: Relationship to behavior modification and implications for special education,*
ed. N. G. Haring and R. J. Whelan. Lawrence, Kansas: Kansas Students in Education, pp. 30–39.

O'Leary, K. P., and Becker, W. C. 1966. Behavior modification of an adjustment class:
A token reinforcement program. Unpublished manuscript, Urbana, University of
Illinois.

Skinner, B. F. 1961. Why we need teaching machines. *Harvard Educational Review* 31:
377–98.

Skinner. B. F. 1965. Why teachers fail. *Saturday Review,* October 16, pp. 80 ff.

1. When given the title of a study in this article, be able to identify:
    a) the current behavior problem(s) and approximate rates;
    b) the target behavior(s);
    c) the behavior-change contingency (both LPB and HPB);
    d) the degree and approximate rate of change from current to
        target behavior(s).

2. What would you suggest to a teacher who complained:

a) I haven't got time to record rate measures.
b) My kids are too old for M&M's.
c) I tried it on six behaviors; it didn't work with a single problem.
d) My principal says I'm substituting a bag of tricks for sound teaching.

unit 12

More Examples of
Applied Behavior
Analysis

OBJECTIVES

The objectives for this unit were listed at the beginning of unit II. Refer to
p. 123, if you need to.

INTRINSIC REINFORCERS IN A
CLASSROOM TOKEN ECONOMY[1]

Thomas F. McLaughlin and John Malaby

Spokane School District 81
and Eastern Washington State College

Many studies have used token reinforcement programs for the management
of classroom behavior (Birnbrauer, Wolf, Kidder, and Tague, 1965; McKensie, Clark, Wolf, Kothera, and Benson, 1968; O'Leary, Becker, Evans, and

Thomas F. McLaughlin and John Malaby, "Intrinsic Reinforcers in a Classroom Token Economy," *Journal of Applied Behavior Analysis* 5 (1972): 263–70. Copyright 1972 by the Society for
the Experimental Analysis of Behavior, Inc. Reprinted with permission.
[1] The authors wish to thank Miss Maxine Davidson, Principal, Columbia Elementary School
for her support of the present study. Reprints may be obtained from Thomas F. McLaughlin,
Columbia Elementary School, East 3817 Sanson, Spokane, Washington, 99207.

Saudargas, 1969). In these studies, token reinforcers were dependent upon back-up reinforcers such as candy, toys, and comic books which are not intrinsic to the natural classroom. The cost for such token programs can be an important factor when considering whether or not to employ such a program. Wolf, Giles, and Hall (1968) estimated an average cost of $250 per subject. Other studies, more appropriately tutorial programs than classroom settings, have reported much lower costs (Staats and Butterfield, 1965; Staats, Minke, Goodwin, and Landeen, 1968).

Most of the past studies that employed token programs took place in non-typical educational settings such as: (a) an adjustment room (O'Leary and Becker, 1967); (b) a remedial classroom (Wolf, *et al.,* 1968), or (c) a special education class (Zimmerman and Zimmerman, 1962). Also, in most cases the number of subjects receiving reinforcement contingencies was small when compared with the typical classload in a public school.

Recently, cost-free group contingencies natural to the classroom have been studied. Osborne (1969) used a free-time contingency to eliminate out-of-seat responses in a classroom of six. Barrish, Saunders, and Wolf (1969) employed a game technique that reduced out-of-seat and talking-out behavior in a class of 24.

The present paper investigated the effects of various contingencies on assignment completion for an entire class. The methods used were: (a) dependent on cost-free back-up reinforcers in the form of privileges, (b) employed in a public school setting, (c) applied to the total class, (d) managed by a single teacher.

METHOD

Subjects and Setting

Members of a combination fifth and sixth grade classroom located in a low socioeconomic area of Spokane, Washington were used. The class size ranged from 25 to 29. The senior author was the teacher of the class for the duration of the study.

Target Behavior

Assignment completion in spelling, language, handwriting, and math was selected for study. Assignment completion was defined as the completion of all the exercises or tasks requested by the teacher in each of the four areas listed above.

Token Economy

The mechanics of a token economy were explained to the class. Token reinforcers were points. The subjects earned points for desirable behaviors and lost points for undesirable behaviors. The teacher often used praise when awarding points. Point removal was done in a calm, matter-of-fact manner. Activities that were naturally available in the school served as back-up reinforcers.

Table 1

Behaviors and the number of points that they earned or lost.

Behaviors That Earned Points	Points
1) Items correct	6 to 12
2) Study behavior 8:50–9:15	5 per day
3) Bring food for animals	1 to 10
4) Bring sawdust for animals	1 to 10
5) Art	1 to 4
6) Listening points	1 to 2 per lesson
7) Extra credit	Assigned value
8) Neatness	1 to 2
9) Taking home assignments	5
10) Taking notes	1 to 3
11) Quiet in lunch line	2
12) Quiet in cafeteria	2
13) Appropriate noon hour behavior	3

Behaviors That Lost Points	Points
1) Assignments incomplete	Amount squared
2) Gum and candy	100
3) Inappropriate verbal behavior	15
4) Inappropriate motor behavior	15
5) Fighting	100
6) Cheating	100

Points awarded. Table 1 shows the number of points that could be earned for various activities. In some instances, the number of points earned could vary. For example, Table 1 shows that a student could earn from 6 to 12 points for working the items in an assignment correctly. This was due to the fact that the assignments at the end of the study units in the textbooks varied in length, and that a subject might answer some items incorrectly. If a 10-item assignment were answered with all 10 items completed and with nine correct answers, then the subject was given nine points. If the same assignment were done with only nine of the questions answered, then it was considered incomplete. An incomplete assignment was never given points, no matter how much of the partially completed assignment was correct.

In the case of study behavior for the 25-min period between 8:50 and 9:15 A.M., the student earned one point per 5-min period of study. Similarly, the amount of food and sawdust brought for the rats that were kept in the classroom determined the number of points awarded to a subject. Other variable awards shown in Table 1 were on the basis of quality of performance.

Penalties. In general, the penalty for an undesirable behavior was severe, as may be seen in Table 1. This was done in an attempt to prevent a payoff following a week in which the student engaged in such behavior. The values of the penalties were determined a year earlier in a similar token economy and simply represent values which, along with point values for desirable behavior, seemed to control the students' behavior in that earlier token economy.

Privileges. The points a subject earned were exchanged weekly (or, see Token II) for the privileges shown in Table 2. Activities that were naturally available in the school served as back-up reinforcers. The privileges were determined by the subjects themselves. One class period at the beginning of school was devoted to asking which activities the subjects considered to be privileged. The subjects then ranked the privileges in terms of their desirability. That ranking determined the relative number of points assigned to the privileges.

The most desirable privilege cost the most; the least desirable privilege cost very few points. In any event, by including the categories of Special jobs and Special projects, which could be chosen by a subject in any given week, and by allowing the subject to choose whatever privileges he wished, the experimenters felt some confidence in the reinforcing properties of the privileges before the token system was introduced.

Mechanics of the token economy. Since the variable of major interest in this study was the number of assignments completed, availability of points was primarily associated with that behavior and with behaviors compatible with

Table 2

Weekly Privileges

| | Privilege | Price in Points | |
		Sixth	Fifth[a]
1)	Sharpening pencils	20	13
2)	Seeing animals	30	25
3)	Taking out balls	5	3
4)	Sports	60	40
5)	Special writing on board	20	16
6)	Being on a committee	30	25
7)	Special jobs	25	15
8)	Playing games	5	3
9)	Listening to records	5	2
10)	Coming in early	10	6
11)	Seeing the gradebook	5	2
12)	Special projects	25	20

[a] Privilege costs were determined separately for the two grades. Also, fifth-grade children were in the room less time per day than were the sixth-grade children.

it. Assignments were usually made daily for math, spelling, and language; there were three assignments per week for handwriting. However, these numbers could vary. Assignments that were due the following day, and assignments to be corrected during a given day were listed on the chalkboard. The student was expected to complete each assignment by class time. At the beginning of each class, papers were corrected. Each student graded his own paper. Corrections were made in pencil if the assignment were in ink or, at least, in some medium other than that used to complete the assignment. At the end of the correction period, the teacher called subjects one at a time to his desk and awarded points for the number of items correct in the assignment, providing it was complete, and gave bonus points for neatness.

The student recorded these points on a special record form on which he kept his point totals. An example of this form is shown in Figure 1. If the assignment were incomplete, he was told to subtract the appropriate number of points. The student could, however, make up the assignment to remove the penalty, but the make-up would not earn points for correct answers. Approximately 50% of the incomplete assignments were made up over the period of the year.

The teacher also recorded the points earned and lost in his grade book in order to cross-check the honesty of the students. Only one student in the course of the year failed to subtract points for an incomplete assignment.

Points were exchanged for privileges each Monday morning. A student was made banker for each of the privileges. Each banker subtracted the necessary number of points from a student's point total and initialed it. At the end of the period, he turned in a list to the teacher of the names of students who purchased privileges. This list enabled the teacher to control the use of privileges.

By having students keep all of their own records and make all of the transactions, and by including relatively simple checks on the system, the token economy was very easy to manage. No more than 20 to 25 min per week were devoted to the system by the teacher.

Experimental Conditions

The experimental design involved a baseline, three token conditions variously arranged, and a quiet-behavior contingency. The data for each academic assignment were collected and recorded in the gradebook.

Baseline. Normal rates of assignment completion were recorded daily. The baseline condition was in effect for the first six weeks of school. During the baseline condition, traditional control techniques were used: (a) staying after school to finish work; (b) parent and student conferences; (c) lectures to the class and individual students on the merits of completing assignments. During this condition, standard letter grades were used to grade assignments.

Points Earned   Points Lost

Language							Assignments
Spelling							
Handwriting							Talking
Science							
Social Studies							
Reading							Break
Math							
Notes							Gum
Taking Home Work							
Sawdust for Rats							
Food for Rats							Library
Quiet Behavior							
Spelling Test							Out-of-Seat
Study							
Other							
						Total	Total Lost

Name _____

Row _____

FIGURE 1.
Point chart used by students to record points earned and lost.

Token I. During this condition the token economy was introduced. Completed assignments and other desirable behaviors as shown in Table 1 were awarded points. Undesirable behaviors were penalized. This condition lasted 75 days.

Token II. This was similar to Token I except that point-exchange days were variable rather than fixed. The time between exchange varied from two to six school days with a mean of 4.25 days. The exchange schedule was as follows: 4, 3, 5, 4, 3, 6, 5, 4, 3, 6, 5, 2. Point values for privileges were increased proportionately if the time between exchanges was greater than five days, and decreased if the exchange occurred in less than five days. Token II was employed twice, once after Token I, and once after the Quiet-Behavior period for an additional 11 days.

Quiet Behavior. The teacher informed the class that assignment completion in language, spelling, math, and handwriting would no longer receive points, but letter grades. The students could still earn or lose points for the other behaviors in Table 1. In addition, a new category of quiet behavior was added to the economy and students could earn approximately the same number of points from this contingency that they had from assignments during Token II. Point-exchange days were again variable with the mean of four days between point exchange, as in Token II. The Quiet-Behavior contingency was in effect for 17 days.

RESULTS

Figure 2 shows the per cent of assignment completion for the total class in the four academic areas under the various experimental conditions. During the first 28 days before token procedures were introduced, the class completed from 69 to 94% of the assignments given. Pre-token records show variability in each area. When Token I was introduced, a noticeable change in variability of performance occurred in spelling, language, and handwriting. Performance in math tended to remain variable, but the mean per cent completed assignments was higher during Token I than it was in the Baseline period.

With the introduction of the variable point-exchange contingency of Token II, assignment completion increased. A majority of 100% data points were

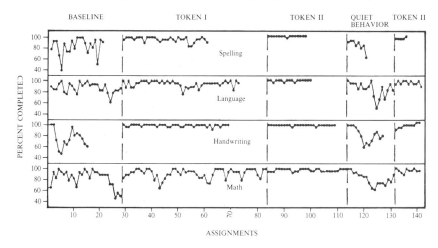

FIGURE 2.

Percent of assignments completed in spelling, language, handwriting, and math under each experimental condition for fifth and sixth grades combined.

found in all four academic areas. Consequently, as Figure 2 shows, the variability evidenced in the first two conditions was virtually eliminated.

The Quiet-Behavior condition resulted in reduced rates of assignment completion. Completion rates ranged from 69 to 99%. The rates tended to show recovery as the condition remained in effect, but assignment completion was variable throughout the condition.

The reapplication of Token II again generated high completion rates for the four academic areas. The data shown in the second Token II are for the last three weeks of the academic year.

Figure 3 shows a comparison between the student with the best and the student with the worst assignment completion records for the year. A mid-way student was not shown due to the relatively low incidence of non-completion of work. Figure 3 shows rather clearly that the effects of such an economy are greatest for so-called poor students. The effects of changing the contingencies for points was dramatic for the poor student for each of the four academic areas.

Inasmuch as assignment completion played such an important role in earning points, a reliability check was made. Three other teachers in the school were given 100 papers and asked to judge the completeness of the assignment according to the criteria used, *i.e.,* whether or not, say, a 10-item assignment had 10 answers. There was 100% agreement among the judges.

DISCUSSION

Token procedures significantly increased assignment completion. The experimental design illustrated that high rates of academic completion could be generated and maintained and that when points and fines were no longer contingent, completion responding decreased. The reapplication of token contingencies increased completion again.

The only analysis of the token system itself involved the manipulation of point-exchange days. The control exerted over assignment completion by the variable-point exchange contingency is perhaps analogous to the control exerted by variable schedules of reinforcement over simple operants with infrahumans in a free-operant paradigm. Figure 2 showed that responding under the variable contingency became stable. It has been widely reported in the literature that variable schedules produce more stable rates of responding than fixed schedules (Ferster and Skinner, 1957). The present design is perhaps lacking in that Token II was not followed by Token I, but the virtual elimination of variability under Token II suggests that one may entertain the possibility of true schedule effects.

One point of interest is the amount of behavior represented in the study. The study was not of short duration nor restricted to isolated behaviors. Instead, the data shown in Figure 2 represent the entire output for an academic year in the four classes reported. Figure 2 represents approximately 12,500 individual assignments. Completion of assignments at a rate of approximately 100%

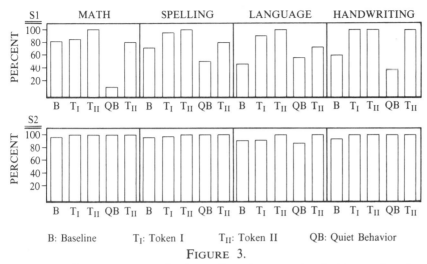

B: Baseline   T$_I$: Token I   T$_{II}$: Token II   QB: Quiet Behavior

FIGURE 3.

Per cent of assignments completed in spelling, language, handwriting, and math under each experimental condition for the student with the lowest completion record in the classroom (S1) and the student with the highest completion record in the classroom (S2).

over 30 assignment days as in Token II, is rather more significant than would be short-term control of a restricted class of behavior.

There are, of course, individual differences with respect to the amount of control exerted by the token economy. Figure 3 shows these differences dramatically. The student with the worst record of assignment completion for the year was influenced much more by the economy than was the best student. When the contingencies were changed, so that points were readily available in the absence of academic performance, the academic performance declined in the poor student. Further, the performance did not return to the previous levels that he had shown under token conditions. There is no way to assess the effects that the token system may have had on the good student as the effects were measured here. His academic completion rate was very high from the beginning. Other types of measures might show an effect on his behavior.

Reactions to the token program were obtained from the class. The program was favored by the students. Twenty students rated the economy favorably; only five rated it unfavorably. Those who liked the token economy made statements such as: "I completed my work on time easier", "I liked to earn the privileges", and "It made school fun". Negative comments included: "I don't like losing points for not doing my work", "The fines were too high", and "Privileges cost too much".

The methods used in this study have definite practical implications for several reasons: (a) the back-up reinforcers were in the natural classroom environment and were cost-free, (b) the study took place in a typical classroom setting, (c) the number of students that received group contingencies was comparable in size with most classloads in a public school, (d) significant gains in academic completion were obtained without specially made assignments for individuals or programmed instruction, (e) the token economy was manageable by one teacher, requiring, on the average, some 20 min per week more than usual to record points, fines, privileges, *etc.* Further, the use of the Quiet-Behavior procedure eliminated the necessity for a reversal procedure, which is sometimes unpleasant to the teacher. (Packard, 1970)

Token reinforcement programs have been used widely in a variety of special settings, but an analysis of their effects on assignment completion behavior for an entire class is not common. These methods using reinforcers natural to most classrooms can be implemented by teachers without expense or drastic instructional changes.

REFERENCES

Barrish, H. H., Saunders, M., and Wolf, M. M. Good behavior game: effects of individual contingencies for group consequences on disruptive behavior in a classroom. *Journal of Applied Behavior Analysis,* 1969, **2,** 119–124.

Birnbrauer, J. S., Wolf, M. M., Kidder, J. D., and Tague, C. Classroom behavior of retarded pupils with token reforcement. *Journal of Experimental Child Psychology,* 1969, **2,** 219–235.

Ferster, C. B. and Skinner, B. F. *Schedules of reinforcement.* New York: Appleton-Century-Crofts, 1957.

McKensie, H., Clark, M., Wolf, M., Kothera, R., and Benso, C. Behavior modification of children with learning disabilities using grades as token reinforcers and allowances as back-up reinforcers. *Exceptional Children,* 1968, **34,** 745–752.

O'Leary, K. D. and Becker, W. C. Behavior modification of an adjustment class: A token reinforcement program. *Exceptional Children,* 1967, **33,** 637–642.

O'Leary, K. D., Becker, W. C., Evans, M. B., and Saudargas, R. A. A token reinforcement program in a public school: a replication and systematic analysis. *Journal of Applied Behavior Analysis,* 1969, **2,** 3–13.

Osborne, J. G. Free-time as a reinforcer in the management of classroom behavior. *Journal of Applied Behavior Analysis,* 1969, **2,** 113–118.

Packard, R. G. The control of "classroom attention": a group contingency for complex behavior. *Journal of Applied Behavior Analysis,* 1970, **3,** 13–28.

Staats, A. W. and Butterfield, W. H. Treatment of non-reading in a culturally deprived juvenile delinquent: an application of reinforcement principles. *Child Development,* 1965, **36,** 925–942.

Staats, W. W., Minke, K. A., Goodwin, W., and Landern, J. Cognitive behavior modification 'motivated learning' reading treatment with subprofessional therapy technicians. *Behavior Research and Therapy,* 1965, **5,** 283–299.

Wolf, M. M., Giles, D., and Hall, R. V. Experiments with token reinforcement in a remedial classroom. *Behavior Research and Therapy,* 1968. **6,** 51–64.

Zimmerman, E. H. and Zimmerman, J. The alteration of behavior in a special classroom situation *Journal of the Experimental Analysis of Behavior,* 1962, **5,** 59–60.

1. Identify: target behavior(s); contingencies; duration of the study.

2. How were the backup reinforcers identified? Where were they obtained?

3. How many points were awarded for a correct but incomplete assignment? Describe a situation in which this kind of contingency would be ineffective.

4. How much of the teacher's time was required to manage the token economy? Cite several time-saving methods used by the teacher.

5. Describe the conditions in each of the four experimental phases and the effect of each on the target behavior.

6. What schedule effect is indicated in Figure 2? What differential effect is indicated in Figure 3?

7. How do the four experimental phases, taken together, support the rule: "what you reinforce is what you get"?

THE EFFECTS OF CONTINGENCY MANAGEMENT PROCEDURES
ON
ACHIEVEMENT SCORES IN A HIGH SCHOOL BIOLOGY CLASS

*Susan B. Kovacs and Robert G. Packard**

The literature on the subject provides abundant evidence and examples of how the principles and procedures of contingency management or behavior modification can be used to achieve impressive improvement in the academic performance of students in elementary, special, and even college classes. Some teachers and students, however, have questioned the applicability of contin-

*Both authors are with the School of Education, University of Missouri, St. Louis.

gency management to high school instruction, particularly because of the higher level objectives and because of the lack of feasible reinforcing events for adolescents.

The purpose of this study was to investigate the effects of a simple contingency management system on the achievement test scores of high school biology students. The procedure involved changing from a traditional lecture-discussion system to an instructional system that (a) provided a degree of self-pacing, (b) provided daily formative evaluation of individual student progress, and (c) used an immediate reinforcement system based on the Premack Principle, with the reinforcing events chosen by the students.

PROCEDURE

The subjects were fifteen biology students who had chosen the class as an elective. There were nine boys and six girls in the class; nine were sophomores, four juniors, and two seniors. The school is in a small-town/rural area, and its students are generally from economically deprived families.

During the baseline phase, which lasted one quarter, the sixty minute classroom procedure was a fairly traditional lecture system, with the teacher explaining the material in the text and asking questions over daily homework assignments. At the end of each chapter of the text (i.e., about once a week), the students took a standardized test over the material of the chapter. These tests were developed and standardized by the author of the textbook used in this class and were of the multiple-choice and completion type. After every three or four chapters, the students took a "Test of Interpretation" (also standardized and accompanying the text), composed of essay type questions requiring integration and application of the material in all the preceding chapters.

The experimental phase was introduced at the start of the second quarter. The teacher simply told the students that they were going to try a new approach since it was the start of a new quarter. He then explained the new procedure and led the students in compiling the Reinforcing Events (RE) menu.

The procedure for the experimental phase was as follows. As in the previous quarter, the teacher gave daily reading assignments of several pages of text from the chapter the class was working on at the time. But during this phase, each class period began with a 10–15 minute session during which the students could discuss and ask the teacher questions about the material assigned for homework reading. Then each student received a quiz of three or four completion or short answer questions covering the assigned reading material. As each student finished this written quiz, the teacher evaluated his answers. If every response was correct, the student selected an item from the RE menu and engaged in that activity for the rest of the class period. If one or more of the student's responses was incorrect, the student joined a remedial group and received teacher assistance and time for re-study. Later in the class period, a second form of the quiz (either oral or written) was available to the remediating students, and the student's responses on this quiz were consequated in the same manner as on the first quiz.

The RE menu (see table 12-1) was a list of activities suggested by the students as events they would like to earn. All student suggestions were accepted except for smoking, which was contrary to school policy. The menu was attractively displayed on red posterboard in plain view during all class sessions of this experimental phase.

A student's grade for each quarter of the class was based exclusively on his scores on the chapter tests. During the experimental phase, the fourteen daily quizzes had no direct effect on the student's grade.

Data were collected on each student's twelve test scores, on the frequency of reinforcement per student, and on the frequency of reinforcing events selected. These data were used to assess (a) the effect of the change in instructional procedure on achievement scores, (b) the relationship between any achievement-score change and the sex or grade level of the student, and (c) any reinforcer preferences by age or sex.

RESULTS

The test data were programmed and computer processed for analysis of variance and individual-student scattergrams. Thirteen of the fifteen students demonstrated significant improvement on their test scores after the contingency management procedure was introduced. The other two students showed minimal or inconsistent change, and their overall improvement was not significant.

Two students improved at a rate that was significant at the .01 level. An example of their scattergrams is shown in Figure 1.

Eleven students showed improvement in their achievement-test scores at a rate that was significant between the .01 and .05 level. An example of their scattergrams is presented in Figure 2.

Figure 3 is representative of the two students whose improvement was not significant. Notice that the two higher scores during the experimental phase are offset by another extremely low score.

One student, a sophomore boy, never reached criterion on any of the fourteen daily quizzes. Most students, however, scored 100 percent on their first attempt on eight or more of the quizzes. The two seniors reached criterion on every daily quiz. They ranked first and second in the class (as measured by their cumulative chapter-test scores) during the baseline quarter, and they maintained that ranking during the experimental phase. Taking the class as a

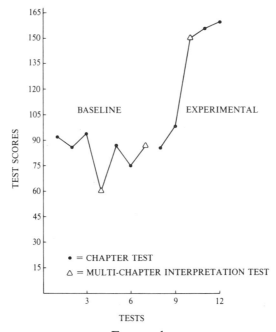

FIGURE 1.
Scattergram of successive test scores for Student No. 4.

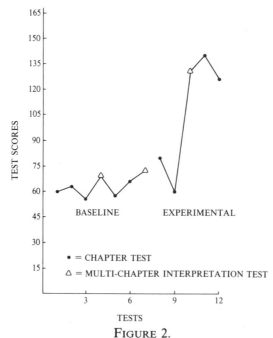

FIGURE 2.
Scattergram of successive test scores for Student No. 1.

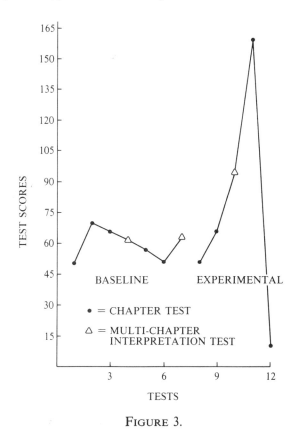

FIGURE 3.

Scattergram of successive test scores for Student No. 11.

whole, the number of times a student reached criterion and was able to choose an RE did not correlate with the amount of his improvement in test scores.

There was no significant difference between males and females in the effectiveness of the instructional change. Agewise, however, there was a difference: the sophomores and juniors as a whole showed significantly more improvement than did the seniors. This may reflect an asymptotic or ceiling effect, due to the seniors' prior learning history. The seniors were already performing at or near the top of the class and had had other biology or related courses. Because of this, the seniors may have had less possibility for improvement than the other students. It could also be that because of their additional years of school experience, the two seniors were motivated more by the course content than by the RE menu. Finally, as is true with all students and especially adolescents, contingencies and reinforcing events outside the classroom may have been exerting an overriding effect on any classroom events or requirements.

Table 12-1 displays the RE menu with the frequency of choices for each event by students who reached quiz criterion on the first attempt. Overall, talking and lab project work were the most preferred consequences. The girls chose talking three times as often as the boys. The boys selected lab projects most frequently. The seniors' most preferred activity was talking; the juniors preferred lab projects and other homework; the sophomores chose reading and homework more often than the other events.

Table 12-1

Available Reinforcing Events and the Number of Times Each Was Chosen

RE	Frequency of Choice
1. Sleep	0
2. Read	4
3. Chess	8
4. Cards	16
5. Homework (any subject)	14
6. Lab Project Work	29
7. Work on Aquariums	2
8. Sew	1
9. Other Games	1
10. Help Other Students	0
11. Eat	0
12. Help Correct Tests	1
13. Join Group for Review	0
14. Talk	30

Though games and talking and other nonacademic activities were popular, the fact that lab work, homework, and other academically related events were also preferred choices underscores the frequently made suggestion that a teacher can achieve significant improvement simply by rearranging the relationships between the various class-related activities. For many students, there is no need to provide academically unrelated reinforcing events. Every high school subject area can include a variety of activities, including study of basic facts, paper-and-pencil work, research projects, group discussion, demonstration projects, application projects, and small-group work. The teacher can frequently take advantage of a student's preferences for certain of these activities over others, without violating prerequisites, and increase the performance rate, mastery level, and enjoyment factor for each student. What is required is that a student's preferences be analyzed and, on the basis of that preference scale, opportunity to engage in certain of these activities be made contingent on quality performance of other less preferred but necessary activities.

This study was marred by several factors. Five snow holidays and twelve scheduled holidays caused interruptions that affected the smoothness of the procedural change and may have had differential retention effects on the test scores. Furthermore the teacher, while agreeing to cooperate in the study, frequently voiced a personal bias against the experimental system. He liked to lecture, and during the experimental sessions he would frequently use part of the discussion-question period to lecture. Occasionally he also allowed a student who had made one error on his quiz to skip the remediation. Since consistency is critical to contingency management, more effective teacher training might have improved the results of this study. The reinforcing effects of seeing marked improvement in many students may be too weak and too delayed for a teacher who is strongly reinforced by his own lecturing.

From these data, it appears that the strongest effect of this contingency management procedure occurred for students who were not seniors and who were functioning at considerably less than their capacity. But the fact that thirteen out of fifteen (i.e., 87 percent) students in this study showed significant improvement in their mastery of the material despite the simplicity of the procedural change, the bias and inconsistency of the teacher, and the unpredictability of the school schedule indicates that careful management of the classroom contingencies may be an important if not essential requirement in high school teaching. Perhaps, as Skinner has suggested, education would be better off placing greater emphasis on the redesign of instructional procedures and less on the redesign of buildings and curricula.

1. Describe the experimental procedure, identifying the contingencies, the two kinds of consequent events, and the general classroom procedure. Contrast these with the corresponding aspects of the baseline procedure.

2. Summarize the effect of the contingency management procedure on achievement scores.

3. What is an RE menu? Describe how the menu in this study was constructed. Identify several events that were reinforcing for the high school students in this study.

4. What difference might it have made if this teacher occasionally let a student choose an RE even though one of his answers was incorrect?

5. Do you think the contingency management procedure was making any difference on the achievement of student # 11? Why? What is needed to be sure?

6. If you were the teacher, what changes would you have considered making when you noticed the one sophmore boy was never reaching criterion on his quizzes?

7. If you were to use a general contingency management system for a high school class you were teaching, how would your procedure differ from the one in this study? Be specific about the subject matter area, the class events and their relationships, and the general classroom routine.

unit 13

Behavior Change
Project

OBJECTIVES

To give you experience and training in the design, implementation, and evaluation of a supervised procedure for modifying a behavior in terms of:

* precisely defining an observable behavior
* systematically recording behavior rates
* identifying the preceding and consequent events which affect the behavior
* specifying the contingencies for modifying the behavior
* implementing the contingencies for modifying the behavior
* gathering data and analyzing the resulting data
* evaluating the effectiveness of the contingencies in the modification of the behavior.

In this unit, you will have the opportunity to put into effect the different procedures, principles, and techniques described in previous units. To best demonstrate the various principles and procedures, you will choose a behavior of some other person and attempt to modify it.

Your project will be evaluated in terms of meeting the objectives of the unit, not in terms of the degree of change in the behavior. Although it is hoped that your design will result in the modification of the behavior problem, it is not always the case that your first attempt at behavior modification will be successful. You are encouraged to seek the advice of the course instructor(s) and to consult the textbook for help in developing your plan. You will also be required to have each component of your project approved by the instructor of the course prior to starting the component.

Choosing a Behavior

To start this unit, you must choose a behavior to modify. A word of caution is necessary here. The behavior you attempt to modify should be some behavior which is worth changing. For example, it should result in the person improving his interpersonal relationships or his study habits, increasing his self-confidence, decreasing a bad habit such as overeating, swearing, smoking cigarettes, or chewing his nails, or becoming easier to live with. The behavior you choose to modify should not be chosen out of curiosity or to see what bizarre behaviors you can shape up since these instances border on the immoral and may very well violate the person's right to be taught useful, functional, and helpful skills. Likewise, you should choose a behavior to modify that is worth the investment of your time and effort.

When you have decided on what behavior you would like to modify, you need to define the behavior in terms of its physical characteristics. What does the behavior look like? Observe the behavior and describe it in terms so that another person could look at your definition and know what the behavior you were modifying looked like. This is extremely important when you begin to record data on the rate of the behavior.

Preceding and Consequent Events

Once you have specified the behavior in observable and measurable terms, you need to identify the preceding and consequent events. Observe the behavior and record what immediately precedes and follows its occurrence. This will help in identifying the controlling variables for the behavior and help in specifying the contingencies for changing the behavior.

Recording the Behavior

Once you have chosen a behavior to modify, you need to determine how often it occurs. You may choose to record the behavior in terms of how many times it occurs *(frequency)*, or you may choose to record the length of time the behavior occurs *(duration)*, or you may choose to record the percentage accuracy or completion of the behavior, or a measure such as weight or distance traveled.

Regardless of the measure you choose to use in recording your behavior, you must be sure that your data are comparable from day to day (or whatever time unit you use); that is, you must be sure that the opportunities for the behavior to occur and be recorded by you are the same for each recording session. If you record the behavior for two hours on one day and for six hours on the next and get different frequency counts for each day, part of the difference may be due to the fact that opportunity was three times greater on the second day.

For instance, if you were recording the number of cigarettes smoked by your husband/wife/lover and were to record some days for two hours and some days for eight hours, the number of cigarettes smoked would be higher on the days you recorded for the longer periods of time simply because there were more opportunities. The same problem exists if you record at different times during the day.

There are several ways to control for opportunity in recording behavior. You can arbitrarily decide to record your data for a fixed period of time each day—the same amount of time and the same time period—both during baseline and experimental phases. If this is impractical (because you don't see the person behave this way at the same times daily) or if this will cause you to omit some data because of varying observation times (for example, you can observe only one hour a day during the week but you can observe eight hours a day on weekends), you can weight each day's records for opportunity per unit time. For each day's records, divide the number of responses that day by the number of time units during which you observed. For example, if you were recording cigarettes smoked per hour and on one day recorded four cigarettes in five hours, the rate would be .8 cigarettes per hour. If the next day you recorded one cigarette in an hour, the rate would be 1.0 cigarettes per hour.

Developing Your Plan

Once you have recorded the rate of the behavior and identified the preceding and consequent events which affect the behavior, you are ready to develop a procedure to modify the behavior. First, you must specify an observable target behavior. Second, you should specify the preceding events after which the target behavior should occur. Next, you should define the consequent events that will be presented when the target behavior occurs. You also should specify a criterion for the consequent events to be presented. This criterion at first should be fairly easy for the person whose behavior is being modified to obtain and then, as the behavior occurs more frequently, the criterion for the consequent events to be presented should be raised. You should also specify the reinforcers you will use in the modification of the behavior. Even if you are attempting to decrease an undesirable behavior, you should reinforce the person for engaging in the appropriate behavior. This procedure will result in the strengthening of the desirable behavior and make the reoccurrence of the undesirable behavior less likely in the future. The reinforcers you use should be chosen in terms of their effect on the person whose behavior is being modified—not on the basis of what you think will be effective. If you are using some kind of token or point system you should specify the frequency of the exchange schedule for the backup reinforcers. Although the points and stars may be effective consequences at first, if they are not paired with the backup reinforcers, they will lose their effectiveness. Finally, if the target behavior is complex or far away from the current behavior, you may have to break the target behavior down into a series of steps and shape toward the target behavior.

Implementing Your Plan

Once you have designed your plan and had it approved, you are ready to implement it. In the experimental phase, you continue to record data and notate the change between the baseline and experimental phase on the graph with a dashed vertical line (see figure 13–1). You also do not connect the data points between the baseline and the experimental phase. Also, you should notate any uncontrolled-for environmental changes should they occur. If you are recording the number of cigarettes smoked and the person gets a sore throat and doesn't smoke due to the sore throat, you should notate that in your data.

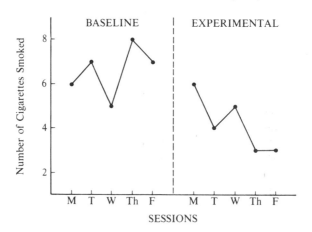

Figure 13–1

When implementing your plan to modify the behavior, you should pay strict attention to the rules for managing behavior found in unit 3. It is extremely important to start where the behavior is and work toward your target behavior. If you have to, break down the target behavior into a series of steps and shape toward the target behavior. It is most important to *be consistent!* Remember to always reinforce the desired behavior and ignore the inappropriate behavior or punish it depending on the procedure. Do not expect a behavior change on the first day or the first week. For the most part, the behaviors you are attempting to modify have been in the person's repertoire for a long time, and it may take longer than a week to effect a change in the behavior.

Writing Up the Results

After implementing your procedure and collecting sufficient data, you need to compile your data and make some judgments as to the results of your project. Data should be summarized in terms of an increase or decrease in the number of responses from X number of responses during baseline to Y number of responses during the experimental phases. *Do not* expect your readers to analyze your data. A composite graph showing baseline and experimental phases should also accompany the results. You should analyze the procedures you have used and explain why your results support or fail to support the defined procedural effect. You also should include information as to other alternative procedures which may result in the same way. If you get no conclusive results, describe some alternative procedures which may be more effective in producing the behavior change.

In addition, you should include an analysis of the overall project in terms of successful features and flaws that should be incorporated or avoided by someone who may do a similar project.

Component One:　　　　　　　　*Behavior Change Project*

A. Specify your name, section, address, and phone number.

B. Specify the name, address, and age of the person or persons whose behavior you will attempt to modify.

C. Define the behavior you want to modify in observable, measurable terms.

D. Why is this behavior worth modifying?

E. What are the preceding events prior to the occurrence of the behavior?

F. What are the consequent events after the occurrence of the behavior?

G. Specify the time and length of each recording session, what will be recorded, and who will record the data.

H. How will you label your horizontal axis? How will you label your vertical axis?

Approved _____

Date _____

Component Two: *Behavior Change Project*

A. Attach your approved Component One.

B. Attach a minimum of two weeks baseline data.

C. Define the target behavior for the behavior change.

D. What are the preceding events after which the target behavior should occur?

E. What are the planned consequent events when the target behavior occurs?

F. What are the contingencies between the behavior and the consequent events?

G. Specify the criteria for consequent events to be delivered. If necessary, specify the various shaping steps.

H. What reinforcers will be used?

I. When will the reinforcers be delivered? If necessary, specify the exchange schedule for the backup reinforcers and the prices for the backup reinforcers.

Component Three: *Behavior Change Project*

A. Attach Components One and Two.

B. Attach graphs of baseline and experimental phases.

C. What were the results of the study? Include an analysis of the recorded data for the baseline and experimental phases.

D. Does your data indicate that you reached your target behavior as defined in Component Two? Specify why or why not in reference to the procedure used.

E. What alternative procedures could you suggest to get the desired results?

F. Specify the weak and strong points in the procedures you used and describe possible modifications to avoid and incorporate these points.

G. What other conclusions can be drawn from this study?

unit 14

Self-Control

OBJECTIVES

When you complete this unit, you should be able to:

* analyze a behavior of your own in terms of measurable events and controlling contingencies;
* analyze the relative effect of consequent events for your own behavior in terms of the relative strength and immediacy of those consequences;
* specify and differentiate between the internal and external procedures for changing your own behavior and differentiate both from the exhortation method.

Most behavior is a function of its preceding and consequent events. A person is likely to do a certain thing in a certain situation because in the past that kind of behavior in that kind of situation frequently was followed by desirable consequences. He is likely not to do a certain thing in a certain situation because in the past that kind of behavior was frequently followed by neutral or undesirable consequent events. The probability of a certain behavior can be changed (increased or decreased) if the frequency or kind of consequent events is changed and also if the preceding events (situations) which signal the usual contingency between the behavior and its consequence are altered.

Frequently behavior change of this type occurs because *someone other than the behaver* changes the preceding or consequent events—or causes them to change. The other person or persons may do this deliberately or accidentally, or the cause of change in these surrounding conditions may be nonhuman agents or events. Whatever the source for the change in preceding or consequent events, that source is frequently not the person whose behavior changes as a result.

We usually think of such preceding and consequent events as being external to the person whose behavior is influenced by them. Not necessarily so. We know that many influential things happen "inside our skin" or "in the head." These events can and often do control what we do and say. The sight of a book can act as the preceding stimulus for your thinking of an exam tomorrow, and you are then reminded of the consequences you can expect if you do or do not study for it. Whether you actually do study or do something else instead, this external behavior is not only the result of your past experience with similar exams and grading contingencies, it is also the result of this internal thinking and imagining chain of events.

In fact most of our behaviors are controlled by *both* external and internal events and contingencies. Furthermore, just as many external events become reinforcers, punishers, or signals by conditioning, that is, by frequent close association with events that already function that way, so many internal events also become effective by a process of conditioning. Just as the sight of a friend can become reinforcing in itself because in the past that event has frequently led to pleasant times, so the internal thought of that same friend can become reinforcing in itself because thinking of him has frequently been followed by pleasant events (internal or external).

Self-control is a special case of behavior control in which the person whose behavior is changed or maintained and the person who changes the antecedent and/or consequent events is the same person. In self-control, the same person is both object and subject, but he influences his behavior precisely the same way he would the behavior of anyone else—by changing the variables of which that behavior is a function. Technically, the person does not change his own behaviors; what he does change or arrange are the events which in turn change his behavior.

1. Choose a behavior that you do regularly, describe it behaviorally, and list several probable reasons why you do it.

2. What do we mean by "self-control"? Why is it not true, technically, that we can change our own behavior?

Changing Your Behavior

If you want to change one of your behaviors without the direct aid of someone else, your probability of success will depend on how well you *rearrange the contingencies* between that behavior and its consequences and/or how well you control the opportunities for doing it. If you want to eliminate overeating, you must change the discriminative stimulus and contingent reinforcement conditions in such a way as to make the probability of saying No to yourself greater than the probability of eating at certain times, or else make food unavailable at certain times. Or if you want to be more cheerful in the morning, you have to arrange some discriminative stimuli which will get you to think cheerful thoughts, smile, and say cheerful things to others, and then arrange for reinforcing consequences to follow. Of course if you succeed in this effort to control your environment, you are more apt to try to do so again because your success will probably reinforce this general kind of self-control behavior.

A major practical problem lies in the *initial strength* of reinforcement for another behavior incompatible to the one you want. Even if you get your new set of stimuli and contingencies started, they are in immediate competition with contingencies that are well established by other strong reinforcers. Instead of studying at night, you usually watch TV or go out somewhere; though you want to diet, there are a variety of preceding stimuli inviting you to eat, and the immediate consequences are very rewarding. Resisting these temptations is a behavior that is likely to have fewer effective preceding stimuli and weaker and less immediate consequences than does the incompatible behavior.

If you choose to watch TV after supper instead of hitting the books, that's simply a way of saying that TV watching at that time is a higher probability event than studying. The next morning as you head for classes, your choice might be the opposite, except that the opportunity for either is no longer available. The trick is to be able to arrange conditions that *overcome a dominant probable response* at a specific time or in a specific situation.

There is experimental evidence to indicate that the *probability of a choice* between two behaviors at a given time depends on both the *strength* of the reinforcing consequence for either choice and also on the *delay* of that consequence.

The reinforcer for watching TV is more immediate than the reinforcer for studying, so that one will choose to watch TV unless the strength of the consequence for studying is much stronger than the enjoyment from watching TV. Similarly, the reinforcer for eating is more immediate than the reinforcer for not eating (losing weight, looking better). The same analysis presumes, of course, that the discriminative stimulus functions are held constant.

If a reinforcing effect is weak, it could be that either the reinforcer itself is weak or there is too much of a time delay between the behavior and the reinforcing event. To change the immediate probabilities of two opposing behaviors, a person must introduce conditioned reinforcers that are strong and *immediate*. There are several ways to do this.

One way is to *arrange external conditions* ahead of time to make sure the undesired response is very unlikely to occur or that the probability of one response will be much greater than the other. There are numerous examples of this in everyday life. We set the alarm clock out of arm's reach or sign up for automatic payroll savings deductions or put a time-lock on the refrigerator. A student who had three papers to write in three weeks gave thirty dollars to her friend with instructions to mail ten dollars each week to her most detested political candidate unless the friend received a completed paper before the weekly deadline. The first paper was a day late, but the student got all three papers done and twenty dollars back. Homer suggested this technique also, when Circe urged Odysseus to plug his boatsmen's ears and have himself tied to the mast in order to avoid turning his boat toward the bewitching songs of the Sirens and crashing on the rocks.

This technique has the drawback that you must either rely on someone else to enforce the contingency or, if you do it yourself, you are liable to cheat. It's easy to say, for example that if I finish this chapter I'll give myself a ten minute break and go get a drink, but until I do I won't let myself have a break; it's not as easy to stick with that contingency. How can that be made easier—that is, more probable?

A second general way is to *arrange internal events and contingencies* with enough strength and immediacy to control the probabilities of opposite behaviors. The potential power of this strategy comes from the fact that you will be able to carry around with you your own source of reinforcement or punishment. Instead of being dependent on certain persons or certain external conditions which are not always available when you need them, your internal events and contingencies can always be called up for service.

This general strategy makes use of the Premack principle which says that a low probability event can be reinforced (strengthened) if it is followed frequently by any high probability event. These are the steps in using the *internal* procedure[1]:

1. Decide what *specific behavior* you want to strengthen or weaken—call it your target behavior. Make it specific.
2. Make a list of many *aversive consequences* of not achieving your target behavior. Be sure the reasons or images are really aversive to you, not someone else.
3. Make a list of many *good consequences* for doing your target behavior, as many as you can think of, but only those that move you.

---

[1] Suggested in part in the excellent self-instructional text by Lloyd Homme and Don Tosti, *Behavior Technology,* Unit 4 (San Rafael, Calif.: Individual Learning Systems, 1971).

4. Select a *preceding stimulus* not associated with your target behavior and one to which you always respond in the same way. For example, reaching for the phone to make a call, lifting a cup of coffee or soda to take a drink, reaching for the faucet to wash your hands, reaching for your keys to open the car or house door. Each of these preceding events occurs regularly during the day but not constantly, each situation is easy to discriminate, and each is always followed by a specific response which is therefore a high probability response.

5. In the presence of the preceding stimulus situation, complete the *chain of responses:*
   a) imagine the list of aversive consequences, as vividly as you can;
   b) imagine the list of good consequences, as vividly as you can;
   c) engage in the high probability event, that is the event that the preceding stimulus always leads to (drink, or wash, or turn the key, etc.).

6. Later on, after the mental chain of good and aversive consequences has become strengthened as a probable event in your mind, you can begin to use the thought of doing or not doing the target behavior as *another* preceding stimulus for going through the chain. Then reinforce this by engaging immediately in either an activity that is highly probable at the moment or some other event that is reinforcing to you —taking a quick break or a sip or nibble (unless dieting is your objective) or simply complimenting yourself on your progress in "mastering your own fate."

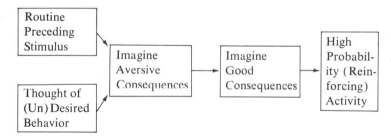

Figure 14-1

After a day or two of practice, the whole chain should only take you several seconds.

7. Keep a continuous *record* of the frequency per day of your target behavior. This is necessary because achieving your target behavior is the ultimate reinforcer, and without clear and regular feedback, your efforts to change through self-control will extinguish.

You usually can't rely simply on step 6 to successfully change your behavior. If you decide that whenever you think of doing (or start to do) the undesired behavior you will remind yourself of the aversive and good consequences, your decision will probably have no effect. Since it has never worked in the past, why should it now? One of the reasons we do things we later wish we hadn't is because we remind ourselves of the good and bad consequences only after the behavior is done. Thinking of doing it, or starting to do it, is usually not enough to remind ourselves of the consequences. The trick is to get us to talk to ourselves *before* we act, not after. But if you try to break this strongly conditioned chain with a new and unstrengthened self-instruction link, the new link will be crushed rather quickly by the old and well-established chain. Instead, the self-instructional thought chain must be hothoused and allowed to gain strength in a neutral situation before it is transplanted into the critical behavior process that you want to change.

By inserting the internal chain of thoughts and imaginings between a strong preceding stimulus and a high probability event, you are not only increasing the likelihood of the internal chain's occurrence *at that time* but you are also reinforcing its occurrence and thereby increasing the likelihood of its occurring again *in the future.* And this increase in the thoughts and imaginings makes the target behavior more probable because its reinforcers, though vicarious and conditioned, are immediate. For example, even though the ultimate reinforcer for not eating is loss of weight, fitting into a bikini, etc., the thought of achieving these things can also be a strong conditioned reinforcer and a very immediate one.

Exhortation

Notice the difference between these two methods of changing one's own behavior (by changing internal or external consequences) and the usual method of arranging for someone to exhort us to change. Throughout history men have relied on exhortations to "think positively!" "have confidence!" "don't eat so much!" "have faith!" "Repent!" This method seems to have worked occasionally, at least temporarily, but we can never rely on it. The reason is that moral persuasion and appeals to "willpower" do not specify ways of accomplishing the desired change. The two procedures for arranging preceding and consequent events and contingencies, however, are effective because they help us *analyze* our own behavior and its relationship to controlling events. They also give us *specific techniques* for achieving the results suggested by good advice.

Exhortation may be of some value, however, especially with the internal chain procedure since the persuasion may lead you to *decide* to change by getting you to think of very powerful *reasons* for deciding to change.[2] Unless

---

[2] Suggested by David Premack, "Mechanisms of Self Control," in *Learning Mechanisms and the Control of Smoking,* ed. W. Hunt (Chicago: Aldine-Atherton, Inc., 1970).

you decide rather firmly and emotionally that a behavior change is desirable, you won't follow through with either external or internal procedures. Unless the initial emotional intent to change is stronger than the reinforcers maintaining the present behavior, you won't begin the procedures which will allow you to change.

And it is not true that once you really decide, you've won. Most smokers, for example, have quit dozens of times. By itself a decision, even with its emotional charge, can't overcome the control that years of learning have established. The emotional charge is very *fragile* and if it does not lead to initial success, it will evaporate rather quickly. Each such failure makes the next failure more likely because through overuse (habituation) the emotional charge dissipates into clinical dispassion, like a joke that has lost its humor at the tenth telling.

Self-control is not magical or supernatural. Self-control is a form of behavior change based on the arrangement of preceding and consequent events. By disrupting and rearranging such events, especially internally so that we can mentally instruct ourselves about the consequences of our behavior, we ourselves can arrange the contingencies which control our own behavior.

Perhaps this is the most useful way to think of terms like conscience, ideals, attitudes, values, and willpower.

Self-Management of Studying

These self-control methods can be applied successfully to a wide variety of behaviors. Students have used them to stop smoking, lose weight, be more cheerful in the morning, be more prompt, be less obnoxious to a specific person, stop pulling one's hair. The choice is wide open, and the success depends on the decision and the methods.

Self-management of study behavior is an especially important area of self-control for students. If you could use some improvement in this area, the following illustrations might help to get you started. If your study habits are already working to your satisfaction, the following will serve as an illustrated application of the internal and external methods of self-control. In either case, remember that the specific detail of the procedures may not be as appropriate in your case as they were for the students who adopted them, but the general procedures are applicable to all.

One college student was just barely getting by in his courses, and was regarded as lazy by his professors, indifferent or slightly slow by some fellow students, and forgetful by his girl friend. He chose to do something about it and decided to use a combination of internal and external change methods.

For the *internal* chain, he had his girl friend make him some stiff-cloth bookmarks of bright colors, on each of which was written "A" and "F" and

"Weekend." He put one in each of the books he used for classes, including notebooks. Their color and the fact that they protruded from the books made them easily noticeable. Each time he noticed one (starting in the morning when he assembled his books for the trip to school), he would mentally go through the chain of thought about the good consequences of regular, persistent study and the bad consequences of sluffing off (marks, panic and long hours at exam time, time for weekend flings with his girl or with the boys, embarrassment at his reputation as a student, pride in being thought of as a good student). Each time he would stop what he was doing (such as heading for the car, starting to leave a class, putting his books down after school) and run through the chain before completing the action he had interrupted. Soon he no longer had to read the bookmarks, and the internal chain took only a few seconds.

Externally, he made arrangements with his girl friend whereby some reinforcers that she had under her control were to be made available to him contingent on weekly persistence and accomplishment in studying for his courses. He had divided his semester's work up into small units for each course and assigned a certain number of units for each week of the semester. At the end of each week, when and if the week's allotment of reading, paper writing, etc. was finished (as mutually agreed to), they could use the weekend time for activities together. Also, on weekdays when the day's allotment of units was finished early, a phone call or even a brief get together was allowed.

He did not always meet the contingencies, and the girl friend was unselfish enough to impose the consequences. But he met all the contingencies after the fourth week, and he ended up with a 3.6 GPA for the semester, which improved his overall GPA considerably. He still maintains that one professor dropped his grade to a B solely because of his past reputation; the professor says he was afraid to give him an A for fear it would be the only one on his transcript. That's no longer a problem.

To get the most out of your study time and effort, there are other kinds of procedures and devices you can use that usually help considerably. The environment in which you study can be very important. The student in the above example posted his daily and weekly schedule at his study desk, and he used the bookmarks as reminders. The same kind of prompting mechanism can operate if you choose for your study area an environment that is as free as possible of outside distractors and has as many study prompts as possible. One way to secure this is to arrange things so that the *only* thing you do in that specific place is study. In that way, the normal stimuli in that place will become associated only with study behavior and will be more likely to prompt you only to study.

Another important procedure is to schedule your time and work in some detail. Students who always get A's usually do this to some extent anyway, but even they can be helped by scheduling, in that they will be more apt to avoid occasional need for late hours spent finishing a paper or preparing for an exam.

To schedule your time, you must first get the detailed *requirements* for the semester for each course: how many papers or projects must you complete and exactly what does each require, etc. If the requirements are not clear or if you've heard that the professor doesn't really insist on some of them, the best procedure is usually to ask the professor directly for the details.

Then break this work up into *small units*—perhaps one to three hours each unless the professor has already done this for you—and schedule these units out over the semester. A paper, for example, is really a series of such units; you have to define the topic, do a literature search, an outline, a rough, and a final writeup. A mid-semester test over 250 pages of text comes out to about 36 pages per week (250/7) and about 6 pages per day (giving yourself 1 day a week off).

It also helps to *graph* your progress through these units. Set up a cumulative graph (like figure 14-2), one for each course, with the units of work on the vertical axis (from bottom to top) and the actual study days (or class days, if you wish) on the horizontal axis. Then you can plot your daily progress through the requirements of each course and be able at any time to know how you are doing relative to your goals for the course. If you fall behind, you will be reminded of this in plenty of time to recover. Graphing your progress also has a very helpful reinforcing effect for most students. And helping yourself in these ways will probably cost you no more than thirty minutes per semester.

You should also try, as much as possible, to schedule your daily use of time. If you want to use a couple of free periods during the day for study, choose an on-campus study area much as you do a home study area (e.g., in the library) and commit yourself to going there every day during those periods. The same applies to your use of after school hours.

Of course, none of these procedures will help unless you *arrange the preceding and consequent events* properly. Posted schedules and graphs, time of day, and even other people can be helpful in prompting you to begin and to continue studying. Reinforcing contingencies, arranged and enforced by yourself and or others, will increase the ease and satisfaction in your study efforts. If you don't have access to a buddy system for reinforcing your efforts, you yourself can arrange to put off the phone calls, the work on your car or bike, TV, other recreation, or even money for a special purchase, until you have finished the day's scheduled units. Of course, in this case you are on your own as far as consistently enforcing the contingencies.

In many cases (perhaps most, at the college level), these methods can make the difference between a poor student and a good student. To explain a poor student's grades in terms of laziness, indifference, or forgetfulness is a pseudo-explanation. The student simply has not learned to manage his own study behavior, and it's unlikely at the level of college that anyone will actually teach him how. At that stage it's probably a case of self-teaching as the only recourse, but with the technology of self-control, that no longer needs to be left to chance or exhortation or magic.

Figure 14-2

Class: _____   Project Due Dates:

Small Tasks

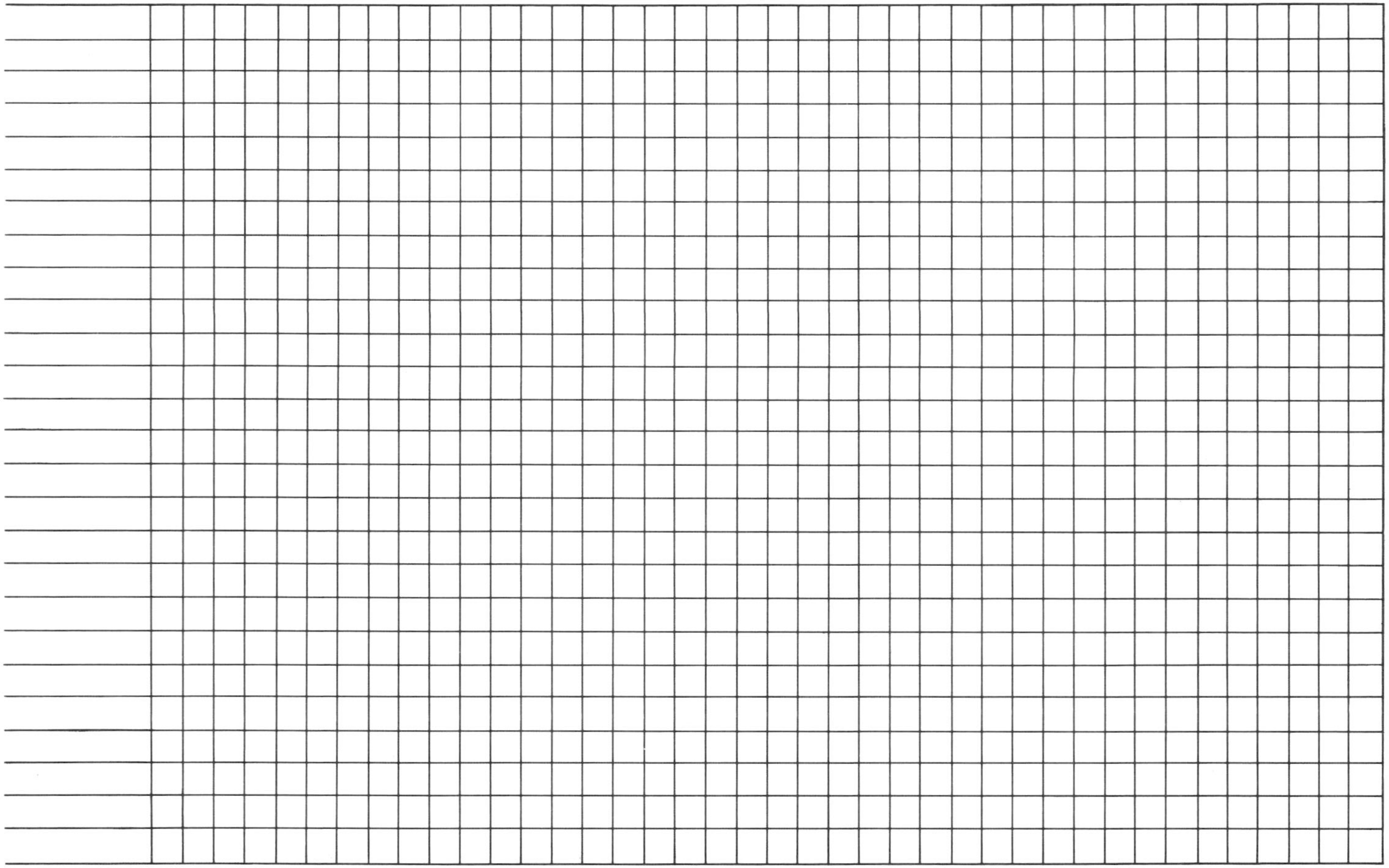

Days

174

3. What are two possible reasons why one consequent event is chosen over another?

4. How does the "internal chain" technique make self-control more probable? How does this differ from the "exhortation" technique? How might exhortation help?

5. Choose a behavior of your own that you might like to change (strengthen or weaken), specify it in measurable terms, and describe two procedures, internal and external, you could use to achieve this change. Your internal procedure must specify several aversive consequences for not changing, several good consequences for changing, a preceding stimulus which occurs regularly, which is not directly related to the target behavior, and which is predictably followed by a high probability or reinforcing event, and a listing of the sequence of steps to be followed.

If you want to apply the methods described in this unit to some behavior of your own, unit 15 (Self-Control Project) and unit 16 (Self-Management of Study Project) outline the steps you should take.

unit 15

Self-Control Project

This project is identical to unit 13 except that the behavior to be changed (shaped, strengthened, or extinguished) is a behavior that *you* do (or don't do but wished you did).

Review unit 13 and follow the same procedures for each component. Before you begin component 2 of the project, review that part of unit 14 which outlines different strategies for self-control. Be especially concerned about the questions of reliability and "cheating" and the steps you might take to be sure that the graph is true and that the contingencies are consistently imposed.

Self-Management of Study Project

OBJECTIVES

* design and carry out a self-management project regarding your management of your study efforts and time.

This project is appropriate and tailor-made for you if you find yourself having serious difficulty managing your study time or deciding what, when, or how to study for this or any of your classes.

If you don't see yourself as really needing help in this area or if you are not very interested in working on the problem at this time, then just skip over this unit. Furthermore, to be of some value for you, this project should be started early in the semester.

This is what you do:

Step 1: *Read* through this whole unit carefully and completely so that you know where you're going and how you're going to get there.

Step 2: *Baseline*

    a) Begin to record the following baselines:

        1) Minutes of actual study time per day of the week and per subject;

        2) Pages read per day per subject.

You may think of other baselines that might be appropriate and important in your particular case; if so, begin measuring these also. Keep separate graphs for each behavior, at least during the baseline.

b) Write up a detailed description of your current study behavior. This should include answers to the following questions:

1) Where do you study? Describe the places. What distractors occur there?

2) What free time do you have available—during the day, after school, at night, on weekends?

3) What do you do during each of these free periods when you don't study?

4) When the thought occurs to you that you should study but you don't, what activities do you frequently choose instead?

5) When you do choose to study, which subjects do you choose first? Why? Which subjects or activities do you frequently put off? Why?

Include in your writeup any other factors which add to a description of your study behavior.

c) Submit the baselines and the writeup to your instructor for approval. If possible, bring along some ideas you have about arranging situations and contingencies for changing your pattern of study. Your instructor will also make some suggestions, based on the data you supply. If necessary, he will also suggest modifications in your writeup or in your procedures for collecting baseline data.

Step 3: The Plan

After you obtain your instructor's approval of step 2 activities, then begin planning the details of your procedures for changing your study behavior. To prepare for this, review unit 14 and perhaps the several units preceding it. Your plan should, wherever appropriate, specify the following:

a) Full details of the internal chain procedure you will use to increase the probability of self-instruction occurring and being effective; be sure to identify the preceding stimulus, the thought chain, the consequent event, and the times when this process will occur during the day.

b) The external control arrangements you intend to make; include details of any contingencies you will arrange for others to impose, how you will arrange your study environments, and how you will graph your progress.

c) Details of your general planned study schedule for the various time slots each day of the week. Perhaps this can be in the form of a chart, with days of the week blocked horizontally and the time periods of the day blocked vertically, and each block identified as a class meeting, a library study period, lunch, study at home, recreation, etc. The intention is that this time schedule be not an inflexible routine but a general guide to be followed whenever possible and feasible.

d) A breakdown of the requirements for each of the courses you are currently taking into small sequential units, dividing this group of units into relatively equal weekly amounts according to the number of weeks available for accomplishing them.

e) Continue taking your baseline measurements while developing these plans.

f) Submit your complete plan, along with your complete baseline records, to your instructor for his analysis and possible modifications.

g) Your credit in this course, dependent on your implementation of the details of this plan, should at this point be arranged with your instructor.

h) After his final approval of these plans, proceed to step 4.

Step 4: Implementation

a) Begin immediately to implement all the details of your plan as approved.

b) Report weekly (unless arranged otherwise) to your instructor with your progress graph for the last week, the list of small units you intend to achieve in the coming week, and any problems that have arisen during the past week.

c) Near the end of the time period, or as arranged with your instructor, collect your data and graphs and writeups, add a summary assessment of the procedures and a note as to what you would do differently if you were to do this again, and submit the complete package to your instructor.

d) Your credit for this unit should be based on criteria established between you and your instructor just prior to implementation.

This unit, if done as outlined above, will undoubtedly teach you how to change your own study behavior, not only in theory but also in practice. But simply being able to do it is not likely to be helpful unless you continue to manage your own behavior. Hopefully the results of your doing it will convince you that it is worth continuing.

Review and Application I

The questions and activities for this unit require you to apply principles and procedures to real situations, to analyze various aspects of original situations, to merge the principles and procedures from several units in solving a particular problem, and to evaluate the results of various methods. Previous units have required some similar skills, but the primary focus of this unit is on these kinds of higher order skills. In addition, this unit serves as a mechanism for reviewing all the preceding material; you will find that some of the objectives are even clearer now that you can view them from a larger perspective.

The evaluation for this unit will probably include one or more questions from each of the subsections of questions listed below. If your evaluation takes the form of an oral interview with your instructor, be sure to make an appointment in advance.

As a part of this review, you may be asked to participate in a group discussion with several other students. Use the Review Discussion Sheet for this unit to record your discussion. Be sure to complete your own private review beforehand, so that the discussion can be as profitable as possible for everyone.

A.

1. Construct an original example in which the use of punishment would likely lead to escape or avoidance behavior.

2. Identify several contingencies and consequences (reinforcing, neutral, punishing) from the procedures in this course.

3. How could you use the Premack principle to get an A in a course?

4. Name one event that has been reinforcing to you recently and explain behaviorally how you know it was reinforcing. Do the same for a punishing event.

5. Using the Premack principle, you arrange to give each student ten minutes of time to talk with one another if and when they complete the assignment. Why might this not have any effect on the work completion of some students?

6. Two students in your class are fighting over a pencil. You don't know "who's fault it is." What might you do that would not reinforce inappropriate behavior?

7. Construct an original example of a classroom behavior you would want to shape.

8. Criticize the following procedure and cite the rule being violated: to reduce thumbsucking a child is reinforced for taking his thumb out of his mouth.

9. Defend with original examples the importance of consistency in reinforcing and extinguishing.

10. Cite three or four of the "rules for managing consequences" and show how they are or are not followed in this course.

11. As a teacher you know you should give reinforcement immediately, but in some situations or with some topics there is simply "no time to do so." How can you overcome this problem without violating the immediacy principle?

12. Give several different examples of how you, as a teacher, could use extinction to improve learning.

B.

13. If a student is clearly not turned on by adult attention (yours and/or others), outline a procedure for reversing this.

14. How can you tell whether or not your contingent praise is a reinforcer for a specific student? If it is not, how can you make it into a reinforcer for that student?

15. Be able to draw and label stylized graphs for each of the five kinds of reinforcement schedules. From these graphs, be able to explain all that the graph tells you about the behavior.

16. What kind of reinforcement schedule is represented by the weekly Friday spelling test? By the midsemester-and-final exam testing procedure? By the take-a-quiz-whenever-you're-ready testing procedure? Describe the different patterns of study behavior each of the above schedules is likely to produce.

17. On the first day of your English class, several students make it clear to you (by word and action) that they do not like English. Outline a specific procedure you could use to change this over the semester, including measures of the effect of your procedures.

18. Choose a behavior of your own which, if modified in some way, would probably make you a better teacher, and outline a feasible way in which you could make this modification.

19. In self-control, how does the "internal chain" method involve the use of the Premack principle?

20. In using the internal chain technique for changing a behavior of your own, why not just skip the neutral preceding stimulus arrangement and simply concentrate from the start on the thought of doing the undesired behavior?

21. I don't do the project work required for a boring course I'm taking. Describe a way I can get myself to do it regularly.

22. A friend of yours wants to go on a diet. He (she) has tried it several times before but hasn't stuck to it for long. Outline several ways in which you could help him (her) make it successful this time.

C.

23. As a teacher, why and how would you collect baseline data; what would you do with it?

24. There are several procedures for determining whether a change in behavior was caused by what *you* did. Which one do you think is most feasible for the teacher in the classroom? Why?

25. How could you demonstrate empirically whether or not a bonus point system for rate of progress was actually reinforcing for a particular student in your course?

26. During an independent study period, every time you look up at Jimmy, he is doing something other than his school work. Before implementing any behavior change procedures, what should you do first?

27. Identify two discriminations and two generalizations you had to learn in order to survive as a student or in order to handle the job you now have.

28. Cite several discriminations and generalizations a child would have to learn in the process of learning to read.

29. Give an example of a generalization and of a discrimination required in this interview.

30. What's the difference between a pseudoexplanation and a simple descriptive label?

D.

31. Outline several procedures you could use to handle the following problems if they occurred in your classroom (your area of specialization):
    a) for the first three days of class, the student sat quietly at his desk and did nothing;
    b) several times a day a student reaches over and hits another student causing an outcry;
    c) a student speaks out "anytime he feels like it."

32. You notice that Freddy Fickle does well when given small tasks and easy problems, but whenever the task is not short and easy or whenever he doesn't get something right the first time, he gets angry and refuses to work anymore. Describe how this behavior might have been learned. Outline the details of a procedure you would use to correct this problem and develop Freddy's perseverance.

33. Sally is constantly talking to the teacher, doing her favors, etc., but she rarely ever interacts with her peers. As a teacher, how could you change this?

34. Several times a day, Johnny throws something at another student, causing a noticeable class disturbance. Outline a procedure for eliminating this disturbance.

35. About six students in your class fail to complete their work assignments in reading each day, usually the same six. Outline a procedure for eliminating this failure. If this didn't work for several students, what other procedures would you consider?

36. In your reading group (six students) a couple of students make a lot of silly mistakes in oral reading, even though on other occasions they have read the same passages perfectly. Outline a procedure for eliminating or reducing these oral mistakes.

37. In the first three of the weekly quizzes you give your math students, one student asks to see the nurse the first time, is absent for the second, and vomits before the third test. Outline some nonmedical procedures you could initiate for this student for the next several tests.

38. Describe a procedure you could use to handle a student who speaks out "any time he feels like it."

39. A student of yours does his homework each night, but never turns it in unless you specifically remind him. You want him to turn it in

when he enters the room in the morning, not when you ask for it. Without adding any new consequent events, how can you bring about this change?

40. A student of yours is continually talking out of turn. When you told him to stand in the hall, he ran up and down the corridor. The principal then told you to carry out your discipline inside the classroom. How will you eliminate this student's talking out behavior? How could you do it using *only* reinforcement?

41. The gym teacher, knowing you are an expert in behavior modification, asks you to help solve some discipline problems he has. Remembering that gym is probably a reinforcer for many students, outline some reinforcing contingencies that he might use effectively.

42. The same gym teacher wants all his students to be ready for gym on time. What procedures would you suggest to him?

E.

43. In the above situations, what are some errors you could make in your initial observation of the student's behavior.

44. In the above situations, what if your original procedure did not work, or worked only partially?

45. In the above situations, how could you arrange it so as to avoid having to reinforce every correct response.

Review Discussion: Unit 17

Date: _____   *Time:* _____

Students (identify chairman, recorder):

Summary of Topics, Questions, and Situations Discussed (identify contributors):

Section II

An arrow indicates that prior units are prerequisites for the next unit. A △ identifies a key application/synthesis unit for purposes of summative evaluation.

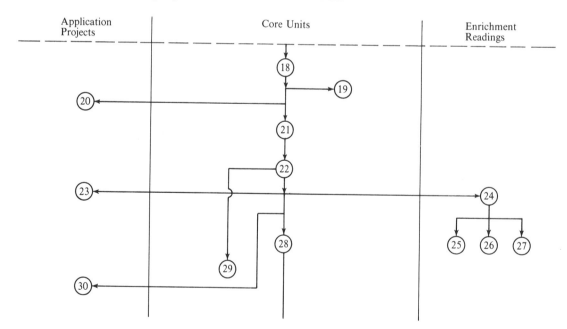

Instruction

The analysis of instruction is a subdivision of the more general analysis of learning. Recall the earlier general definition of teaching as the arranging of preceding and consequent events in such a way that students learn. When a student learns, his behavior changes. The process of instruction is a behavior-change process in which the focus is usually on academic or skill/knowledge behaviors.

In section II you will analyze the various components of effective instruction, and you will notice many similarities with the previous analysis of learning, though many terms will be different (educational). For example, effective instruction requires the specification of objectives (that is, specification of observable behaviors, preceding stimulus conditions in the testing situation, and other important properties of the behavior such as frequency or rate), a taxonomy or hierarchy of objectives (that is, a shaping plan of steps leading from the current to the target skill/knowledge level), a plan for presenting new material (that is, a plan for arranging preceding and consequent events which will elicit and reinforce appropriate responses), an evaluation plan (that is, a system for recording student responses and comparing them with baseline performance and with preset criteria), etc. In section II, you will focus more closely on specific instructional skills such as these.

Units 18–20 teach you to write and evaluate behavioral objectives relating both to academic skill/knowledge and to attitudes and values.

Despite the very real advantages of behavioral objectives, they don't guarantee that a student will learn anything. A detailed plan of instruction must be designed to bring the student from his current skill/knowledge level to the point of mastering the overall objective.

Before a child can run, he must learn to walk. Before a student learns creative writing skills, he must learn basic reading and writing skills. Before a student can tackle calculus, physics, or chemistry, he must learn basic math. Most unit objectives can and must be subdivided into a large set of subobjectives, each of which is a prerequisite for the main terminal objective, and these objectives must be sequenced in the proper order so that a student is not asked to do something for which he is not prepared.

Units 21–23 will teach you the fundamentals of task analysis and sequencing.

For a change of pace, the next four units deal exclusively with *theories* of instruction and learning. The first of these units gives a brief overview of four prominent, important, and current theories: those of Jean Piaget, Jerome Bruner, Robert Gagné, and Benjamin Bloom. This overview is followed by two articles which add further detail to the theories of Piaget and Bruner. A third article reviews the progress, contributions, and promises of the field of educational technology, which some educators feel is a kind of theory in its own right.

These units will not teach you how to implement the theories in actual instruction. Instead they introduce the basic characteristics of each theory and show how they contrast with each other.

Units 28–30 will teach you some skills that you need when you actually present a unit of instruction to your students. There are a variety of methods for presenting instruction; the appropriateness of each depends in large part on the particular objectives you have for the unit. But there are also some basic methods that apply generally to all instructional purposes, such as requiring active responding, sequencing by successive approximation, allowing self-pacing, choosing media and resources to serve the specific objective, choosing and phrasing questions to fit the desired response.

In addition, you as a teacher need special skills in interpersonal relations. You must be able to clearly identify your feelings toward your students and your work and be perceptive of the feelings your students have toward you and their learning. The way in which these attitudes are expressed and interpreted can greatly influence the effectiveness of your instruction. Unit 30 is a workshop of eight sessions in which you will work with other students to improve your ability to:

* attend to and interpret the feelings expressed by others or held by yourself;
* respond to others in a way that shows understanding and invites trust;
* express your own feelings honestly, courteously, and assertively.

Behavioral Objectives

OBJECTIVES

Objectives, as used in education, are statements that describe what students will be able to do after completing a specific unit of instructions. For example, this unit has several objectives; after working through it, you should be able to

* differentiate educational, instructional, and behavioral objectives on the bases of characteristics and uses, constructing original examples of each;
* construct an original cognitive behavioral objective which specifies the conditions, the behavior, and the criteria precisely enough so that another person knowledgeable in the field could construct and grade a fair test of how well your students mastered that objective;
* identify major defects in one or more of the three components of defective sample objectives;
* rewrite deficient objectives according to the three criteria.

The Need

The skill of constructing clear and precise objectives is an important one for the teacher for several reasons. Without clear objectives, choosing *materials and activities* for instruction is largely a random effort. It's a difficult job to choose and arrange a set of curricular materials and activities and to design teaching procedures that actually produce the kinds of student behaviors you want; it is impossible to do this if you are not clear and precise about what those end-result behaviors are before you begin to choose and design.

Second, without clear objectives it is difficult for a teacher to give himself and a student day-to-day feedback on how he is progressing, where he needs additional help or practice, and so on. If you don't know ahead of time precisely where you are heading, it is difficult to tell where you are along the way. On the other hand, with precise and measurable objectives both the teacher and the student can tell what has already been learned, what still needs to be taught, and where the problems are.

As a student you have probably experienced the frustration of vague objectives. You are assigned chapters 1–10 of the class text, you put off reading them (partly because you are not quite sure what "read" really means) until a few days before the test, then you cram (knowing you can't memorize or become an expert on all ten chapters and hoping you have emphasized the same points the prof will when he makes out the exam the night before), you take the quiz and find out you missed on some points and hit on others, and then you find out a week later that many other students had medium luck too.

Third, since without clear objectives a teacher can't get reliable feedback on the effectiveness of the instruction, he also can't identify *problems* as they occur or design effective *remedial* activities when they are identified. Waiting until the end (or even the middle) of a course or a school year to identify those students who are "behind" means that a lot of time and instruction has been wasted for those students. But with clear and precise objectives, problems and errors can quickly be detected and remedied, and a great deal of valuable learning time can be saved.

Finally, without precise objectives there is no valid way to measure the *effectiveness* of the instruction. A final test might tell you who does better than whom, but without measurable objectives there is no way to measure how well each student performs weighed against the goals for the instruction. This is because the test-maker will not be able to select test items which clearly measure the student's mastery of the goals of the instruction. With measurable objectives, however, it is a relatively straightforward matter to construct test items which measure each student's mastery and the effectiveness of the instruction for each student.

The Components of a Behavioral Objective

Behaviorally stated objectives begin to solve this problem. If the objective is stated in terms of measurable behaviors and situations (e.g., "when presented with a written list of ten randomly chosen, single digit multiplication problems, the student will write the correct answers to at least nine of them within ten minutes), the teacher and the student both know what the desired behavior is, appropriate materials and activities can be selected, and the change in student behavior can be measured, remedied if necessary, and communicated to all concerned.

A precise behavioral objective has three parts:

1. The *conditions:* the situation, in all-important *detail,* in which the student is expected to *perform* the desired behavior. For example; "when presented with a written list of ten randomly chosen single digit multiplication problems . . ."
2. The *action:* the response or behavior we want the student to be able to do, always in terms of an action we can observe and *measure.* For example: " . . . the student will write the correct answers . . ."
3. The *criterion:* the precise quantity, quality, and the rate of responses which you will accept as mastery of the desired skill. For example: " . . . to at least nine within ten minutes."

Condition

The condition or situation in which the desired behavior will be measured should be complete and clear enough to indicate the kind of test items, resources, and prompts that the student will have when he demonstrates his mastery (or nonmastery) of the objective. Think of the condition as the test situation. When you write a condition, it helps to require yourself to begin with a phrase like "Given . . . ," or "When presented with. . . ." That way the wording forces you to specify precisely what the student will be provided with in the test situation and what he will not be able to use.

If, for example, your general aim is to teach the student some basic facts about the Korean War, the condition component of a behavioral objective requires you to state the test situation in which you want him to show you he knows those facts. Perhaps you want him to state the facts when asked the appropriate questions; in that case your condition would be something like "When asked 'Who was the President of the U.S. when the Korean War ended,' the student will. . . ." Or perhaps you want him to demonstrate this knowledge in a written paragraph; in this case you must specify whether you want him to write this paragraph in a closed book situation (that is, given nothing but the test question), or whether he can use library resources and notes in a kind of take-home exam.

Whatever kind of test situation you decide is most appropriate for your general instructional goals, your condition component must be detailed enough so that others will understand and be able to duplicate the givens and the not-givens just as you planned.

In stating your condition component, you must be careful to make sure that the test situation matches the situation in which the student has been taught to respond.

For example, you actually may have taught a student how to identify the various stages of cellular mitosis, but he might very well fail your test if he learned from illustrations in the text and you test him on slides under a microscope; the response is basically the same (identifying stages), but the preceding stimulus situation (illustrations vs. slides) is different. This difference can be critical.

The fact that you have taught your students to add and subtract any sets of numbers does not mean that they will be able to solve word problems calling for addition and subtraction; word problems involve other skills in translating words into numbers before adding or subtracting, and your students may not have learned these translation skills. It's poor teaching to "presume" that some skills don't need deliberate specification and teaching. Elementary students have been known to become confused when given addition problems with the numbers arranged in a horizontal list, instead of the usual vertical list. And if mastery of a given skill is to be demonstrated in an oral situation, the student may fail if all his learning activities have been written. From your own experience you know that a multiple-choice exam, for example, does not test exactly the same skills as a short-answer or essay exam.

Notice that this component does *not* deal with the conditions under which the student will be taught (e.g., "after studying the unit on . . ."). It only deals with the conditions under which he will demonstrate his *mastery,* usually after instruction is given. In other sources you will come across many objectives that begin with a phrase like "After studying. . . ." A phrase like that states the situation in which the student presumably learned, but it doesn't state a test situation. There may be nothing wrong with including a learning situation as long as it is not used as a copout for stating the givens and not-givens of the test situation. Furthermore, in most cases you as a teacher don't care how or when or where a student learned something, just *whether* or not he learned it. The condition component states the precise test situation in which you intend to find that out.

Action

The action identifies the observable behavior of the student that you will accept as evidence of his mastery. Such words as "know," "understand" (even "really understand"), or "appreciate" are not useful in specifying an objective so that it can be measured or communicated. Since the teacher can't get into a student's mind (or "heart") to measure knowledge, understanding, or appreciation, the teacher must observe some form of overt behavior, such as what the student writes or says or defines or differentiates or solves or lists or compares or constructs.

This is not to say that understanding or appreciation are worthless goals. The problem is that these words do not help the teacher or the student to *arrange* appropriate instruction or *decide* when the goal has been reached. For example, it may be important for a student to understand the theory of evolution. But what does this mean? How can we tell when a student has achieved this? Which of the following does it include: defining such terms as genetic equilibrium, diagraming the Hardy-Weinberg Law, identifying the causes of mutation, comparing Lamarckism to Darwinism? Perhaps all of these and many other discrete behaviors.

How can you tell whether a student appreciates music; do you simply ask him, or count how much money he spends on Bach or Stones records, or ask him to hum three themes from Beethoven's Ninth, or ask him who Mel Torme's drummer is? Any *one* of these behaviors might not be enough to convince you that the student has developed an appreciation for some form of music, but a *set* of them together might.

The point is that in defining precisely what it is you intend to teach, be sure that the words you use, especially in describing the action, are clearly *measurable* and observable *behaviors*. Then it is much easier to decide whether those are really the behaviors you want and whether you actually teach them.

Criterion

The criterion specifies how well you want the student to perform the action and what measure you will use. It specifies the standard of success clearly enough for any knowledgeable person to decide whether your objectives have been achieved, and they specify what kind of measure you will use.

For example, you might specify a *time limit*. Sometimes this is unstated, presuming a reasonable time limit (one addition problem in one hour is usually considered unreasonable), but sometimes it is important to specify a time limit, and if part of your criterion is rate, then include it in the criterion. Or you may want a certain amount of work (*quantity* of behavior) or a specific degree of *quality* (a certain percentage, or in a certain order, or other qualitative aspect).

Frequently the criterion must also specify other characteristics of performance *accuracy* that you deem important. If you ask a TV repair man to adjust your set, you may be interested not only in how long it takes him, but whether your set still has any distortion when he finishes. The quality of the picture is an important measure of his performance. In the sciences, objectives frequently specify the criterion with such phrases as " . . . rounded off to the nearest whole number" or " . . . to the nearest milliliter."

Remember that the *best test* for a useful and clear behavioral objective is to ask: If this was someone else's objective and he had already attempted to bring the students to mastery of the objective, could I (presuming I knew the subject matter) devise a *fair test* for these students, using only the information in the objectives itself? If you can, then it's a good objective; if you can't, then the objective is unclear—not only to you but probably also to the teacher and his students.

Another version of the best test method for checking your objectives is to ask: If this was someone else's objective, could I devise an exam that would not violate any part of the objective, but would really burn the students by asking for things they never expected. If you could, then the objective needs more clarity and precision.

1. Describe four ways in which behavioral objectives can contribute to instructional effectiveness.

2. Describe the three components of a cognitive behavioral objective.

3. What test is suggested to determine the clarity and usefulness of a behavioral objective?

Educational Objectives

Let's look at some sample objectives to see whether the conditions, the action, and the measure and criterion are stated in sufficient detail. Consider this objective; try to pinpoint its deficiencies, if any, on your own before reading on:

The student will develop the rational thinking powers which underlie scientific modes of inquiry.

Of course there is no way this could be considered a clear behavioral objective; neither the conditions, the action, nor the criterion are stated measurably, and it would be impossible to fairly test students on their achievement of this objective. (If you have any doubts about this, be sure to review the previous pages.) This objective is a good example of what is called an *Educational Objective*—a very broad and nonspecific statement of general goals. Educational objectives are typically used by institutions or groups to indicate their *overall direction* and purpose.

We could rewrite the above objectives into a behavioral form in a variety of ways: "When given a microscope and yeast culture and asked to give empirical support to the theory that yeast is alive, the student will establish an observation schedule and record the time and frequency of observed growth and reproduction events (90 percent of which agree with those of another observer) and describe the series of events in writing." Or: "After having demonstrated his ability to explain the bending of bimetallic strip under heat, the student will cite the same principles to explain how a thermostat works, when given a diagram of a thermostat." Notice that in this last example the criterion is more implied than stated, since there is no time limit or percentage correct criterion stated. The implied criterion is 100 percent since there are a set number of facts and sequences all of which must be identified to "explain" the thermostat's workings. Someone who already knows the principles involved would have no trouble in developing a test for this objective.

Instructional Objectives

Consider this objective: "The student will be able to list the steps a bill follows through the state legislature, specifying requirements for passage in each step.

This kind of objective is usually an *Instructional Objective* because it omits the conditions and the criterion. An instructional objective has many uses in communicating one's instructional intentions to others in an abbreviated form. They are usually written after the behavioral objectives have been completely specified. For example, the above objectives might be an abbreviation of the following behavioral objective: "In a half-hour closed book test, the student will be able to list, in correct order, the steps a bill follows through the state legislature, specifying the requirements for passage (matching those in the text) in each step."

When evaluating or writing behavioral objectives, you might find it helpful to use the following prompts:

Condition: resources or restrictions; testing situation; skills which have actually been taught.

Action: what the student will do to demonstrate mastery; measurable words.

Measure-Criterion: how to evaluate; lower limit of acceptable performance.

Practice Problems

Work the following self-test problems to pinpoint for yourself any details you may have missed. Don't look back or forward in the text while you are working these problems since your purpose is to find out how well you can do without extra resources. Remember the test; could you construct and grade a test fairly, just from the information given.

Rewrite the following objectives into acceptable form *if* they have serious faults; otherwise mark them acceptable.

1. The student will state in sequence the six basic steps in typing a business letter.

2. The student will play the C major scale through two octaves on the violin, in third position.

3. Given whatever equipment he requests, the student will determine experimentally the density of an unknown solid.

4. On a written test, the student will demonstrate his thorough understanding of Newton's three laws.

5. The student will correctly identify 80 percent of the chords as dominant, subdominant, seventh, or tonic, when played singly on a piano.

6. When given any paragraph from the class text, the student will identify the tense and mood of the main verb in every sentence or main clause.

7. When shown any unknown organism, the student will correctly name its genus and species.

8. The student will know the eight rules for managing consequences.

9. On a written, closed book test, the student will be able to define reinforcement.

10. After studying the unit on organic compounds, the student will correctly identify the structural formula of 80 percent of the compounds, when given the name.

Answers to Practice Problems

1. Conditionally acceptable; depends on whether or not we can assume the condition (oral or written, no prompts) and criterion (100 percent).

2. Needs further criteria details, e.g., regarding speed, accuracy, and perhaps even tone quality.

3. In this case, the criterion probably can't be assumed. Perhaps you would want to allow, say, a 3 percent margin of error.

4. Understanding, by itself, is not measurable (even when the words "demonstrate" and "thorough" are added); therefore the action is faulty. And the criterion is also faulty, since you can't specify a measure for an unmeasurable.

5. Probably acceptable, although you might want to indicate that the chord will be played only once, with a ten second pause between chords.

6. Acceptable. The criterion is presumed to be 100 percent.

7. While the criterion is presumed to be 100 percent (which may not be reasonable in many classes), the condition is not clear enough. In cases like this, it can make quite a difference whether the organism is shown live, via picture, or in a slide.

8. "Know" is not an action word. And because we don't know what action is really intended, we can't tell if the condition can be assumed or not.

9. Acceptable though it should probably also state whether a paraphrase or a literal definition is expected.

10. Unacceptable, though it appears to have all the components. Study the objective again, before reading the discussion below.

Superficial Objectives

Consider this objective and try to analyze it before reading on.

> "After completing a unit on behavioral objectives and when given a twenty-item, closed book exam designed by the instructor to test comprehension of the topic, the student will correctly answer 75 percent of the questions."

This objective seems to state a condition ("After completing . . ."), an action (". . . answering . . ."), and a criterion (". . . 75 percent correct . . ."). We can presume that the action implies writing, but apply the basic test to this objective—could you write a fair test for it? What specific questions would you include in the post-test? Would you ask the student to write behavioral objectives which clearly specify the three components, or would you ask him to identify the components of sample objectives; would you require him to distinguish good from poor objectives; would you require psychomotor and affective as well as cognitive objectives; would you require cognitive objectives at various levels? Or would you require all of these skills to be demonstrated? Even though this objective seems to include all the right things, it ends up telling you very little about precisely what the student will be taught to do, and you would be hard pressed to develop a fair test just on the basis of the information in this objective. The basic problem with this objective is that the specified action (answering questions), has no useful meaning for the purposes of instruction or evaluation. You still need to know what kinds of questions, that is, a *specific* statement of what the student is expected to be able to do after studying the unit. Notice the difference between the above objective and the kinds of objectives for the unit you are now studying. Which test would you rather take?

The fault with the objective in question 10, and with many objectives, is the lack of specificity in what the student is expected to do. The student's action is *superficially clear* (say, write, choose, etc.), but it is not clear *what* he will say or write. For example, "answer 8 out of 10 questions correctly" doesn't specify the expected behavior very well; "answer" may imply writing (and that's acceptable unless the student is very young), but the action doesn't identify anything about the ten questions— we still have the question "*which* ten questions?" It's no better than saying "after reading chapter 5, the student will pass (80 percent) a multiple-choice exam over the material of the chapter." Superficially, this objective meets all the criteria for a good objective, but it doesn't pass the test for a good objective—being able to create and grade a fair exam just from the objective.

A behavioral objective must clearly state *exactly what the student is expected to be able to do* after the instruction, even if the student will be tested over only a sample of these desired behaviors. The action component of an objective must state (or clearly refer to) not only the physical action (write, or say) but the *content* and precise *preceding stimulus* event for the desired behavior.

Another way of looking at it is this: your objective must *narrow down the field* of possible behaviors to a reasonable and clear limit. Someplace (in the objective or in the text or in a handout) the student should be able to pinpoint *all* the behaviors he is expected to master and might be required to demonstrate—all the behaviors from which you take a sample for your test.

For example, in the objective, "After reading the unit on the contemporary novel, the student will correctly match eight authors with titles, when given a scrambled list of ten authors and ten titles," the action is too vague. It doesn't specify *which* matches or *how many* the teacher expects the student to be able to make. Someone creating and/or grading a test from this objective might ask; can I include any twentieth-century novelist, or just those in the chapter? Can I include any novelist mentioned in the chapter or should I exclude some (a problem if the chapter refers to several hundred novelists and/or novels)? If the teacher has decided on only ten, which ten are they—and why not tell the students beforehand (in the objective) which they are.

A better objective would indicate (in the objective or by means of study guide questions or handouts) precisely which novelists and novels are thought to be important to learn and might be included in this quiz.

Remember that however and wherever you specify the action, you must clearly *communicate* to others (especially the students) exactly what you expect as a minimum. Study guide questions or handouts must themselves be specific and measurable to qualify as usable components of an objective.

Few if any objectives do this perfectly for a large class of students, but imperfect objectives are better than no objectives.

4. Cite several examples of objectives that contain defective elements (conditions, action, measure and criterion) and a *corrected* version of each example.

5. Be able to identify and correct defects in new examples of cognitive behavioral objectives, when you see them on a quiz.

6. Differentiate educational, instructional, and behavioral objectives on the bases of characteristics and uses, with an original example of each.

Practice Problems

Now try your hand at writing some behavioral objectives of your own.

Below are some global educational objectives related to a variety of subject matter areas and levels. To reach each general objective would of course require many specific objectives. Just pick one or two of these subobjectives and write them up, remembering the test for a useful objective. Afterwards you should also practice writing some objectives that are appropriate for the specific tasks you will be teaching.

1. Familiarity with the styles of the five major romantic poets.

2. The student will understand the simple proofs in Euclidean geometry.

3. Familiarity with the basic theory of classical harmony.

4. Understanding of cubism and dadaism.

5. Develop proficiency in sports.

6. Develop in each student a more creative ability through art.

Answers to Practice Problems

For these problems, there are many possible correct answers and you will have to evaluate the acceptability of your examples, using the criteria explained in the unit. Below are some suggested objectives and some hints on specific problems.

1. With this objective, your first task is to define precisely what you want to include by "familiarity." Perhaps you want the students to be able to identify new passages as to its author. A matching test would be appropriate, so your objective might be: "When given ten passages of 4–10 lines each, written by Wordsworth, Shelley, Keats, Byron, or Coleridge and included in the student's text, the student will correctly identify the author of nine of them." If you want your students to "compare and contrast" these styles, then you have to specify on what bases they should make these comparisons (structure, symbolism, etc.), and how many comparisons you expect as a minimum.

2. Again, you must decide what you mean by "understand simple proofs." If you want your students to be able to reconstruct the proof for a given theorem, then state that—or just to identify a proof as being for a specific theorem—or perhaps simply to be able to find the circumference of a circle. State the specific tasks you want them to be able to do. Also, do you want to allow them to use some resources (tables, slide rules, etc.)?

3. "Basic" might include harmonic recognition (e.g., identify major, minor, augmented chords when played on the piano singly, with a ten second pause between each), or it might extend to actual composition (e.g., in an overnight take-home exam, the student will compose an original four part piece of eight lines in the style of Palestrina, J. S. Bach, Handel, and Mozart, according to the style criteria sheets handed out). If you want to include quality norms, be sure to specify.

4. Some possibilities: When shown twenty prints of twentieth century paintings, the student will identify at least 90 percent of the works representing cubism. Or . . . identify at least one feature of each work which characterizes it as cubist, Or . . . produce an original work that has at least three characteristics of cubism. The "characteristics" referred to in these examples must, of course, be specified in a text handout.

5. Given three tries on the athletic field, the student will throw a softball at least 70 feet, with no more than a 10-foot deviation on either side of a criterion straight-line marker. Or: the student will mount the

trampoline from either side, using the jump-sit-swing method, when given three tries and ten minutes. Perhaps this later objective should include criteria regarding style and smoothness, if these can be specified.

6. See the discussion on creativity which follows.

Objectives for Creativity

To teach creativity in any area, you must first ask yourself "What is creativity (and is your answer something observable)?" "When I say that someone or something shows creativity, on what bases do I say that—what signs prompt me to say it?"

One sign we usually use is *unusualness*. A student shows increased creativity when his art product is *different* in some important aspect—perhaps he used a new color or new color combinations, a style that was different in some specified respect, a new medium or media combination he hadn't used before. So your objective would be that the student will produce one or more art products of his own that successively show features that are new and different for that student. You should also specify the classes of features in which you want originality to be shown.

For example: "Each student will produce ten drawings during the semester (the noncreativity criteria should be specified also), dealing with ten different subject matters, and each drawing will show a noticeable difference from his previous works in terms of color, style, or medium." For some advanced art students, your objectives for creativity might be more demanding and detailed.

Of course, there are other aspects of creativity that are important. For example, the degree of unusualness must to a certain extent be tempored by *acceptability standards* of the culture. Perverts can be highly creative, but the mainstream of society does not reinforce such creativity. On the other hand, there are many examples of creativity in the history of, say, music, art, and science which were initially rejected by professionals as being bizarre and yet eventually helped reshape society's views about the acceptable limits of creativity. This is one respect in which the criteria for creativity cannot easily be specified until long after the fact.

But a great deal of creativity can be developed systematically in students before the issue of public acceptability becomes crucial. The school can provide a supportive environment for creative experimentation so that the skills and the preferences associated with creative effort can become reliable.

To Use or Not To Use

From this brief introduction to behavioral objectives, you can see that the specification of objectives for a unit of instruction is not an easy task; it requires a lot of work and attention to detail *before* the instruction even starts. For this reason, teachers are tempted to use published collections of objectives. These can be of help, but they usually do not relieve you of all the work because many (perhaps most) of the sets of objectives currently available are nonbehavioral and nonmeasurable. After you eliminate the "know's" and "familiar with's," the "appreciation of's" and the "awareness of's," very few useful objectives are left.

Some educators argue that behavioral objectives are useful only for teaching trivial or very basic skills because the other more important goals of education (like teaching creativity, attitudes, etc.) are "intangible" and can't be specified measurably. The argument is frequently voiced by those who have just recently become acquainted with behavioral objectives.

Of course, it's difficult. It's not easy to specify objectives for basic skills either, but that's no excuse for escaping the responsibility to measure what is taught. English teachers often claim that it is next to impossible to identify acceptable essays—yet they do it every time they grade an essay. An English teacher must have criteria in order to make judgments. What behavioral objectives force him to do is put his criteria on the line, out in the open for examination. He won't do this if he is defensive and insecure about his teaching, but if he can relax with the fact that even teachers can learn and improve, stating his objectives and criteria will help him to make them more precise and valid. Only when we begin the task of specifying the conditions, action, and the measure and criterion for such "intangible" skills can we design more effective procedures to teach them systematically and replicably.

For another example, consider the social studies teacher who says that his objective is to develop in his students a commitment to the democratic way. Who could criticize such a profound and worthwhile objective? Yet his measure of success might be simply how well his students do on a multiple-choice exam concerning what the "loyal American citizen" does. A large amount of trivia is hidden beneath noble statements. Precise specification of behavioral objectives (cognitive and affective) allows us to choose only important goals.

The basic instructional requirement cannot be avoided: *what you attempt to teach you must attempt to measure.* Whether your instructional goals are cognitive or affective, concerned with basic skills or aesthetic refinements, you as a teacher have the responsibility of designing some way to detect the effect of your teaching in the student's behavior. The burden of proof is on you. You need to know this effect in order to know where you and the student are going, whether and when you've arrived at mastery of each objective, and whether remediation is called for at a given time.

The criticality of measuring what you teach has led some experts to advise teachers to focus on the *posttest* items rather than on behavioral objectives. They argue that current objectives are too vague and unmeasurable and that educators spend too much time arguing about the theory of objectives and neglect the actual improvement of instruction. Instead, they suggest that the teacher devise a complete list of posttest items which he feels are clear, fair, and comprehensive. When the teacher can say: "If a student can handle all these items, then I've achieved all my goals," the posttest items become a true statement of the teacher's objectives. In this sense, posttest items are the best way to express what you are really teaching; they clearly state what you expect the students to be able to do as a result of your teaching, and a student's performance on such items tells you and the student about the quality of that instruction.

7. Construct ten *original* behavioral objectives concerning different goals in your field of concentration, some of which require the student to do more than just memorize. Have your instructor evaluate them before you complete this unit. (Ask yourself, with each objective: Could someone else construct and grade a test fairly after reading this objective?)

8. What's the basic rule relating teaching and measurement? State one way that behavioral objectives help in meeting this requirement.

9. State the argument against the claim that "Behavioral objectives apply only to trivia."

10. Explain the usefulness of a posttest as a statement of instructional objectives.

unit 19

Attitudes and Affective Objectives

OBJECTIVES

When you complete this unit, you should be able to:
* describe attitudes in terms of measurable behaviors;
* specify and apply the steps for teaching an attitude to an example of your own choosing;
* describe the three components of an affective behavioral objective;
* rewrite deficient affective objectives according to the three criteria;
* construct several original affective behavioral objectives which include the three components and which are designed to contribute to your general objectives as a teacher.

Most educators insist that attitudes play a very important role in learning. They argue that the attitudes and values a student brings to school play a large role in determining the quality and quantity of what the student learns, remembers, and uses. The teacher, they say, must therefore be very concerned about teaching and changing attitudes. There is, of course, some disagreement about which attitudes and values are most useful and should be taught, especially regarding so-called middle-class values.

Most educators also admit that the questions of defining an attitude, measuring it, and teaching it are confusing and puzzling. Usually an attitude is defined as a feeling toward something or someone. Since feelings can't be directly measured, we usually rely on a person's verbal report of how he feels toward the object. And the teaching or changing of attitudes usually involves a mixture of talking about different feelings, endorsement and models from important people, feeding the person more information, and giving encouragement.

During the 1930s and '40s, many educators considered attitudes more important than subject matter. The "whole child" philosophy of the progressive education movement focused on personality development, creativity, spontaneity, and citizenship for democracy. Critics pointed out, among other things, that such goals were too vague to be recognized, let alone achieved.

But difficulties, vagueness, and failures do not mean that attitudes are imaginary or trivial. What is needed is a more careful analysis of the topic, so that training can be measured for its real effectiveness in achieving what we wish it to achieve. A behavioral analysis may be as helpful here as with other types of learning.

What Is an Attitude

We say an attitude is a feeling. Even though we can sometimes be fairly certain about our own feelings, we can never *directly* observe the feelings—and therefore the attitudes—of others. What we do observe are outward behaviors—words about something, facial expressions, the speed of movements toward or away from something. We see a student reading for long periods without distraction, asking questions or initiating discussion about what he has read, requesting to have time to read, going to the library frequently to get books, and taking books home to read. What we say is "he likes to read" or "he has a good attitude toward books," but what we have observed is not the attitude or the feeling, but instead a group of *approach behaviors* toward the object of the presumed attitude.

Or we see a student who never smiles at the teacher and sometimes scowls when she talks to him, who avoids the teacher whenever possible, talks negatively about the teacher and sometimes to the teacher. We say that this student has a bad attitude toward the teacher, that he dislikes the teacher. We say this on the basis of a set of *avoidance behaviors* regarding the teacher.

For another example, think of a person's "attitude" toward long hair. We infer it from whether he mixes with longhairs, whether he approaches short-hair and long-hair strangers with equal ease, and from the type of comments he makes about such strangers.

How did these attitudes develop? Probably in the same way as most other behaviors are developed and maintained—by the reinforcing or punishing consequences of many previous similar behaviors. These behaviors may not have been taught deliberately, but in any case the student does learn the effectiveness of certain kinds of behaviors by experiencing their consequences.

In this sense, an attitude is a verbal *shorthand* way of referring to a *set* of approach or avoidance behaviors toward someone or something. In common conversation, there may be no problem in using such shorthand, but if we wish to teach or modify attitudes effectively, we are better off focusing on the behaviors rather than on the feelings. The feeling or attitude is a result of learning experiences with consequences, not the cause of learning.

Teaching Attitudes

This analysis of attitude suggests a rather straightforward method for teaching or modifying what we call attitudes. The first step is to *specify* in detail the *behaviors* implied in the attitude you want. One way is to think of a person (real or imaginary) who has the attitude you want to an ideal degree, and then *list all the behaviors* that person would do to indicate to someone else that he has this attitude, being sure that each behavior is described in specific observable terms. An example is the list of behaviors noted above for the "like to read" attitude.

Then when you have decided which of these behaviors you want to teach, *arrange reinforcing contingencies for each of them,* or in certain cases for gradual approximations to the desired behavior (shaping). Shape each of these behaviors in the same way you would any behavior. Frequently this will mean arranging for the student to achieve frequent success at a certain kind of task and immediate reinforcement for that success. In this way, the student will learn to expect success and good consequences for effort in that area and will be more apt to approach similar situations in the future.

Third, prompt the student to *verbalize* to you (or to others) the *good consequences* of this kind of behavior and the *bad consequences* of the opposite behavior. And, of course, reinforce these verbalizations when they occur. In this way you are helping the student to firm up and clarify his *discrimination* concerning the *consequences* of his behavior. Furthermore, you are teaching the student skills that are indispensible for his own self-control and independence. There is a good deal of evidence that the ability to discriminate cues and signals (preceding stimulus events) and probable consequences and to make appropriate decisions is greater when the ability to clearly verbalize these discriminations is greater.

Finally, arrange ways to prompt the student's *discrimination* of *relevant preceding stimuli* for the behavior you want. Teaching a behavior involves teaching not only what to do but also when (in what situations) to do it. This applies also to teaching the behaviors which make up an attitude. This might include describing these cues to him in detail at first. The reason for this is the same: understanding at the verbal level enhances the ability to discriminate appropriately.

This general procedure can be applied to the teaching of a variety of attitudes: self-esteem and personal pride, confidence in one's judgment, liking one's school mates, liking music, persistence (the "I can do it if I keep working at it" attitude), liking school, liking learning, and so forth. These and similar attitudes can be taught by specifying and then teaching the behaviors from which they are inferred.

1. Behaviorally, what is an attitude? Why is this a better way to think of attitudes than the "feeling" definition?

2. Choose an original attitude, specify it behaviorally (in terms of a set of approach/avoidance behaviors), and apply the other three steps for teaching an attitude to this example (arrange contingencies for each chosen behavior, verbalize consequences, prompt discriminations).

Affective Objectives

In a previous unit we studied behavioral objectives that dealt primarily with cognitive skills. But as we have seen, objectives that deal with attitudes, values, feelings, and appreciations are also appropriate goals for instruction. As with cognitive objectives, the same care must be taken in defining affective objectives. Once you have defined the desired attitude or interest in terms of a set of measurable behaviors, you are in a position to specify objectives for teaching these behaviors.

An affective behavioral objective, like a cognitive behavioral objective, has three components: condition, action, and measure and criterion.

The Condition

The condition of an affective objective indicates a test situation and restrictions. The testing problem is somewhat different here; when dealing with attitudes or interests, what we are testing is a *preference,* so the testing situation must give the student at least two options in a free-choice situation. To take an extreme example, if your affective objective was to teach the students to like you as a teacher, asking them in class to raise their hands if they like you would not be a valid testing situation for that attitude. Technically, they do have a choice of raising or not raising their hand, but this approach behavior is more strongly influenced by the teacher's presence than by a liking preference for the teacher.

A better statement of the objective might be: "each student will *initiate* an exchange of greetings or a conversation with the teacher, outside of the usual class period, at least three times during the month."

The absence of cues (of any type) indicating what the teacher hopes the behavior will be is important in testing the achievement of affective objectives. Consider this situation: the teacher wants to teach her students an attitude of respect for other people. Now if, at lunch time, what she really wants is to decrease the likelihood that her students will make a lot of noise, knock things over, or bump into other students, then she might be wise to give a cue before leading her students to the lunch room (e.g., "remember our discussion yesterday about how we show respect for others.") But if she wants to test to see if she has actually taught these attitudes she must eliminate this and other prompts and perhaps even have another teacher lead the students to the lunch room.

The Action

The action of an affective objective is usually one or more approach behaviors, although the desired outcome may be an avoidance behavior (think of using drugs, smoking, etc.). And, as with cognitive objectives, the behavior must be observable and measurable, a statement of what you expect the student to *do*. However, for any given attitude or interest, there are a great many possible approach behaviors that could indicate the attitude. You can't teach them all, so how do you choose the appropriate behaviors to teach and then to test? Perhaps the most efficient way is to choose several behaviors that would be very likely to occur *commonly* among students who have that attitude or interest. We might label this a high probability behavior in someone with such an attitude, and this would include such behavior categories as taking time to engage oneself in the topic, talking about the topic more than usual, going to sources of information about the topic, and asking relevant questions.

For example, if your general affective goal is to develop an interest in art, "the student collects paint brushes" is not a reasonable action statement because it is not a common behavior of students interested in art, nor is it an approach behavior to the specific attitude. "The student pick-pockets for a month and uses the money to travel to New York to visit the Metropolitan Museum of Art" specifies an approach behavior that few students in art class would be likely to exhibit.

A more useful affective objective might look like this: each student will do one of the following things during the semester without being prompted or required to do so:

1. ask the teacher for reference materials on a specific art topic;
2. tell the teacher about the student's visit to an art museum or show;
3. initiate discussion with the teacher on an art topic not discussed in class;
4. display an art product of his own.

The Criterion

The criterion and measure of an affective objective must, as always, include a precise statement of how success will be *measured* and of what *level* of performance will be accepted as evidence of the attitude. You might indicate the number of the percentage of students in your class who will exhibit the behaviors (e.g., at least half of the students will attend a concert or recital sometime during the semester). Usually it is better (and more realistic) to aim for teaching all your students at least some of the behaviors (e.g., each student will voluntarily complete at least five of the ten optional activities), as with the examples given above. In either case, the criterion statement should include a number; that is, be precise enough so that an outside observer could tell whether or not the objective has been reached.

When evaluating or constructing affective behavioral objectives, you might find it helpful to use the following prompts:

Condition: test situation; alternatives; free-choice; no-cue.
Action: observable behavior; approach or avoidance behavior; high probability.
Criterion: measurable words; number of behaviors, realistic criteria.

Remember the general test for a useful and clear objective. It works for affective as well as cognitive objectives.

In the previous pages you have examples of affective objectives (or parts of affective objectives) related to a variety of attitudes, such as liking someone, respecting one's classmates, and being interested in a particular subject matter. Following are some further examples of attitudes which you can use to practice constructing affective objectives of your own. Use the prompts listed above to check your objectives.

Practice Problems

1. In your social studies class, one of your affective goals is to develop in your student a positive attitude towards the equality of women in terms of basic rights and responsibilities. How could you specify this objective?

2. You want to teach your students about the skills, duties, and benefits of the career of politics (or any career, for that matter), and also develop in them a positive attitude toward the career. How would you specify the affective aspect of this goal?

3. Several of your students seem completely lacking in self-confidence. Presuming this attitude is not completely justified, write an affective objective aimed at remedying the deficit.

4. Similarly, several students downgrade themselves at every opportunity. Write an affective objective aimed at improving their self-esteem.

5. As an official of the student council of your campus, one of your main goals is to improve the attitude of students toward campus social life and extracurricular activities. How would you state this objective behaviorally?

Notes on the Practice Problems

1. Your first task is to specify the attitude in terms of behaviors that are highly probable from someone who already has the positive attitude. These might include: saying that he believes in equal rights, when asked; identifying local examples of discrimination against women; working to eliminate such instances; listening as attentively to the opinions of women as he does to those of men; using the description "dumb broad" no more frequently than the phrase "dumb stud"; choosing the topic for an essay of a speech (presuming no heavy prompts), etc. From an extensive list of such behaviors, you are able to choose a variety of options by which the students can demonstrate whether or not they have the attitude you desire, making sure that the options are free-choice and that you define how many behaviors by how many students you will accept as meeting your objective. It would probably not be sufficient to ask them to write a paragraph or a paper on how they feel about women's rights since they know very well how you feel, and they might question your ability to be completely objective. On the other hand, say you spend one hour a week in small-group discussion about a variety of topics (and your class is half male and half female); your objective might be that during the remaining weeks of the semester, the small groups will elect a female student as discussion leader at least 40 percent of the time.

2. What does a person do who has a high regard for a particular type of occupation? He reads about it, follows the activities of certain

people in that profession, talks about it, speaks highly of people in that profession, etc. If you wanted to rely strictly on verbal behavior as evidence, you might set up something like this: Given a paragraph that presents a noncommittal and purely factual account of the daily activities of a politician, the student will rewrite the paragraph, slanting it with loaded adjectives or phrases so as to create a favorable or unfavorable impression of politicians. Such an objective would be appropriate in a composition or journalism class and would presume some intermediate writing skills.

3. A person who has self-confidence is usually one who does not hesitate to accept responsibility, to begin difficult tasks, to appear relaxed in the face of challenge, and to say things that indicate he expects to succeed. Stating this objective is done similarly to those above, but in this case you must pay special attention to the feasibility of the action and the criterion, since only a fool would be self-confident in the face of a task for which he obviously had none of the required skills. To teach self-confidence, a shaping process is called for, so that the student experiences frequent success and praise while working through a series of progressively more difficult tasks.

4. Self-esteem is similar to self-confidence, except that self-esteem seems to refer more to one's verbal behavior about oneself. If he speaks highly of himself to others, we conclude that he must think highly of himself (i.e., say similar things to himself). In this case, however, the criterion must include some measure of the social appropriateness of the comments. People can have admirable self-esteem but come off sounding like conceited and naive brats. Socially acceptable expression of self-esteem must also be taught.

5. During the coming academic year, student attendance or participation will increase by at least 10 percent in half and by at least 20 percent in one-quarter of the following categories: number of student volunteers as representatives on academic committees; student attendance at plays, concerts; number of students working or contributing articles for the student paper; student membership in campus organizations; student attendance at athletic events.

3. Differentiate between cognitive and affective objectives on the basis of the kinds of behavior with which they deal.

4. Describe the three components of an affective behavioral objective. Cite several examples of objectives containing defective elements and a *corrected* version of each example.

5. Be able to identify and correct defects in a new sample of affective behavioral objectives, when you see them on a quiz.

6. Construct several original affective behavioral objectives which would contribute to your general objectives as a teacher. (Be sure your condition tests a preference and offers free options and that your action component requires several actions common to persons with the attitude.)

7. Describe one method suggested for choosing the behaviors appropriate to the desired attitude.

unit 20

Behavioral Objectives Project

This project will give you a chance to look closely at a current set of curricular materials in a subject matter area of your own choosing. This unit will also give you practice at analyzing behavioral objectives and clarifying them when necessary.

You are to complete this unit in two steps:

1. Search through a curriculum library or resource center and identify a small set of curricular materials that is appropriate to your interests, is current, and is adaptable to a behavioral objectives analysis. Even though a curriculum does not list its behavioral objectives under that caption, objectives may still be identifiable in other ways, particularly by means of the posttests attached to each small unit. Get your instructor's approval *before* proceeding to analyze the materials.

2. Your analysis and report should include the following:
   a) identify each objective in the sequence in which it is taught;
   b) rate its clarity and measurability (i.e., apply the test for a good objective);
   c) rate the degree to which the skill/knowledge of that objective is actually taught to the student or is simply expected of the student.

unit 21

Analysis of Skills

OBJECTIVES

When you complete unit 21, you should be able to:

* name and describe the components of task analysis;
* choose an original short task, analyze its component subskills, analyze the interdependencies among these subskills, and arrange them in a logical teaching order;
* define discriminative stimulus and show its function in an original example of a discrimination learning process;
* describe the nature and uses of a pretest and identify several entry behaviors for a sample instructional unit;
* specify Gagné's rule for determining the level of detail needed in a task analysis.

The analysis of teaching, like the analysis of learning, is a complex task, requiring the analysis of many components of teaching and of their interrelatedness. The act of teaching involves the tasks of specifying the objectives, subdividing these objectives into smaller discrete tasks, arranging these learning tasks into a logical dependency sequence, designing materials and procedures for teaching each of these successive subtasks, and designing methods and formats for evaluating a student's ability at each subtask level. All of these tasks must be done before a teacher can begin to interact effectively with the student. In this sense, a great deal of teaching goes on outside the classroom before the teacher and the student interact on an instructional unit.

Analyzing Terminal Skills

You have already learned how to construct clear and complete behavioral objectives. Typically, however, your objectives have been terminal objectives —that is, skills which you intend the student to have at the conclusion of a process of instruction. To bring the student from his current skill level to this terminal objective requires that he master a sequence of *intermediate* objectives, that is, a series of subskills, progressively more and more complex, many of which require or include previous subskills, and all of them required by the terminal skill.

As an example, consider this objective: The student will divide any real numbers (including decimal fractions) up to four digits with 90 percent accuracy when presented in the form: NN.N)ddd.d. Before you can begin to teach to this objective, you have to analyze the various skills involved in the total task. In the analysis of skills, or task analysis, you must identify the various intermediate skills the student must acquire, and the logical order in which he must acquire them, in order to be able to do the task specified in the objective.

Briefly, a task analysis for the above objective might be outlined as follows:

1. The first thing a student must do is adjust the decimal point, if necessary:

$$120.4 \,) \, \overline{748.31}$$

2. Then the student estimates how many times the divisor goes into a portion of the dividend and writes that number above the line and the appropriate digit.

$$1204 \,) \, \overline{7483.1}^{\,6.}$$

3. Then the student multiplies the estimated number by the divisor and enters the product below a portion of the dividend.

$$1204 \,) \, \overline{7483.1}^{\,6.}$$
$$7224$$

4. Then the student subtracts the product from part of the dividend and enters the difference below those numbers.

$$6. \atop 1204 \overline{\smash{)} 7483.1} \atop \underline{7224} \atop 259$$

5. Then the student "brings down" more digits of the dividend and repeats the process of estimating, multiplying, subtracting, etc.

$$6.2 \atop 1204 \overline{\smash{)} 7483.1} \atop \underline{7224} \atop 2591$$

Obviously, the above is only an outline and not a thorough task analysis. Rules must be specified more precisely, variations from the above example must be analyzed, and other methods for achieving the skill must be analyzed so that the most efficient and effective set of subskills can be chosen and arranged for instruction. Furthermore, this analysis presumes that the student already can discriminate numbers, subtract, multiply, etc. If these skills are not already a part of the student's entering abilities, they must also be taught.

Components of a Task Analysis

A complete task analysis identifies the list and order of specific intermediate objectives a student must acquire to move from his current skill level to the skill level identified in the terminal objective. It is a master blueprint specifying in detail the intermediate objectives and their relationships.

A complete task analysis is an analysis of:

1. the subskills that the student must have in order to acquire the more complex terminal skill;
2. the relationships and interdependencies between these subskills;
3. the most efficient order or sequence in which to teach these subskills;
4. the conditions under which each of the subskills should be performed in performing the terminal task.

1. Briefly describe what is meant by task analysis, including a paraphrase of its four components. (Specify entry, intermediate, and

terminal skills, interdependencies, sequence, performance conditions.)

Identifying Subskills

An analysis of a terminal objective must specify *all* of the component subskills. Although this is an obvious statement, it is very easy for adults who are already proficient in the terminal skill to take for granted or overlook several subskills, with the result that some students fail to reach criterion even though they can perform all of the identified subskills.

In beginning a task analysis it sometimes helps to rehearse in your imagination and in slow motion all the small steps a student must go through in performing the terminal objective. This is not difficult to do with such operations as arithmetic or with such concept discriminations as common animals. With less tangible concepts and rapidly performed skills, the rehearsal process is more difficult. A tennis pro, for example, reacts quickly with a finely coordinated and sequenced series of movements. But the good instructor can teach each of these movements separately and then in small sets before putting the complete series together. The subskills include positions of the body with respect to the net (plus such features as slight bend in knees, body weight slightly forward, feet shoulder-width apart), the backswing movement parallel to the ground with the elbow slightly bent and close to the body and the weight shifted to the right foot, and the forward swing with wrist firm, racket parallel to the ground, the racket head slightly higher than the wrist, and the weight shifting to the left foot. A slow motion analysis of such a skill helps to isolate each discrete movement and feature.

Interdependence among Subskills

A complete set of subskills usually cannot be taught in random order because some of the subskills are prerequisites to others within the set and must therefore be learned before the others. In fact some skills must be taught in a very exact order, or the student will be faced with a subtask for which he lacks prerequisites.

Take, for example, the task of long division. In order of their appearance in the actual performance, there are five major skills involved:

1. adjusting the decimal point,
2. estimating the quotient,
3. multiplying,
4. subtracting, and
5. bringing down another set of digits from the quotient.

While this is the order in which these skills are used, it is clearly *not* the order in which they are taught. Skills 1 and 5 could probably be taught at anytime since none of the other skills depends on them as prerequisites—that is, a student might be able to do 2,3, or 4 without being able to do 1 or 5. But to multiply, one must first be able to add and probably also be able to subtract. And estimating the quotient is best taught to a student who already can add, subtract, and multiply.

On the basis of interdepencies, it appears that addition and subtraction must be taught before multiplication, that estimating the quotient should follow next, and that finally the student should be taught when, under what conditions, and in what order to perform each of these skills. The skill of adjusting the decimal point could be taught anytime before the final integration skill.

In analyzing interdepencies, there are three possible relationships:

1. Skill C must be taught sometime after skill B and before the terminal skill;
2. Skill C must be taught after skill B and before skill D;
3. Skill C can be taught anytime before the terminal skill is taught.

2. Choose an original but simple task and analyze its component subskills. Then review your analysis to see if you have isolated all the important behaviors. Be sure to state each subskill in measurable terms. Study the sample task analyses at the end of this unit.

3. Analyze the interdependencies among the subskills identified in question 2. Then rearrange the subskills according to the order in which you think they should be taught. Justify each interdependency.

4. For each of the subskills identified in questions 2 and 3, determine which of the three possible relationships it has to the other component and terminal skills.

Temporal Relationships Among Subskills: Stimulus Control

A student must learn not only what do do but also when to do it. To perform long division, a student must not only be able to add, subtract, multiply, and adjust the decimal point, but he must also know the proper order in which to exercise these skills, the conditions under which he adjusts the decimal or brings down another set of digits, etc.

Knowing when and under what conditions to perform a skill is itself a skill and must be identified and taught as a distinct subskill. A student learning division must be taught that $\sqrt{}$ means $\div$. He must also be taught other cues for dividing when they are found in word problems or in less contrived "real life" situations. If he is not deliberately taught these discrimination skills, he may do well with a sheet of division problems but be mathematically illiterate outside the classroom.

Teaching this ability to discriminate the appropriate situation for the use of a skill involves bringing that response under the control of a specific preceding stimulus. This kind of preceding stimulus is called a discriminative stimulus (S^D). As you already know, discrimination refers to responding differently to differing preceding stimuli which may have many attributes in common. Each preceding stimulus is an S^D for a different response.

Teaching the temporal relationships among subskills requires maximizing the probability that a certain S^D will evoke a certain kind of response. (Notice that this statement avoids the notion of absolute causality and refers merely to the probability of evoking a response; probability, unlike causation, is measurable and usually sufficient for instructional purposes.) This can best be done using differential reinforcement. If in the presence of the letter b (the S^D) we reinforce the response "Bee" and never reinforce the response "Dee," the future probability of the response "bee" to that S^D is increased. Learning to discriminate between the doorbell and a telephone ring is differentially reinforced automatically.

Frequently the S^D for performing one subskill is the completion of the previous response. In swinging a tennis racket, for example, the pro relies on the "feel" of the previous small movement to prompt the exact features of the next small movement he makes. Or consider your knowledge of the alphabet; though you can undoubtedly whip through the alphabet quickly from A to Z, you might have trouble answering the question "What letter comes before J?" Most of us learned the alphabet as a chain, with each response depending on the previous one, so that we have no trouble answering "What letter comes after J?" When the terminal objective involves a chain of responses that always occur in a set sequence, then it is appropriate to teach the student to make each response on the basis of the previous response—i.e., with the previous response acting as an S^D for the next.

Sometimes, however, the appropriateness of a given subskill depends on the situation. In long division, for example, the student must learn that he is to adjust the decimal point only if the divisor is a decimal fraction; otherwise he is to skip that step. The S^D for this discrimination is, therefore, the presence of a decimal fraction in the divisor, and the student must be taught to discriminate this cue as a part of his being taught to perform long division. As another example, the student who is being taught to write behavioral objectives must also be taught when such a behavioral statement is appropriate and when an educational or instructional statement is sufficient. Finally, the skill of driving a car includes the skills of discriminating when to accelerate, brake, or maintain current speed at the sight of a yellow light.

Like all discriminations, these S^D's are taught by requiring differential responding in their presence or absence, and the test for these discriminations is likewise a test for differential responding.

These discriminations and generalization skills do not happen automatically; they must be taught. Of course, a person can and does learn to discriminate and generalize without deliberate teaching because nature and society do reinforce some responses differentially, though often haphazardly. But teaching, by definition, is the careful and deliberate arrangement of preceding and consequent events. Teachers often blame the student for not being able to transfer a set of subskills to other situations; the fault lies with the instruction. The ability to discriminate the situation that calls for a set of component skills is as critical a subskill as any other.

5. Define: S^D, discriminative stimulus, discrimination.

6. Construct an original example of a discrimination you have learned, identify its S^D, and describe how you learned it. (Remember to pair the intended S^D with the S^D that is already effective.)

7. Cite a stimulus control reason why many elementary students have trouble with arithmetic word problems.

Entry Behavior

Entry behavior refers to the skills a student already has mastered before your instruction begins. It is important to measure or estimate a student's entry behavior before you begin your instruction for two reasons: (1) if his entry behavior includes some or all of the skills you are about to teach him, you probably won't want him to go through the motions of "learning" them again; (2) if his entry behavior does not include some of the prerequisite skills which you think you won't have to teach, your instruction will fail unless you first teach him these prerequisites skills.

In analyzing a task, you must break the terminal objective down into smaller and smaller subskills. Of course, this subdivision could go on indefinitely; you could break down the long division objectives into minute subskills such as grasping the pencil between the fingers, lifting the hand, placing the pencil point on the paper, etc. This amount of detail might be necessary for preschool students, but probably not for eighth graders.

How far you go in breaking down the terminal objective depends on the entry behavior of the students you will be instructing. When you come to the point where each subskill is, by itself, part of the student's entry behavior, you have subdivided far enough. Gagné suggests a simple method: Each time you subdivide a task, ask yourself whether the student could do this subskill when simply requested to do so. If he could, then your analysis is sufficiently detailed; if not, or if there is doubt, then subdivide it again and repeat the question.

In analyzing the task of long division, you identify subtraction as a subskill. If your students can perform subtraction when asked to do so, then you need not go into more detail with that subskill; but if they can't, then you must further analyze the subskill of subtraction into its set of component operations. The same is true with the other component skills of division. Some of them will require further analysis (e.g., estimating the quotient), while others might already be part of the student's entry behavior (e.g., adjusting the decimal point, although you must still teach the student when to do this adjusting).

In effect, what you are doing is treating each subskill as a kind of terminal objective and analyzing it to see whether its component skills need to be taught or are already learned. In this sense, any specific skill can be considered a terminal objective (for the instruction that leads to it), an entry behavior (for instruction that presumes it and builds on it), or an intermediate objective (for instruction that both builds to it and on it). Which one it actually is depends on the specific objectives of your instruction and on your students' entry behavior.

How do you know when you have subdivided a task in sufficient detail to match the entry behavior of the students? In practice, what you do is estimate and then verify your estimate by a pretest. That is, in analyzing your total task and designing your instructional unit, you decide, on the basis of what you already know about the students, what skills they probably already have, categorizing these as entry or prerequisite behaviors. Then you categorize all the other component skills as intermediate objectives leading to your terminal objective. See figures 21-1 and 21-2 for examples.

Before beginning your instruction, you design and give a pretest which measures:

1. the skills you have categorized as entry or prerequisite skills;
2. the intermediate subskills; and
3. the terminal objective skills.

You need to test for all three categories for the reasons mentioned at the beginning of this section on entry behavior. The topics of evaluation and test construction are treated in subsequent units. At this point you should simply note that pretests, posttests, and all achievement tests depend for their usefulness and for their ease of construction on the clarity and measurability of the objectives and on the precision of the analysis of component skills.

8. What categories of skills must a pretest measure?

9. Describe two uses of a pretest.

10. How can you determine when your task analysis is sufficiently detailed?

11. Where does task analysis start? Where does it end?

12. Explain: an entry behavior is an intermediate skill is a terminal objective. Cite an original example for illustration.

13. State several probable entry behaviors for the task identified in questions 2, 3, and 4.

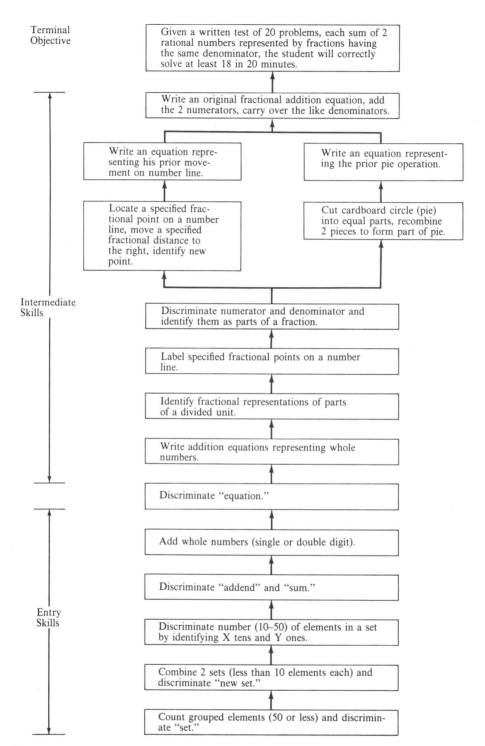

Terminal Objective

Given a written test of 20 problems, each sum of 2 rational numbers represented by fractions having the same denominator, the student will correctly solve at least 18 in 20 minutes.

Write an original fractional addition equation, add the 2 numerators, carry over the like denominators.

Write an equation representing his prior movement on number line.

Write an equation representing the prior pie operation.

Locate a specified fractional point on a number line, move a specified fractional distance to the right, identify new point.

Cut cardboard circle (pie) into equal parts, recombine 2 pieces to form part of pie.

Intermediate Skills

Discriminate numerator and denominator and identify them as parts of a fraction.

Label specified fractional points on a number line.

Identify fractional representations of parts of a divided unit.

Write addition equations representing whole numbers.

Discriminate "equation."

Add whole numbers (single or double digit).

Discriminate "addend" and "sum."

Entry Skills

Discriminate number (10–50) of elements in a set by identifying X tens and Y ones.

Combine 2 sets (less than 10 elements each) and discriminate "new set."

Count grouped elements (50 or less) and discriminate "set."

Figure 21–1

An Example of a Simple Task Analysis

232

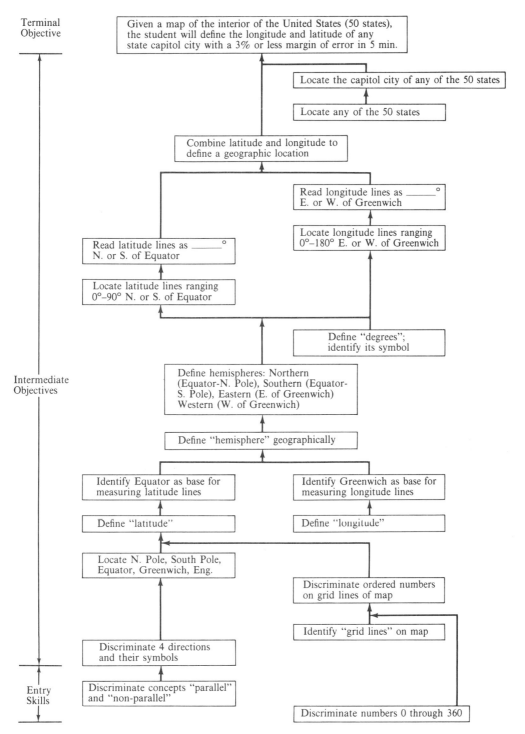

Terminal Objective

Given a map of the interior of the United States (50 states), the student will define the longitude and latitude of any state capitol city with a 3% or less margin of error in 5 min.

Locate the capitol city of any of the 50 states

Locate any of the 50 states

Combine latitude and longitude to define a geographic location

Read longitude lines as _____° E. or W. of Greenwich

Locate longitude lines ranging 0°–180° E. or W. of Greenwich

Read latitude lines as _____° N. or S. of Equator

Locate latitude lines ranging 0°–90° N. or S. of Equator

Define "degrees"; identify its symbol

Intermediate Objectives

Define hemispheres: Northern (Equator-N. Pole), Southern (Equator-S. Pole), Eastern (E. of Greenwich) Western (W. of Greenwich)

Define "hemisphere" geographically

Identify Equator as base for measuring latitude lines

Identify Greenwich as base for measuring longitude lines

Define "latitude"

Define "longitude"

Locate N. Pole, South Pole, Equator, Greenwich, Eng.

Discriminate ordered numbers on grid lines of map

Identify "grid lines" on map

Discriminate 4 directions and their symbols

Entry Skills

Discriminate concepts "parallel" and "non-parallel"

Discriminate numbers 0 through 360

Figure 21–2
A Sample Task Analysis

unit 22

Analysis of Skills: Concepts and Principles

OBJECTIVES

When you finish unit 22, you should be able to:

* give a behavioral definition of concept, essential attribute, irrelevant attribute, and principle;
* differentiate between principle and verbal chain on the basis of the discrimination required in each;
* analyze a concept and a principle and outline a method for teaching both, specifying the entry behaviors, the intermediate objectives and their interdependencies, the sequencing of subtasks, and the use of positive and negative examples and of prompts.

The last unit outlined the important features of task analysis, though the examples focused primarily on motor skills and operations. Concepts and principles also refer to skills that must be analyzed before they can be taught systematically. Task analysis of concepts requires the same general procedures; identifying the subskills, their interdependencies, and their teaching sequence, and identifying the appropriate stimulus control features.

A concept is a pattern of *discrimination responding* to a set of attributes shared by some examples and not shared by other examples. As with all discrimination responses, a person who "has a concept" responds in one way to things that have certain characteristics and in another way to things that don't have all those characteristics. This definition also implies that the person *generalizes* across other attributes—that is, his responding is not affected by the presence or absence of certain other features of the examples.

A simple example is the concept of "red." When we say a person "has the concept of red," we mean that he responds one way in the presence of something that is red (perhaps by saying "red") and another way to things that are not red. The response is under the control of the stimulus properties associated with the wavelength range we call red; when the wavelength falls outside this range, the person responds differently. The wavelength properties of red comprise the set of essential characteristics (the S^D's) in this discrimination. The person ignores other characteristics (what kind of thing it is that is red, how big it is, etc.), which is to say that he generalizes across these irrelevant attributes.

Essential Attributes

Usually the dictionary definition identifies the essential or critical attributes of a concept. An object must possess a *set* of attributes to be an example of the concept. If it lacks any one of these essential attributes, it is by definition not an example of that concept (but instead an example of another concept). In other words, an essential attribute is a stimulus characteristic that is shared by all examples of the concept.

For example, the dictionary defines a square as a parallelogram having four equal sides and four right angles. Analyzing this definition reveals that the concept square has three essential stimulus attributes:

1. four equal sides,
2. opposite sides are parallel,
3. four right angles.

The concept of square then requires that all three of these attributes have stimulus control over the response "square." The person must discriminate when all three of these S^D's are present; if any one of them is absent in an object, then he must not respond "square" in relation to that object.

As another example, the dictionary defines life as a state characterized by metabolism and growth, reproduction, and internally initiated adaptations to the environment. According to this definition, the set of attributes shared by all examples of living things includes metabolism and growth, reproduction, and adaptation. The concept then is a pattern of discriminating these three attributes together, responding to every example which has all three of these attributes as having life and responding to every example that lacks one or more of these attributes as not having life.

Any thing or event that has all the essential attributes is called an example or an instance. To distinguish an example from a nonexample, sometimes the words positive and negative are used; a positive example or positive instance is one which has all the essential characteristics, all the discriminative stimulus features called for by the concept, and a negative example or instance lacks at least one essential attribute.

Irrelevant Attributes

Irrelevent attributes are stimulus characteristics that do not (or at least should not) control the responding. They can be present in an example or be absent, and the response is the same. The person does not discriminate these attributes (at least for the purpose of responding to this particular concept), but generalizes across them and responds differentially only to the essential attributes.

The concept of square has a variety of irrelevant attributes, including size, color, texture, position (although in one position it is sometimes called a diamond). The concept of square calls for generalizing across these types of attributes.

The concept of life also has a variety of irrelevant attributes, including the attributes specific to humans, to animals, or to plants, as well as attributes of size, shape, color, environment, frequency and type of reproduction, and type of metabolism.

Complex Concepts

At first glance, it might seem that learning to generalize across the irrelevant attributes of "living" things might be more difficult than generalizing across the irrelevant attributes of "square" things. But for a student who does not "know" the concept of square (i.e., can't make the necessary discriminations and generalizations), learning these discriminations and generalizations is just as involved as his subsequent learning of the concept of life. Complexity is primarily a matter of a student's *entry* skills.

There are other ways in which a concept can be thought of as a complex. Consider, for example, *relational* concepts which require a person to discriminate essential attributes which are defined only in relation to the attributes of other negative examples. The concepts of "larger" and "sooner" require discriminating essential attributes in contrast to essential attributes of "smaller" and "later." But, like all concepts, relational concepts can be defined in terms of discriminating essential attributes and generalizing across irrelevant attributes.

Some concepts are *disjunctive,* requiring an either-or discrimination. The concept of reinforcer includes, as an essential attribute, a behavioral effect—either the effect of the behavior being strengthened or the effect of the behavior being maintained at current strength. Both effects can't occur in a given example, but one or the other must be discriminated as an essential attribute if the concept response is to be correct. Some religious denominations define membership in a disjunctive way; a person is a member of that denomination if he was so baptized in infancy or if he subsequently converted in a public ceremony.

Finally, concepts can be considered complex because of *variations* in usage and meaning. Consider the concept of "democratic." The concept sometimes requires a person to discriminate essential attributes concerning political party affiliation, at other times concerning group behavior patterns or "life-style," and at other times concerning governmental decision-making processes. The essential attributes vary somewhat in each case, so we are really dealing with several different concepts carrying the same label.

Only superficially could you consider democratic as being a single concept. While it's true that the response "democratic" may be common to all three cases, the discrimination responding can be very different in all other respects. A person could speak and work enthusiastically for democratic group behavior patterns, be uninvolved behaviorally with the Democratic Party, and work and speak against the "democratic" governmental processes in his country. Since the only way we can measure a concept (or any discrimination skill) is in terms of differential responding, we must judge that this person "has" three distinct concepts.

"Here, Have a Concept!"

The above heading is only partly facetious. The way in which you, as a teacher, think of concepts can have an important effect on your students' learning of concepts.

On the one hand, you can think of a concept as a mental construct, a mental classification system. It is clear, of course, that concepts do not exist outside the mind as things in the world. But you could think of a concept as a thing in the mind, as a set of characteristics mentally abstracted from real examples, or as a mental picture of a set of features common to many real examples.

There may be no problem in speaking this way about concepts in ordinary conversation. The problem arises when you apply this way of thinking to the teaching of concepts. How does one rearrange the mental constructs or mental classification systems of a student? How does one establish in a student's mind a mental picture of essential attributes? A teacher must try to measure what he tries to teach. But how can you find and measure an idea, mental construct, set of neural connections, or blob of gray matter in a student's mind?

On the other hand, we can define concept as a behavior pattern of discrimination *responding*. We are then dealing exclusively with observables—observable responses and observable characteristics of real objects. You have already learned how to strengthen, weaken, or shape behaviors of various types. The discrimination and generalization behaviors involved in concept learning are also behaviors and are amenable to the same behavior change procedures. The procedures associated with differential reinforcement and stimulus control are the critical factors in teaching concept discrimination and generalization.

Principle Learning

A principle is two or more concepts combined to form a rule. Principle learning, then, is learning to discriminate on the basis of several *combined* sets of essential attributes. A person who has learned a principle has learned to respond in the same way whenever examples of several concepts occur together. After the student has learned the concepts of variable and of exponent, he then can learn to respond in a new way whenever examples of these concepts occur together; he learns that "X^n" is an S^D for the response of multiplying X by itself n times.

The Premack principle is a principle which combines the essential properties of several concepts: higher probability, lower probability, contingent, and reinforcing effect. The student who learns this principle learns to respond in a certain way when examples of these concepts occur *together* in new situations. He learns to arrange a contingency relationship between any lower and any higher probability event so as to reinforce the lower probability event.

In one sense, a principle is simply a higher order concept. When a student consistently responds differently to Schnauzers than he does to any other living or nonliving things, he has learned the concept of Schnauzer. When a student responds differentially to examples of dogs (whether Schnauzer, Basset, or whatever) he has learned a higher order concept, which can be thought of as a principle in that he responds differentially whenever the object has attributes common to several subconcepts (i.e., occur together).

More often the term principle refers to a set of key discriminations and generalizations which are operationally important in a special area of study. In this sense, the Premack principle is a key rule in the analysis of behavior, and the exponent principle is a key rule in mathematics. Usually the less important discriminations and generalizations such as facts and definitions are referred to as concepts (higher or lower order, depending on the frame of reference.).

It is important, however, to distinguish between what Gagné calls verbal chaining and principle learning. In a verbal chain, the S^D for the verbal response is another word or words (e.g., memorizing a poem or reciting a definition). This stimulus word may be a previous word in the chain or a word in the question that sounds similar to the response or is a synonym for it. The danger is that this form of discrimination learning may be confused with principle learning. A student who can recite the exponential principle may not "understand what he is saying"—i.e., he may not respond appropriately when the rule should be used. Verbal S^D's are frequently essential attributes in a verbal chain response, but in principle learning, verbal S^D's are often irrelevant attributes, and the student must be taught to generalize across these characteristics and discriminate other essential attributes.

1. Construct your own paraphrased definition of:

    concept
    essential attribute
    irrelevant attribute
    principle

2. Cite, with original examples, four ways in which concepts can be considered complex.

3. Contrast the mentalistic and behavioral view of concepts in terms of instructional usefulness.

4. Differentiate between principle and verbal chain on the basis of the discrimination required.

Practice Problems

Before continuing, spend some time attempting to analyze the following concepts. "Analyze a concept" means identify all the essential attributes which the learner must discriminate and several irrelevant attributes across which the learner must generalize.

1. Human being
2. To roll
3. Round things roll
4. Dying
5. Reinforcer
6. Reinforcement
7. Concept
8. Principle

Notes on Practice Problems

1. A primate with erect posture, highly developed brain, articulate language.

   Irrelevant attributes include sex, age, color, size (within some limits), etc. The essential attribute of language is now somewhat in question since we have discovered that some animals communicate with each other, and some can be taught to construct complex sentences (in dialogue with man) and solve complex problems.

2. Straight motion on a surface, continuous and smooth rotation around the axis.

   Irrelevants include the thing that is rolling, its size, speed, direction.

3. The essential attributes of rolling (as above) plus the essential attributes of roundness (smoothness over entire surface area, circular, from all points on the surface). Notice in this case that both concepts must be learned well before the principle can be learned.

4. Refer to the example of "living" in the text.

5. This and the following concepts and principles you should be able to analyze from the text itself.

Teaching Concept and Principle Skills

A student has learned a concept or principle when his behavior is under the control of critical attributes which define the concept of principle. Presumably the appropriate response is already a part of the student's skills (or can easily be taught). The critical task in concept learning is to bring that response under the control of the appropriate set of S^D's.

In teaching a concept or principle, two things must be taught:

1. discriminating *all* of the essential attributes or characteristics, whenever they occur together in an example;
2. generalizing across *any* irrelevant attribute or characteristic which might be present in an example.

Generally, you will be most effective if you teach these skills in the above order.

Discrimination of Essential Attributes

The first stage of concept (or principle) learning is learning to discriminate the essential attributes. This can best be done in the following ways:

1. Make the essential characteristics very prominent and obvious in the examples you give. Point them out, highlight them one by one, exaggerate them if necessary.
2. At the same time, eliminate from your examples all the irrelevant features you can. If you must include some irrelevant attributes, don't let them change from example to example.
3. Use many examples that are highly familiar to the student. If necessary, introduce examples of each essential attribute singly, before giving examples of the set of essential attributes.
4. Contrast these positive examples with negative examples; at first make the negative examples widely different from the positive examples (i.e., having few if any of the essential attributes).
5. Require the student to make the appropriate response(s) frequently (naming, identifying characteristics, defining, applying, etc.)

For example, if you are teaching a student to discriminate the letter *d* whenever he sees it, it might be best to start out by exaggerating the stem and the circle, by using very simple print (as opposed to script, for example, which introduces irrelevant features), by pointing out how part of the letter looks like a ball or circle (something familiar) and by contrasting this letter with other letters (at first letters like *x* or *m,* then with letters that share some common attributes, like *b* or a *t*). The contrasting might take the form of a matching-to-sample exercise of this variety:

"This is the letter b:"   b

"Which of these is a b?"   b   d   +

Since complexity is primarily a function of the entry behaviors of the students, with some students and some concepts you will not need to use all of the above methods. You may simply have to define the concept, briefly describe the essential attributes, perhaps give several examples, and the students may then be able to discriminate new examples of the concept or new uses of the principle. In such cases it is best not to exaggerate the essential attributes or eliminate the irrelevant attributes because whenever you do this, you must eventually fade the highlights and introduce the irrelevant attributes in order to teach the discriminations as they must occur in real life.

But if the concept and the current skills of the students call for careful and deliberate instruction, then the above methods are useful and often necessary if *all* students are to learn the discrimination.

Generalization across Irrelevant Attributes

The second stage of concept (or principle) learning is learning to generalize across any irrelevant characteristic that might occur in an example. A student must learn not only to discriminate the essential features of a positive example but also to do this even when there are many other attributes present which could tend to confuse him. First you teach him to discriminate in the presence of as few distractors as possible, and then you begin to introduce the distractors:

1. Introduce and/or begin to vary the irrelevant attributes in the examples. At first introduce one irrelevant attribute at a time, then several. By the end of the instruction, many irrelevant attributes should have been exemplified.
2. Then begin to fade the highlighting and exaggeration in your examples, so that the essential attributes appear exactly as they do in real examples.
3. During this stage, contrast the positive examples with negative examples, being sure that at least some of the time both positive and negative examples have the same irrelevant attributes. Otherwise, the student might learn to discriminate on the basis of an irrelevant attribute.

For example, in teaching the concept of the letter *b,* you would begin to introduce some irrelevant attributes (such as script or slant of the letter, its position on a page or in a word), reduce the exaggerated stem and circle and drop most of your verbal prompts, and then require the student to identify the letter when it is juxtaposed with very similar negative examples having the same irrelevant attributes. For example, "find all the b's in this list:"

t b double b d d boy dog

In both stages, when you begin to introduce positive and negative examples, change only one attribute at a time in switching from one example to the next. This procedure emphasizes the attribute and helps the student learn from the series of examples.

Special Cases and Special Methods

If the concept you are teaching has more than one essential attribute and the student's entry behavior is limited, then highlight one essential attribute at a time, beginning with the one that eliminates the greatest number of incorrect responses. For example, in the concept of animal the characteristic of life eliminates all inanimate objects and should be taught first.

If the concept you are teaching has an essential attribute with a *range* (for example, the color red ranges from pink to burgundy), then teach this range by presenting a series of positive examples in which nothing changes but the range of this essential attribute.

You must include *negative* examples in your instruction if the student is to learn the limits of the essential attributes he is to discriminate. Without negative examples, the student may learn to discriminate on the basis of attributes that are shared by higher order concepts (e.g., though a student is able to identify examples of democratic government, he may only be discriminating forms of government in general).

5. Choose an original concept or principle and outline how it could be taught most effectively. Include illustrations of the kinds of examples (positive and negative) and prompts you might use and the kinds of responses you would require. (Be sure to identify the essential and some irrelevant attributes.)

6. How do you teach discrimination of an attribute that has a range? Illustrate with an original example.

7. In teaching a student to discriminate the small letter *c,* why must you use letters like *e* and *o* as negative examples?

8. Be able to analyze a concept which you have been taught in a previous unit. (Be sure to specify the essential and some irrelevant attributes.)

Evaluating Concept or Principle Learning

The crucial test for the understanding of a concept is very simple: ask the student to identify *new examples* of the concept. Since all examples, whether or not they were used in the instruction, contain all the essential attributes, "new" here means a different set of irrelevant characteristics in positive examples contrasted with new negative examples.

If, after teaching the letter *b,* you ask the student to pick out the letter *b* from an assortment of letters including *b,* and he does so, has he learned the concept? Perhaps, but he may have learned to discriminate only the presence of a tall stem and your list did not include a letter *d.* In evaluating the learning of a concept, you must arrange the test so that you can tell if the student has learned to discriminate *all* or only some of the essential attributes and if he has learned to generalize across any or only some of the irrelevant attributes.

You can, of course, test mastery of a concept or a principle by asking the student to repeat what you have taught him. But if your test items use words and examples that are identical or very similar to those used in the instruction, the student may respond correctly only on the basis of verbal chain learning. Test items of this variety should use substantially *different* words and examples.

The measure of a concept or principle is a test which requires the student to use his learning in new situations. In other words, the best test for a concept or principle, as with any discrimination task, is the same as the definition: does the student consistently respond differently to new positive and negative examples?[1]

9. What's the best test for a concept or principle?
    What two skills must you measure?

---

[1] For research on this approach to the analysis and evaluation of concept and principle learning, see: R. Anderson, "Learning Principles from Text," *Journal of Educational Psychology* 64(1973): 26–30; and R. Anderson and R. Kulhany, "Learning Concepts from Definitions," *American Educational Research Journal* 42(1972): 145–70.

Task Analysis Project

OBJECTIVES

To give you experience and training in developing a detailed analysis of:
a task in terms of:

* defining a series of skills in behavioral terms
* specifying criteria and conditions for mastery of the skills
* identifying a series of skills from entry behaviors to the terminal objectives
* defining the learning interdependencies between the skills.

In this unit, you will apply what you have learned about the procedure of task analysis to a small instructional unit. This will involve the specifying of a series of behaviors or skills and the arrangement of these skills as to entry behaviors, intermediate behaviors, and the terminal behavior along with specifying the learning interdependencies between these skills.

Choosing a Task

The task you choose to analyze should be small and relatively simple. It is to your advantage to choose a task in your field of specialization, for ease in identifying the intermediate skills and the interdependencies between these skills. A small enough task is one that would involve one to two hours of instruction for the mastery of the task. When you have determined the task, you should define your terminal objective—defining the behavior, criteria, and condition for the terminal objective to be mastered.

Specifying the Entry Behaviors

Once you have determined your terminal objective, you are ready to define your entry behaviors for the task. These entry behaviors should be stated in terms of instructional objectives. The behaviors defined should be in *behavioral* terms—not in terms of demonstrating understanding of the topic or in terms of knowledge of the subject matter.

Defining the Intermediate Skills

The intermediate skills should include all skills or behaviors that must be mastered prior to meeting the terminal objective. Look at your terminal objective and the entry behaviors and determine the skills that must be taught to reach the terminal objective. Once you have identified them, look at the series of behaviors you have defined and again think through the task from the point of view of a student who has the defined entry behaviors. It is easy to overlook a skill that must be taught to reach the terminal objective. Be careful! **For** example, the ability of a student to circle or underline or match some **terms** does *not* insure he can generate original examples of the terms.

Defining the Learning Interdependencies

When you have identified the various intermediate skills, you then are ready to identify the learning interdependencies. The learning interdependencies are *not* necessarily the same thing as the instructional sequence or the performance sequence. The learning interdependencies involve the identification of what skills *must be taught* prior to other skills. In many task analyses, there are a number of intermediate skills that can be taught at any time as long as they are taught *prior* to the terminal objective. An analysis of the interdependencies will show the relationship between these skills. A completed analysis of the interdependencies would look similar to those found in the chapter on task analysis (unit 21).[1]

---

[1] For a similar approach to Task Analysis and a detailed example, see: L. Resnik, M. Wang, and J. Kaplan, "Task Analysis in Curriculum Design: A Hierarchically Sequenced Introductory Mathematics Curriculum," *Journal of Applied Behavior Analysis,* 6 (1973): 679–710.

Approved_____

Date_____

Component One   *Task Analysis Project*

1. What is the task you are going to analyze?

2. What is the makeup of the student population you would teach the task to? Identify the grade level, age, possible background of the students.

3. Specify the terminal objective-behavior, criteria, and conditions for mastery.

4. What are the entry behaviors for this task?

Approved_____
Date _____

Component Two   *Task Analysis Project*

1. What are the intermediate skills? Specify the behaviors, criteria, and conditions of mastery for each skill.

2. What are the interdependencies between the intermediate skills?

3. Diagram your task analysis using the flowchart format as found in unit 21—Task Analysis.

unit 24

Theories of Instruction: Piaget, Bruner, Gagné, Bloom

OBJECTIVES

When you complete this unit, you should be able to:

* name and describe the developmental stages proposed by Piaget and Bruner;
* name and describe, with original examples, each of the levels of Gagné's hierarchy and Bloom's Cognitive, Psychomotor, and Affective domains;
* compare and contrast the theories of Piaget, Bruner, and Gagné relative to readiness, developmental and learning stages, and optimal method of instruction;
* contrast the theories of Bruner and Bloom regarding aptitude.

In this unit you will learn to differentiate several current theories of instruction on the bases of their proponents and basic propositions. You will be introduced to the basic characteristics of each theory and how these characteristics contrast with those of other current theories. This will serve as background for other units and future courses in which you will learn specific methods appropriate to the various theories.

A theory is a systematic integration and interpretation of a set of data and/or subjective observations relating to a certain area of knowledge. It attempts to summarize and crystalize this body of information and insight into a few simple and short statements which adequately cover all the facts and emphasize those considered most important. A theory should also be testable so that its validity can be thoroughly investigated. A theory's usefulness is, in the end, determined on the basis of how well it helps us explain why things happen the way they do, predicts what will happen in given circumstances, and controls the occurrence of related events.

Theories are not always testable nor noticeably useful. Specifically with regard to learning and instruction, students in the classroom are usually not touched in any clear way by the variety of educationally related theories that come and go. Some theories, however, do lead to changes in curriculum, teaching methods, administrative procedures, environmental arrangements, and so on and thus do affect the classroom experiences of students—sometimes resulting in better learning, sometimes in poorer learning, and sometimes making no learning difference whatsoever.

The four theories described in this unit have affected the instructional practices of many schools, and most educators would agree that each has made some worthwhile contributions to the practice of teaching and to the understanding of the teaching-learning process.

Piaget

Jean Piaget (born 1896) is a Swiss develomental psychologist who continues to have considerable influence on the psychology of instruction. Piaget sees the child as a developing organism passing through biologically determined *cognitive stages*. These stages are more or less age-related, though the rate of progress through them can vary somewhat dependent on the culture and environment. Progress through these states is continuous, but each stage is describable by the kind of *logical structures* a child uses in each.

In the *sensorimotor* stage (birth to about 18 months), the child learns solely through the senses and through sensory manipulations of objects. Objects are known only sensually, not by thought, and this sensual experience forms the basis for later cognitive development.

In the *preoperational* stage (up to about 7–8 years) the child begins to use symbols to represent things and events, but he still does not think symbolically. He tends to discriminate things on the basis of a single attribute, many "apparent" contradictions are not apparent to him, and he solves problems by trial-and-error manipulation of things, rather than through cognitive manipulation.

In the third stage, that of *concrete operations* (from about 7 years to about 11–12 years), "logical thought" begins to develop; that is, the child begins to differentiate groups of things and events on the basis of common characteristics. It is then that the child comes to learn such basic concepts as conservation of mass, weight, and number, serial organization of things, and reversibility in thought and action (e.g., subtraction as the reverse operation of addition).

In the final *formal operations* stage, the child is able to manipulate symbols and deal with ideas without direct contact with physical things (i.e., he can think abstractly). He can hypothesize what will happen in certain situations (as opposed to a trial-and-error approach). He can also combine things in all the ways possible, on the basis of different common characteristics, and he can combine propositions on the basis of logical consistency.

Piaget's theory proposes that a child progresses through these four stages in a sequence of successive disequilibria followed by adaptations leading to a new state of equilibrium. Each state of cognitive imbalance can be caused either by a biological change as maturation progresses or by input from the environment that conflicts with past experience. The child resolves the disequilibrium by modifying his present cognitive structure.

To tell if a child is ready to be taught something, you must not only analyze the logical structure of the child whom you will teach but also the logical structure of the concept or principle you want to teach. If the child is already operating at the cognitive level consonant with the structure of the new concept, then you can teach it to him. If the dissonance between the two structures is substantial, then you must wait for further maturation. While Piaget admits the theoretical possibility of teaching a child to move from one stage to another, he favors waiting for the more natural development to occur.

Bruner

Jerome Bruner (born in 1915 in New York) proposes a learning-by-discovery theory that combines an interpretation of Piaget's developmental stages theory with the Socratic idea that learning is primarily a matter of reorganizing what you already know.

Bruner theorizes a three-stage developmental process through which a child progresses cognitively. Each stage identifies the way in which the child represents real things to himself.

In the *enactive stage,* a thing is real only when the child is directly interacting with it. This stage is similar to Piaget's sensorimotor stage. At first, a thing is real to the child only when he is actually manipulating it; gradually the thing begins to have reality to him when it is seen or heard from a distance; eventually the thing is recognized as existing even when it is not in the child's presence. The thing takes on an autonomy that is not dependent on personal interaction; it can now be pictured or thought of without action.

And this represents the second stage, the *iconic stage* (from the Greek word *icon,* meaning image) in which the child imagines, mentally visualizes, or remembers the visual or auditory features of a thing. Though in the iconic stage the child deals with images in the sense of recognizing and remembering them, he does not actually manipulate them until the third stage.

In the third stage, the *symbolic stage,* the child does manipulate and transform images into symbols. Where images were more or less exact representations of the things, symbols are arbitrary and often remote from the nature of the thing. Language, for example, involves symbolic representation and is far more versatile than are images; with language the child can begin to test and eliminate alternatives and make deductive conclusions without being limited by the availability or visibility of things. He can now use symbols both to deduce conclusions and to induce principles—each in resulting symbolic form.

Since, according to Bruner's theory, this is the way a student develops his cognitive ability, it follows that instruction should be tailored to the stage that the student is currently in. Heavy reliance on language may be appropriate when instructing a student who is in the symbolic stage, but the teacher must use a variety of visual and auditory illustrations (such as pictures, color, movement, and sound recordings) in teaching a student who is in the iconic stage.

In this sense, aptitude becomes primarily a question of the match between the student's cognitive stage and the instruction's mode. The student must be able to handle the kind of vehicles (e.g., images or symbols) in which the instruction comes, and the teacher must be able to present instruction in a form that is appropriate to the student's current stage.

Bruner also argues that instruction should not be a presentation of facts and principles for the student's memorization and analysis, but a presentation of a variety of things and events which the child can manipulate (actually and symbolically), put together and take apart, rearrange, until in the process he intuitively discovers a new, more generalizable arrangement (a concept or principle). "We teach a subject not to produce little living libraries on the subject, but rather to get a student to think mathematically for himself, to consider matters as an historian does, to take part in the process of knowledge getting. Knowing is a process, not a product."[1]

Bruner believes that in each area of knowledge there are a few fundamental ideas around which everything else in the area is structured (e.g., the commutative, associative, and distributive laws of mathematics). These fundamental ideas or structures of discipline are essentially simple. They can be made complex, of course, if we use symbolism for which the student is not ready, but these fundamental ideas can also be manipulated and presented via visual representations. In this sense, "any subject can be taught effectively in some intellectually honest form to any child at any stage of development."[2]

---

[1] Jerome S. Bruner, *Toward a Theory of Instruction* (Cambridge: Harvard University Press, 1966), p. 72.

[2] Jerome S. Bruner, "Readiness for Learning," in *The Process of Education* (Cambridge: Harvard University Press, 1960).

In manipulating things, the child first discovers incongruities that conflict with intuitive regularities he has already come to understand; that is, the child cannot match what he is doing with his own mental model of things. In reconciling these irregularities, what the child discovers is not something about the world, but a different and better reorganization of ideas he already knew.

Thus Bruner theorizes that good instruction focuses on a series of incongruities presented to the student. As soon as a child is confident of his mastery of a concept or principle, he should be "torpedoed" by an example which obviously contradicts the principle, forcing him to resolve this disequilibrium by reorganizing his understanding—a new discovery. Just as Socrates was a "torpedo fish" to his students, forcing them to modify and refine their understanding in the face of self-contradiction, just as change in scientific theory is considered to be a dialectic process, so each student's learning is a disequilibrium-to-equilibrium process of discovering a new cognitive state.

1. Give an example of a theory related to education (other than those discussed in the unit) and show how it meets the criteria for a theory.

2. Name and describe the developmental stages proposed by Piaget and by Bruner.

Gagné

Robert Gagné is a psychologist and educator whose influence on instructional practice is impressive. In contrast to Piaget and Bruner, however, Gagné's theory focuses on task analysis rather than developmental analysis. To him the critical first question is: What is it you want the student to be able to do? The next question is: What does the student have to be able to do in order to do this? A succession of such questions leads to a pyramid of subskills, many of them prerequisites to other subskills which in turn are prerequisites to the terminal objective.

Figure 22–1 outlines the basic stages of learning Gagné has identified, from the most simple to the most complex.

As an example of Gagné's classification hierarchy, consider the skill of finding the weight of an object when no scale is available. The initial levels of prerequisites for solving this problem involve signal and motor responses, of course, and also verbal skills (remember that "thinking" involves, and perhaps

Signal Learning:	Giving a specific response to a specific stimulus event; e.g., reaching out at the sight of food, or attending when your name is called.
Motor Chaining:	Giving chains of (stimulus-)responses; e.g., walking which involves a series of leg, arm, and trunk responses (including balancing reactions) to changing stimulus events (many of which are kinesthetic or "feel" feedback events).
Verbal Learning:	Giving a verbal labeling response to a specific stimulus or thing; notice that this requires basic motor skills of seeing, hearing, vocalizing, etc.; e.g., saying "duh" when shown the letter d.
Verbal Chaining:	Forming chains of words into a phrase, sentence, or series of sentences; e.g., "every cell has a nucleus containing chromosomes, which . . ."
Multiple Discrimination:	Responding differently to various stimuli which have some things in common but also some physical differences: note that this skill requires both motor and verbal chaining skills; e.g., naming the letters d, p, b, g, h; identifying the different animals in the lion house at the zoo.
Concept Learning:	Classifying different stimuli which all have some characteristics in common; generalizing; e.g., grouping oak, pine, elm into one category labeled "tree"; e.g., identifying changes in motor behavior and in verbal behavior as examples of "learning." (Notice that the separate discriminations must first be learned before they can be classified on the basis of common properties.)
Principle Learning:	Combining two concepts to form a rule and using this rule in new situations involving instances of these two concepts; responding to instances of 2 concepts whenever they occur together, by recognizing that "these can always be put together in such and such a way"; e.g., variable and exponent (X^2) form the rule "multiply X by itself N times"; e.g., the concepts of relative probability of a behavior and the concept of reinforcement form the Premack principle.
Problem Solving:	Combining two or more rules (principles) into a higher order rule and applying this new rule to solve a new problem involving the original lower order rules; e.g., combining a rule for multiplication (add X to itself Y times) with the rules for exponents (multiply X by itself N times) to get the higher order rule for multiplying numbers with exponents (add the N's, as in X^2 times $X^3 = X^5$).

Figure 22–1

Stages of Learning in Gagné's Hierarchy

is, talking to oneself). Building on these skills, we find that the terminal skill also requires the ability to discriminate the degree of heaviness of different objects and the ability to discriminate the need to differentiate some objects by weight (multiple discrimination). Next, the student must be able to classify things by weight (concept learning) and to use the rules regarding how scales function and regarding gravity and equalization of weights when balanced equidistant from a fulcrum (principle formation). Finally the student must be able to combine these rules into a higher order rule to determine the unknown weight without a scale. As an alternative route, the student must have learned the use of the rule "when you don't know, ask Joe"—or Teacher—a rule which many children and adults have learned too well.

While Gagné agrees with Bruner that, in the long run, strategy or process objectives should receive more emphasis than information objectives, Gagné sees these process objectives as intellectual skills that are to a great extent specific to particular areas of knowledge and are dependent on a mass of subordinate facts and skills. Gagné has said:

> If it is a mathematical problem the individual is engaged in solving, he may have acquired a strategy of applying relevant subordinate rules in a certain order—but he must also have available the mathematical rules themselves. . . . Knowing strategies, then, is not all that is required for thinking; it is not even a substantial part of what is needed. To be an effective problem-solver, the individual must somehow have acquired masses of organized intellectual skills.[3]

For Gagné, readiness is essentially a function of the presence or absence of *prerequisite* learning. Gagné is not concerned with genetic developmental processes, except in their extreme cases. If a five-year-old child has trouble grasping the concept of conservation of liquid volume, it is simply because he has not had the necessary prior learning experiences. Teach him the prerequisite skills, and he will be able to conserve.

In contrast to Bruner, Gagné's theory views instruction as a smoothly guided climb through a hierarchy of learning tasks, from motor and verbal skills, through concepts, principles, and problem solving, provided the hierarchy is carefully constructed beforehand.

3. Describe and give an original example (in the form of an instructional objective) of each of Gagné's levels.

---

[3] R. Gagné, *Condition of Learning,* 2d ed. (New York: Holt, Rinehart, and Winston, Inc., 1970).

4. Choose an original problem-solving skill in a specific area and show how this skill involves prerequisite learning at each of the other levels in Gagné's heirarchy. Be able to arrange a scrambled list of Gagné's levels into their proper sequence.

Bloom

Benjamin Bloom and his associates,[4] adopting the general features of Gagné's theory of instruction, have devised a different learning hierarchy, one that is perhaps less precise but including an affective domain. Bloom's taxonomy arranges intellectual behavior into a hierarchy of six categories, each progressively more complex and therefore dependent on the preceding category as its prerequisite. See p. 259 for an illustration of Bloom's taxonomy.

5. Describe and give an original example (in the form of an instructional objective) of each of Bloom's levels of cognitive learning, when given the name of the level. Be able to arrange a scrambled list of Bloom's levels into their proper sequence.

6. Describe each level of Bloom's Psychomotor and Affective domains, when given the name of the level. Be able to arrange a scrambled list of these levels into their proper sequence.

These classifications are not airtight final answers to the problem of classifying and sequencing learning, but they can be helpful to instruction in several ways. They guide educators in the process of sequencing objectives in terms of prerequisities. They prompt teachers to ask whether they are teaching all the levels of learning they desire. And they encourage all of us to be more precise and careful in our terminology and our specifications for instruction.

In addition to his classification schemes, Bloom adds an important consideration to the current theories of instruction. Adopting an earlier proposition

---

[4] Benjamin Bloom, *Taxonomy of Educational Objectives* (New York: David McKay Co., Inc., 1956).

Cognitive Domain

Knowledge: remembering and relating facts, definitions, methods, processes, structures, categories, and settings.

Comprehension: paraphrasing, summarizing, predicting, inferring, putting facts together in a new way to form a concept or rule.

Application: using concepts or abstractions in concrete situations, without the need for detailed directions.

Analysis: breaking down concepts or rules into their component parts, showing how they are related and arranged, showing which parts are relevant and which are irrelevant.

Synthesis: putting the parts of concept or rules together so as to form a pattern or structure not clearly there before, with originality.

Evaluation: judging the accuracy or value of something for a given purpose, using personally defined criteria for this evaluation.

Affective Domain

Attending: being aware, willing to receive and to look for certain features of what is being presented.

Responding: showing some degree of interest by complying with response instructions and perhaps even showing some satisfaction in responding.

Valuing: tentatively or firmly demonstrating (usually verbally) a commitment to a point of view.

Organizing: arranging several values into a system, with some values dominant over others in conflicting situations.

Being Characterized by a Value: the person is so controlled by these values in a variety of situations that they constitute a total philosophy, and the person is described in terms of this.

Psychomotor Domain

Gross Body Movements: moving limbs separately or with other body parts.

Finely Coordinated Movements: hand-eye coordination (e.g., speed typing), eye-ear-hand coordination (piano tuning), eye-ear-hand-foot coordination (driving a car), etc.

Non-Verbal Communication: facial expressions, gestures, body movements that convey a message (as in dance, theatre)

Speech: all forms of verbal labeling, chaining, and communication.

made by John Carroll[5] that aptitude is the amount of time required by the learner to attain mastery of a learning task, Bloom[6] suggests that mastery of any cognitive skill is theoretically possible for any student, providing only that we know how to arrange the instruction. In this view, aptitude is not a matter of a student's genetically based intelligence or of the natural unfolding of developmental processes, but rather aptitude is simply a measure of the *rate* at which a student can master an objective. Since this rate is primarily determined by the extent to which the student has mastered *prerequisites* to that skill,[7] a student's readiness (entry behavior) and his aptitude tend to coincide. To put it another way, a student's aptitude does not determine whether or how much a student can learn but only how long it will take him to master it.

7. Compare and contrast (i.e., cite one similar or contrasting characteristic) the theories of Piaget, Bruner, and Gagné relative to each of the following aspects of their theories;

a) readiness
b) developmental and learning stages
c) optimal method of instruction

8. Cite one point of contrast in the theories of Bruner and Bloom regarding "aptitude."

[5] John Carroll, "A Model of School Learning," *Teaching College Record* 64(1963): 723–33.
[6] Benjamin Bloom, *Handbook on Summative and Formative Evaluation of Student Learning* (New York: McGraw-Hill, Inc., 1971), pp. 43–56.
[7] Benjamin Bloom, "The Acquisition of Knowledge," *Psychological Review* 69(1962): 355–65.

unit 25

Piaget on Learning and Instruction

OBJECTIVES

When you complete this unit, you should be able to:

* define and sequence the developmental stages proposed by Piaget;
* cite several implications of Piaget's studies for teachers.

This article gives you a more detailed explanation of Piaget's developmental stages, describes some research support for the theory, and suggests some implications for instructional application.

JEAN PIAGET AND THE TEACHER*

R. D. Kitchen

INTRODUCTION

For the past forty years Jean Piaget, a Swiss psychologist, has carried out numerous experimental studies into the processes of children's intellectual

* Reprinted from *The Forum of Education,* Vol. 28, No. 1 (March 1969), by permission of the author and publisher.

development. His published works range over the language and thought of children,[1] their ability to reason and form judgments about their physical world,[2] their conception of number[3] and reality,[4] and other mental operations. All these studies provide mutually supporting evidence for his belief that intellectual growth[5, 6] stems from an individual's active interaction with his environment. Unlike many of his contemporaries, who have seen intelligence as a fairly fixed and rather undefinable quantity, Piaget elaborates upon a number of major stages in intellectual growth; the sensori-motor period, preoperational and intuitive thought, and concrete and formal operations in thinking.

His original and stimulating work and the supporting results of further studies are having a considerable effect on curricula content and teaching methods, particularly in mathematics. It is being increasingly recognized that children, especially at the primary stage, need a variety of experiences with tangible and visible objects to help them build up the essential basic concepts for an understanding of their environment. This kind of practical and active experience appears necessary as a basis for the development of more difficult and abstract modes of thinking at the adolescent and adult stages.[7]

Intellectual Growth

According to Piaget, the starting point of a child's intellectual development is not sensory perception or anything pressed upon him from outside, but is an internal and continuous growth, stemming from his own actions. In the most literal and physical sense of the term, these actions govern his life from the very beginning. It is through his own activities that he gains new and ever widening experiences of his surroundings. Each child takes a controlling hand in procuring and organizing his contact with the outside world. A baby in a cot, for example, turns his head, moves his eyes and explores with them. He grips with his hands, lets go, pushes and gains knowledge of the objects around him. Through constant repetition of these same actions, he builds up internally mental structures of his environment. In fact, it is his actions which fashion and shape his viewpoint, support it, and provide him with the essential key to his understanding.

[1] Piaget, J.: *The Language and Thought of the Child.* London: Routledge and Kegan Paul, 1926.

[2] Piaget, J.: *Judgment and Reasoning in the Child.* London: Routledge and Kegan Paul, 1928.

[3] Piaget, J.: *The Child's Conception of Number.* London: Routledge and Kegan Paul, 1952.

[4] Piaget, J.: *The Construction of Reality in the Child.* London: Routledge and Kegan Paul, 1954.

[5] Piaget, J.: *The Psychology of Intelligence.* London: Routledge and Kegan Paul, 1950.

[6] Piaget, J.: *The Origins of Intelligence in Children.* London: Routledge and Kegan Paul, 1952.

[7] Piaget, J.: *Les Mécanismes Perceptifs.* Paris: Universitaires de Paris, 1961.

As the baby grows, he becomes involved in more and more complex procedures, partly to fit himself into this world, and party to fit it to himself. It is
an adaptive process whereby he "assimilates," or takes in mentally his surroundings, like an organism assimilating food. He also fits himself to his
environment. That is, he "accommodates" himself to the objects and people
outside himself. He has to learn, for example, that some things are hard, others
soft; some small, others big; and each needs to be handled in a particular way.
These distinguishing features he accepts and acknowledges as he adapts himself to the nature of his surroundings.

These patterns and processes of assimilation and accommodation are, for
Piaget, chief factors in intellectual growth, and both functions are present in
every intellectual act. They both lead towards a "state of equilibrium" in the
human being. That is, in simplest terms, each individual strives to arrive at a
meaningful and realistic understanding of his environment. This is attained
when a balance, or state of equilibrium, prevails between assimilation and
accommodation.

Experiments with young babies led Piaget to state that, in the earliest
months, they have no awareness of the world outside themselves. A young
baby has sensations and is capable of making movements, but has no knowledge of the objects or things that surround him. He has no awareness of their
existence as something permanent outside of himself. In the earliest months,
a baby reacts to objects presented to him as a rattle, doll, or feeding bottle, but
if these same objects are placed out of sight, he gives no indication of being
aware of their existence and makes no attempts to search for them.

At this time, however, the constant appearance of the same object gives a
baby opportunity and experience in acquiring movements of touch, feeling and
seeing. These repeated actions with the same objects allow him to build up an
awareness of them. The process has to continue for many months, for it is not
until about the age of two years that a child appears capable of accepting the
existence of an object and looks for it if out of sight. Piaget maintains that
children build up an internal structure of objects in gradual sequential stages
over these first two years. Perhaps the playful child who throws an object from
his pram for others to pick up, and return to him, is confirming his recent
achievement. He has come to realize that objects have a permanence, identity
and existence of their own.

Following upon the sensori-motor stage of the first two years, a young child
gradually becomes able to identify different objects and separates them to some
extent from each other. He begins to place objects into groups, as apple, pear,
and orange under "fruit," but he has not yet the means of grouping objects
into sub-groups. Each of his judgments at this stage, the preoperational, is
isolated and self-sufficient. For example, if some wooden beads which may be
brown in colour with a few white beads added are given to a child, he may

judge that there are more brown beads than wooden beads. He finds it impossible at this period to reason about the whole (in this instance, wooden beads) and its parts (the two colours) at the same time.

With increasing age and experience; through looking, handling, manipulating; through striving to walk, talk and through the mastery of every kind of new activity, a child enlarges and organizes internally his view of the world. His actions become progressively internalized through learning of language and his expanding experience in play till they culminate in a more organized scheme of mental operations. A child builds up within him a kind of working model of his surroundings to which he refers in his thinking. This structure remains basically the same, but he enriches it and enlarges upon it. He draws upon it in his thinking and behaviour, and relies upon it when he has to think out a course of action. It is his internal model of the real world.

PRIMARY SCHOOL AGE

A young child of about school age continues incessantly expanding, enriching, organizing and re-organizing this inward model of his surroundings. He develops knowledge by experimenting, through combining questions with listening and talking. He extends his world by being able to walk further, manipulate paper, cloth and other materials. He is beginning to extend his activities through more contact with children of his own age; with them he explores. He is constantly repeating actions and gaining greater confidence in his physical and mental abilities. Yes, most of his thoughts and ideas tend to be vague and unstable. His thinking depends upon present activities, upon the "here and now" situation, and he is lost if he moves away from the visible and tangible objects before him. According to Piaget, a child's mind at this period of growth is in a stage of flux; nothing is clear or stays put. The judgments of most five year old children are uncertain, fragmentary and lack clear settled notions. Their thoughts are "intuitive." If, for example, a child at this stage is presented with two balls of plasticine made up of equal amounts he will admit they are equal. But if one of them is drawn out to sausage shape, he will probably say that the sausage shape has more plasticine because it is longer or thinner.

It is a period of half-truths, for he is able to count and give an impression of being number-wise, but he most likely cannot match two groups of objects, arrange members of a class in order of size, judge two amounts of beads in a jar as equal, even after counting them one by one into the jar. In other words, a child of around five years old, may have learnt [sic] to count correctly ten bricks or other objects when placed before him. But, if these same objects are piled up together, or re-arranged in a more complex pattern of say four together, another four, then two, he will not always give the correct total answer of ten objects. Piaget[3] has shown repeatedly that "there is no connection between the acquired ability to count and the actual operations of which the child is capable." That a child can count is no sure sign that he understands the principles of number essential to a fundamental knowledge of mathematics.

To count intelligently, a child must first understand the one-to-one correspondence between one object and another object; to understand the oneness of one, and its relationship to another object. It is obvious that until children do fully understand the relationship of objects to each other, calculations on a blackboard or on paper with the symbols "4" plus "4" plus "2," or any other combination have only very limited meaning. An understanding of the underlying principles in mathematics cannot be implanted by rote-learning into a individual child, like an imprint upon a plastic record. Children need time and opportunity to compare and contrast objects of different size and shape. They have to learn by their own actions, through manipulations and seeing for themselves, the meaning of "much," "less," "less than," "more than," "equal to," and other basic mathematical notions.

It is during the primary stage that a child's actions on the environment becomes more and more internalized, resulting in an ability to classify objects into size, shape, and work with numbers. His mental system of operations (internalized actions) begins to take on a simple logical basis that gives order to his world. He attains "reversibility" of thought, that is, when he is faced with such problems as the "sausage" problem mentioned earlier, he is no longer led astray by perceptual features. Mental operations can revert back, stabilizing his judgments. He can now "conserve" the quantity and know that whatever the shape of a ball of plasticine may be pulled into, it remains the same in quantity. A child's intellectual structure at this period is defined as a "concrete" operation, that is a reversible internalized action.

These new achievements appear to be the direct result of playing and working with real objects, particularly in school. Beard,[8] testing children's conceptions of conservation in primary schools, concluded that experience and opportunity to play with water, see-saw balances and other play objects are an important part of helping a child to obtain an understanding of conservation. On the other hand, a recent attempt[9] in Canada to develop formal "training techniques" in school to encourage the development of conservation and reversibility were not successful.

Not all children attain conservation and reversibility at the same age. Lovell,[10] reporting research in an English junior school, examined 322 children individually to study the growth of the concept of conservation of substance. He noted that at an age of seven years plus, only 35 percent of the total number

---

[8] Beard, R. M.: The order of concept development in two fields. Section I, *Educational Review,* 15.2, Section II, *Educational Review,* 15.3, 1963.

[9] Mermelstein, E. and others: The training techniques for the concept of conservation. Edmonton: *Alberta Jour. Educ. Research,* XIII. 3., 185–200, September, 1967.

[10] Lovell, K.: *The Growth of Mathematical and Scientific Concepts in Children.* London: University of London, 1961.

of children tested and attained the concept of conservation, and that even at the age of 10 years plus, 14 percent had no understanding that quantity remained the same, whatever the change in shape. His results would seem to suggest that there lies a wide difference in individual attainment in the understanding of the concept of conservation.

It is highly probable that slower learning children fail to achieve real understanding of their school work, and merely follow the rote-learning processes of habit and repetition. Academic instruction can go beyond a child's actual intellectual growth, so that he counts and writes without fully grasping the essential basis of his work. He performs a school task like a "good boy"—or like a good parrot! The mind of a child can only deal effectively with a quantity of material, a glass of water, or a number of objects, if they are understood to remain permanent in amount and independent of any re-arrangement of their individual parts.

Peel[11] quotes an experimental study on Piagetian lines to test children's logical judgments. A number of questions, based on simple historical passages, were graded to different levels of mental growth. From the children's answers, it was evident that a young child is unable to reason about or explain set passages, except within the contents of the passages themselves, and is not able to see causal relationships. Peel argues that the results obtained imply, ". . . more active questioning, answering and discussion in relation to reading in History and English would do much more than passive reading in providing concrete experience (parallel to that of handling models and materials in arithmetic, geography and simple science) necessary for a child to progress to the stage of being able to reason more formally."

If we agree with Piaget's insistence that intellectual growth depends upon an individual's active interaction with his environment, then children must be given more opportunity in our primary schools to learn for themselves the basic principles, the master ideas, that underlie the world in which they live and play. Teachers need greater freedom to provide for the right kind of learning-teaching situations within the classroom and school. Piaget's work emphasizes again and again, how necessary it is to understand the laws of a child's internal growth, and by cooperating with these laws, draw upon them to lead him on, and guide him through his active interest. By so doing, teachers can then give opportunity for real understanding to take place.

Churchill,[12] summing up the results of a teachers' conference, wrote, "It was generally agreed that one of the problems even today, is still that too many teachers see their role as one of imparting information and that it would be

[11] Peel, E. A.: Experimental examination of some of Piaget's schemata concerning children's perception and thinking, and a discussion of their educational significance. *Brit. J. Educ. Psychol.* XXIX. 89–103, 1959.

[12] Churchill, E. M.: *Piaget's Findings and the Teacher.* London: National Froebel Foundation, 1961, pp. 12–13.

very useful if more headteachers could be persuaded to release teachers from a syllabus to be covered and a standard to be reached. What matters is that children are active, inquiring and experimenting and that where this is happening teachers learn as well as the children and come in time to provide increasingly challenging and satisfying experience for them."

The new approach to science in the primary school is essentially an active way of finding out about the immediate environment, and often forms the basis of what goes on at other times in reading, writing, talking, art and other subjects. According to one science teacher's experience[13] in an English junior school, this approach allows children to learn more effectively, because they become involved in practical problems which arise from their own questions and enquiries. He tells us that he ". . . does not decide in advance what will be studied and then proceeds to direct the children along preconceived paths." Rather he encourages discussion and offers suggestions towards further discovery on active lines. Some of his children, for example, finding that the cog in the centre of a bicycle wheel would turn only in one direction, got together as a group to investigate gears, ball bearings and other related items. There followed a lively amount of mathematics. This kind of activity supports one of Piaget's major tenets, stressed from his earliest writings, that group activities liberate the child from his egocentricism. Social cooperation is one of the principal formative factors in intellectual growth.

During most of the primary stage, a child's thinking is limited by being tied to tangible and visible objects, for he can only deal satisfactorily with a "real" world. He is unable to consider possible explanations and form hypotheses. In addition, his thought processes do not form as yet an integral comprehensive mental system of operations for general application. It is not until he attains the next stage in thinking, the "formal" stage, that he begins to work out problems on lines similar to that of the adult.

SECONDARY SCHOOL AGE

Towards the beginning of the secondary school stage pupils start to carry out logical operations on symbolic and abstract material. They can refer to objects that are not visible to them and classify them into sub-groups. For example, they can understand "fruit" as a collective term, and relate it to apple, orange, pear; sweet, sour; cooking; eating; large, small and other distinguishing features. They can make decisions as a result of their mental abstract operations. The arithmetical calculations at the earlier stage which were carried out best on actual quantities of material and objects, can be coped with at this later period in arithmetical symbols of quantities. The underlying process is the capacity to operate internally with abstract entities.

---

[13] Rose, A. J.: The science scene. *New Education*, 2.4, 10–13, April, 1966.

Piaget and a colleague Inhelder[14] have demonstrated that young adolescents begin to be concerned with possibilities and probable explanations. They start to free their thinking from slavish concern about "real" things, and become involved in trying to envisage relationships which might or might not be true to data. They begin to grope with possible answers, and from manipulations of their mental operations, deduce certain conclusions. They calculate with more variables, and know that if they fill, for example, a kettle with water, place it on a stove, and according to the heat applied and quantity of water, it will boil in so many minutes.

An essential element of his hypothesis formulation is an ability to create in the mind relationships between symbolic representations. Young children at the primary stage would have no difficulty in saying who was the fastest runner in a race, but not until the "formal" stage of thinking is reached, would they be able to reason out in a formal way, the following problem. "John runs faster than Bill. Tom runs slower than Bill. Who runs the fastest?"

Formal operations are ways of transforming propositions about reality so that the relevant variable can be isolated and relations between them deduced. They enable a student to combine propositions internally, and to isolate in an abstract way those which confirm his hypothesis. For instance, a young adolescent can find out a certain number of facts about rods of metal and formulate them as propositions from which to hypothesise about the determinants of flexibility. He maybe says to himself; "This rod is made of steel. It is long. This rod is steel, but shorter" and then on to, "This rod is made of brass" and so on. From experiments with such rods, a student can discover that long steel rods bend, but a short brass rod does not. According to Piaget, it is an adolescent's combinatorial system of mental structures which enable him to manipulate a combination of facts.

To gain further information about adolescents' capacity to reason and note differences from young children, Piaget and Inhelder carried out many experiments. One of the better known is the "Oscillation of a Pendulum." The problem utilizes a simple apparatus consisting of string which can be shortened or lengthened and a set of varying weights. The other variables that might be considered relevant by the student are the height of the release point and the force of the push given to the weight to make it swing. The subject is asked to explain the varying frequency of oscillation. That is, what makes the pendulum go fast or slow—the weight, the push, the height, or the length of string?

The solution to the problem lies in isolating the length of string from the other variables, and thereby gaining an understanding of the principle involved. When, however, this experiment is given to a child at the "intuitive" stage of thinking the subject's physical action dominates his mental operations,

[14] Inhelder, B. and Piaget, J.: *The Growth of Logical Thinking.* London: Routledge and Kegan Paul, 1958, p. 72.

and nearly all his explanations imply the real cause of the variations in frequency of the oscillations is due to his pushes. The child at this stage is unable to give an objective account of the experiment or give consistent explanations.

At the "concrete" stage, subjects can vary the length of string serially, and judge differences in oscillations. That is, they generally achieve correspondence, but are unable to separate the variables and draw conclusions. Inhelder and Piaget[14] state that at this stage "... it is evident that the subjects still lack some logical instrument for interpreting the experimental data and that their failure to separate out the factors is not simply the result of mental laziness." The thinking of adolescents differs fundamentally from that of the child.

The formulation of hypotheses and the testing of them against actual data appears to form an essential part of adolescent thinking. Adolescents seek explanations, reasons and answers to the many problems that daily confront them, and school subjects appropriately taught can form a strong link with the environment in which they live.

Progress in school depends much upon pupils' capacity to think, and as teachers we ought to promote intellectual growth at all levels of school work. We need to give ample opportunity for effective mental operations. Piaget's studies emphasize the psychological gulf that lies between "true learning" that is "growth," and the so-called learning that comes from mere verbal training, habit formation, and the mechanical mastery of skills. True learning develops through "doing" and genuine understanding.

Possibly the new science projects at secondary level[15] are beginning to give a lead for "discovery through doing" is their keystone. Many science teachers are guided by the belief that "... the best way to awaken original thinking in children studying science is to engage them in experiments and practical enquiry." Traditional science tends to confirm foregone conclusions which, according to one writer[16] is "damaging to lively minds."

CONCLUSIONS

Jean Piaget, possibly more than any other writer, has shown how children build up a structural model of the world in their minds as they interact with their environment. He has demonstrated that children are not born with this knowledge, nor is it an automatic growth, but has to be constructed internally piece by piece from birth on a very active basis. Thought processes evolve in accord with an identifiable developmental direction which he prescribes into major stages.

During the first two years, a child learns to coordinate sense and movement, and give direction to his movements. Through active manipulation of objects

---

[15] Nuffield Foundation, *Science Teaching Report.* Longmans-Penguin Books, October, 1964, p. 15.

[16] Schools Council, *Science for the Young School Leaver.* Working Paper No. 1. London: H.M.S.O., 1966.

and substances, there comes knowledge of some of the fundamental concepts in his environment. These processes form the basis for the growth of abstract and propositional thinking with symbolic material at the formal stage in adolescence.

The educational implications of Piaget's studies are many. For teachers concerned with curricula planning and methodology, his work provides a detailed normative frame of reference about cognitive structures. If a teacher has an idea of what and how children are likely to think at a given stage, some idea of children's possibilities and limitations, whether they are likely to understand their school work, then much greater harmony and achievement between child and teacher must ensue.

One of the most important aspects of Piaget's teaching is that a child must experience and manipulate material objects and substances to develop his intellectual powers. Stable and enduring learning about the world in which he lives comes about only through a very active intercourse with the world on the part of the learner. The teacher's task is to give pupils at all stages of learning opportunity for them to learn from their own experiences. What matters most is not verbal learning of rules and facts but growth of complex functional structures or internal organizations that permit children to understand their environment in a meaningful way.

1. Define and sequence the following, according to Piaget's theory:

> discrimination of things
> a working mental model of the world develops
> internalized reversibility
> acceptance of the existence of things
> hypothesis formulation
> intuitive thoughts and half-truths

2. Cite two implications of Piaget's studies for teachers.

Bruner on Learning and Instruction

OBJECTIVES

When you finish unit 26, you should be able to:

* define discovery learning and state Bruner's hypothesis about the relationship between discovery learning and motivation to learn and between discovery learning and memory;
* differentiate several problem-solving methods discussed by Bruner;
* describe Bruner's theory regarding the basic reward for discovery and the type of attitudes and practice required for problem solving.

In this article, Bruner describes his theories about problem solving and discovery learning, the heuristics of discovering, and the relation of discovery to motivation and to memory.

THE ACT OF DISCOVERY*

Jerome S. Bruner

Maimonides, in his *Guide for the Perplexed,*[1] speaks of four forms of perfection that men might seek. The first and lowest form is perfection in the acquisition

---

* Jerome Bruner, "The Act of Discovery," *Harvard Educational Review,* 31(Winter 1961), 21–32. Copyright © 1961 by President and Fellows of Harvard College.

of worldly goods. The great philosopher dismisses such perfection on the ground that the possessions one acquires bear no meaningful relation to the possessor: "A great king may one morning find that there is no difference between him and the lowest person." A second perfection is of the body, its conformation and skills. Its failing is that it does not reflect on what is uniquely human about man: "he could [in any case] not be as strong as a mule." Moral perfection is the third, "the highest degree of excellency in man's character." Of this perfection Maimonides says: "Imagine a person being alone, and having no connection whatever with any other person; all his good moral principles are at rest, they are not required and give man no perfection whatever. These principles are only necessary and useful when man comes in contact with others." The fourth kind of perfection is the true perfection of man; the possession of the highest intellectual faculties. . . ." In justification of his assertion, this extraordinary Spanish-Judaic philosopher urges: "Examine the first three kinds of perfection; you will find that if you possess them, they are not your property, but the property of others. . . . But the last kind of perfection is exclusively yours; no one else owns any part of it."

It is a conjecture much like that of Maimonides that leads me to examine the act of discovery in man's intellectual life. For if man's intellectual excellence is the most his own among his perfections, it is also the case that the most uniquely personal of all that he knows is that which he has discovered for himself. What difference does it make, then, that we encourage discovery in the learning of the young? Does it, as Maimonides would say, create a special and unique relation between knowledge possessed and the possessor? And what may such a unique relation do for a man—or for a child, if you will, for our concern is with the education of the young?

The immediate occasion for my concern with discovery—and I do not restrict discovery to the act of finding out something that before was unknown to mankind, but rather include all forms of obtaining knowledge for oneself by the use of one's own mind—the immediate occasion is the work of the various new curriculum projects that have grown up in America during the last six or seven years. For whether one speaks to mathematicians or physicists or historians, one encounters repeatedly an expression of faith in the powerful effects that come from permitting the student to put things together for himself, to be his own discoverer.

First, let it be clear what the act of discovery entails. It is rarely, on the frontier of knowledge or elsewhere, that new facts are "discovered" in the sense of being encountered as Newton suggested in the form of islands of truth in an uncharted sea of ignorance. Or if they appear to be discovered in this way, it is almost always thanks to some happy hypotheses about where to navigate. Discovery, like surprise, favors the well prepared mind. In playing bridge, one is surprised by a hand with no honors in it at all and also by hands that are all in one suit. Yet all hands in bridge are equiprobable: one must know to be surprised. So too in discovery. The history of science is studded with examples of men "finding out" something and not knowing it. I shall operate on the assumption that discovery, whether by a schoolboy going it on his own or by a scientist cultivating the growing edge of his field, is in its essence a matter of rearranging or transforming evidence in such a way that one is enabled to go beyond the evidence so reassembled to additional new insights. It may well be that an additional fact or shred of evidence makes this larger transformation of evidence possible. But it is often not even dependent on new information.

It goes without saying that, left to himself, the child will go about discovering things for himself within limits. It also goes without saying that there are certain forms of child rearing, certain home atmospheres that lead some children to be their own discoverers more than other children. These are both topics of great interest, but I shall not be discussing them. Rather, I should like to confine myself to the consideration of discovery and "finding-out-for-oneself" within an educational setting—specifically the school. Our aim as teachers is to give our student as firm a grasp of a subject as we can, and to make him as autonomous and self-propelled a thinker as we can—one who will go along on his own after formal schooling has ended. I shall return in the end to the question of the kind of classroom and the style of teaching that encourages an attitude of wanting to discover. For purposes of orienting the discussion, however, I would like to make an overly simplified distinction between teaching that takes place in the *expository mode* and teaching that utilizes the *hypothetical mode.* In the former, the decisions concerning the mode and pace and style of exposition are principally determined by the teacher as expositor; the student is the listener. If I can put the matter in terms of structural linguistics, the speaker has a quite different set of decisions to make than the listener: the former has a wide choice of alternatives for structuring, he is anticipating paragraph content while the listener is still intent on the words, he is manipulating the content of the material by various transformations, while the listener is quite unaware of these internal manipulations. In the hypothetical mode, the teacher and the student are in a more cooperative position with respect to what in linguistics would be called "speaker's decisions." The student is not a bench-bound listener, but is taking a part in the formulation and at times may play the principal role in it. He will be aware of alternatives and may even have an "as if" attitude toward these and, as he receives information he may evaluate it as it comes. One cannot describe the process in either mode with great precision as to detail, but I think the foregoing may serve to illustrate what is meant.

Consider now what benefit might be derived from the experience of learning through discoveries that one makes for oneself. I should like to discuss these under four headings: (1) The increase in intellectual potency, (2) the shift from extrinsic to intrinsic rewards, (3) learning the heuristics of discovering, and (4) the aid to memory processing.

1. Intellectual Potency. If you will permit me, I would like to consider the difference between subjects in a highly constrained psychological experiment involving a two-choice apparatus. In order to win chips, they must depress a key either on the right or the left side of the machine. A pattern of payoff is designed such that, say, they will be paid off on the right side 70 percent of the time, on the left 30 percent, although this detail is not important. What is important is that the payoff sequence is arranged at random, and there is no pattern. I should like to contrast the behavior of subjects who think that there *is* some pattern to be found in the sequence—who think that regularities are discoverable—in contrast to subjects who think that things are happening quite by *chance*. The former group adopts what is called an "event-matching" strategy in which the number of responses given to each side is roughly equal to the proportion of times it pays off: in the present case R70:L30. The group that believes there is no pattern very soon reverts to a much more primitive strategy wherein *all* responses are allocated to the side that has the greater payoff. A little arithmetic will show you that the lazy all-and-none strategy pays off more if indeed the environment is random: namely, they win seventy percent of the time. The event-matching subjects win about 70 percent on the 70 percent payoff side (or 49 percent of the time there) and 30 percent of the time on the side that pays off 30 percent of the time (another 9 percent for a total take-home wage of 58 percent return for their labors of decision). But the world is not always or not even frequently random, and if one analyzes carefully what the event-matchers are doing, it turns out that they are trying out hypotheses one after the other, all of them containing a term such that they distribute bets on the two sides with a frequency to match the actual occurrence of events. If it should turn out that there is a pattern to be discovered, their payoff would become 100 percent. The other group would go on at the middling rate of 70 percent.

What has this to do with the subject at hand? For the person to search out and find regularities and relationships in his environment, he must be armed with an expectancy that there will be something to find and, once aroused by expectancy, he must devise ways of searching and finding. One of the chief enemies of such expectancy is the assumption that there is nothing one can find in the environment by way of regularity or relationship. In the experiment just cited, subjects often fall into a habitual attitude that there is either nothing to be found or that they can find a pattern by looking. There is an important sequel in behavior to the two attitudes, and to this I should like to turn now.

We have been conducting a series of experimental studies on a group of some seventy school children over the last four years. The studies have led us to distinguish an interesting dimension of cognitive activity that can be described as ranging from *episodic empiricism* at one end to *cumulative constructionism* at the other. The two attitudes in the choice experiments just cited are illustrative of the extremes of the dimension. I might mention some other illustrations. One of the experiments employs the game of Twenty Questions. A child—in this case he is between 10 and 12—is told that a car has gone off the road and hit a tree. He is to ask questions that can be answered by "yes" or "no" to discover the cause of the accident. After completing the problem, the same task is given him again, though he is told that the accident had a different cause this time. In all, the procedure is repeated four times. Children enjoy playing the game. They also differ quite markedly in the approach or strategy they bring to the task. There are various elements in the strategies employed. In the first place, one may distinguish clearly between two types of questions asked: the one is designed for locating constraints in the problem, constraints that will eventually give shape to an hypothesis; the other is the hypothesis as question. It is the difference between, "Was there anything wrong with the driver?" and "Was the driver rushing to the doctor's office for an appointment and the car got out of control?" There are children who precede hypotheses with efforts to locate constraint and there are those who, to use our local slang, are "pot-shotters," who string out hypotheses non-cumulatively one after the other. A second element of strategy is its connectivity of information gathering: the extent to which questions asked utilize or ignore or violate information previously obtained. The questions asked by children tend to be organized in cycles, each cycle of questions usually being given over to the pursuit of some particular notion. Both within cycles and between cycles one can discern a marked difference on the connectivity of the child's performance. Needless to say children who employ constraint location as a technique preliminary to the formulation of hypotheses tend to be far more connected in their harvesting of information. Persistence is another feature of strategy, a characteristic compounded of what appear to be two components: a sheer doggedness component, and a persistence that stems from the sequential organization that a child brings to the task. Doggedness is probably just animal spirits or the need for achievement—what has come to be called *n-ach*. Organized persistence is a maneuver for protecting our fragile cognitive apparatus from overload. The child who has flooded himself with disorganized information from unconnected hypotheses will become discouraged and confused sooner than the child who has shown a certain cunning in his strategy of getting information—a cunning whose principal component is the recognition that the value of information is not simply in getting it but in being able to carry it. The persistence of the organized child stems from his knowledge of how to organize questions in cycles, how to summarize things to himself, and the like.

Episodic empiricism is illustrated by information gathering that is unbound by prior constraints, that lacks connectivity, and that is deficient in organizational persistence. The opposite extreme is illustrated by an approach that is characterized by constraint sensitivity, by connective maneuvers, and by organized persistence. Brute persistence seems to be one of those gifts from the gods that make people more exaggeratedly what they are*

Before returning to the issue of discovery and its role in the development of thinking, let me say a word more about the ways in which information may get transformed when the problem solver has actively processed it. There is first of all a pragmatic question: what does it take to get information processed into a form best designed to fit some future use? Take an experiment by Zajonc[2] as a case in point. He gives groups of subjects information of a controlled kind, some groups being told that their task is to transmit the information to others, others that it is merely to be kept in mind. In general, he finds more differentiation and organization of the information received with the intention of being transmitted than there is for information received passively. An active set leads to a transformation related to a task to be performed. The risk, to be sure, is in possible overspecialization of information processing that may lead to such a high degree of specific organization that information is lost for general use.

I would urge now in the spirit of an hypothesis that emphasis upon discovery in learning has precisely the effect upon the learner of leading him to be a constructionist, to organize what he is encountering in a manner not only designed to discover regularity and relatedness, but also to avoid the kind of information drift that fails to keep account of the uses to which information might have to be put. It is, if you will, a necessary condition for learning the variety of techniques of problem solving, of transforming information for better use, indeed for learning how to go about the very task of learning. Practice in discovering for oneself teaches one to acquire information in a way that makes that information more readily viable in problem solving. So goes the hypothesis. It is still in need of testing. But it is an hypothesis of such important human implications that we cannot afford not to test it—and testing will have to be in the schools.

2. Intrinsic and Extrinsic Motives. Much of the problem in leading a child to effective cognitive activity is to free him from the immediate control of environmental rewards and punishments. That is to say, learning that starts in response to the rewards of parental or teacher approval or the avoidance of failure can too readily develop a pattern in which the child is seeking cues as to how to conform to what is expected of him. We know from studies of children who tend to be early over-achievers in school that they are likely to be seekers after the "right way to do it" and that their capacity for transforming their learning into viable thought structures tends to be lower than children

---

* I should also remark in passing that the two extremes also characterize concept attainment strategies as reported in *A Study of Thinking* by J. S. Bruner *et al.* (New York: John Wiley, 1956). Successive scanning illustrates well what is meant here by episodic empiricism; conservative focussing is an example of cumulative constructionism.

merely achieving at levels predicted by intelligence tests. Our tests on such children show them to be lower in analytic ability than those who are not conspicuous in over-achievement.[3] As we shall see later, they develop rote abilities and depend upon being able to "give back" what is expected rather than to make it into something that relates to the rest of their cognitive life. As Maimonides would say, their learning is not their own.

The hypothesis that I would propose here is that to the degree that one is able to approach learning as a task of discovering something rather than "learning about" it, to that degree will there be a tendency for the child to carry out his learning activities with the autonomy of self-reward or, more properly by reward that is discovery itself.

To those of you familiar with the battles of the last half-century in the field of motivation, the above hypothesis will be recognized as controversial. For the classic view of motivation in learning has been, until very recently, couched in terms of a theory of drives and reinforcement: that learning occurred by virtue of the fact that a response produced by a stimulus was followed by the reduction in a primary drive state. The doctrine is greatly extended by the idea of secondary reinforcement: any state associated even remotely with the reduction of a primary drive could also have the effect of producing learning. There has recently appeared a most searching and important criticism of this position written by Professor Robert White, reviewing the evidence of recently published animal studies, of work in the field of psychoanalysis, and of research on the development of cognitive processes in children. Professor White comes to the conclusion, quite rightly I think, that the drive-reduction model of learning runs counter to too many important phenomena of learning and development to be either regarded as general in its applicability or even correct in its general approach. Let me summarize some of his principal conclusions and explore their applicability to the hypothesis stated above.

I now propose that we gather the various kinds of behavior just mentioned, all of which have to do with effective interaction with the environment, under the general heading of competence. According to Webster, competence means fitness or ability and the suggested synonyms include capability, capacity, efficiency, proficiency, and skill. It is therefore a suitable word to describe such things as grasping and exploring, crawling and walking, attention and perception, language and thinking, manipulating and changing the surroundings, all of which promote an effective—a competent—interaction with the environment. It is true of course, that maturation plays a part in all these developments, but this part is heavily overshadowed by learning in all the more complex accomplishments like speech or skilled manipulation. I shall argue that it is necessary to make competence a motivational concept; there is *competence motivation* as well as competence in its more familiar sense of achieved capacity. The behavior that leads to the building up of effective grasping, handling, and letting go of objects, to take one example, is not random behavior that is directed, selective, and persistent, and it continues not because it serves primary drives, which indeed it cannot serve until it is almost perfected, but because it satisfies an intrinsic need to deal with the environment.[5]

I am suggesting that there are forms of activity that serve to enlist and develop the competence motive, that serve to make it the driving force behind behavior. I should like to add to White's general premise that the *exercise* of competence motives has the effect of strengthening the degree to which they gain control over behavior and thereby reduce the effects of extrinsic rewards or drive gratification.

The brilliant Russian psychologist Vigotsky[6] characterizes the growth of thought processes as starting with a dialogue of speech and gesture between child and parent; autonomous thinking begins at the stage when the child is first able to internalize these conversations and "run them off" himself. This is a typical sequence in the development of competence. So too in instruction. The narrative of teaching is of the order of the conversation. The next move in the development of competence is the internalization of the narrative and its "rules of generation" so that the child is now capable of running off the narrative on his own. The hypothetical mode in teaching by encouraging the child to participate in "speaker's decisions" speeds this process along. Once internalization has occurred, the child is in a vastly improved position from several obvious points of view—notably that he is able to go beyond the information he has been given to generate additional ideas that can either be checked immediately from experience or can, at least, be used as a basis for formulating reasonable hypotheses. But over and beyond that, the child is now in a position to experience success and failure not as reward and punishment, but as information. For when the task is his own rather than a matter of matching environmental demands, he becomes his own paymaster in a certain measure. Seeking to gain control over his environment, he can now treat success as indicating that he is on the right track, failure as indicating he is on the wrong one.

In the end, this development has the effect of freeing learning from immediate stimulus control. When learning in the short run leads only to pellets of this or that rather than to mastery in the long run, then behavior can be readily "shaped" by extrinsic rewards. When behavior becomes more long-range and competence-oriented, it comes under the control of more complex cognitive structures, plans and the like, and operates more from the inside out. It is interesting that even Pavlov, whose early account of the learning process was based entirely on a notion of stimulus control of behavior through the conditioning mechanism in which, through contiguity a new conditioned stimulus was substituted for an old unconditioned stimulus by the mechanism of stimulus substitution, that even Pavlov recognized his account as insufficient to deal with higher forms of learning. To supplement the account, he introduced the idea of the "second signalling system," with central importance placed on symbolic systems such as language in mediating and giving shape to mental life. Or as Luria[7] has put it, "the first signal system [is] concerned with directly perceived stimuli, the second with systems of verbal elaboration." Luria, commenting on the importance of the transition from first to second signal system, says: "It would be mistaken to suppose that verbal intercourse with adults merely changes the contents of the child's conscious activity without changing its form. . . . The word has a basic function not only because it indicates a corresponding object in the external world, but also because it abstracts, isolates the necessary signal, generalizes perceived signals and relates them to certain categories; it is this systematization of direct experience that makes the role of the word in the formation of mental processes so exceptionally important."[8,9]

It is interesting that the final rejection of the universality of the doctrine of reinforcement in direct conditioning came from some of Pavlov's own students. Ivanov-Smolensky[10] and Krasnogorsky[11] published papers showing the manner in which symbolized linguistic messages could take over the place of the unconditioned stimulus and of the unconditioned response (gratification of hunger) in children. In all instances, they speak of these as *replacements* of lower, first-system mental or neural processes by higher order or second-system controls. A strange irony, then, that Russian psychology that gave us the notion of the conditioned response and the assumption that higher order activities are built up out of colligations or structurings of such primitive units, rejected this notion while much of American learning psychology has stayed until quite recently within the early Pavlovian fold (see, for example, a recent article by Spence[12] in the *Harvard Educational Review* or Skinner's treatment of language[13] and the attacks that have been made upon it by linguists such as Chomsky[14] who have become concerned with the relation of language and cognitive activity). What is the more interesting is that Russian pedagogical theory has become deeply influenced by this new trend and is now placing much stress upon the importance of building up a more active symbolical approach to problem solving among children.

To sum up the matter of the control of learning, then, I am proposing that the degree to which competence or mastery motives come to control behavior, to that degree the role of reinforcement or "extrinsic pleasure" wanes in shaping behavior. The child comes to manipulate his environment more actively and achieves his gratification from coping with problems. Symbolic modes of representing and transforming the environment arise and the importance of stimulus-response-reward sequences declines. To use the metaphor that David Riesman developed in a quite different context, mental life moves from a state of outer-directedness in which the fortuity of stimuli and reinforcement are crucial to a state of inner-directedness in which the growth and maintenance of mastery become central and dominant.

3. Learning the Heuristics of Discovery. Lincoln Steffens,[15] reflecting in his *Autobiography* on his undergraduate education at Berkeley, comments that his schooling was overly specialized in learning about the known and that too little attention was given to the task of finding out about what was not known. But how does one train a student in the techniques of discovery? Again I would like to offer some hypotheses. There are many ways of coming to the arts of inquiry. One of them is by careful study of its formalization in logic, statistics, mathematics, and the like. If a person is going to pursue inquiry as a way of life, particularly in the sciences, certainly such study is essential. Yet, whoever has taught kindergarten and the early primary grades or has had graduate students working with him on their theses—I choose the two extremes for they are both periods of intense inquiry—knows that an understanding of the formal aspect of inquiry is not sufficient. There appear to be, rather, a series of activities and attitudes, some directly related to a particular subject and some of them fairly generalized, that go with inquiry and research. These have to do with the *process* of trying to find out something and while they provide no guarantee that the *product* will be any *great* discovery, their absence is likely to lead to awkwardness or aridity or confusion. How difficult it is to describe these matters—the heuristics of inquiry. There is one set of attitudes or ways of doing that has to do with sensing the relevance of variables—how to avoid getting stuck with edge effects and getting instead to the big sources of variance. Partly this gift comes from intuitive familiarity with a range of phenomena, sheer "knowing the stuff." But it also comes out of a sense of what things among an ensemble of things "smell right" in the sense of being of the right order of magnitude or scope or severity.

The English philosopher Weldon describes problem solving in an interesting and picturesque way. He distinguishes between difficulties, puzzles, and problems. We solve a problem or make a discovery when we impose a puzzle form on to a difficulty that converts it into a problem that can be solved in such a way that it gets us where we want to be. That is to say, we recast the difficulty into a form that we know how to work with, then work it. Much of what we speak of as discovery consists of knowing how to impose what kind of form on various kinds of difficulties. A small part but a crucial part of discovery of the highest order is to invent and develop models or "puzzle forms" that can be imposed on difficulties with good effect. It is in this area that the truly powerful mind shines. But it is interesting to what degree perfectly ordinary people can, given the benefit of instruction, construct quite interesting and what, a century ago, would have been considered greatly original models.

Now to the hypothesis. It is my hunch that it is only through the exercise of problem solving and the effort of discovery that one learns the working heuristic of discovery, and the more one has practice, the more likely is one to generalize what one has learned into a style of problem solving or inquiry that serves for any kind of task one may encounter—or almost any kind of task. I think the matter is self-evident, but what is unclear is what kinds of training and teaching produce the best effects. How do we teach a child to, say, cut his losses but at the same time be persistent in trying out an idea; to risk forming an early hunch without at the same time formulating one *so* early and with so little evidence as to be stuck with it waiting for appropriate evidence to materialize; to pose good testable guesses that are neither too brittle nor too sinuously incorrigible; etc., etc. Practice in inquiry, in trying to figure out things for oneself is indeed what is needed, but in what form? Of only one thing I am convinced, I have never seen anybody improve in the art and technique of inquiry by any means other than engaging in inquiry.

4. Conservation of Memory. I should like to take what some psychologists might consider a rather drastic view of the memory process. It is a view that in large measure derives from the work of my colleague, Professor George Miller.[16] Its first premise is that the principal problem of human memory is not storage, but retrieval. In spite of the biological unlikeliness of it, we seem to be able to store a huge quantity of information—perhaps not a full tape recording, though at times it seems we even do that, but a great sufficiency of impressions. We may infer this from the fact that recognition (i.e., recall with the aid of maximum prompts) is so extraordinarily good in human beings—particularly in comparison with spontaneous recall where, so to speak, we must get out stored information without external aids or prompts. The key to retrieval is organization or, in even simpler terms, knowing where to find information and how to get there.

Let me illustrate the point with a simple experiment. We present pairs of words to twelve-year-old children, One group is simply told to remember the pairs, that they will be asked to repeat them later. Another is told to remember them by producing a word or idea that will tie the pair together in a way that will make sense to them. A third group is given the mediators used by the second group when presented with the pairs to aid them in tying the pairs into working units. The word pairs include such juxtapositions as "chair-forest," "sidewalk-square," and the like. One can distinguish three styles of mediators and children can be scaled in terms of their relative preference for each: *generic mediation* in which a pair is tied together by a superordinate idea: "chair and forest are both made of wood"; *thematic mediation* in which the two terms are imbedded in a theme or little story: "the lost child sat on a chair in the middle of the forest"; and *part-whole mediation* where "chairs are made from trees in the forest" is typical. Now, the chief result, as you would all predict, is that children who provide their own mediators do best—indeed, one time through a set of thirty pairs, they recover up to 95 percent of the second words when presented with the first ones of the pairs, whereas the uninstructed children reach a maximum of less than 50 percent recovered. Interestingly enough, children do best in recovering materials tied together by the form of mediator they most often use.

One can cite a myriad of findings to indicate that any organization of information that reduces the aggregate complexity of material by imbedding it into a cognitive structure a person has constructed will make that material more accessible for retrieval. In short, we may say that the process of memory, looked at from the retrieval side, is also a process of problem solving: how can material be "placed" in memory so that it can be got on demand?

We can take as a point of departure the example of the children who developed their own technique for relating the members of each word pair. You will recall that they did better than the children who were given by exposition the mediators they had developed. Let me suggest that in general, material that is organized in terms of a person's own interests and cognitive structures is material that has the best chance of being accessible in memory. That is to say, it is more likely to be placed along routes that are connected to one's own ways of intellectual travel.

In sum, the very attitudes and activities that characterize "figuring out" or "discovering" things for oneself also seem to have the effect of making material more readily accessible in memory.

REFERENCES

1. Maimonides, *Guide for the Perplexed* (New York: Dover Publications, 1956).
2. R. B. Zajonc (Personal communication, 1957).
3. J. S. Bruner and A. J. Caron, "Cognition, Anxiety, and Achievement in the Pre-adolescent," *Journal of Educational Psychology* (in press).
4. R. W. White, "Motivation Reconsidered: The Concept of Competence," *Psychological Review,* LXVI (1959), 297–33.
5. *Ibid.,* pp. 317–18.
6. L. S. Vigotsky, *Thinking and Speech* (Moscow, 1934).
7. A. L. Luria, "The Directive Function of Speech in Development and Dissolution," *Word,* XV (1959), 341–464.
8. *Ibid.,* p. 12.
9. For an elaboration of the view expressed by Luria, the reader is referred to the forthcoming translation of L. S. Vigotsky's 1934 book being published by John Wiley and Sons and the Technology Press.
10. A. G. Ivanov-Smolensky, "Concerning the Study of the Joint Activity of the First and Second Signal Systems," *Journal of Higher Nervous Activity,* I (1951), 1.
11. N. D. Krasnogorsky, *Studies of Higher Nervous Activity in Animals and in Man,* Vol. I (Moscow, 1954).
12. K. W. Spence, "The Relation of Learning Theory to the Technique of Education," *Harvard Educational Review,* XXIX (1959), 84–95.
13. B. F. Skinner, *Verbal Behavior* (New York: Appleton-Century-Crofts, 1957).
14. N. Chomsky, *Syntactic Structure* (The Hague, The Netherlands: Mouton & Co., 1957).

15. L. Steffens, *Autobiography of Lincoln Steffens* (New York: Harcourt, Brace, 1931).
16. G. A. Miller, "The Magical Number Seven, Plus or Minus Two," *Psychological Review,* LXIII (1956), 81–97.

1. How does Bruner define discovery?

2. Differentiate between "episododic empiricism" and "cumulative constructionism" as two extremes among problem-solving methods. For each, describe an example of Bruner's or of your own.

3. Explain Bruner's hypothesis about the relationship between constructionism and practice in discovering.

4. According to Bruner, what is the relationship between discovery learning and motivation to learn. If this hypothesis is true, explain how it could be applied to the "slow-to-average" student.

5. According to Bruner, what's the basic reward for discovering something? Is it measurable?

6. According to Bruner, to learn how to discover requires practice in problem solving and also a particular set of attitudes toward discovery. What kind of practice? How can the attitudes be taught or learned?

7. According to Bruner, what's the relationship between memory and discovery?

unit 27

Educational Technology: Myth and Reality

OBJECTIVES

When you finish this unit, you should be able to:

* cite several definitions and several criticisms of educational technology and several predictions about its future impact on schooling.

The authors of this article attempt to put educational technology into a realistic perspective by examining its present capabilities and cautiously predicting what we can and cannot hope for in the 1980s.

RUN, STRAWMAN, RUN:
A CRITIQUE OF RUN, COMPUTER, RUN*,1

Robert W. Locke
David Engler

It was bound to happen. After all the hoopla these past four or five years about the salvation of education by technology, it was time for somebody to throw

  * Reprinted with permission from *Educational Technology* 10(1970): 47–50. Copyright © 1968 by McGraw-Hill Book Company.
  [1] A critique of the essay on educational technology "Run, Computer, Run" by Anthony G. Oettinger and Sema Marks. Cambridge, Mass.: Harvard University Press, copyright, 1969, by the President and Fellows of Harvard College, pp. 215–230.

some cold water on the subject, and that role has fallen—rather, been aggressively seized by—Dr. Anthony G. Oettinger of Harvard. In his essay, *Run, Computer, Run,* he takes on the Office of Education, the education companies, the systems analysts, the computer people and just about everybody else, raising serious doubts about the claims that all of them have made. Dr. Oettinger's doubts are all the more dramatic because in 1965 he published a mini-essay called *A Vision of Educational Technology* in which he made some far-out claims of his own about what the marriage of technology and education might produce. He closed that piece, however, with some warnings about how long the product of the marriage might take to mature, and the present essay (isn't "essay" too modest for a work of this length?) is essentially an elaboration of those warnings. Dr. Oettinger says he is still confident that technology will bring great and beneficial changes to education—but not for a long time to come. The wonder is that he thinks they will ever come, considering the force of his own arguments. We agree with much of Dr. Oettinger's analysis and with some of his conclusions. However, we disagree with him on some fundamental points and this commentary is therefore more critical than not. We bring to the task, of course, our own frame of reference. It is neither as academic nor as technological as Dr. Oettinger's but perhaps this is an advantage. We have no technological axes to grind and are not lusting for the advent of educational technology so that we might sell our computers or tape recorders or overhead projectors. Nor do we have any particular point of view about what the curriculum should be or how schools should be organized or what educational theories are most desirable. We tend to look upon the sprawl which is American education with what we hope is an enlightened and objective eye. In our business the greatest successes usually come when we anticipate correctly and satisfy effectively the real, practical needs of schools and universities. In this review we make our own predictions for the changing needs of teaching and learning in the next decade, and speculate about the contributions that will be made by the so-called education business. Oddly enough, our confidence in technology appears to be greater than Dr. Oettinger's, but we also define technology differently than he does.

Oettinger's Thesis

Oettinger bases his gloomy view on an impressive piece of logic, made all the more interesting and lively because he supports much of it by quoting the very proponents of technology whose predictions he challenges. His analysis goes something like this:

1. *Claims for Technology—Myth versus Reality.* Many of the assumptions about the *future* value of technology in education are, according to Dr. Oettinger, based on false assumptions about its *present* accom-

plishments, resulting largely from exaggerated and even irresponsible claims made by technology's proponents. Since the assumptions about the present are false, it follows that the predictions of the future may turn out to be inaccurate.

2. *Systems.* One of the most questionable assumptions about educational technology is that systems analysis can be as useful in solving educational problems as it has been in solving military and space problems. Oettinger is particularly effective in puncturing this balloon.

3. *Individualized Instruction.* Dr. Oettinger recognizes that the main goal of educational technology is to help individualize instruction, but says there is little evidence that it has so far, and suggests that the problems of individualization are much greater than we realize.

4. *Economics.* The cost of the hardware, Dr. Oettinger maintains, will be far beyond the means of all but the wealthiest school districts, based on the present costs of conventional equipment like language labs and experimental equipment like computers.

5. *Innovation-Proof Schools.* Schools are probably the most innovation-proof institutions in American society, Oettinger believes, and the normal assumptions that might apply elsewhere about technology and rates of change do not apply to schools.

6. *Timing, Short-term.* In brief, he says, "educational technology is most unlikely to have significant impact on instruction and learning . . . within, say, the next decade."

7. *Timing, Long-term.* But he leaves us on a hopeful note. Although he sees little reason to expect progress in the short term, he is still confident about the longer term. In fact, his main disagreement with the proponents of technology in education appears to be not whether, but when.

COMMENTS ON OETTINGER'S THESIS

Oettinger's analysis is worth closer examination. The individual arguments are always lively, generally perceptive and sometimes convincing. Taken at face value, they clearly support his pessimistic short-term conclusion. In fact, they would appear to support a more pessimistic vision of the longer term than he professes. But more on that later. First, we want to comment on each of his arguments.

Myth Versus Reality

Oettinger devotes much of his introduction and first three sections to parallel and highly revealing examinations of what, on the one hand, is claimed for technology by computer experts, education industry spokesmen, Office of

Education officials and educational researchers; and, on the other hand, what is actually happening in the schools. He finds that the claims bear no relationship to the reality of schools as they now exist, and accuses the proponents of technology of creating a myth that "may serve worthwhile political purposes [but] utterly obscure[s] the small fund of genuine knowledge now available to us in this area." In effect, he puts Lou Bright and Bel Kaufman in the same room (he quotes both extensively) and then concludes that they are talking about two different worlds.

While we might quibble that Oettinger does neither Bright nor Miss Kaufman justice by quoting them in juxtaposition, he has performed a useful service by calling to task the publicists of educational technology. In a presumably well-intentioned effort to focus attention on the *potential* importance of technology to education, too many of technology's champions have described their hopes for the future as if it were the present, as for example, in the Republic Steel advertisement: "He is learning to read from a computer." In a country with unbounded faith in technology, it is hardly surprising that large numbers of the public have assumed that such technological innovations as computer-assisted instruction are just around the corner, but it is more serious that some school officials, whose understanding of technology is generally superficial, are diverting time and money into projects for which neither they nor their teachers are ready. (However, their students probably *are* ready.)

The tragedy of unrealistic expectations is that disappointments can lead to confusion at best, and at worst to the sort of disillusionment that can seriously increase education's resistance to change. We may even be in for a repetition of the teaching machine fiasco of the early 1960's when disillusionment about the machines obscured the growing evidence that programed instruction itself had the potential to make a significant contribution to teaching and learning. The "I-told-you-so's" in education are still beating the dead horse of the teaching machines and no one will ever know how many good teachers have failed to experiment with programed instruction as a result.

Systems

Oettinger devotes much of his second and third sections to the argument that if educational technology depends on the successful application of systems analysis to school problems, we're in for some major disappointments. Education simply doesn't meet either of two criteria he gives for the systems approach to be worthwhile:

1. It isn't independent enough of the other systems which interact with it, e.g., the family and the community.
2. There are not well-developed and reliable research and design tools available to either describe or study cause and effect in education.

Oettinger even goes so far as to suggest that systems analysis has been less of a panacea in better-defined fields, but his main point is that it will not contribute greatly to the solution of educational problems, including those for which technology appears on the surface to have considerable potential. To give his contention the force of specificity, he quotes extensively from a number of sources, including a report on the Watertown Schools of the Harvard Graduate School of Education, a report of a one-day visit which he and an associate made to two high schools in an unidentified city (which sounds very much like New Haven), plus Bel Kaufman (again), Jonathan Kozol, James Coleman, Peter Schrag, and other commentators on the educational scene.

For the most part we agree with Oettinger. Most of the talk about the virtues of systems analysis and education has come from people who know a lot more about systems analysis than they do about education, and the arrogance of their assumptions is astonishing. As a system to analyze, education is infinitely more complex than the areas in which the technique has already been successful, and less ambitious claims might be more realistic. The believers in the systems approach could well take a look at economics, another field in which the elements are more often human than physical and in which we now have over two decades of experience in applying sophisticated quantitative techniques to the analysis of cause and effect. The economists, whose progress has actually been considerable, are more cautious in their claims than the defense and space analysts turned educator.

However, we are not at all sure that Oettinger's conclusion about systems analysis has as much to do with educational technology as he believes. He bases his argument on the difficulty of coming to grips with the large, sprawling and complex organism of education—as in Watertown or "Small City"—but, as we shall suggest later, the significant contributions of technology to education are more likely to come in much smaller and more manageable areas of education; that is, specific areas of instruction where goals can be defined with a good deal more clarity than the generalized and fatuous goals of Calvin Coolidge High School in *Up the Down Staircase*.

Individualized Instruction

At one point in his essay, Oettinger refers to individualized instruction as the *idée fixe* of present-day education and for a moment it appears that he is ready to question the ends of educational technology along with its means. However, his interest in individualized instruction turns out to be as genuine as his doubts about the value of efforts so far to adapt instruction to individual differences.

The Harvard report on Watertown apparently contains a detailed description of how that school's language laboratory is being used, and Oettinger quotes extensively from it, including an appalling set of procedures that indicate only that Watertown may be using its equipment very badly. From that single case study, Oettinger constructs an elaborate analysis of what technology (by his definition, hardware) has so far contributed to the individualization of instruction, concluding: Not much. In another section, he discusses the Oakleaf experiment but argues that its principal contribution so far has been a modest improvement in the capacity to adjust *rate* of instruction according to the different abilities of individual children—and not much else. This is a far cry from the claims about individualized instruction being made by the above-mentioned advocates of educational technology. Oettinger says that any prediction about the future capacity of technology to individualize instruction has to be tempered by the fact of life that its impact so far has been minuscule.

He even suggests that individualized instruction, when it does come, may present school superintendents and principals with severe problems of parental dissatisfaction. Mothers and fathers who care about the education of their children generally want them to conform to predetermined standards and may find it difficult to accept the notion that what's the proper instructional strategy for the boy next door may not be best for their own child.

Oettinger's concerns about individualized instruction are the most important in his essay because if educational technology does not significantly reduce the lockstep of most classroom instruction, then the ball game is over. His thesis is not that technology will fail, but that it will take a long time to succeed. However, this careful assessment of the present state of individualized instruction is more disturbing than he may have intended because he attaches so little importance to what seems to us like genuine signs of progress. We don't agree with his assessment and wonder about the conclusions he draws from it (of which more later).

Economics

Few people doubt that educational technology, be it defined as process or product, is expensive in comparison to conventional instruction today. Thus one would expect that Oettinger's case against technology would rest on a solid economic base. In effect, he shows us the Watertown school budget, presumably typical, plus the cost of their language laboratory and their teachers' median salaries; and by way of contrast, the cost of commercial computer time-sharing services, as well as typical salaries of motion picture directors, film editors and computer programmers. He cites projections of expenditures for education over the next decade. From an economic point of view, he concludes that educational technology, especially that involving computers, is a pipe dream.

It seems to us that there are two major omissions in Oettinger's argument. Nowhere does Oettinger give any serious consideration to the marked downward trend of the cost of technology, particularly computers. For example, the cost of a transistor in 1960 was about $2. Today, an integrated circuit with a capacity equal to 50 transistors, costs $3; and this cost will probably go down to about $1 by 1970. Couple the declining cost with an exponential increase in reliability which went from one failure per 1000 every ten hours to one failure per 350,000 every year, all of which was accomplished in about a decade, and you begin to question the kinds of projections which consider costs in static terms.

The cost of performing 125 million multiplications on the ENIAC was $12,800; on the UNIVAC 1103 it was $1,420; on the IBM 7030 it was $29. Undoubtedly, current equipment can perform for well under the $29 figure of a few years ago.

Thus to look at current commercial time-sharing rates of $20 to $40 per hour and come to the conclusion that CAI will not be economically feasible for at least a decade is to ignore completely the fact that the cost of computer technology is in the grip of a sharply downward trend. Nowhere in his look at the next decade does Oettinger take this trend into account.

Instead of comparing Watertown's expenditure of $2.80 per child per day with the $20 to $40 per hour rates of commercial time-sharing, Oettinger might have contributed more to our understanding of the problem by analyzing the Kopstein and Seidel study of last year which compared the economics of computer-administered instruction and traditionally administered instruction. Their conclusion indicated that although CAI, as exemplified by the use of an IBM 1500 system in a public school, was about ten times more expensive than conventional instruction ($3.73 per student hours versus $.36 per student hour), the probability is that in the near future the cost per student hour of CAI will be as low as $.11. Obviously, Oettinger does not consider this as a justifiable probability; but it is not enough to dismiss this kind of projection by citing the relatively high costs of commercial time-sharing. The burden is on Oettinger to explain why the Kopstein-Seidel study does not stand up to analysis and why we must not accept what they consider to be "extravagantly conservative" estimates.

One of the critical assumptions made by Kopstein and Seidel in predicting an $.11 per hour student cost is a major drop in the cost of student terminal equipment. The engineering of such low-cost-terminal devices has been accomplished. The plasma display device developed at the University of Illinois is one example. We understand that other terminal configurations using conventional television receivers exist and are now being tested. If Oettinger does not believe that such devices are technically or economically feasible now or in the near future, he must tell us why. Otherwise, we *must* assume that these devices, and others like them, will be produced, will both help create and fill the demand for CAI, and will dramatically lower the cost per student hour of CAI.

Oettinger's second omission is even more significant. Instead of juxtaposing quotations from Bel Kaufman and Lou Bright, Oettinger might gain more by quoting Fred Hechinger on the Higher Horizons Project after citing excerpts from *Up the Down Staircase* and *The Blackboard Jungle.* The Higher Horizons pilot project, in which, incidentally, one of the present writers participated, took place in the real counterparts of the fictional schools of those novels. If Oettinger recognizes that the conditions described in these novels are deplorable, then an additional cost per student of $250 per year to improve these conditions dramatically should not strike him as being beyond the limits of rational possibility. On the basis of his own projections, this would come to something on the order of $4 billion per year, less than one-half of 1% of our gross national product.

Indeed, if the political leadership and the public in New York City had known seven or eight years ago that the situation in the ghetto schools would deteriorate to the extent that it has in the course of those years, they might have recognized that $25 million in additional expenditures would be a relatively cheap price to pay to avoid the human and economic damage wrought by ineffective and inferior slum schools. How much better the situation in those schools—and in the community at large—might be today if that investment had been made!

This brings us to the crux of the economic argument and compels us to cite what we consider to be fundamental and obvious factors which have been largely ignored in Oettinger's analysis.

The conditions of life in our urban ghettos pose the most critical problem our society faces, perhaps the most critical problem we have ever faced. The sources of that problem are many and complex, but few people would argue with the proposition that one of the basic factors underlying the problem is technological change in American society in general. Technological revolution in agriculture led to the migration of millions of rural Negroes to urban industrial areas. Technological change in industry eliminated substantially the need for their unskilled labor. The ghettos were thus packed with undereducated, unemployable people who quickly became the social dynamite that now threatens to blow this society apart. Jobs, better housing, more effective education and improved health services for the inner city poor are in the process of moving to the top of our list of national priorities. To accomplish these things will take staggering amounts of money. Quite aside from the moral imperatives which alone should be enough to justify the kind of effort we must make, the political and social realities of this problem are such that they leave us with only one viable solution: to invest whatever is necessary to eliminate the problem. This is not to say that we need only invest heavily in educational technology to solve all the problems of our ghetto schools. In fact, as one reads Kaufman, Kozol, Kohl, Schrag and others, it is almost easy to conclude that educational technology is irrelevant to the problems they are discussing. For the most part their focus is on the "people" problems which underlie the distress in the schools they have written about. These problems are psychological, emotional, ethical; they are concerned with racism, class bias, double standards, hypocrisy, dehumanization and assorted neuroses. These problems are pervasive and probably more difficult to solve than the kinds of instructional problems to which technology may offer solutions.

However, these problems and the problems of instruction *per se,* as well as their solutions, are not mutually exclusive; in fact, at various junctures they are often related. To maintain that we can or should address ourselves to only one or the other seems to us to be an untenable position.

Yes, we need better teachers and administrators in our inner city schools. Yes, we need better human relations and more relevant curriculum. But we also need better defined instructional objectives, more varied and effective instructional strategies, greater accommodation of individual differences and better evaluation of the instructional process. In short, we also need educational technology. It seems to us that Oettinger fails to recognize this because he thinks of technology as hardware rather than process. Hardware, considered in a vacuum, obviously can provide no solutions. The process, however, is what is relevant.

Innovation-Proof Schools

The contention that American schools are innovation-proof is frequently used as an argument against the feasibility of introducing educational technology into the schools on any significant scale. Paul Mort's classic study of some years back, indicating that it took 50 years for a new idea to make its way through the warp and woof of American education, is often cited as evidence of how resistant schools are to change. However, this contention overlooks two important factors. First, the historic gap between invention and wide-scale application is changing. Approximately 100 years elapsed between the discovery of electricity and the general use of the electric light. Photography was invented 100 years before the development of the photography industry.

In fact, gaps of 50 and 100 years were typical until the middle of the 20th century. One of the significant features of contemporary technology is the general narrowing of that gap, a phenomenon which has probably been the product of the post-World War II advent of research and development as a widespread *modus operandi.* The transistor is probably the best example of innovation which has rapidly passed into common, everyday use, although one could cite innumerable other examples.

This emphasis on research and development has, in the last few years, become a significant part of the educational enterprise. It seems likely that the results of research and development in education will similarly shorten the gap between the introduction and the widespread dissemination of innovation practices in the schools.

Second, the curriculum reform movement of the last decade has resulted in more innovation in the content of what is taught in schools than one would consider feasible using Mort's model. If schools are innovation-proof, how can one explain the extent of curriculum reform which has pervaded education from preschool to junior college during the past ten years? How does one explain the fact that 40% of our high schools have adopted PSSC physics, 30% Chem. Study? Or that 30% use programed instruction? Or that 40% use team teaching? Or that 30% use data processing equipment? Textbook publishers have learned—some of them the hard way—that the influence of the curriculum reform movement has been so broad as to make a great many traditional programs economically untenable. One would be hard put to find a major textbook publisher whose mathematics list is not modern in every sense of the word. All of these changes have taken place in less than ten years.

In fact, on the strength of the changes in basic curriculum during the last ten years, a good argument could be made for the proposition that we are in the midst of the most innovative era in the history of American education and that our schools have never before been so innovation-*prone*.

Again, we must cite the changing nature of American society in order to remind ourselves about the environment in which this receptivity to innovation is emerging. We have already mentioned how technological change in agriculture and industry has made the undereducated, unskilled individual economically obsolete and socially maladjusted. These same factors have created other problems with the majority of the rest of our population. Because the rate of change in society is accelerating so much, because the so-called knowledge explosion continues to have ramifications in so many fields, we can no longer assume as we once did (rightly or wrongly) that there is a finite body of knowledge that one must master as a generalist and/or as a specialist in a given field. Rapid obsolescence has become characteristic of most scientific and technical fields and is becoming increasingly so in many nontechnical fields as well.

Educators are now much more concerned with teaching youngsters to become effective learners than with trying to teach them mastery of a fixed amount of subject matter. The interest in inquiry, discovery, structure, problem solving and the like is evidence, on the one hand, of considerable ferment in the most fundamental aspect of education—the aspect of goals and objectives. On the other hand, the interest in non-graded schools, continuous progress, flexible scheduling and individualized instruction is evidence of an analogous ferment in another fundamental aspect of education—the aspect of method.

Introducing innovations such as these in the schools is enormously difficult, but if Oettinger had visited a larger and perhaps more representative sample of schools, we believe he would have encountered the kind of evidence that has convinced us that a large number of our schools are by no means innovation-proof and that, indeed, change is the order of the day.

A Different Conclusion

Oettinger concludes his essay on a strangely ambivalent note. On the one hand, he professes confidence in his own research, in the *Vision*, which he quotes at the beginning of the essay; on the other hand, he expresses strong reservations about the techniques being used (systems analysis, especially) to reach the goals of his *Vision*, and makes it clear he expects little of any real value to be accomplished in the next decade or two. He even confesses at the very end that he is quite unsure about what should be done about all this.

Actually, it is hard to see how Oettinger can maintain any confidence about the longer term either. Having established his own *Vision* as the goal of educational technology, and having specified that effective systems analysis is required to reach the goal, he demonstrates the great unlikelihood that schools such as those in either Watertown or "Small City" will be any closer to the goal in 1978 than they are now. What he fails to conclude, however, is that if he's correct, the prospects for 1988 or 1998 will be equally dim. In short, Oettinger has constructed a neat piece of logic but failed to follow it to its conclusion. If we accept his premises, his goals seem unattainable.

Run Strawman Run

But maybe neither the premises nor the goals are reasonable. Perhaps his *Vision* is a strawman that represents an unrealizable (and even undesirable) goal; and perhaps it is equally unreasonable to require that systems analysis constitutes the chief means of reaching it. As he says himself, he wrote his *Vision* to "present a vision of technological possibility deliberately unclouded by economic or temporary realism." That may be how progressive attitudes are developed, but it seems unfair to describe a fanciful future and then turn around and show that it may be impossible to achieve. It would have been both more impressive and also more discouraging if Oettinger a) had set more realistic goals for education, b) had required that they be reached through techniques that are now available, and c) had *then* concluded that progress would be very slow.

Although Oettinger professes to believe in his *Vision*, he never comes to grips with the problem of how we get there from here. He quotes Stolurow on this:

> It would be a mistake today to introduce CAI as an active instrument of education. This would be like introducing the Wright brother's first plane to a group of business men who were running transportation companies so that they would

begin immediately to use it for commercial purposes. Even the first Ford car did not start the taxi business. On the other hand, it also would be a grave mistake to proceed the way many have counseled, namely, to reject CAI as a short-lived phenomenon or curiosity which should not be taken seriously until it has been proved. This would be like saying that we would not take seriously the idea of using the car for a taxi or the plane for passenger service until the car was like today's Cadillac and the plane like today's 727 jet.

We have problems with today's cars and aircraft designs, but we do not stop using cars or planes. We might reject certain models, like the Edsel, but we do not reject the whole idea of the car. The fact is that the engineering designs of cars and aircraft have reached their present state of development only because earlier designs were used for practical purposes and provided us with information on ways they could be improved.

But nowhere does he deal with this aspect of technology. He would leave us exactly where we are today, awaiting that distant day when the capabilities of technology, the capabilities of teachers and administrators, and the economies of both education and technology will all fit neatly into an elegant algorithm of change.

Had he been at Kitty Hawk on December 18, 1903, he might have argued that Orville and Wilbur's feat of flying 120 feet in 12 seconds was impressive but, after all, he could cover the same distance faster by horse, and a horse was a lot cheaper than a flying machine. Besides, the flying machine was not very reliable and only the Wright boys knew how to operate them.

And had he been around at the time of the invention of the rotary press and convinced the incipient publishing industry to wait until we knew how to use textbooks effectively before undertaking to publish any, we too would probably still be back on the farm, and so, we suspect, would everyone else!

Meanwhile, we believe there are some quite realistic goals for significant improvement in education, and that technology will contribute importantly to their accomplishment. We will describe them here, but first we need to define educational technology in broader terms than Oettinger's.

Defining Educational Technology

Oettinger's essay is extraordinary in the narrowness of its view of educational technology. By and large he defines it as hardware—language laboratories, slide projectors, computers—although there seem to be times when he simply means computers. The narrowness of this definition inevitably limits his view of why and how technology should play a role in education.

A broader definition is essential. If technology is defined as the application of knowledge to practical purposes or, more concisely, as applied science, then educational technology must surely be considered as being more than just hardware.

In education, we must apply what we know about learning, about child development, about human relations, about communications, about statistics, about any subject matter area, in short, about any discipline—and apply this to the processes of teaching and learning.

Obviously, we do not know enough in any of these fields to solve all of the problems we face in education. However, to dismiss cavalierly what we do know as being inadequate is to throw out both the content and method of science and to leave the process of education to intuition and the mystical arts.

. Thus, educational technology must be considered as the process of applying relevant knowledge to the practical purpose of instructing youngsters. In the context of this definition of educational technology, the role of hardware is subsumed by the broader process of instructional design.

There are a number of good definitions of educational technology as a process, and we could cite any one of them to support our point here. We particularly like Robert Glaser's conception of instructional design because he has stated it in a context which makes clear its relationship to the emergence of educational technology in the schools. We interpret him this way:

> As behavioral science begins to play a significant role in instructional practice, the design of instruction will change in four main areas. First, objectives will be defined after analysis of the relationship between subject matter content and student behavior. Second, preinstructional behavior will be diagnosed in terms of the learner's readiness, aptitude and achievement. Third, materials and methods of instruction will be selected and developed in relation to both preinstructional behavior and the desired target performance by the learner, as well as in relation to the intrinsic characteristics of the subject matter. Finally, the evaluation of the student's performance will be accomplished through criteria which are directly related to the objectives and tasks specified for any particular instructional situation rather than to norms which provide comparisons to performances by other students.

These changes will, in turn, lead to four significant changes in the way schools operate. First, the teacher's role will become more involved in the progress of the individual student. Next, this increasing focus on individualized instruction will lead to change in school organization and practice. Also, instructional materials will be more carefully evaluated in relation to instructional objectives and effectiveness. Lastly, more students will successfully achieve competence in various subject matter areas, while tests which measure this mastery will also help measure the general quality of education.

It seems clear that behavioral psychology, however inadequate it may be as a science when compared to the physical sciences, nevertheless offers us the possibility of organizing and developing instructional programs on a more rational, measurable and presumably more effective basis than heretofore.

Actually, what Oettinger is talking about can better be defined as educational gadgetry, a malady which has afflicted American education in recent years.

Fascination with gadgets is, after all, an old American custom, so it shouldn't be surprising that schoolmen are just as susceptible to the blandishments of gadgeteers as is the rest of our population. Some gadgets have been around for a long time and have proved useful on a pragmatic basis. Motion pictures, filmstrips, phonographs, tape recorders and other such instruments have been used as supplementary aids to instruction for many years. Research has reassured us that these media are at least no worse than teacher-textbook instruction, while intuition tells us that for some instructional objectives they are markedly superior and for some learners they are considerably more effective, perhaps essential.

We seem to be at the beginning of a period in which we will see the increasing use of these media in the central instructional process itself and on a more rational basis than heretofore. This rational basis can be developed only through the *process* of educational technology.

It's useful to compare the school use of three major hardware systems— television, language laboratories and computers—on the basis of the degree to which they represent educational gadgetry or educational technology in the sense of our definition.

Television has, in a relatively short time, become widely available in schools. However, one searches in vain for the scientific rationale which undergirded the introduction of television to the instructional process. This was gadgetry at its worst in the sense that people assumed that the communications capabilities were in and of themselves valuable in the process of instruction. The research that went on focused on questions about whether or not one could accomplish by means of television what one accomplished through lecture.

The language laboratory had the virtue of being the product of the influence of science on foreign language instruction. The science of linguistics contributed a new rationale for teaching foreign languages. The language laboratory was, to a large extent, designed to meet the needs created by this new rationale. One could argue that this change and the introduction of the language laboratory took place with inadequate experimentation. Nevertheless, this was in part technology in our sense of the word: the application of scientific knowledge to a practical purpose.

When one compares the introduction of the computer to the instructional process to previous experiences with television and language laboratories, one is even more struck by the influence of the process of educational technology. Experimentation with computer-assisted instruction either because of the great expense involved or because of the exotic nature of the system has tended to proceed on a much more scientific and experimental basis. In fact, many people suspect that one of the major contributions of CAI will be in helping us learn how to develop empirically validated instructional materials. Certainly the initial impetus for much of the experimentation with CAI has come out of an interest in doing research on how learning takes place. Thus, the entire framework and atmosphere in which computer-assisted instruction is being developed is markedly different from our experience with other pieces of hardware precisely because it is being developed as part of the process which we define as educational technology.

SOME PREDICTIONS ABOUT SCHOOLS IN 1978

When we at McGraw-Hill think about technology and the future of education, we tend to concentrate on what is likely to happen rather than on what life could be like if things went a certain way. This is not to say that we don't dream, or that as individuals and citizens we don't feel strongly about the condition of our schools. But as a corporation, we must respond to the realities of our marketplace and not simply to our visions about it. So our predictions about the future do not constitute a "vision" although they come from the same crystal ball, as do all predictions. And yet, despite our response to reality, our outlook is more optimistic than Oettinger's.

By 1978, we believe that the influence of technology will be such that the self-contained classroom featuring conventional modes of teacher/textbook centered instruction at a lock-step pace will be characteristic of a minority of the schools in this country. It will still be a large minority, but it will be declining.

By 1978, the majority of schools will demand systems of instructional materials which include precisely stated behavioral objectives, diagnostic tests of preinstructional behavior, criterion-referenced tests of achievement, and instructional programs which are delivered through a variety of media, which engage the student actively, which permit him to progress at his own rate and which are designed to generate in the learner a maximum amount of self-direction.

By 1978, the majority of schools will have independent study facilities equipped with audio and visual components. These will range from sophisticated dial-access systems to simple combinations of tape recorder and projector. It is also likely that a versatile, low-cost, easy-to-operate audio-visual device designed for self-instructional use will be used in significant numbers of these facilities.

By 1978, about 25 percent of the schools will have on-line use of computers for instructional purpose—drill, tutorial, simulation, problem solving and information retrieval.

By 1978, purveyors of instructional materials designed to fill the needs created by these changes in education will carry on substantial in-service teacher training programs.

By 1978, many schools will require evaluation data from the distributors of new instructional materials and equipment.

These predictions imply many far-reaching changes in education. They are by no means certain to happen. There are strong counter-trends in the world of education, of which Oettinger's paper is an articulate example. Social and political forces will be more important determinants of the shape of things to come than will the evolution of instructional theory and practice. Nevertheless, we think that the probabilities lie closer to our predictions than to Oettinger's.

INDUSTRY AND EDUCATION

A myth overlooked by Dr. Oettinger is that critical decisions in education are rarely if ever made by people in the businesses associated with teaching and learning. This was never true, even in the simpler days when the only business interests were the textbook publishers—partly because the publishers were among the few organizations with national outlooks at a time when almost all of the decisions in education were made at the state and local level. It is even less true now. Business firms have themselves become major institutions for education and training, a handful of them have contracted to manage such public institutions as Job Corps centers, and more important to the present discussion, some of the effort to apply technology to education is being undertaken or at least paid for by industry. Therefore, a careful examination of the so-called "knowledge industry" or "education business" may be instructive.

Not One But Several Businesses

Actually, there is a good deal of confusion about the businesses associated with information, learning and communications because they are, in fact, several distinctly different businesses, only one of which is directly concerned with educational technology. Part of the confusion about these several businesses is because information and education are too often considered the same, which they are not.

First, there is the business of generating, collecting, organizing, and selling information, usually in the form of data: business and financial data, technical data, scientific data, and data for almost every other field of human endeavor. This is the information business, and it is different from the education business; in fact, most of the customers for information aren't in education at all. They're in business firms, research libraries and the government. (The federal government is both the largest generator and the most voracious user of data.) The leaders of the information business are commercial firms like Standard & Poor's and non-profits like the Chemical Abstracts Service of the American Chemical Society, and it is well ahead of the education business in its use of such newer techniques as data processing and reprography.

Then there is the business of creating, manufacturing and marketing systems of instruction, from textbooks to computer-assisted instruction, and all combinations of everything in between. This is what can properly be called the cducation or learning business, made up of firms which create and sell books, films, instructional equipment and other products designed to help teachers teach and children learn.

Third, there are communications businesses, like the broacasting companies, which help transmit both knowledge (or information) and education. Some of them appear to be more concerned with entertainment than either information or education, but their capacity both to inform and to educate is obviously great.

Finally, for some companies, education is a market for service rather than products. Traditionally, educational services have been provided by educational consulting firms, school magazines, and in a sense by test publishers; more recently, schools have bought curriculum planning (as Oakland Community College did from Litton Industries), systems analysis (General Learning), and computer time (any number of service bureaus). Some of these businesses have a peripheral relationship to the instructional side of education, but for the most part their services are of interest to administrators rather than teachers.

The Education or Learning Companies

Our concern is with the companies in the second category, which produce instruments of teaching and learning. They differ greatly one from another, often to a much greater degree than most observers in and out of education suspect, particularly with respect to their ability to deal with the technology of education.

The great majority of these companies are either independent publishers and film producers or else industrial firms that now have publishing subsidiaries. The independent companies generally fall into two categories.

1. First, small firms that deliberately eschew the risky and unfamiliar territory of educational technology and limit their efforts to the publication of good books, films and other conventional materials of instruction, for which there will clearly continue to be a large demand and important place in teaching and learning. Since this is a business that can be started without a large amount of capital, the list of such firms 10 years from now will undoubtedly include some new names.
2. Second, much larger and more diversified publishing firms which have the resources to develop complex and sophisticated instructional systems, and even to acquire or build their own hardware capabilities as needed. Significantly, the companies in this category are among the strongest educational publishing firms, and it is no

accident that they have so far chosen to avoid being acquired by larger industrial firms. They include McGraw-Hill, Harcourt-Brace & World, Prentice-Hall (which had a brief engagement with RCA), Scott-Foresman and Encyclopedia Brittanica. As we shall suggest, there is at least as much chance that these companies will make significant contributions to educational technology as that their industrial competitors will.

Then there are the publishing firms that have been absorbed by industrial firms—or to put it less parochially, the industrial giants which have picked up publishing bedfellows. They, too, differ greatly, and it's a mistake to lump them all together.

One model is IBM's, the one that started it all. IBM's acquisition of SRA in 1963 was in some respects the shrewdest move of the lot because SRA had a well deserved reputation for innovative publishing and excellent profits. Considering that this first marriage is approaching its fifth anniversary, it has produced less of an innovative character than many had expected. It's a matter of speculation whether this is because IBM management has deliberately decided to let its subsidiary operate with maximum independence, or the IBM engineers and SRA editors are basically incompatible, or even whether both groups are simply taking a very cautious public position about new developments in order to avoid the trap of selling the sizzle before the steak is even over the fire. (Dr. Oettinger take note: compared with its actual accomplishments in the development of computer-assisted instruction, IBM's pronouncements have been decidedly modest, and have contributed less than some others to the myth of educational technology.) Regardless of what IBM and SRA have *appeared* to do, between them they should be in an unusually good position to contribute to and profit from educational technology: through IBM's long lead in computer-assisted instruction, SRA's record as an innovating publisher, and (each in its own way) superb marketing operations.

RCA, with Random House, genrally fits the IBM-SRA model, but with qualitative differences. RCA has also done some work in computer-assisted instruction and Random House, through one of its subsidiaries, Singer, has experience in the production and sale of textbooks. Unlike IBM, RCA is a major producer of educational equipment other than computers, such as television sets and motion picture projectors; and unlike SRA, Random House publishes widely in general, non-educational areas. As in the case of IBM and SRA, there is little evidence so far that the RCA and Random House people have learned how to work together to produce the hardware-software systems that were predicted at the time of their merger (Sarnoff: "We've got the hardware and they've got the software). On the contrary, RCA took the lead among the computer companies in making it clear that it would work with any and all publishing firms that wished to develop CAI programs for use on its computer equipment. This enlightened policy, which was subsequently adopted by IBM, simply appears to say that it is a mistake for an electronics firm to put all of its hardware eggs in one software basket. (Or vice versa.)

Of course, this throws some doubt on the logic behind the mergers of computer companies and publishers, because if the computer companies are going to develop *ad hoc* relationships with competitors of their own publishing subsidiaries, why acquire publishers in the first place? It may be one of the reasons why some other computer companies, such as Philco-Ford and Honeywell have so far failed to acquire publishing firms. In fact, there are no other combinations that quite fit the model created by IBM and SRA, and then followed later by RCA and Random House. The closest is General Learning, the joint venture of GE and Time, Inc., but it really belongs in a category all of its own.

In its initial efforts General Learning epitomized the wide conceptual differences between the people whose experience has been in education itself (e.g., publishers, individuals like Frank Keppel) and the engineers and systems men whose experience has been in manufacturing firms or in fields related to defense and space. Leaving aside the financial arrangements between GE and Time, the two basic assets of the new company were a conventional school publishing firm, Silver-Burdett, and a large number of systems analysts from the ranks of GE—plus, of course, access to GE's computer capabilities. During the first year or so of General Learning's existence, its most visible activity was what amounted to management consulting services for schools, in which the systems people went to work solving problems that were primarily administrative rather than instructional. It was this activity that was largely stopped in the early 1967 shake-out at General Learning that was widely interpreted as a triumph of the educators over the engineers. Whether it was or not, General Learning is now primarily a publishing firm, plus modest activities in educational planning and systems analysis. There is no public evidence that the Silver-Burdett people and the GE people have together done any work that fits our definition of educational technology.

Westinghouse has taken a very different approach. In fact, the only real similarities between the educational efforts of GE and Westinghouse are that both are running Job Corps centers and both used the word "learning" in the names of their education companies. (As a word to describe the business involved, "learning" is more basic and probably better than "education," and far more appropriate than "book.") Westinghouse is almost unique among the new education companies in that it has organized a business and established long-term goals without acquiring a publishing firm as a base. Its only acquisitions to date have been people, including a few of the men who did pioneering work in programed instruction almost 10 years ago. It remains to be seen whether Westinghouse can build a viable business from scratch—and remember that it will take products more than services to make the business viable

—or whether it will eventually build its base through the acquisition of companies that are already producing educational materials and equipment, e.g. publishers, film companies, and equipment suppliers.

Another variant is Xerox, which has acquired not one but several publishing businesses, and in the process is becoming one of the major producers of printed educational materials and information services. (When its acquisition of Ginn is completed later this year, the Xerox Education Division will have sales of somewhere around $90 million.) Part of the Xerox strategy seems to be that a diversified product line is highly desirable in and of itself, even if much of it offers little opportunity for the application of reprographic techniques. In fact, the Xerox Education Division, which houses all of these subsidiaries, appears determined to remain machine-independent. Given our concept of educational technology as a process rather than as hardware systems, the present writers consider machine-independence an asset rather than a liability. However, the balance sheet on Xerox should also include a note to the effect that it is neither a manufacturer of computers nor a producer (on any significant scale) of audiovisual materials. Lawrence Lipsitz, editorializing in the February 28, 1968 issue of *Educational Technology,* feels that Xerox "has behaved in a conservative fashion" and is "an example of non-innovation in education," but there are some signs that the *process* of educational technology is better understood at Xerox than in some of the firms that are more dependent on a particular kind of hardware, like computers.

The Raytheon Education Company looks somewhat like Xerox, but is smaller and has a different mix of components. It is comprised of four acquisitions: D. C. Heath, like Ginn, a relatively conventional school publishing firm; Macalaster Scientific, a producer of science equipment for schools and colleges; Edex, a manufacturer of an electronic student response system for classrooms; and Dage-Bell, which manufactures both school television and language lab equipment. Raytheon appears to have made a conscious decision to bring these four subsidiaries close together in one place in order to get the benefits of interaction between them, and this may turn out to be a strategic decision of major importance. (It is a decision that geography would make considerably more difficult for Xerox.)

Our final variation on the theme is the CBS acquisition of Holt, Rinehart and Winston. Unlike IBM, RCA, GE, Westinghouse, Xerox and Raytheon, CBS is not a manufacturer of equipment, educational or otherwise, but rather a proprietor of communications networks and a producer of programs, primarily for entertainment rather than education. (CBS does have, however, an exceptional capacity under Peter Goldmark for equipment research, which could presumably lead to equipment production.) The new CBS-Holt group will presumably be machine-independent and, like the independent publishers, free to make *ad hoc* arrangements with different equipment manufacturers, particularly in the field of computer-assisted instruction. The CBS-Holt group also includes Creative Playthings (educational games and toys, especially for pre-school programs, are of considerable current interest) and two producers of films and filmstrips. It will be interesting to see what CBS and Holt between them can produce. Both are in the business of dissemination, CBS through programming and broadcasting and Holt through the printed page (and more recently films); neither is essentially hardware-oriented although CBS has some important hardware competence.

There are other major industrial firms with new interests in education—Litton Industries, for example, which has acquired the American Book Company—but these few are among the more visible, and they serve to illustrate the differences between the new education companies, differences which will almost certainly lead them in different directions. There are also major industrial firms quite similar to those described, which have not as yet made any major moves into the education or learning market, and which must wonder if they are missing a major opportunity. It remains to be seen. It also remains to be seen whether the major accomplishments (both educational and financial) will be made by the strong independent publishers like McGraw-Hill, Harcourt and Crowell-Collier and Macmillan, by the computer-oriented combinations like IBM-SRA and RCA-Random House, by the *de novo* operations like Westinghouse, by the *potpourri* combinations like Xerox and Raytheon, like the communications firms like CBS-Holt, or by some other types still to come.

A Look at Capabilities

A better clue to the ability of business firms to develop a process of educational technology and to compete effectively in a highly diversified educational marketplace may be to examine the capabilities that will be required. The more obvious ones are a) developmental research, b) an understanding of behavioral psychology, c) subject-matter competence, d) equipment competence but machine independence, e) broad marketing operations, f) systems analysis experience, and g) money to invest over a long period of time. Good management is assumed.

Strong research departments have been one of the strengths of many of the industrial firms that have entered the education business, while *bona fide* research has been notably absent in educational publishing. How important is it to the applications of technology to education? Our view is that pure research, which here would primarily be research in learning itself, need not be done by the business firms themselves, but that they must be prepared to do a great deal of developmental research towards the creation of specific products or systems—or to give it a less dignified designation, experimental product development. Given the objective of creating an innovative learning system, the early steps would include at least the following:

1. research in learning, on which new instructional strategies can be based;
2. experimental applications of this research in the form of methodologies, e.g., graded vs. ungraded primary education, or other changes between the teacher and the learner;
3. experimental products to implement the experimental strategies, e.g., programed books;
4. research to develop entirely new types of products, e.g., computers to apply programed instruction;
5. subject-matter or skills analysis to determine the content of units of instruction, or what to teach when and in what sequence, to whom;
6. the production of models for field-testing;
7. and evaluation under conditions that approximate the real world of education.

Of these seven steps, the first two and the fourth come closest to being true research. The first two are clearly the responsibility of educational researchers in universities and other non-profit organizations associated with education; and while more power to any business firm that undertakes them, this may not be the best allocation of resources for either education itself or the stockholders of the companies involved. The fourth could well be in responsibility of university research groups, but in fact has largely been carried out by business firms. The most expensive research towards new types of educational products has been in the computer field, most of which has been done and paid for by the computer manufacturers, particularly IBM. (Consider, of course, who would have paid if computers for education had the same priority as jet engines for national defense.)

None of the other steps can realistically be called research. Instead they are either basic decision-making to determine the scope and sequence of instruction (which is largely but not entirely the responsibility of educators), or else experimental product development and testing (which is largely but not entirely the responsibility of business). Thus it appears that the capacity to do pure research is not of critical importance to the companies pursuing educational technology, but that the willingness and ability to experiment and test is critically important. Some firms have this ability to a greater degree than others, and some clues as to their relative abilities can be seen in the degree to which they have been willing to create new product lines that have the potential to make their own proven and successful product lines obsolete.

Behavioral psychology is increasingly the foundation of the process of educational technology, and it is unlikely that much significant work can be done without reference to it. The problem for the designers of instructional systems is not to conduct behavioral research but to apply its findings where they are applicable.

Subject-matter competence is necessary because development of skills and mastery of content are the ends of education. Even in the creation of a fairly stable medium like a textbook, in-house subject-matter competence has been extremely important, and it is even more important in the creation of a new learning system in which individual components and the juxtaposition of components are innovative. During the early days of programed instruction there were arguments about whether the best work would be done by programming experts who learned the subject-matter or by subject-matter experts who learned programming. By and large the latter won out, and they are even more likely to maintain their pre-eminence as several methodologies and instructional media are combined. This is not to suggest that the producers of instructional systems will no longer need the help of outside independent authors, but rather that the producer's side of the developmental group must have people who know in depth the structure of the skill or subject that the system is being designed to teach.

Equipment competence is important to the extent that equipment is an integral part of the instructional system and is not relatively standard. The various equipment technologies are not all alike in this respect. On the one hand, audio-visual technology is now so standardized that the producer of audio-visual materials of instruction need only know the technical characteristics of different kinds of equipment—and have good relations with their manufacturers. On the other hand, computer technology is so complex that the developer of computer-assisted systems of instruction either needs his own computer competence or else a close working relationship with one or more computer manufacturers. More important, the customer will require continuing service of both the equipment and the programs. Equally as important as a technical knowledge of equipment is an independence to choose the equipment that is most appropriate for the particular instructional task. One of the weaknesses of textbook publishers has been a tendency to depend exclusively on the printed page to help students accomplish specific learning or skills, and a potential pitfall for the computer-oriented companies will be to turn first to the computer to deliver a given unit of instruction. The best systems of instruction will be developed by the people who make equipment decisions late in the game, and make them without undue regard to what equipment they make in their own shops.

The marketing of educational technology is more of an unknown than its development because so little has yet been sold. However, it seems likely that it will require at least three ingredients. First, a sure knowledge of the educational community, primarily at the state and local level where almost all of the buying decisions are made. This is a particularly long suit of the educational publishers, and it's an important one because the education market is sprawling, complex, highly idiosyncratic, and often slow to respond.

Second, the marketing of instructional systems created through educational technology will take a major commitment to teacher-training. These systems will require teaching techniques with which most teachers are unfamiliar (and for which the schools of education are giving them little training), and the only way their producers will get them sold and used properly is to run thoroughly professional in-service training programs. This is an expensive proposition, as we have discovered who have done it on a large scale.

Third, it will require custom selling of the sort done routinely by computer manufacturers. Almost by definition, an instructional system will be tailored to the needs of the individual school system, even though it may be made up of off-the-shelf components.

The two final capabilities required by business firms that apply technology to education are systems analysis or management and capital. The first has been discussed at more length than it deserves both in Dr. Oettinger's essay and in this commentary, and therefore needs no further elaboration here. It is a competence that has importance and value, but no greater than any other mentioned here.

Money is more important, along with the willingness to allow bets to ride for three, four or five years. The development of sophisticated systems is a complex and expensive job and although the investment in absolute dollars is not great for companies that have gambled on the manufacture of computers or television sets, it is large relative to the potential pay-off. Rates of profit are anybody's guess, but they are apt to be lower than for textbook publishing (8 to 9% after taxes). If so, they would be lower than the normal rates of profit for Xerox and IBM, but higher than those of RCA, Raytheon and Westinghouse. Cash flow is apt to be poor in a business involving long-term investments, slow inventory turnover (schools buy once a year) and large receivables (schools being slow to pay). No quick buck business, this. (It helps, obviously, to have a large base of profitable business out of which to finance the new developments—like textbooks.)

Diversity and Integration

As must be entirely obvious by now, we attach great importance to diversity of capabilities and resources. The teaching-learning environment is becoming highly fluid, and the greatest contributions to it (and profits from it) are likely to be made by the organizations with the capacity to move in the greatest number of different directions. The companies that can produce films as well as books are in a better position than those which produce books alone; and the companies that can produce a full array of materials and equipment, from books to computer programs to instructional equipment, have the greatest chance to help make instruction responsive to the needs of individual learners. The companies that have deliberately diversified, from either a publishing base or a hardware base, are better off than those which haven't, and the more diversity the better.

However, diversity without integration may not pay off, and integration can be the more complex side of the equation. The creation, through the process of educational technology, of sophisticated instructional systems requires *by definition* that people with different capabilities work together and have at their disposal all of the applicable resources of the organization. This means that the different components of a diversified education company should either be put together or at least have easy access to each other. To cite a specific example, Raytheon's work on the PSSC project will presumably improve as the Heath and Macalaster people work more closely together. When PSSC was first developed, Heath and Macalaster were separate companies, and the entire job of integrating the different components of that instructional program fell to the PSSC group at ESI. Now both Heath and Macalaster are part of Raytheon and the opportunity exists, at least, to create from both companies a project team with multi-media capabilities to work on PSSC. However, not much is apt to happen unless the Raytheon management is willing to violate the organizational integrity of Heath and Macalaster, both of which so recently were independent companies. Raytheon's current institutional advertising suggests that it is now an integrated education company, so perhaps it has taken this difficult step which we consider essential.

All of the other education companies face the same problem. Integration is easier to accomplish if new capabilities are created internally rather than acquired, and it probably comes easier in a company that diversifies from a programming (or publishing) base than in one that diversifies from a hardware base—simply because the programming process is closer to the process of educational technology or instructional design than is the process of designing hardware. If you want to make your own judgments about which companies are most likely to solve some of the problems of educational technology posed by Dr. Oettinger, make a list of the different kinds of educational products they now have, the functional capabilities they appear to have, and then examine the degree to which they have integrated them.

1. Summarize Oettinger's seven-point critique of educational technology, and the authors' response to each point.

2. Contrast Oettinger's "definition" of educational technology with that of the authors.

3. Cite several bases for the authors' claim that "our schools have never been so innovation-prone."

4. Which of the "1978 predictions" do you think are coming true? What's the basis for your opinion?

Presenting Instruction

OBJECTIVES

When you complete unit 28, you should be able to:

* contrast the discovery and presentation methods of instruction on the bases of efficiency and effectiveness;
* identify the four components of Programmed Instruction in an original example and construct a Mathetics form of PI material to teach a student to find an average;
* outline an errorless procedure for teaching an original concept or principle;
* cite the bases for choosing media, resources, type of instruction, and type of responding;
* describe conditions under which active responding facilitates learning and one in which it impedes learning.

After you have specified your objectives for a unit of instruction and analyzed and sequenced the subskills in detail, you are ready to decide on the materials, mode, and method of presenting the instructional unit.

Presentation Methods and Their Uses

There are a variety of specific approaches to the presenting of instruction currently in use. You can verbally deliver the material to the students in a note-taking class session or you can write out your lecture as clearly as possible on a one-time basis and distribute this written material to the students. When appropriate, you can demonstrate the skill you are teaching. Or you can lead the students in a class discussion about the topic, perhaps but not necessarily preceded by a lecture presentation on the topic. Or you might choose a discovery approach, in which you provide the materials and require the students to identify facts, define concepts, or solve problems on their own or with some guidance from you.

In any of these specific approaches there are a variety of resources that can be used, including texts, film, recordings, and real examples. These resources can be brought into the classroom, or the students can be taken on a field trip to a natural or community resource setting. The main instructional advantage possible in the use of these resources lies in the increased reality of what is observed or done. The essential attributes of a certain plant species may be able to be learned in the classroom, but the plant's natural setting includes many irrelevant but typically associated stimuli. An athlete might be able to demonstrate a skill in his own gym class, but a competitive meet before an unfamiliar crowd could add powerful (though irrelevant) S^D's which might affect his performance. The same kind of phenomenon can occur when a student who has learned to solve problems presented in a text attempts to solve similar problems occuring in a live community action effort.

The choice of method, modes, and resources should be made after the objectives are defined and the task analysis is completed because in instruction the medium is not the message, even in instruction about media. Method and media and other resources are basically *servants* of the *instruction*. Of course, they can add pleasure and be of interest in their own right, but they should be selected primarily on the basis of how well they can be expected to contribute to the achievement of the objectives.

The objectives and the task analysis should be the primary determinants of the resources used to achieve them. If a student's ability to identify the components of a cell when shown a diagram or picture is the objective, then there's no need for microscopes. But there is such a need if you want him to be able to identify and describe real cells. Travelogues and copies of *National Geographic* might be very useful if your objective regarding differences in culture among peoples is not only cognitive but affective as well. If your objective is to teach the student to use not only the school library but also any local library, then you might start out with some textual material and classroom demonstration, but you would want to move to the school library and the city library to give your students practice and skill development in those real situations.

Each major content area has a variety of resources and special methods that have been found to be especially appropriate and effective in teaching about those topics. You will find that specialists in these areas can provide a variety of suggestions, but seldom any hard and fast rules about when to use which method or resource. Furthermore, the educational enterprise is not as amply financed as you might require or wish, and you will undoubtedly have to make compromises and settle for approximating the ideal conditions under which a skill should be learned and demonstrated. It may well be that the most valuable presentation skill you can learn is the ability to be *adaptive* and ingenious in using common ordinary resources in uniquely helpful ways.

Shaping and Errorless Learning

Recall your prior learning of the procedures involved in shaping a new behavior, and you will note the similarities between shaping and the learning of a new skill. Building on a student's entry behavior, you differentially reinforce successive approximations to the desired skill level. In the case of concept learning, for example, the successive approximations involve learning finer and finer discriminations. At first the S^D's are highlighted and the potentially confusing features are minimized; then the S^D's are reduced to real proportion with reference to the irrelevant stimuli. Thus by a gradual process the new behavior is shaped until it is under the control of the appropriate features of any example.

In the past it was thought that student errors during learning were inevitable and even desirable. We now know that errors are not inevitable when learning to discriminate or generalize. The classic experiment was performed by Herbert Terrace[1] and is worth studying as a model. His purpose was to teach pigeons to discriminate the color red from green without making any errors. The key that the pigeon pecked was translucent, and Terrace could make the key red or green by shining a colored light through it. He first taught the pigeon to peck the key when it was red, differentially reinforcing such responses with food. Then he began to introduce green through the key, but at first he did this only for a few seconds at a time and only when the pigeon had moved away from the key. Furthermore, initially the green light was very dim, almost black. He continued, of course, to reinforce pecking only when the key was red. Very *gradually* he increased the duration of the green light, increased its intensity, and allowed the key to be green when the pigeon was closer to the key. Using this procedure, the pigeons acquired the discrimination of red and generalization across green (and black) with virtually no errors. A control

[1] Herbert Terrace, "Discrimination Learning With and Without Errors," *Journal of the Experimental Analysis of Behavior* 6(1963): 1–27.

group of pigeons was taught the same discrimination by a process of differential reinforcement that began with green and red lights of equal duration and brightness, and these pigeons made several thousand errors each in the learning process.

Notice that Terrace began by teaching the pigeon to discriminate the *essential* attributes, using *prompts* (contrasting brightness and duration of the lights), and then he gradually introduced *irrelevant* characteristics and *negative* examples, while *fading* the prompts. This procedure can and has been used effectively in human learning of discriminations (see, for example, the previous illustration of teaching the letter *b*).

Though we can learn by our mistakes, research indicates that it is far better to learn without mistakes. Terrace found that even after the discrimination was learned, the pigeons who learned with errors continued to make hundreds of errors, usually in bursts after periods of correct responding. Classroom research has repeatedly shown the same phenomenon of continued error probability.

1. Using an original example, outline an errorless procedure you could use to teach a concept or principle. (Remember all the appropriate steps.)

Presentation versus Discovery Method

In a broad sense, the aforementioned procedures can be used in teaching a skill, concept, or principle in one of two general ways, inductive or deductive. The inductive approach is often referred to as *discovery* learning, in which the student is not shown the skill, not told the fact, not given the definition of the concept or its critical attributes, but instead is given a set of materials or a series of examples and must induce or discover the fact or concept for himself. Sometimes these examples are carefully arranged so as to increase the probability that the student will discriminate the essential features, and often prompts and hints are supplied along the way. There is even a method called "Guided Discovery," in which the student begins only with examples and materials, but is provided with progressively more explicit prompts until he is finally able to state and apply the fact or concept.

The presentation or expository approach presents the student immediately with the skill or concept by defining and/or demonstrating its essential properties. In the case of a concept, examples are then given illustrating the essential attributes as well as the irrelevant features, until the student demonstrates that he can identify new examples and uses of the concept or principle.

Research indicates that the presentation method is considerably more *efficient* than the discovery method; more students actually master the objectives, and in less time. The main argument for discovery learning is that it will make the student a better problem solver because he is given a lot of practice at discovering solutions to problems.

Here the research is at best inconclusive, but the reason may be in the poor research designs of many of the studies. Obviously, if a discovery lesson is to be successful, it must be arranged so that the student actually is *able* to discover, and do so soon enough to have time to discover other important things as well. This means, among other things, that the student actually has the prerequisite skills for learning the task of problem solving. Problem solving is a *skill* in itself, and like all other skills it is best taught systematically, not by chance.

It seems clear from the research to date that if your objective is to teach a particular task or concept, then the presentation method will be more effective and efficient than the discovery method. If your objective is to teach the student to discover solutions to problems, then the discovery method might be very useful, especially in giving the student practice at applying general problem-solving rules he has already learned *directly*.

Programmed Instruction

Programmed instruction (PI) is a method that is equally adaptable to either of the general approaches outlined above. As a general method, PI has several variations. You are probably familiar with the programming technique of presenting the material in small frames of one or several sentences, each of which requires a student response (either constructed or multiple-choice). These frames can be arranged in a linear fashion, which offers only one route through the material, or in a branching fashion, which provides several optional routes as indicated by the acceptability of each response by the student.

PI as a general technique is not limited to the small frame variety. The term embraces both materials and procedures which have the following components:

1. Instruction is organized into *small units*. A unit means the amount of material presented before a criterion test, after which a *decision* is made about the kind of instruction that should follow for the student. "Small" is a variable term; the unit might range from several sentences or an exercise to several pages or exercises.

2. The material presented in the units and within each unit is *sequenced* according to the shaping dictates of task analysis, so that the terminal objectives are successively approximated.

3. Each unit requires active student *responding* at frequent intervals throughout the unit, with the final responding being the mastery **test** for the unit objectives. Student responses during and at the end of **the** unit receive immediate *feedback.*

4. Student progress through the units is *self-paced,* determined primarily by the adequacy of the student's responses.

One variant of the programmed instruction approach is called *Mathetics.* It calls for a three-step process in teaching each subskill identified in the task analysis: demonstrating, prompting, and releasing the intended response. First the response is demonstrated or, in the case of a concept, the essential attributes are highlighted. Then the student is required to practice the appropriate responses in the presence of prompts (heavy, fading to light). Finally the response is released from the prior guidance and prompting so that it is made in a realistic situation.

As an illustration, consider the following small sample of mathetics instruction. Each frame would be on a different page.

Demonstration (p. 1)

You have already learned to multiply fractions.
You **DIVIDE** fractions in the same way, except you must do one step first:

$1/2 \div 1/3$ Turn this number upside down (3/1), then

$1/2 \times 3/1$ multiply as you have learned

You do this one: $1/5 \div 1/4$

Prompt (p. 2)

Work these problems: (Remember to turn upside down first)

$5/6 \div 8/9 =$

$8/9 \div 5/6 =$

Release (p. 3)

Work these problems:

$7/9 \div 3/5 =$

$3/4 \div 2/3 =$

$8/4 \div 3/5 =$

$2/5 \div 5/2 =$

Mathetics is easy to learn and easy to use, and the teacher will find it flexibly applicable to just about any instructional task.

> 2. Contrast the presentation and discovery methods of instruction on the bases of efficiency and effectiveness. (Remember that effectiveness is relative to the objective.)
>
> 3. Cite an original example of programmed instruction and identify the specific ways in which it meets the four general criteria for PI.
>
> 4. Construct a mathetics sequence to teach a student how to find an average. Presume the student can already add and divide.

Learning by Doing

It should be clear that there is one principle basic to every aspect of careful teaching; a student learns best by actively doing what he is being taught to do. A teacher who has described the instructional objectives in measurable terms has also identified the kinds of responding that are involved in that terminal skill. Even if the terminal objectives are purely mental or affective, these can be expressed in terms of directly observable behaviors. The student will best learn to do these skills and subskills to criterion if the instruction carefully and frequently requires active responding.

Types of Active Responding

There are many varieties of student responding, ranging from covert listening, reading, and watching through thinking to overt verbal responding and demonstration (such as on a test). The appropriateness of each type depends primarily on the particular nature of objective behaviors, but there are several qualities (identified by research) which the required responding must have if it is to serve instruction.[2]

First, the required responding must be *relevant* to the key *objectives;* if it is not, it will not improve instruction and may in fact hinder it. This principle may seem very obvious but it is frequently violated. Consider the following question for a unit of instruction which has the objective of mastery of the concept of concept:

A concept is a pattern of discrimination_____(1) to a set of attributes shared by some examples and not shared by other_____.(2)

The required responses are not only of doubtful criticality in relation to the objective but also are heavily prompted; the student who makes these responses is probably not assisted in learning the definition of concept. Furthermore, mastery of the objective includes more than the definition; the student must also be able to identify essential attributes, construct and discriminate between examples and nonexamples, etc. Some of these skills call for *constructed* responding (that is constructing the correct response without any prompts except for the question itself, as for example in an essay or short-answer type question); others simply require a *choice* (that is, choosing the correct answer when it is given with incorrect answers, as in a multiple-choice type question. But for the skill of constructing original examples, a multiple-choice type of responding is invalid because choice behavior requires the student to choose an item when given several, not to construct one without prompts. Most of the research studies that show no advantage for programmed instruction used programs in which the responses were trivial to the objectives or in which the students could easily get the answers without making the responses.

Second, the student must be *able* to make the response correctly; that is, he must have been taught to make the response not long before he is required to make it. Requiring the student to exhibit a skill for which he has not been prepared, as is done in many forms of discovery learning, or a skill he was taught months before and has since forgotten, as is done in some expository systems, will hinder instructional effectiveness and frustrate most students.

Frequency of Active Responding

Third, research strongly indicates that active responding is most beneficial when it is required *immediately* after small units.[3] Not only does this proce-

---

[2] See, for example, the report by Holland and Kemp "A Measure of Programing in Teaching-Machine Material," *Journal of Educational Psychology* 56(1965): 264–69.

[3] For example, see the article by G. J. Margolius and F. O. Sheffield, "Optimum Methods of Combining Practice with Filmed Demonstrations in Teaching Complex Response Sequences: Serial Learning of a Mechanical-Assembly Task," in *Student Response in Programed Instruction,* ed., A. A. Lumsdaine (Washington, D.C.: National Academy of Sciences—National Research Council, 1961).

dure produce needed feedback about the student's learning, but it also guarantees that the student will *retain* more. Research indicates that most forgetting occurs during the first twenty-four hours after learning. Requiring active and relevant responding immediately after learning helps preserve what the student has learned and still remembers.

For this reason, simply throwing out a question now and then during instruction won't help much at all. Occasional quizzes (monthly or even weekly) will have only minimal effect on student achievement, in comparison with procedures that require a student to practice each subskill as soon as possible after instruction on that subskill.

This evidence also relates closely to the optimal size of a unit. The question is how many skills should be taught before active responding is required as a basis for deciding whether to remediate or continue with the instruction? The answer has very little to do with the length of the material in pages or minutes or class periods. Instead, the size of a unit depends on the *current skills* of each student and on the difficulty of the skill being taught.

The general principle is that *a unit should teach only as many skills as a student can be expected to be able to handle without having his possible errors snowball.* If a student has failed to learn a segment of the unit, that need not be a serious problem since the required responding will make this error evident and it can be corrected. The danger is that his error will in turn lead to further errors and these compounded misconceptions will interact to produce a serious problem. If in a statistics or calculus course you fail to learn to use some basic procedures correctly, further instruction is not only a waste but a hindrance to learning.

The errors must be identified *immediately.* Some suggest that you can estimate the proper length of a unit by determining whether each student could be expected to respond with 75–80 percent accuracy after finishing the unit. Since the basic skills of students can be expected to vary considerably from student to student, it is easiest to design your unit for the student who needs the most immediate feedback; then it is no problem to combine several units for students who are less likely to make snowballing errors.

5.   What's the most important basis for choosing media? extra resources? instructional method? type of responding to require?

6.   Describe three conditions under which active responding will facilitate learning.

7. Why is it dangerous to require only covert responses until the post-test?

8. How soon after material is presented should you require each student to respond? Cite several reasons for your answer.

9. What kind of required overt response might do more harm than good in instruction?

10. Four groups of students with the same entry skills are given the same unit of instruction. Group A receives an immediate posttest; Group B takes a posttest the next day; Group C takes its posttest one week later, and Group D one month later. If all four groups then take another form of the posttest six months after their first posttest, which group would you expect to do better, or would you expect no clear difference between the groups? Why?

unit 29

Questioning

OBJECTIVES

When you complete this unit, you should be able to:

* define and differentiate between narrow and broad questions and differentiate memory, convergent, divergent, and evaluative questions on the bases of the uses of each and the type of responding elicited by each;
* construct original examples of the four kinds of questions and classify a new sample of questions according to the four categories;
* describe four suggested questioning strategies with original illustrations.

Questions are one type of *preceding stimulus* event. Questions function in the same general way as do words and instructions in a workbook, announcements or directions on the blackboard, sounds that are heard, or pictures or diagrams that are seen. Each kind of preceding event tends to elicit a certain kind of response from the student, such as working a problem in the workbook, starting the spelling assignment after finishing the math assignment as indicated on the blackboard, looking around to see who just screamed, attending to the details of a picture.

But the effectiveness of these preceding events in eliciting a response depends, in the long run, on the *consequent* events that follow the behavior. A person who lives near the airport may eventually "adapt" to the intermittent roar of the jets and never "hear" or attend to the noise; the response to that preceding event extinguishes. In the same way, a student can cease responding (outwardly and inwardly) to verbal directions or questions because he has learned that such responding gets him nothing that he finds worthwhile.

The question is a frequently used preceding stimulus event in the classroom. Some teachers spend up to 80 percent of their time asking questions. When used well, questions can elicit a variety of kinds of responses, especially mental responses, and at all levels from memory recitation to thinking of new ways to combine rules for solving problems. In this unit, you will learn how to construct different kinds of questions to get your students to think or act in different ways. But remember that even the best question will not achieve its purposes unless the teacher also pays close attention to the consequences he provides for responding to questions.

The questions you direct to your students can greatly influence the cognitive level at which they *think*. Many research studies report a high correlation between the level of student thought displayed in student answers and the type of question asked. When you think about this, it's an obvious point; a student is very likely to think only at the knowledge level when he is asked a purely recall question because there's no payoff for doing otherwise. It is equally obvious that if your objective is at the application or problem-solving level, then you should choose a question that requires responding at that level.

The next few pages outline a system for classifying questions on the basis of the level of thought required to answer them.[1] Your knowledge of this system will help you to identify different kinds of questions and to choose the type that best fits your instructional purpose.

Classifying and Choosing Questions

In very general terms, questions fall into two classes: narrow and broad. *Narrow* questions call for answers that are very predictable because there is only *one* specific answer that is appropriate. Narrow questions typically require more *memory* than original thought, more discrimination and comprehension skills than application or principle learning skills. Here are some examples of narrow questions:

What time is it?

---

[1] This classification system is adapted from the following sources, which you might wish to consult for elaboration: Edmund Amidon and Elizabeth Hunter, *Improving Teaching: The Analysis of Classroom Verbal Interaction* (New York: Holt, Rinehart and Winston, Inc., 1966); James Gallagher, *Productive Thinking in Gifted Children* (Urbana, Ill.: University of Illinois Press, 1965); and James Weigand, *Developing Teacher Competencies* (Englewood Cliffs, N.J.: Prentice-Hall, Inc., 1971).

What is the area contained in this circle?
What is the definition of energy?
Do you have your lunch money with you?
What is a cell?
What is the name of Hamlet's sister?

Narrow questions are useful for collecting information, testing knowledge and comprehension of basic facts and skills. The teacher needs this kind of information to manage the instruction and to make decisions about whether each student is ready for more complex learning. If these questions are overused, however, higher level cognitive skills may receive less deliberate training than they should.

Broad questions, on the other hand, permit a *variety* of answers, any of which might be appropriate. Broad questions require the student to do more than simply recall; the student must *put facts together* to form concepts, put concepts together to form principles, or put principles together to form higher order rules. Frequently there are several ways in which this kind of putting-together can be accomplished, and so there may be several "right" answers to the question. Here are some examples of broad questions:

How could you communicate in the classroom if you could not ask questions?
How might education be different if all teachers were men?
Why do you want to be a teacher?
How could you determine the volume of this box without using a ruler?
Name several works of literature or music based on the Faust theme.
What might happen if we mixed chemical X with chemical Y?
If Jesus were alive today, what might he say and do?

Broad questions can be used to stimulate a student to exhibit independence in using information, to become more creative in analyzing and synthesizing facts and rules, and to become more precise in evaluating his own cognitive principles.

Practice constructing some examples of your own of narrow and broad questions, and compare them with the above descriptions and criteria, before continuing.

1. How do the questions you ask affect the cognitive level at which they think?

2. Differentiate between narrow and broad questions on the basis of

a) the type of answer each elicits or the kind of skill required of the respondent;

b) the uses of each.

Within these two general classes of questions, there are further useful distinctions that can be made. Narrow questions can be subdivided into *memory* and *convergent* questions; broad questions can be subdivided into *divergent* and *evaluative* questions (figure 29-1). Notice as you study these subclasses that they are not exhaustive; there are other types of questions that can elicit other kinds of responses, for example, concerned with analyzing and synthesizing or with developing new rules and applying them to new problems

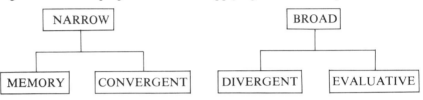

Figure 29-1

Narrow Question Categories

Memory questions are a type of narrow question requiring no more than *recall* of memorized information. Memory questions ask for naming, identifying, or defining something and frequently call for a one-word or yes-no answer.

Convergent questions are also narrow, but not as narrow as memory questions. Convergent questions still "converge" on one right answer, but they require the student to put *together* some facts, compare and contrast several concepts, or paraphrase in his own words in order to get that correct response.

Examine each of the following questions and decide whether they are memory or convergent questions: if you have trouble, review the above descriptions.

_____ What is identical about the angles of a square and any triangle?
_____ What is a square?
_____ What did I just do in this demonstration?
_____ Why does the sun appear to rise and set?

Questions 1 and 4 are convergent questions since they converge on one answer and the student must put several facts or concepts together (squareness, triangleness, angles and degrees, earth's rotation, relationship of sun and earth). Questions 2 and 3 call for naming and defining and are therefore memory questions.

Notice that convergent questions can become pure memory questions after some instruction. Question 1, for example, is convergent for a student who is being asked to find these common characteristics for the first time. But if he is asked the same question later, he may be able simply to recall the answer he gave the first time. In this unit, we will presume this has not happened.

Broad Question Categories

Divergent questions comprise one class of broad questions since they admit more than one correct response; they "diverge" into *more than one* acceptable answer. They might require the student to infer, hypothesize, or in some way predict an event on the basis of facts or concepts that he already knows. Not only do they require the student to put together such information (as do convergent questions) but, once he has done this, they allow him to repeat the process with different combinations of facts or concepts to arrive at a different answer.

Evaluative questions are the broadest type of question; they not only admit more than one acceptable response, but they also require the student to *judge the merit* of several possible answers. The student must put together information in several ways, then make a judgment about the relative merits of each possible answer, and perhaps justify his choice or defend his judgment.

Examine the following questions and classify each one as memory, convergent, divergent, or evaluative. If you have trouble, review the descriptions of each.

_____ 1. How could you communicate to someone from a foreign country that you wanted his friendship?
_____ 2. Explain why the brick did not float.
_____ 3. Why is this novel better than the other one?
_____ 4. How will the Presidency of the United States be different ten years from now?
_____ 5. Is syphillis contagious?
_____ 6. How is a cell like a person?
_____ 7. What might your life be like if you were a Neanderthal?
_____ 8. Who is your favorite musician and why?

Question 5 is a memory question requiring a recall answer. Questions 2 and 6 are convergent questions requiring explanation and comparison. Questions 1 and 7 require the student to infer, hypothesize, or predict and thus are divergent. Questions 3, 4, and 8 are evaluative, requiring not only the combination of information but also the evaluation of these facts and an evaluative judgment.

There are some cues that are often helpful in identifying one kind of question or another. Memory questions often begin with words like who, what, where, which, when, and sometimes how and why. Convergent questions more often begin with words like how or why or compare. Divergent questions might begin with if or what if or what would happen. Evaluative questions might include phrases like do you think, in your opinion, or superlatives like best or most. But you can't rely on these clues; the rest of the sentence can change the nature of the question completely.

Sometimes the distinction between divergent and evaluative questions is a difficult one to make. Both kinds of questions can lead to several acceptable answers; both require the putting together of several known facts or concepts; both can require some hypothesizing. But evaluative questions also require a subjective merit judgment. This requirement is clear in question 3 (above), but not as clear in question 4. Notice, however, that question 4 admits of several acceptable answers, but none of them are necessarily correct since they all refer to the future, about which we can't be sure. A student can integrate several things he knows about past and present presidential trends and come up with some plausible predictions, but he can also come up with contradictory predictions based on a different set of facts. He must therefore make a subjective judgment as to which are more likely. In contrast, question 7 is divergent because it does not necessarily require a merit judgment; one can make some true and sure statements about the Neanderthal's life.

To further illustrate the similarities and differences between these four types of questions, let's see what it might be like to move from memory to evaluative questions with a specific topic of study.

Let's say you and your music class are studying Beethoven's Ninth Symphony. After some introductory listening and study, you might then play excerpts of themes on the piano and ask your students what movement each belongs to. This is a memory question and it is important because this knowledge is prerequisite to other things you want to teach them about the symphony.

Later in the study you might ask them to identify the first time a variant of the Choral Movement's main theme is introduced in the symphony. This is a convergent question because it requires the student to put together several facts in arriving at the correct answer.

At a more advanced stage of study, you might ask the students to identify several devices Beethoven used to build up to the last movement. This is a divergent question because it requires the student not only to remember facts and put them together, but also to repeat these processes in coming up with several correct answers.

Finally you can prompt the students to evaluate different aspects of the work as a whole in comparison with other symphonies. You might ask them "What is your favorite movement?" or "What do you think has made the Choral Movement so famous?"

3. Be able to write an *original* example of each of the four general kinds of questions.

4.   Be able to classify a new sample of sentences as one of the four kinds of questions and justify your choices.

Phrasing Questions

It is important for you to know not only what type of question to use for specific types of responding but also how to phrase the question so as to make it as effective as possible. A properly chosen type of question can still cause confusion or prompt an undesired type of response if it is poorly phrased.

Confusing questions violate the basic need for clarity. If you want your question to prompt a certain kind of thinking, then you must be sure that your intent is clearly communicated. Questions like "tell me about evolution" or "are you sure?" are often so vague and ambiguous that the student doesn't have any useful criteria to guide the direction of his thinking and responding. Even when such questions are placed in the context of a topic and an ongoing dialogue, they unfairly require more of the student than what he has been taught. When a student has to guess at the point of the question, he can easily be wrong for irrelevant reasons; he will of course find this punishing and may learn ways to avoid answering questions.

Simple yes-no questions are poor for a somewhat different reason. Questions like "Is there another way to solve this problem?" require the student only to respond with a yes or a no. Without thinking at all, he will be right about half the time. Furthermore, when the teacher gets a yes or a no, he will have to come back with another question, like how or what is it, and that is an uneconomical use of time. Such questions can be rephrased easily by using an interrogatory term at the start, such as who, what, or why. For example, "What is another way to solve this problem, without using a ruler?"

Too obvious questions are poorly phrased questions because they include so much information that the student is not required to contribute anything. For an example, a question like "Is this block white or black?" or "So this weighs more than this, is that right?" simply force an answer on the student without requiring much independent responding at any level. Such questions can be rephrased by asking, for example, "What color is this?" or "How can you tell which weighs more?"

Presenting Questions

The best measure of an effective question is the answer it elicits. Effective questioning depends not only on proper choices and clear phrasing but also on your presentation strategies. Here are four general rules that will make your question asking more effective.

1. *Mix your types of questions.* If you rely solely on a multitude of narrow questions, your students won't have the opportunity they need to develop skill in analysis, application, and evaluation. At first you need some narrow questions to prompt the student to clarify his knowledge and understanding of basic facts. Once this stage has been set, however, broad questions are necessary to prompt thinking and responding at higher levels.

2. *Mix your rate of questioning.* A rapid fire pattern (question-answer-question-answer) is an economical and attention-producing method for many types of narrow questions. However, quantity does not ensure quality. With many types of broad questions, a rapid fire pattern can be counterproductive. In answering a broad question the student must do more than simply recall; he must compare ideas, put them together, evaluate, and then phrase a clear response. This takes some time to be done well, and the student can't be expected to do it well if the questions are fired rapidly at him. The teacher must learn to be comfortable with a few seconds of silence.

3. *Encourage everyone's participation.* If you must work with large groups in your questioning process, you have to find methods that tend to keep *all* your students thinking *all* the time. This means that you must avoid directing most of your questions to the "bright volunteers" (a sort of mutual reinforcement clique); mix the questions up between volunteers and nonvolunteers, and attempt to tailor the type of question to an individual student's current abilities. It is best not to identify the respondent until after you have stated the question; otherwise the other students might tend to tune you out until their name is called. Instead, state the question and then call on someone to answer it. Best of all, whenever possible, phrase your broad questions so that they can be answered by several students, each with an answer that contributes something to the general point. For example: "There are several ways we could solve this problem; who can think of one?"

4. *Reinforce individual improvement.* Be sure that every student is reinforced for the slightest improvement in the quality of his response, even though his current skill may be not nearly as well developed as another student's. This requires, first of all, that you set the stage for reinforcement by asking individual students the kinds of questions they can probably handle. Levels of learning are interdependent. A student who does not yet understand some basic facts will surely not be able to formulate new principles. The purpose of questioning (and of teaching in general) is not to categorize students into "dumbs" and "brights" but to bring each student from the level he is at to the

highest level possible. When a student's response is wrong or incomplete, it is often wise to supply some prompts or rephrase the question into a narrower type so as to encourage his eventual correct response. Incomplete answers can also be handled with prompts that elicit the rest of the answer. In all cases, appropriate and desirable aspects of a student's response should be reinforced, even if all the student produced was a good try.

5. Be able to rephrase correctly: confusing, yes-no, too obvious questions.

6. Be able to summarize and illustrate each of the four suggested presentation strategies, when given its title.

Workshop: Dealing with Feelings

"I never suspected that he felt that strongly about it. Boy, I bet he thought I was hard. I just never got the message."

"I wish I could get my parents to understand how I feel about their nagging, but every time I try we get into a big argument and things get blown all out of proportion."

"Letting your feelings show just buys trouble. When I'm happy and excited and I show it, I come off looking like some kind of childish nut. When I'm bugged about something and say so, it sounds like I'm uptight and selfish about petty things. I say stay cool or be a fool."

These are statements of fairly common attitudes. They are said—or thought —by students and by teachers in thousands of schools, and they represent one important hindrance to effective instruction in the schools and to effective interpersonal relationships everywhere.

Feelings are states of mind or emotion a person has toward someone or something. Of course, we usually are not in a position to measure these states directly. We sometimes even find it difficult to identify our own feelings accurately and are surprised when our actions reveal different feelings.

But we can and do identify feelings on the basis of what a person says and does. A person's statements may clearly express his attitude toward someone or something, or they may vaguely hint at such an attitude. A person's actions (including facial expression, tone of voice, and posture) may give nonverbal indication of his feelings. In this sense, feelings—like attitudes—are sets of *approach or avoidance behaviors,* especially verbal behaviors, regarding the object of the feeling.

Whether we like it or not, the way we express (or don't express) our feelings about people and things has a great deal of influence on the satisfaction and achievement we and others get out of life. You already know how important it is that you exercise care in arranging contingencies and consequences for others and for yourself. Trusting relationships can be developed or stunted, understanding can be deepened or destroyed, self-satisfaction can be nurtured or perverted—all dependent to a large extent on your ability to accurately read the feelings of yourself and others and to respond appropriately.

This unit will not make you an expert in reading and responding to feelings, but it will probably make you much better at it than you are now. It will improve your ability to attend to and interpret the feelings expressed by others or held by yourself, to respond to others in a way that shows understanding and invites trust, and to express your own feelings honestly, courteously, and productively.

Of course there are times when it is not appropriate or advisable to lay out your feelings, but you can't really make a *choice* unless you already have the skills. This unit will give you information, practice, and feedback on these skills.

Introduction to Session 1

This unit takes the form of a workshop with other students. The unit's objectives are, in part, social skills, and they are best learned in a setting that is, in part, social.

To complete this unit you will need at least five other students (total group membership of no less than six and no more than nine) who can all meet at the same time twice a week for 50–60 minutes each.

When this group has agreed on a schedule for the sessions, submit the names of the members and the date and time for your first session to your instructor, who may want to make some recommendations to the group.

All members should read the Introduction to this unit before the first session, and all should bring the complete unit to each session.[1] The directions for conducting each session are included in the pages for each session.

It might be helpful to learn one definition before Session 1.

Empathy: feeling for and with another person. Putting yourself in the other person's shoes so that you understand exactly how the other person is experiencing something, no matter how superficial or deep his feelings are.

---

[1] For a complete training guide, see: G. Gazda, *Human Relations Development* (Boston: Allyn and Bacon, Inc., 1973).

Session 1

Organization

1. Each member should *introduce* himself to the group and state several things about himself that he thinks might help the others know and understand him.

2. Choose a *moderator,* if you wish. The moderator participates as a member in all the activities of the workshop, but he is also responsible when necessary to get a session started, to keep discussion on the topic, to keep track of time spent on each step, and to turn in the record sheets for all members.

3. Begin with Step 1. *Check off each step* as it is completed. As a general rule, you should not remain at any step longer than the time indicated for each step. During the first session, you will probably not be able to complete all the steps. *Be sure to save 15 minutes for steps 8 and 10.*

Each member privately and quickly completes steps 1, 2, 3, and 4 by writing a one or two-sentence *response* you would most likely make in the following situations:

_____Step 1
(2 min.)

A good friend says to you: "I'm pretty worried. I don't think Joe likes me any more. He hasn't called me all week, and yesterday I think he saw me on campus and deliberately avoided me. I wish I knew what I did wrong." *Write your response on the Session 1 Record Sheet.*

_____Step 2
(2 min.)

A close friend says: "Well, the team I play for finally got an invitation to the NCAA finals in St. Louis." *Write your response on the Session 1 Record Sheet.*

_____Step 3
(4 min.)

How do you feel right now about any or all aspects of this interpersonal workshop? *Write your response on the Session 1 Record Sheet.*

_____Step 4
(2 min.)

Your professor has just handed you back a term paper you wrote. He marked it C, with no comments. You thought you had done A or at least B work. What would you most likely do or say? *Write your response on the Session 1 Record Sheet.*

_____Step 5
(after 25 min. on steps 5, 6, and 7, skip to step 8— even if some steps must be skipped)

One member of the group reads his response to *Step 1* aloud. The group then discusses his response in terms of the following questions:
  a) Might the response in some way make the friend feel *foolish* or unreasonable for being worried?
  b) Does the response *avoid* the issue of how the friend is feeling?
  c) Does the response show some degree of acceptance or *empathy* for the friend's anxiety?

Be sure to save 10–15 minutes for Steps 8 and 10.

_____Step 6

Other members of the group take turns reading their responses to Step 1 and the group discusses the response in terms of the above questions. No member should be required to read his response unwillingly.

_____Step 7

Each member then reads his response to Step 2, and after each response the group discusses it in terms of the following questions:
   a) Does the response *belittle* the accomplishment?
   b) Does the response *focus* on the unstated enthusiasm the friend probably feels but is hiding?
   c) Does the response reflect *enthusiasm* for the accomplishment and the opportunity?
   d) Can anyone think of other responses that would do this?

_____Step 8
(10–15 min., be
sure to save 5
min. for c, d, and
e)

Each member then reads his response to Step 3, and after each response the group discusses it in terms of the following questions:
   a) Does the response actually express some *feeling,* or is it noncommittal?
   b) Ask each other if there are *other* feelings about some aspect of the workshop that were *not* expressed. If so, *why* were they not expressed—out of reluctance or because of not being able to describe them precisely? (Here again, discussion should be voluntary only).
   c) At this point, the group might spend a minute or two in complete *silence,* with each member using the time to try to identify more precisely how he or she feels at this time about the workshop or the other members.
   d) Can anyone think of a clearer or more straightforward response to Step 3 than the one he first made?
   e) Did anyone feel uncomfortable with the silence?

_____Step 9
(if there is time)

Each member reads his response to Step 4, and after each response is read, the group discusses it in terms of the following questions:
   a) Does the response include an *honest,* direct expression of what the student feels are his rights for information?
   b) Does the response show *respect* for the rights of the professor?
   c) Can anyone think of other responses that include both of the above?

_____Step 10
(2–4 min.)

Preparation for Next Session
   a) Agree on a date and time for the next session of the group and write it below *and* at the top of the Session 2 Record Sheet.
      Date and Time: _____
   b) Review the activities and study materials which are expected. Each member is expected to study some material and complete some activities *before* the next meeting. The worthwhileness of the workshop for each member depends on each member's preparation and participation.
      Things to do before the next session:
         1) Study the Introduction to Session 2.
         2) Learn the 5-point rating scale.
   c) Turn in the Session 1 Record Sheets to your instructor.

Session 1 Record Sheet

NAME: _____   CLASS &
                                        SECTION: _____

DATE: _____   TIME: _____

Response to Step 1:

Response to Step 2:

Response to Step 3:

Response to Step 4:

Introduction to Session 2

If your first session included some honest and serious discussion, you may be feeling uneasy right now about your own abilities to understand feelings, express them openly and clearly, give honest reactions, and take them from others. That's understandable and normal after one session, and it's a good sign that your workshop will actually be profitable for you and the others. The anxiety should pass rather quickly, whereas the improved skills will remain.

Perhaps, however, you feel that your first session was rather superficial, an exercise in the avoidance of the topic of feelings. If so, why not *tell the group* that you feel this way at your next session. But be prepared to make serious contributions of your own by listening closely, expressing clearly, admitting to your own feelings, and by being willing to try something.

Avoiding the Affective

Many people find it very easy to participate in a conversation about things that they do not feel strongly about, focusing on factual information at a cognitive level without revealing their feelings. Many people find it very difficult to talk about things that are very important to them and share their real feelings about them.

From childhood, most of us have been deliberately taught how to discuss at a cognitive and unemotional level; far less frequently are we deliberately taught to converse on an affective level. As a result, without the necessary skills we feel uneasy with periods of deliberate silence, uncomfortable in dealing with another's expressed feelings, and fearful of expressing our own. We learn to avoid these consequences by changing the topic, by expressing opinions rather than feelings, by putting someone down, by pretending to agree, by avoiding periods of silence, and in a variety of other ways.

These ways of responding are not always bad or inappropriate. But when they occur so frequently as to become a general pattern in our dealings with others, they prevent us from learning much about ourselves and others and from relating in helpful ways.

Compare this pair of statements:

"I feel uncomfortable in this workshop—I guess it's because this is a new experience for me."

"Everyone can expect to feel a little uneasy in a new situation."

and these statements:

"I'm really happy about my new stereo."

"I think that this stereo was a good buy."

Perhaps you can begin to see how small differences in wording can make important differences in the message conveyed. They can change the focus and avoid the important.

Advice

Typically when a person tells us about a problem, a worry, or a fear, we tend to jump right in with a suggestion that will fix it up or with strong agreement or vague reassurance. In live situations this might be an avoidance device for closing the topic quickly, avoiding any prolonged discussion of feelings, or even a subtle way of patronizing the other person and putting him down. Often a sense of understanding and empathy is more helpful than words of wisdom.

In any case, it is foolish to attempt advice until you are sure you really *understand* how the other person feels and at what level. For that reason, in the remaining sessions of this workshop, try to *avoid responding with advice,* and concentrate instead on practicing responses that show empathy, acceptance, and a desire to understand more completely.

Acceptance

When you express acceptance of another's feelings, you are, in effect, saying that you sense what he is feeling and that it's all right with you if he feels that way. Whether or not you share or would share his attitude in his situation, you are telling him that his attitude is perfectly understandable and acceptable. And by implication you are also saying that it's okay for him to continue expressing these feelings in his attempt to gain a better understanding of them himself.

For example, if your date says "I don't know if I want to go to this party —I won't know any of the people there," you might respond, "Aw, just relax —they are all good kids and you'll have fun if you just relax." You probably have told your date that the worry is foolish, not worth talking about any more. If instead you had said something like "It can be pretty frightening going into a new situation and thinking you might be ignored all evening," your date would probably have a better chance of understanding and coming to grips with his or her own feelings. Of course, a few people learn to take constant advantage of that device to get attention and sympathy, in which case selective extinction might be appropriate. But, as with the law, a person deserves the benefit of the doubt until proven guilty.

Levels and Rating Scales

In several of the following sessions (including Session 2) of your group, you will need to know and use the following scale for rating the levels of statements and responses made by yourself and your fellow members. It's about the only memorization that this unit requires, but you will have to know the levels well enough to use them without rereading them during the session.

This is a 5-point scale for rating a statement for its empathy, clarity, and depth of feeling expressed.[2]

Level 1:   The statement expresses *no feeling or awareness* of another's feeling, not even the most obvious surface feelings.

> e.g. "I feel uneasy about the test coming up."
> "Let's get going. Class starts in ten minutes."

Level 2:   The statement expresses *some feeling or awareness* of another's feeling, but somewhat *camouflaged* or at a very *superficial* level. A level 2 response tends to *distort* the feeling actually felt or expressed by the other person.

> e.g. "I don't know whether I want to go to the party tonight."
> "Don't be silly. You look fine."

Level 3:   The statement expresses *accurately* the *surface* feelings or responds with an accurate awareness of the surface feelings of another, but *hides deeper feelings* or *misinterprets the deeper feelings* of another.

> e.g. "It's starting to irritate me a little that you always borrow my class notes but never return them unless I bug you for them."
> "I'm glad you told me that that annoys you. I'll try to get the notes back sooner in the future, ok?"

Level 4:   The statement expresses feelings somewhat *beneath the surface* or, as a response, *adds something* to the stated feelings in terms of either precision or depth.

> e.g. "Boy, these students around here are something else—curve-busters, working like crazy for the Almighty A. And if you don't have a 3.5 grade point average, they think you're a misplaced half-wit from the hills. Just because you get a couple of Cs doesn't mean you'll be digging ditches for the rest of your life. What a bunch of phonies."
> "The grades and expectations of other students make you furious. I'm sure that makes your school life miserable. It probably also makes it more difficult to socialize with the A students."

Level 5:   The statement expresses *deep feelings* with accuracy and understanding or, as a response to another's stated feelings, it *adds much* to the statement and shows accurate understanding and empathy at

---

[2] Adapted and revised from several levels suggested by Robert Carkhuff in Vol. 1 of *Helping and Human Relations: A Primer for Lay and Professional Helpers* (New York: Holt, Rinehart and Winston, Inc., 1969).

the deepest level of the other's feelings.

e.g. as a response to the statement under Level 4:

> "I can easily sense how furious you must feel because of the grades and expectations of other students. I'm sure that makes your school life miserable also. But I sense that this problem also touches on something in you that you are unsure about—how to handle your relations with these people. I sense that you are perhaps unsure and anxious about who you are in relation to them."

Review these five levels several times until you feel comfortable with them and *able to use them* in your next session. Check the examples to see why they were judged to be at the stated level.

Remember: Just because a level 5 response is the highest type doesn't mean that it's always the best response in any situation. But unless you *can* respond at a higher level, you won't be able to choose the right response for the right situation. In the hypothetical situations you use in this workshop, *presume* that a high level response *is* appropriate.

Presume also that focusing immediately on *solving* the problem is *not* the best way to respond. In real life, immediately suggesting a solution may be a way of avoiding the issue of the person's feelings. Besides a good solution may be impossible until the feelings are thoroughly probed and clarified. Finally, in some real situations empathy may not be the most appropriate initial response, but in these workshop situations it is the best because the purpose here is simply to learn how.

Consider the following questions about your group:

1. Are *all* members participating? If not, what can you do to improve this?
2. Are any members being put down, becoming defensive or fearful? If so, what can you do to make a person more comfortable and able to test his thoughts and feelings?
3. Are any members dominating the discussion or in some ways frustrating others? If so, consider making these feelings known to the person or the group.

Session 2

Before beginning Session 2, the group moderator should pick up the record sheets for the *first* session from the instructor and give each member his sheet.

_____Step 1	The group forms into *pairs* (and one threesome, if the number of members is uneven). Each pair moves away from the other pairs a little distance.
_____Step 2 (3–5 min.)	Each member rates his *own* written response to each of the first three situations in Session 1 (Steps 1, 2, and 3). Write the ratings on the response sheet for Session 2. Do not share them with your partner at this time; make the best rating you can simply on the basis of what was written.
_____Step 3 (3–5 min.)	Each member *exchanges* his written *responses* (from Session 1) with his partner (do not exchange the ratings) and *rates* his partner's responses to the same three situations.
_____Step 4 (5–10 min.)	Now each pair *compares* the ratings they gave to each others responses and discusses the agreements and differences in the ratings.
_____Step 5 (5–10 min.)	The group as a whole discusses any questions or doubts that pairs of members may have found regarding the empathy and acceptance scales or the ratings.
_____Step 6 (10–15 min.)	The group forms into *different pairs* for some brief role playing. One member assumes the role of a parent and says to his partner (in the role of a high-school-age son or daughter) "Please, can we save your problem until tomorrow? I've got a splitting headache and I've had a very bad day and I'm very upset. Later, ok?" The partner responds, and the discussion continues for a minute or so, or until a logical conclusion is reached. Each member writes his rating of the level of his own responding and of his partner's responding on the Session 2 Record Sheet. Then both members analyze the responses for: a) the *stated* feelings expressed; b) the *unstated* feelings implied; c) the level of *empathy* and accuracy shown by each member's responses; d) ideas on how the responses might have been improved.
_____Step 7 (10–15 min.)	One member (the one who did not initiate the Step 6 dialogue) assumes the role of a high school student and says to his partner (in the role of the student's teacher), just as he (she) is about to begin class: "Mr. (or Ms.) _____, I know the deadline for our project is today, but our family has had the flu the last several days, and I just

couldn't get to the project. I've got part of it done, but could I have a few more days to finish it up?"

The partner responds and the discussion continues for a minute or so, or until a logical conclusion is reached.
Each member rates his and his partner's responding.
Both members analyze the responses for:
  a) the *stated* feelings expressed;
  b) the *unstated* feelings implied;
  c) the level of *empathy* or acceptance shown by each member's responses;
  d) ideas on how the responses might have been improved.

_____Step 8
(5 min.)

_____Step 9
(2 min.)

The group as a whole discusses questions and ratings coming out of the pair dialogues and discussions.

Preparation for Session 3
  a) Agree on a date and time for the next session of the group, and write it below and at the top of the Session 3 Record Sheet. Date and Time: _____
  b) Things to do before Session 3:
      1) Restudy the Introduction to Session 2.
      2) Construct several *original situations* of your own for use during the next session.
  c) Moderator collects record sheets for Sessions 1 and 2 and gives them to the instructor.

Session 2 Record Sheet

NAME: _____   CLASS &
                                    SECTION: _____

DATE: _____   TIME: _____

Step 2: Self-Ratings (check the appropriate level number)

Response to Step 1,   Response to Step 2   Response to Step 3

1 2 3 4 5   1 2 3 4 5   1 2 3 4 5

Step 3: Ratings of Partner's Responses

Response to Step 1   Response to Step 2   Response to Step 3

1 2 3 4 5   1 2 3 4 5   1 2 3 4 5

                             Partner's Name: _____

Step 6: Ratings

                My Own Response   Partner's Response
                1 2 3 4 5   1 2 3 4 5

                             Partner's Name: _____

Step 7: Ratings

                My Own Response   Partner's Response
                1 2 3 4 5   1 2 3 4 5

                             Partner's Name: _____

Introduction to Session 3

Don't be discouraged if you had trouble responding at a 4 or 5 level. These responses are fairly rare in the real world, even among trained counselors. If, by the end of the workshop, you are able to express and respond with ease at one or perhaps two levels higher than when you started, your ability to relate to others will have been improved tremendously.

To prepare for the next session, you should do three things:

1. Reread the *Introduction to Session 2.* These brief notes will probably mean more to you now that you've had some live practice. Pay particular attention to the description and examples of the five levels so that your ratings can be more precise during the next sessions.
2. *Construct original situations* or initiating statements which can be used in the next session. The statements should express a feeling at some level, and the situation should be realistic—one that members of the group can easily respond to. Plan to bring at least two different situational statements to the next session. It might be best to write them out for easy memory and easy use.
3. Consider the advisability of asking your instructor to sit in on a session or part of one. Consider other procedures that might improve the functioning of your workshop and its helpfulness to each member.

Session 3

_____Step 1
(15–20 min.)

Members form into groups of *three,* with each member taking his turn at being discussant initiator, respondent, or recorder.

The discussant initiator says the opening statement in the original situation supplied by the recorder; the respondent responds to that statement, and while the discussion continues, the recorder rates the level of responding by both discussors.

The situation is repeated twice, giving each member a turn at being discussant initiator, respondent, or recorder.

_____Step 2
(15–20 min.)

The whole group comes together again and new groups of three are formed. The procedures of Step 1 are repeated, using new situations.

_____Step 3
(15–20 min.)

The whole group comes together for a brief discussion of ways in which the group might make its remaining sessions more profitable for all members. This discussion might also give members the opportunity to express their own feelings honestly, courteously, and constructively.

_____Step 4

Preparation for Session 4.
    a) Agree on a date and time for the next session (record here and on Session 4's Record Sheet).
       Date and Time: _____
    b) Things to do before Session 4:
       1) Read the Introduction to Session 4.
       2) Prepare to state your own feelings about a topic of your choice.
    c) Turn in Session 3 Record Sheets.

Session 3 Record Sheet

NAME: _____   CLASS &
                                       SECTION: _____

DATE: _____   TIME: _____

Step 1: Recorder's Ratings

Initiator's Statements   Respondent's Statements

1   2   3   4   5   1   2   3   4   5

Initiator's Name _____   Respondent's Name _____

Step 2: Recorder's Ratings

Initiator's Statements   Respondent's Statements

1   2   3   4   5   1   2   3   4   5

Initiator's Name _____   Respondent's Name _____

Introduction to Session 4

During the next two sessions, you will be asked to make a brief *statement* about your feelings regarding someone or something—a friend, a parent, a brother or sister, your job, an aspect of your school life or social life, a specific event in which you were involved, this workshop—whatever you have some feelings about that you want to discuss. Try to be as *clear* and *honest* as you can, but keep your statement brief.

You will also be responding to similar statements by other members of your group to test your understanding of the feelings expressed.

Before the next session, give some thought to the topic you want to discuss and also to exactly what your feelings are about it. One way to do this is to get yourself relaxed in an undistracting environment, bring the person, thing, or event into your imagination and watch (or feel) what happens, as if you were a bystander.

Remember that *depth* of feeling is not the same as intensity. A statement that expresses very intense and strongly felt feelings may not be getting at the deeper, perhaps less clearly identified feelings. Your task as initiator is to express your feelings as clearly and deeply as possible. Your task as a respondent is to probe the initiator's statement for accuracy and depth regarding the feelings.

Try also not to talk *about* but *to* another member of the group about his statements or feelings.

Session 4

_____Step 1
(2–4 min.)

One member of the group (meeting as a whole) initiates a discussion about the feelings that member has toward someone or something. This initiator *briefly* states how he or she feels about the topic, as clearly and honestly as possible.

Each member then rates the initiator's statement for its level of clarity and depth of feeling.

_____Step 2
(5–10 min.)

The other members discuss the feeling *with the initiator.* They test their understanding of the initiator's feelings by attempting to paraphrase and/or interpret what the initiator expressed and getting the initiator's reaction about the accuracy of the response. This discussion will, in many cases, also help the initiator clarify more precisely his own feelings toward the topic.

Remember: All discussion should concern *only* the initiator's *feelings* toward the topic he or she raised. Any discussion of the person or thing involved in causing the feeling or of the level of statement should be avoided or redirected.

The initiating member may terminate the discussion at any time simply by informing the group that he wishes to do so.

_____Step 3
(5 min.)

The group as a whole briefly discusses the following:
1) To what extent was the statement *clear* and perceptive?
2) Did the discussion focus only on the initiator's *feelings?*
3) Did the discussion tend to put down, embarrass, or give *advice?*
4) Did the discussion help to *clarify* the initiator's feelings?

_____Step 4
(10–15 min.)

The procedures in Steps 1 and 2 are repeated with a new member expressing his feelings, and the other members checking their understanding and helping to clarify.

_____Step 5
(10–15 min.)

Repeat the procedure with another member.

_____Step 6

If there are ten or more minutes left, repeat the procedure with another member.

_____Step 7

Preparation for Session 5
  a) Agree on a date and time for Session 5 and write it below and at the top of the Session 5 Record Sheet
     Date and Time: _____
  b) Activities for Session 5
     1) Do some thinking about the statements and responses you made this session and the comments of the other members. Consider how you could improve your statements.
     2) Prepare to repeat Session 4's procedures next time, with new topics.
  c) Turn in the Session 4 Record Sheets to your instructor.

Session 4 Record Sheet

NAME: _____   CLASS &
                                       SECTION: _____

DATE: _____   TIME: _____

Step 1: Rating Statement of Feeling by (name): _____   1 2 3 4 5

   Rating of my response: 1   2   3   4   5

Step 4: Rating Statement of Feeling by (name): _____   1 2 3 4 5

   Rating of my response: 1   2   3   4   5

Step 5: Rating Statement of Feeling by (name): _____   1 2 3 4 5

   Rating of my response: 1   2   3   4   5

Session 5

_____Step 1 | Repeat the procedures in Session 4, beginning with members who were
(10–20 min.) | not initiators in expressing a personal feeling during session 4.

_____Step 2 | The initiating member verbally rates each of the other members on:
(5–10 min.) |
    a) the *accuracy* of each member's paraphrases of the feeling;
    b) the degree of *empathy* expressed.
The group discusses the initiator's ratings.

_____Step 3 | The procedures in Steps *1 and 2* are repeated, with a new member
(15–25 min.) | introducing his feelings.

_____Step 4 | If there are 10–15 minutes left, steps 1 and 2 are repeated again, with
another member initiating.

_____Step 5 | Preparation for Session 6
(2 min.) |
    a) Enter date and time for Session 6 both here and on Session 6's
       Record Sheet.
       Date and Time: _____

    b) Things to do before Session 6:
       1) Study the Introduction to Session 6.
       2) Construct several *original statements* calling for assertive
          responses.
       3) Decide on how you want to use Session 7.
    c) Turn in the Session 5 Record Sheets to your instructor.

Session 5 Record Sheet

NAME: _____   CLASS &
                                        SECTION: _____

DATE: _____   TIME: _____

Step 1: Rating of Statement of Feeling by (name): _____   1 2 3 4 5

Rating of my response: 1 2 3 4 5

Step 3: Rating of Statement of Feeling by (name): _____   1 2 3 4 5

Rating of my response: 1 2 3 4 5

Step 4: Rating of Statement of Feeling by (name): _____   1 2 3 4 5

Rating of my response: 1 2 3 4 5

Introduction to Session 6

So far we've concentrated on developing the ability to express your feelings honestly and clearly and to respond to another's expression of his feelings with understanding and acceptance. And we've avoided any direct focus on the causes of those feelings.

But as you know, sometimes the causes of your feelings are important, and an attempt must be made to *change* those causes in some way. In these cases the cause is usually another person's behavior.

One way you can attempt to change that behavior is by telling the person his behavior is bad and he should change it. This method doesn't often change the behavior unless you include an effective threat. And when it does work, the relationship is usually a little less open than before.

When someone tells you to change your behavior because it's bothersome, you are probably tempted to *justify* your behavior and make him stop showing his feelings. The next easy step is an argument (or at least bad feelings) in which the discussion can get off onto many irrelevant tangents with exaggerated references to every irritant ever experienced.

On the other hand, your chances of improving both the situation and the relationship are better if your statement states *your* feelings about the behavior.

For example:

"It's insane the way you try to get even with other drivers."

or

"I really get frightened when you take after another driver."

In the first statement, you are accusing the other person; this focuses on *his* behavior and is more likely to lead to nonproductive argument. The second statement focuses on *your* feelings, invites him to do the same with your feelings and his own, and is more likely to lead to an honest and better understanding of each other. A behavior change is more likely here than if he is put on the defensive, but whether or not he changes his behavior, you are both better able to understand each other's behavior.

An accusation implies that the other person's behavior must change. You are implying that he must change if you are going to continue liking him. On the other hand, when you state your feelings, you are avoiding the implication that you are blaming him; instead you are making it clear that you are talking about yourself and your own feelings.

Of course we usually try to avoid arguments, but the method we choose is to avoid the problem altogether—don't mention it at all. That usually avoids an argument all right, at least temporarily. But denying your own feelings in order to avoid a disagreement is frequently a big price to pay. You don't have to pay this price; you can learn how to express your negative feelings without arguing or accusing.

Assertiveness

Often a person wants to and should express his feelings about another person's behavior because his *rights* are being violated in some way. If he avoids such an assertion, whether deliberately or indeliberately, or if he expresses his feelings indirectly and vaguely (perhaps in a nonverbal way by his tone of voice or facial expression or other action), he is being *nonassertive.* But if he asserts his own rights in a way that does not violate the rights of another, if he gives honest and direct expression of his feelings, while showing respect for the other person, he is being *assertive.* Notice that assertiveness does not imply respect for the other person's behavior, nor does it mean deference or indecisiveness.

If a person asserts his rights in a way that violates the rights of others, if he attempts to dominate, humiliate, or verbally attack the other person with a hostile outburst, then we say that person is being *aggressive,* not assertive.

For example: A fellow student asks to borrow your class notes, something he has done regularly for most of the semester, and you don't like it. You might say:

1. "Well, all right, but I wish you would do your own work," and you put a scowl on your face and march off.
2. "I've become very irritated by your borrowing my notes all the time. I hate not being able to study them when I want to, and I don't like the condition they come back in. I'm sorry, but I don't want to lend you my notes anymore. I hope you'll understand."
3. "Who was your slave last year? I've had enough of your parasite behavior. Get lost!"

The first response is a mild, somewhat deferential indication of the person's feelings about the note borrowing. Notice that most of the bad feeling is expressed nonverbally. This response is clearly a nonassertive response.

The second response is an assertive one. The focus is on the person's feelings, and even though there is properly some implied criticism of the other person's behavior, the speaker talks mostly about *his own feelings* and his own reactions.

The third response blasts the borrower and violates his right to be free from abusive personal attack. The focus is almost entirely on the other person and his behavior. This is clearly an aggressive response.

An assertive response, like most behavior , is a *learned* response; so is nonassertiveness. Nonassertiveness is primarily *avoidance* behavior; on the basis of painful experiences in the past with attempts to express our feelings and assert our rights (perhaps with some aggression), we decide that we would rather live with the bad personal feelings. Often a tendency to nonassertiveness is situation specific; that is, we experience difficulty in asserting ourselves only in one or a few situations (e.g., with one's spouse or a boss), but not with other people.

To become assertive, we must first of all *learn* how to express ourselves assertively without aggression and without minimizing our feelings; that is, we must first learn how to do it. We must also learn that it is *worth doing*—that in the long run we are better off being able to exercise our rights, express our feelings, and have honest and open relationships with our friends, even though we run the risk of displeasing some people on occasion or being called selfish.

Of course there is no guarantee that in every case asserting your rights and expressing your feelings honestly and openly will improve your relationships with other people. Remember, again, that sometimes it is wise to be cautious and keep your feelings to yourself. But until you have the appropriate skills and learn to value openness, you do not have the *choice* of being flexible, depending on the circumstances.

In the sixth session, you will be able to practice making assertive responses to hypothetical situations. To prepare for this session, you should *construct several original situations* of your own, ones which might be familiar to the members of the group and ones which call for an assertive response if one's rights are to be exercised. Be sure to come prepared with these situations, written out for easy memory and use.

At the end of the sixth session, your group will spend a few minutes deciding on the topic and procedures for the final session. This is intended to allow the group itself to decide on which aspect of the workshop the members feel they would like more practice in. To prepare for this mutual decision, you might want to review the previous units and evaluate your current skills and needs. Once you have decided the area in which you want more practice, then decide whether one of the methods used in the previous sessions might be the best way of proceeding or whether a modified procedure would best serve the purpose. If it happens that the group comes to no decision about the seventh session, then by default the topic and procedures of the sixth session are repeated.

Session 6

_____ Step 1
(15–20 min.)

The members form into *threesomes.* Each member takes a turn at attempting an *assertive* response to *each* of the following situations. The other members score the response as nonassertive, assertive, or aggressive. Then the group discusses the ratings briefly.

    a) You've had your car in twice this week to the local mechanic because it stalls out at about 40 m.p.h. The first time he said it was the tuning and he adjusted it; the second time he said it was the carburetor and he fixed it. But it still stalls out. You drive in the next morning and say:

    b) A good friend calls and asks to use some of your records for a party. Records are the one item you are definitely not willing to lend out to anyone. You say to your friend:

Questions to consider:

    1. Did the response assert honest *feelings* (not just a decision)?

    2. Did the response *avoid* or soften the feelings?

    3. Did the response *focus* on the other person's actions?

    4. Did the response show *respect* for the other person (not necessarily for his behavior)?

_____ Step 2
(5 min.)

The group then discusses other assertive but nonaggressive ways of responding to the above situations. Refer to the Introduction to Session 6, if necessary, for clarification and examples.

_____ Step 3
(15–20 min.)

Different groups of three are formed, and steps 1 and 2 are repeated, using *original situations* suggested by the members. Be sure to save ten minutes for Step 4.

_____ Step 4
(10 min.)

The group as a whole decides on

    a) The topic for Session 7:

        1) expressing understanding and empathy for another's feelings;

        2) understanding and expressing one's own feelings clearly;

        3) asserting one's rights without violating the rights of others.

    b) The procedures for Session 7:

        1) using a format from a previous session;

        2) using a format especially designed by the members for their topic.

    In either case, the emphasis should be on individual *practice of a skill,* with feedback from the others.

Please Turn in Session 6 Record Sheets to Your Instructor.

Session 6 Record Sheet

NAME: _____ CLASS & SECTION: _____

DATE: _____ TIME: _____

Step 1: Assertive Rating

Respondent_____

____Nonassertive ____Assertive ____Aggressive

Respondent_____

____Nonassertive ____Assertive ____Aggressive

Respondent_____

____Nonassertive ____Assertive ____Aggressive

Respondent_____

____Nonassertive ____Assertive ____Aggressive

Respondent_____

____Nonassertive ____Assertive ____Aggressive

Respondent_____

____Nonassertive ____Assertive ____Aggressive

Respondent_____

____Nonassertive ____Assertive ____Aggressive

Respondent_____

____Nonassertive ____Assertive ____Aggressive

Session 6 Record Sheet—Continued

NAME: _____   CLASS &
                                       SECTION: _____

DATE: _____   TIME: _____

Step 3: Assertive Rating

Respondent _____

_____Nonassertive   _____Assertive   _____Aggressive

Respondent _____

_____Nonassertive   _____Assertive   _____Aggressive

Respondent _____

_____Nonassertive   _____Assertive   _____Aggressive

Respondent _____

_____Nonassertive   _____Assertive   _____Aggressive

Respondent _____

_____Nonassertive   _____Assertive   _____Aggressive

Respondent _____

_____Nonassertive   _____Assertive   _____Aggressive

Respondent _____

_____Nonassertive   _____Assertive   _____Aggressive

Respondent _____

_____Nonassertive   _____Assertive   _____Aggressive

Session 7

_____Step 1   The group uses the topic and procedures decided on at the last meeting,
                        reserving the last 10–15 minutes for Step 2.

_____Step 2   Each member individually writes the response he personally would
       (10–15 min.)   most likely make to the following statements: *(Write on Session 7
                        Record Sheet)*

                             1. A good friend says to you: "I'm pretty worried. I don't think Joe
                                likes me any more. He hasn't called me all week, and yesterday
                                I think he saw me on campus and deliberately avoided me. I wish
                                I knew what I did wrong."
                             2. A close friend says: "Well, the team I play for finally got an
                                invitation to the NCAA finals in St. Louis."
                             3. How do you feel right now about any or all aspects of this
                                interpersonal workshop?
                             4. Your professor has just handed you back a term paper you wrote.
                                He marked it C, with no comments. You thought that you had
                                done A or at least B work. What would you most likely do or
                                say?

_____Step 3   Turn in the record sheet for Session 7.
                        Also turn in your personal reaction sheet.

Session 7 Record Sheet

NAME: _____   CLASS &
                                        SECTION: _____

DATE: _____   TIME: _____

Use this page to record ratings and names, as appropriate to topic and procedures used.

Use the *next page* to record *Step 2.*

Session 7 Record Sheet—Continued

Step 2:

Response to statement 1:

Response to statement 2:

Response to statement 3:

Response to statement 4:

Section III

An arrow indicates that prior units are prerequisites for the next unit. A △ identifies a key application/synthesis unit for purposes of summative evaluation.

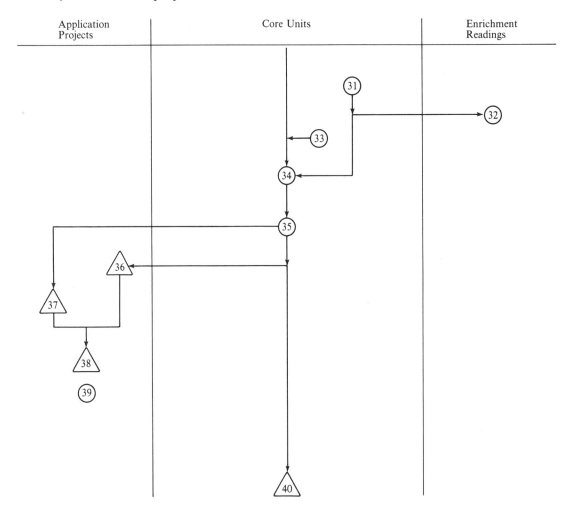

Evaluation

Instruction requires evaluation. Without it you can only guess at how effective your instruction is for the class as a whole and for individual students. You need evaluation skills in order to know from day to day which students have mastered which objectives, where remediation is needed, and in what ways you should revise your instructional materials and methods.

There are a variety of methods and devices for evaluating instruction. You need to know which ones best suit your particular purposes. As the need arises, you must be able to construct and use evaluation devices in such a way that you can rely on the results.

It's rather easy to construct or report the results of a test in such a way that the truth is camouflaged. Whether intentional or not, the student suffers when this happens. Since the primary responsibility for a student's academic progress is the teacher's (not the salesman's or the researcher's), you must be able to interpret the results of tests and assess their trustworthiness.

Units 31–33 deal with traditional methods of test construction and interpretation. Other approaches to evaluation are dealt with in later units. The traditional methods may not always be the most suited ones for your teaching needs, but it is important that you be able to handle them well in order that you can use them effectively and make intelligent decisions about their appropriateness in specific situations.

The current trend toward individualized instruction has been accompanied by a reexamination of traditional evaluation methods and the development of alternatives that are often more informative and productive. Units 34–35 examine several of these new methods, their rationale, and uses. Some of these methods also suggest individualized methods for arranging other aspects of your instructional system, so that your system can flexibly adapt to the changing needs of individual students.

Putting It All Together

Having skills in evaluation will not make you an effective teacher; the same is true for the kinds of skills taught in previous units. Effective teaching requires that these skills be brought together and integrated in practice. Synthesis objectives have necessarily been left until the end since sound evaluation devices must be integrated within the design of an instructional unit before it can be usefully taught. The concluding five units of this section provide you with guidelines for bringing together in one project all the skills taught in prior units, so that you can have a live experience of teaching and analyzing a carefully designed instructional unit.

unit 31

Interpreting Standardized Tests and Statistics

OBJECTIVES

When you complete this unit, you should be able to:

* describe the general contents and uses of the four kinds of educational standardized tests;
* define the following: $\bar{x}$, mode, median, mean, s, Σ, two measures of variability, three measures of central tendency, variability, central tendency, percentile, z, T, and Z scores, age-equivalent, and grade-equivalent scores;
* describe and draw a normal curve and label its areas; describe and draw a skewed curve, and identify a learning situation likely to produce skewed results;
* describe and interpret correlation coefficient scores and coefficient of determination scores.

Especially since World War I, schools have been given the primary responsibility for assessing the abilities and characteristics of citizens, sorting and then training them, and the schools have turned to standardized tests as a basis for doing this. Today there are about 150 organizations turning out over 1200 different kinds of standardized tests for elementary and secondary schools, college admission boards, business and industry, government, and the military.

In our elementary and secondary schools alone, it is conservatively estimated that over 200 million tests are given a year; this represents three to five standardized tests per pupil per year.

Standardization

A standardized test is a measure of a sample of behavior which is obtained and scored in a uniform way for all samples. A standardized test contains a number of items intended to represent the general kind of behavior being tested. The items were administered to a large sample of the kind of people for whom the test was designed, and the scores of this "standardization sample" of people are used to establish the national *norms* or average performance on this test. The test is then administered to different individuals under the same administration conditions of time limits, oral instructions, preliminary demonstrations, etc., and each person's score is compared to the norm or average of the standardization sample to see how far from the norm this person's score falls. By inference, the person's skill or ability in a particular area is rated *relative to the average* for all people of his category in the nation.

Types of Standardized Tests

There are four basic types of standardized tests, classified on the basis of the behavior they aim to measure.

Intelligence or IQ tests measure the general level of intellectual functioning, that is, the person's ability to learn and to think abstractly. Although the intelligence test directly measures only the person's current level of *performance* (and primarily in the areas of verbal and numerical reasoning), it presumes that this performance level is fully or largely determined by the person's *innate* potential or inborn capacity. The most widely used intelligence tests are the Revised Stanford-Binet Intelligence Scale, the Wechsler Intelligence Scale for Children (WISC), and the Wechsler Adult Intelligence Scale (WAIS).

Aptitude tests are very similar to intelligence tests in what they attempt to measure. But an aptitude test is typically a group or *battery* of tests each of which measures presumably independent intellectual components. The Differential Aptitude Tests (DAT) battery has eight tests, including verbal reasoning, numerical ability, abstract reasoning, space relations, and mechanical reasoning. The General Aptitude Test Battery (GATB), which tests for nine abilities, is used by federal and state employment services.

Personality tests measure a variety of character traits, interests, and attitudes, as well as emotional and social adjustment. Since these aspects of personality can't be measured directly, personality tests rely on the person's *verbal* response to questions about his likes and dislikes, how he thinks he would react to hypothetical situations, etc., and personality traits are inferred from these reponses. Some of the most commonly used are the Kuder Preference Record, the Strong Vocational Interest Blanks, the California Psychological Inventory, and the Minnesota Multiphasic Personality Inventory (MMPI).

Achievement tests are usually batteries of short tests which measure the attainment of instructional *objectives*. The best known batteries include the California Achievement Tests (CAT, grades 1–4), the Iowa Tests of Educational Development (ITED, grades 9–12), the Metropolitan Achievement Tests (MAT, grades 1–12), the SRA Achievement Series (grades 1–9), and the Stanford Achievement Test (grades 1–12).

In schools, test results are frequently used to make practical and vital decisions about the individual students, such as assigning students to classrooms and to subjects and grouping students within classes, identifying the special academic, personal, and social problems of students, and informing parents and the community about a student.

In order to interpret and use the scores from standardized tests, you must have at least an elementary knowledge of descriptive statistics. First, we'll review some basic information on graphing.

Frequency Distribution

Anything that can be measured and that can vary in value from case to case or from time to time is called a *variable*. Scores on standardized tests, weights of different aged children, or occurrences of a certain behavior each day are potential variables. The *frequency* of one variable is the number of times that value occurs in the data. If an IQ test produced these scores:

Students	Scores
Bill	96
Mary	100
Susan	98
Sam	100
Ted	109
Henry	98
Sally	100

the frequency of the value (score) of 100 is 3, and the frequency of 98 is 2. When we arrange these scores in order of magnitude, we have a *distribution*. And when this ordered arrangement of scores is accompanied by their corresponding frequencies, we have what is called a *frequency distribution.* If we rearranged the above IQ scores into a frequency distribution, we would get:

Scores	Frequency	
109	1	
100	3	
98	____	(you complete the rest)
____	____	

Usually frequency distributions are plotted on a graph. With the above data, the frequency always is plotted on the vertical axis and the score values themselves on the horizontal axis, like figure 31–1.

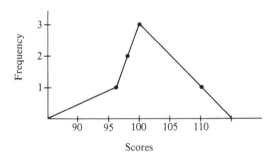

Figure 31–1

Notice that direction of increase is upward for the vertical axis (frequency) and from left to right for the horizontal axis (scores).

Test yourself to see how well you remember so far:

1. Something that is measurable and can change in value is called a
   _____.

2. A list of ordered scores and the number of times each occurred is called a _____.

3. Pretend the following is the list of scores your students got on a test you gave them. Arrange the scores in a frequency distribution and then graph that distribution.

70	65	75	80	75
85	90	85	80	90
90	95	90	90	100

When you've finished all three questions, compare your answers with the ones listed.

Answers:

1. Variable
2. Frequency distribution
3. Your frequency distribution should look like this:

Scores	*Frequency*
65	1
70	1
75	2
80	2
85	2
90	5
95	1
100	1

And your graph something like figure 31-2.

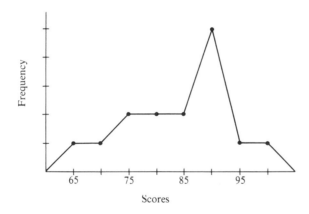

Figure 31-2

Not bad so far? Good! If you correct any confusion you have as soon as you notice it, this unit won't give you any trouble.

Statistical Language

There are many things that can be done with a frequency distribution to emphasize some of its characteristics or to make the set of numbers more useful. We will limit ourselves to a few of the less complicated manipulations —those that will be most useful to you in making sense out of test scores or other data. But first you must learn (or review) some basic statistical language:

X usually means a quantity or a score. Sometimes X stands for a variable, and Y then identifies another different variable.

N is a symbol indicating the number of scores or data points with which we are dealing. For example, if we give the same test to 30 students, then each student's score is an X, and $N = 30$ because we have 30 scores.

X^2 means square the quantity X, or multiply it by itself.

Σ is a symbol which means sum (add up) all the quantities which follow it. For example, ΣX means add up all the X's.

When these symbols are put together, they give shorthand directions for a series of computations. For example:

$$\frac{\Sigma X}{N}$$ means sum all the X's, then divide by the number of X's.

Be sure that you have the meaning of these symbols thoroughly memorized before you continue with the unit.

For this set of scores, 2   10   12   7   9, compute $\frac{\Sigma X}{N}$.

The answer is:

$$\Sigma X = 2 + 10 + 12 + 7 + 9 = 40$$

$$\frac{\Sigma X}{N} = \frac{40}{5} = 8$$

Central Tendency

Frequency distributions are often used to calculate various measures of the average or typical performance of the group as a whole. These are sometimes referred to as measures of *central tendency* or the tendency of scores to cluster around a certain value. The most useful and common measure of central tendency is called the *mean* or arithmetic mean. The symbol of the mean is $\bar{x}$ (called "X Bar"), or sometimes M, and you have already seen the formula for computing the mean:

$$\bar{x} = \frac{\Sigma X}{N}$$

In the answer calculated at the top of this page, the mean turned out to be 8 for the five scores reported. What does this imply? For one thing, the mean is the balanced point within the range of all the scores (See figure 31-3).

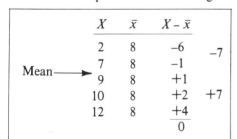

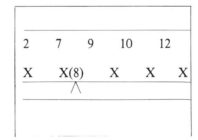

Figure 31–3   Figure 31–4

The *mean* is the true balance point because when we subtract the mean from each score (in the $X-\bar{x}$ column) and then add up all these deviations, we get zero. The sum of the negative deviations (–7) exactly offsets the sum of the positive deviations (+7) (See figure 31-4).

The mean can be very useful in describing the typical or average performance of a group and comparing that with the average performance of another group. There is one major danger, however. The mean is affected by extreme numbers. Compare the original set of scores (column A) in table 31–1 with two other sets in which only one of the scores changes:

Table 31–1

A	B	C
2	2	2
7	7	2
9	9	9
10	10	10
12	22	12
40	50	35
$\bar{x}=8$	$\bar{x}=10$	$\bar{x}=7$

The *median* is another measure of central tendency. It's simply the *middle* number in a frequency distribution. The median in the 3 columns of data in table 1 is 9; half the numbers fall below nine, and half above 9. But when you have an even number of scores (instead of an odd number, as in the examples) there are two middle values; in that case, the median is the mean of the two middle scores. The median of the scores 2, 4, 6, 8 is the mean of 4 and 6 (4+6/2) which is 5.

The *mode,* another measure of central tendency, is simply the score with the *highest frequency* of occurrence. In Column C of table 31–1, the mode is 2. Some sets of data have two modes, that is two scores with the same highest frequency. Such distributions are termed bimodal distributions.

Try your hand at computing both the median and the mode for the following data:

1   3   3   5   7   9   10   10

Answers: The median is 6. The two middle values are 5 and 7, since there are the same number of scores (3) on either side of these numbers. The mean of 5 and 7 is 5+7/2 or 6.

The mode lies at two values, 3 and 10, since both occur twice, more than any other score.

Which to Use

The *mean* is generally the most *useful* of the measures of central tendency; it is sensitive, gives the best average of the data, and can be used in more sophisticated analysis of the same data. The *median* is a better overall describer of the data, however, when there are a few *extreme* scores. For example, consider this frequency distribution of annual incomes for nine residents of one block:

$$
\begin{array}{ll}
\$\ 3,000 & \\
4,000 & \\
5,000 & \\
6,000 & \text{Mean} = \$10,667 \\
6,000 & \\
7,000 & \text{Median} = \$6,000 \\
8,000 & \\
50,000 & \\
\end{array}
$$

Eight of the nine residents earn less than the mean because of the one extreme score. So the mean gives a false impression of the central tendency of the block's income. Obviously the median is more typical of the income of these residents.

As for the mode, it's rarely used as a measure. The word itself is used occasionally and you should know it's meaning, but the measure is too crude to have much value.

Before going on to the topic of variability, let's quickly review:

1. What's the statistical symbol for mean?
2. What's the formula for computing the mean?
3. For the following set of test scores—
   50, 40, 80, 70, 60, 90, 60, 70, 80, 70
   a. arrange the data in a frequency distribution
   b. graph the data
   c. calculate the mean
   d. calculate the median.

Check your answers. If there are any errors, be sure you've resolved them before continuing.

Answers:

1. $\bar{x}$

2. $\bar{x} = \dfrac{\Sigma X}{N}$

3. a.

Scores	Frequency	Totals		
40	1	40		40
50	1	50		50
60	2	120	or	60
70	3	210		60
80	2	160		70
90	1	90		70
	$N=10$	$\Sigma X=670$		70
				80
				80
				90
				$\Sigma X=670$

b.

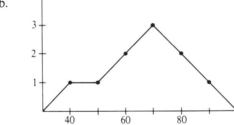

c. $\bar{x} = \dfrac{\Sigma X}{N} = \dfrac{670}{10} = 67$

d. Median = 70

Variability

When you report a set of scores by using a measure of central tendency, you always *lose* a lot of data. The mean, for example, may be the best *single* descriptor of a set of scores, but it can't describe the whole set completely. It's like the man who had his feet in the freezer and his head in the oven; when asked how he felt, he said "OK, on the average." The mean may not describe all the important information.

Measures of *variability* are measures of how *dispersed* or spread out the scores are around the *center.* Consider the two sets of IQ scores in table 31-2.

Table 31–2

Group A	Group B
96	80
98	90
100	100
102	110
104	120
Mean = 100	Mean = 100
Median = 100	Median = 100

When we describe these two groups by using measures of central tendency, they appear identical. But when we look at the variability of the data—the measure of dispersion around the mean—the two sets of data are clearly quite different. *Range* is one common measure of variability. The range of a set of scores is simply the distance between the lowest and the highest score. To find the range, subtract the lowest score from the highest score. In the above examples, the range for Group A is (104–96) 8; the range for Group B is (120–80) 40.

The range is very useful because it is easy to use and understand, and it often is a good quick descriptor of variability. But the range doesn't tell you about the variability *between* the mean and the extremes, where most of the data falls.

The *standard deviation* is the most important measure of variability. It's statistical symbol is s, or sometimes the Greek equivalent σ. Unlike the range, the standard deviation is based on *all* the scores in the group, not just two. There are more complicated ways of calculating the standard deviation, but for your purposes the following method of estimating the standard deviation comes close enough and is easy to work.[1]

1. Arrange all scores in ascending or descending order;
2. Find the *two scores* that mark off the upper and the lower 1/6 of all the scores: to do this, divide N by 6, raise or lower the result to the nearest whole number, and use that result (which is one-sixth of the number of scores) to count off one-sixth of the scores from the top and one-sixth from the bottom;

[1] Robert L. Lathrop, "A Quick but Accurate Estimation of a Distribution," *Journal of Experimental Education* 29(1961): 319–21.

3. Add all the upper 1/6 scores; then all the lower 1/6 scores;
4. Subtract the lower 1/6 sum from the upper 1/6 sum;
5. Divide this result by 1/2 of N.

For example, examine these IQ scores:

87	To estimate the standard deviation:
90	
91	$N = 29$; 1/6 of 29 is $29/6 = 4.8$; raise it to 5;
95	
95	Add the top 5 scores and the bottom 5 scores together:
97	
98	
100	
101	
102	
103	
103	
103	
104	
105	
106	

87	128
90	122
91	118
95	116
95	113
458	597

Subtract the 2 sums:
$$597 - 458 = 139$$

Divide by ½ of 29:
$$14.5 \overline{)139.} = 9.6$$

106	
107	If you calculated the standard deviation of this data using the more
107	complicated way (involving taking the square root of deviation scores),
107	you would come up with ——→ $s = 9.15$
108	
110	For ease of memory, here is the formula for this estimated standard
111	deviation:[1]
112	
113	$$\frac{\Sigma \text{ (highest 1/6 score)} - \Sigma \text{ (lowest 1/6 score)}}{\text{½ } N}$$
116	
118	Try it yourself. Use the same data, but don't peek any more than you
122	have to.
128	

The larger the standard deviation is, the more variability there is around the mean. And when you add measures of variability to measures of central tendency, you get a more complete and reliable picture of the data. This is particularly helpful when you compare one set of statistics with another. For example look at table 31-3.

Table 31–3

	Group A	Group B
Mean	105	97
Median	105	94
s	10	14
Range	129–87=42	140–73=67

Notice that Group B has a lower mean and much more variability around that mean than Group A. There is more homogeneity or alikeness in Group A than in Group B. If a teacher were using this data to decide what and how to teach, she might be inclined to devise special programs for some of the atypical students in Group B because the data suggest that these students would have more trouble adjusting to a single program for all than would the students in Group A.

Normal Curve

A major use of the standard deviation is in connection with what is called the normal curve. You've heard of "grading on the curve." A graph of scores can take on many different kinds of slopes, but the grade curve usually refers to the normal curve.

If you had nothing to do one week and decided to spend it clocking and graphing the speed of the cars using a campus drive, you might end up with something like figure 31–6.

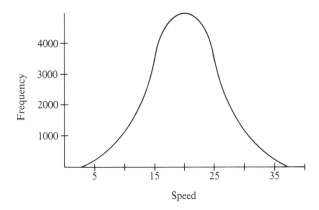

Figure 31–6

Notice that the distribution of the speed scores cluster around the middle (about 20 m.p.h.) and that the curve of variation around that middle is bell-shaped and symmetrical.

A normal curve has the following characteristics:

1. The mode, median, and mean are all represented by the *same point;*
2. The curve is *bell-shaped,* with both concave and convex curves;
3. The curve is *symmetrical,* with half of the scores falling in each half of the curve;
4. The curve represents a *large number* of scores or cases.

Rarely if ever does a large sample of data fit the normal curve perfectly, but data from a variety of natural phenomena *tend* to fit the normal curve fairly closely. Most *standardized tests* assume that if all possible scores were obtained, they would be distributed in a perfect normal curve.

From the mean to the point of inflection in the curve is regarded as one unit of distance or deviation from the mean. This standard unit or *standard deviation* can be used to divide the curve into equal baseline parts.

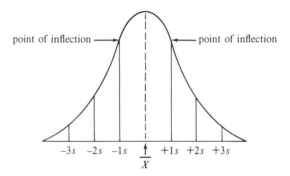

Figure 31–7

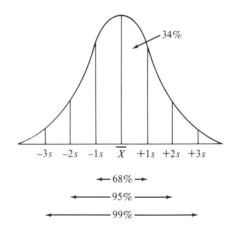

Figure 31–8

As shown in figure 31-7, the points –1 and +1 are situated one standard deviation (one unit of distance) from the central point (the point of the mean, median, and mode). Two units of standard deviation from the mean are labeled as +2 and –2.

Notice that the number of scores falling between $\bar{x}$ and +1 is the same as the number of scores falling between $\bar{x}$ and –1; that is, the area under the curve in both cases is the same.

Mathematically, the data in a normal curve are distributed in this way (see figure 31-8):

    1. About 68 percent of the scores fall between +1s and –1s; 34 percent of the scores, therefore, fall between $\bar{x}$ and either +1s or –1s;

2. About 95 percent of the scores fall between $+2s$ and $-2s$;
3. Over 99 percent of the cases fall between $+3s$ and $-3s$.

When the distribution of scores is not normal, the curve is called a *skewed* curve because the scores cluster to the right or left of the mean. Or it may be that the scores, though clustering in the middle, form a curve that is not bell-shaped (too flat or too peaked). See figure 31-9 for examples.

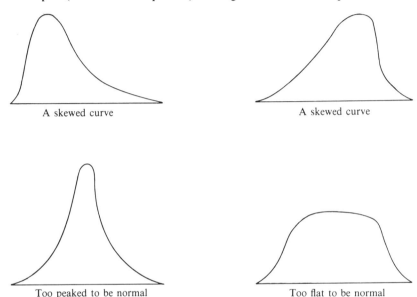

A skewed curve   A skewed curve

Too peaked to be normal   Too flat to be normal

Figure 31–9

Time for a review before the final section.

Given the scores on a final exam for this course ⟶

Score	Frequency
75	1
84	1
90	1
93	2
94	6
95	7
96	8
98	4
99	2

1. What is the mean? _____
2. What is the range? _____
3. Estimate the standard deviation. $s = $ _____
4. Graph the data and describe the curve.

5. Fill in all the underlined blanks; for item a, identify the 7 distribution units in a normal curve, and for items b through e, identify the percentage of scores falling within the area indicated by the arrows.

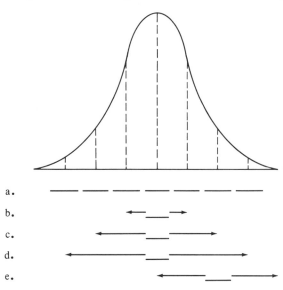

a. ⎯ ⎯ ⎯ ⎯ ⎯ ⎯ ⎯

b. ←⎯→

c. ←⎯⎯⎯→

d. ←⎯⎯⎯⎯→

e. ←⎯⎯⎯→

6. If we assumed that the final exam data (questions 1–4) were *normally* distributed,

  a. about how many scores should have fallen between 94 and 100?

  _____

  b. about what percentage of scores should have fallen between 94.4 and 97? _____

Answers

1. $\bar{x} = \dfrac{\Sigma X}{N} = \dfrac{3022}{32} = 94.4$

2. Range $= 99-75 = 24$

3. $N = 32$ 32 divided by 6 $= 5.3 = 5$
   sum of 5 highest scores $= 492$
   sum of 5 lowest scores $= \underline{435}$
                      57

   divide by ½N or 16
   $s = 3.6$

4.

5.   a. $-3s, -2s, -1s, \bar{x}, +1s, +2s, +3s$
   b. 68%
   c. 95%
   d. 99%
   e. 50%

6.   a. about 50% or 16. Because the curve is skewed, however, more than half the scores fall to the right of the mean.
   b. about 34% should fall between the mean and 1 standard deviation (3.6) from the mean, but more did.

Derived Scores

When you score a test according to the directions in the manual, you end up with what is called a *raw score*. When you then change that raw score in order to make it more understandable and easier to compare with other scores, you have what is called a *derived score*.

For example, many test publishers provide tables for converting raw scores into *percentile rank* scores. If all the scores are arranged in descending order and then grouped into 100 equal sized sets, each of these sets is a percentile. An individual student's score is then determined by how many sets his score *exceeds*. If his percentile rank is 45, that means he scored higher than 45 percent of the others who took the same test; if another student's actual score was 86 and his percentile rank was 99, that means that his score of 86 was as high or higher than anyone's.

Frequently test scores are converted into standard scores—scores based on the standard deviation in a normal curve. The basic standard score is the *z score*. A *z* score of zero means that the score falls right at the mean, or zero standard deviations from the mean. A negative *z* score, like a negative standard deviation, means that the score falls below the mean. A *z* score of +2.00 is a very high score because, as you remember, 95 percent of the other scores fall below +2 standard deviations.

To get rid of the negative signs and decimal points, sometimes the *z* score is converted into another derived score—the *T score*, which is simply the *z* score multiplied by 10 and then added to 50. Thus a *z* score of zero is a *T* score of 50, a *z* score of +1 is a *T* score of 60 (1 × 10 + 50), and a *z* score of –2 is a *T* score of 30 (–2 × 10 + 50 = –20 + 50). The *Z score* (capital *Z*, not a small *z*) is for all practical purposes the same as the *T* score.

Another frequently used derived score is the age-grade score, often called the *age-equivalent* or the grade-equivalent score. A student's raw score on a test is compared with the mean of a large sample of scores by other students of the same age or grade. If a student gets a grade-equivalent score of 3.1 in reading and an 8.4 age-equivalent score, this means that according to the test publisher's data he is reading at the same level as the average student in the first month of the third grade and at the same level as an eight-year, four-month-old student. Notice, however, that age-grade scores presume that the curricula, instruction, and emphases are uniform in city and suburban schools throughout the country and that students learn at a uniform rate from September to June but not during the summer.

Correlation

To this point, we have been concerned with plotting and analyzing only one variable and its data. The relationship between *two variables* is another important concept. The idea of correlation is common. As *X* changes, so does *Y*. Sometimes *Y* changes in the same direction as *X*. As the rainfall increases, so does the water level in the rivers. Sometimes *Y* changes in the opposite direction of *X*. As altitude increases, temperature decreases (to a point, of course). And sometimes *Y* doesn't change much at all when *X* changes. In many cases, an increase in school funding hasn't made much difference in the achievement of the school's students.

Many studies are conducted with the express purpose of identifying the amount of correlation between two variables. These studies attempt, of course, to hold everything else *constant* and to make sure they are really measuring the two variables they say they are measuring. To report their findings, these studies boil down the data for the two variables into one index score, usually called a *correlation coefficient*—a number which describes the degree of relationship between the two sets of scores. The correlational coefficient can vary from

$$-1.00 \qquad -.50 \qquad 0 \qquad +.50 \qquad +1.00$$

Negative   Positive

If the correlational coefficient is around zero, there appears to be little if any relationship between the two variables. A negative coefficient indicates that the variables are inversely related (as one increases, the other decreases in value). But whether the sign is plus or minus, it is the *size* of the coefficient that indicates the degree of relationship.

While you probably won't need to know how to compute the correlational coefficient, you might find it useful to know a simple transformation of this coefficient. When you square the correlational coefficient, you get what is called the *coefficient of determination,* which is a percentage measure indicating how much of one variable actually determines the other. If, for example, the correlation between IQ scores and academic achievement is +.30, the coefficient of determination is .30 X .30, which is .09. This indicates either that 9 percent of one's IQ determines one's level of achievement, or that 9 percent of one's achievement determines one's IQ. To put it another way, the remaining 91 percent of the relationship is determined by other factors besides IQ and achievement.

When there is a high correlation between two variables, this suggests that you will usually have success in *predicting* one variable if you know the value of the other variable, but this does not allow you to say that one variable *causes* the other. As beer sales go up, so do the number of drownings, and you would be fairly accurate in predicting one from the other. But beer may or may not have a causal relation with drowning; other variables such as heat and the opening of beaches may also be factors. In fact, correlation is usually mediated; that is, X is related to Y through Z, and maybe also through $A, B, C,$ etc. The most reliable and honest approach is to stick very close to the data and focus on the observable relationships between observable events and forget about inferring causality.

1. Briefly describe the four kinds of educational standardized tests.

2. Identify: $\bar{x}$, mode, median, mean, s, Σ, 2 measures of variability, three measures of central tendency, variability, central tendency.

3. Be able to compute the median, mean, range, and standard deviation for a new set of scores.

4. Draw and label a normal curve and indicate where 34%, 68%, 95%, and 99% of the data fall.

5. What does "skewed" mean? Give an original example of a learning situation from which you might expect skewed results.

6. Describe the meaning of the following scores:
    percentile
    z, T, Z
    age-equivalent, grade-equivalent

7. Define correlation coefficient, specify its possible range, and be able to interpret the meaning of an actual coefficient.

8. How is the coefficient of determination computed, what does it mean, and what does it not mean?

IQ: God's Gift or the School's Failure

OBJECTIVES

When you complete unit 32, you should be able to:

* describe the origins, and the historical and current uses of IQ tests, and identify several assumptions of such a test;
* outline Jensen's position on racial differences in IQ scores and several criticisms of this position.

Do IQ scores tell how much native learning ability a person was born with? If so, schools should use IQ scores to label the bright and the slow student. If so, schools need not worry about their 50 percent success rate; the IQ test, being standardized to produce a normal curve, guarantees that half of the student population has a below average IQ score and therefore will not succeed.

Do IQ scores tell how well a person has learned certain cognitive skills/ knowledge? If so, schools should use IQ scores to identify each student's past progress, current general abilities, and future needs. If so, then schools should use tests which more precisely define each student's skills, abilities, and specific needs so that the results can be directly translated into instructional programs tailored to each student's current needs.

Perhaps the true answer lies in between these extremes; perhaps both heredity and learning experiences contribute to each individual's intellectual capacity to learn. We know that human genes make a difference in a wide variety
of physical characteristics, so it should not be surprising to find that genes also
make a difference in the detailed physical makeup of the human brain and
nerve system. But is the difference substantial and important in a person's
educational potential?

There is considerable evidence that the effectiveness and the rate of instruction are critical determinants of a person's IQ score—perhaps the only critical
determinants for 95 percent of our students. Englemann[1], for example, reports
on an experiment in which fifteen disadvantaged four-year-olds were taught
basic academic concepts in a program which emphasized rapid achievement
using the basic methods of performance-based instruction and behavior modification. After two years, the mean IQ of these children rose from 95 to 121
(with a final range of 103 to 139). In a disadvantaged Head Start comparison
group, the mean IQ rose from 95 to 99.

An average IQ gain of 26 points in two years in this program seems to
indicate rather strongly that the reason many children fail in school is not
because they are genetically inferior but because they receive poor instruction
—instruction that is not tailored to their skill needs of the moment.

Perhaps in the future, when we are able to measure the precise impact of
heredity on learning ability, we will no longer care, because our schools will
have adopted effective individualized instructional technologies which override any genetic cognitive differences between students.

In the following article, the author describes the current IQ debate and how
the usage of IQ scores has been perverted. The author also notes the fallacy
in using Head Start as an argument for racial IQ differences.

THE IQ DEBATE*

Lillian Zach

Intelligence testing, from basis to implications, continues to be the center of
heated debate. Despite a history which is almost three quarters of a century
long and despite the fact that the IQ is by now a household term in America,
mental tests are still reeling under the impact of criticisms which term them,
among other things, invalid, misleading, and based upon false assumptions of
human development.

---

[1] S. Englemann, "The Effectiveness of Direct Verbal Instruction on IQ Performance and
Achievement in Reading and Arithmetic," in W. C. Becker (Ed.), *An Empirical Basis for Change
in Education* (Chicago: Science Research Associates, 1971), pp. 461–83.

* Lillian Zach, "The IQ Debate," from *Today's Education*, September 1972. Reprinted by
permission.

In a highly controversial article published in December 1969, Arthur Jensen, a professor at the University of California at Berkeley, proposed that compensatory education failed to raise the IQ of black children because of a biological difference in the way these children learn. The topic became incendiary; psychological, educational, political, and racist groups began interpreting the data to suit their views. Arguments and criticisms continue. Yet, unquestionably, the Stanford-Binet, the Wechsler Scales, and certain group tests do provide useful information, and the tests remain the most relied-on source for sorting children according to their presumed learning ability. Is it any wonder that teachers are uncertain what to believe about intelligence testing?

Binet's original intent was to develop an instrument to determine which children in Paris were retarded and in need of special education. In 1905, he produced the first Binet scale, designed to measure a retarded child's intelligence and compare it to the intelligence of normal children the same age. There was no attempt to determine whether the child's retarded learning was genetic or curable.

In 1912, German psychologist Wilhelm Stern suggested that one could express the developmental level, or mental age, of a given child as the age at which the average child achieved equivalent ability. If mental age (MA) were used as a ratio to the child's chronological age (CA), one could arrive at a brightness index, now called the Intelligence Quotient (IQ).

Like Binet, Stern did not claim that the test measured inborn capacity. In 1914, he wrote, "No series of tests, however skillfully selected it may be, does reach the innate intellecutal endowment, stripped of all complications, but rather this endowment, in conjunction with all influences to which the examinee has been subjected up to the moment of testing. And it is just these external influences that are different in the lower social classes. Children of higher social status are much more often in the company of adults, are stimulated in manifold ways, are busy in play and amusement with things that require thinking, acquire a totally different vocabulary, and receive better school instruction. All this must bring it about that they meet the demands of the test better than children of the uncultured classes." But H. H. Goddard, who brought the test to America in 1910, had a very different viewpoint. Dr. Goddard translated the test into English for use at the Vineland Training School for the mentally defective. Perhaps it was an act of fate that the man who brought mental testing to this country was someone who emphasized the importance of heredity on human behavior.

Goddard was working with grossly defective children, and one can speculate that he was probably not convinced they could be educated. (Further, the chances are they were biologically defective as well as mentally retarded.) Goddard became intrigued with the notion that, being able to measure innate intelligence, we had the means for a sweeping program of social reform, with every man working on his own mental level. Soon, mental testing was adopted in every training school and teachers college in the country. Few stopped to consider that perhaps the innate intelligence which Goddard postulated and the intelligence measured by the test were not the same. Shortly thereafter, in 1916, L. M. Terman revised the Binet Scale at Stanford University to give birth to the Stanford-Binet, the standard of today's intelligence test. The test was revised and updated in 1937 and 1960. The rapid growth of compulsory education in the United States required some means to identify the intellecutal capacities of pupils in the schools, and the Stanford-Binet seemed to fill the bill.

When the intelligence test is evaluated solely in terms of its value to meet specifically defined, immediate situations, its usefulness has proven itself. A good case in point can be seen in its use since the start of World War I to screen men for the armed forces. In these instances, the mental test has provided the means for appraising what an individual could do, here and now, as the product of his biological inheritance and his training and background.

But as testing proliferated, some problems became apparent. Testing in America was growing along two separate paths. One was in the real world of the school, the armed forces, and the industrial plant. The other was in the halls of academe, where the basic theoretical issues of intelligence were not yet settled. This lack of a universally accepted theoretical framework led to the anomolous situation in which intelligence is defined as that which intelligence tests test.

Herein lies a dilemma: Intelligence was only vaguely defined by the test maker, but the tests were used to define intelligence. This is perhaps the greatest failure of the testing movement in the United States. The pragmatic value of the mental test is undiminished. Test scores are good indicators of functioning abilities as long as their limitations are clearly understood, but these scores should not be used outside of their immediate significance. The failure lies not in the mental tests themselves, but in the perversion of the test results by investigators and social philosophers who use numbers in support of particular far-reaching positions. It is unfair both to the person tested and to the test itself to say that the scores of any one individual represent support for broad statements concerning human development.

There is nothing inherently wrong with practical definitions as long as they are clearly understood. The tests, after all, were developed to measure those aspects of human behavior which correlate well with scholastic achievement. In order to succeed in school, an individual must demonstrate certain types of abilities. If we develop tests to measure these abilities and if they prove to be valid and reliable instruments, we are measuring some form of intellectual ability. But if we lose sight of what we are measuring and if we claim for the test qualities for which it was never intended, we can be led into invalid implications.

Moratorium on Standardized Testing

"This Representative Assembly directs the NEA to immediately call a national moratorium on standardized testing, and at the same time to set up a task force on standardized testing to research and make its findings available to the 1975 Representative Assembly for further action."

The above "Item of New Business" was passed by the NEA Representative Assembly in Atlantic City, New Jersey, in June 1972. In another action on this subject, the Representative Assembly passed Resolution 72–44, Standardized Tests, which says:

"The NEA strongly encourages the elimination of group standardized intelligence, aptitude, and achievement tests to assess student potential or achievement until completion of a critical appraisal, review, and revision of current testing programs."

The IQ, like the MA, is nothing but a score. The IQ indicates a child's performance on a test in the same way that a score of 80 on an arithmetic test does, except that intelligence tests purport to measure more general learning skills. Further, the scores merely reflect the child's performance on a specific test at a given time. The difference between the IQ and other test scores is that intelligence tests are standardized. Standardization means that the same test items are developed and revised on a large group, representative of the population for whom the test is designed—U.S. elementary school students, for example. Standardization also requires that the same test be administered under the same carefully controlled conditions to all who take the test. This means that a given child's score can be compared with scores obtained by other children of the same age on whom the test was originally standardized. It also permits prediction of the chances that in later testing a given child will obtain a score which is close to the original score, and further, to what extent a given child's performance is the result of the construction of the test rather than his own ability.

In order to interpret the results of standardized tests, certain fundamental assumptions are implicit. It is assumed, for example, that the test norms are fair, since they are based on a representative national sampling of children. But this does not take into consideration the fact that the national sample is weighted heavily by average white children.

Since the mental test purports to measure basic learning capacities, it is also assumed that the items which make up the test are of two types—information which for the most part all children have been exposed to or situations to which no one has been exposed.

For items based upon supposedly equal opportunities of exposure, it is possible to reason that a child who has learned what he has been exposed to is bright; one who has not done so is not bright. Observation tells us that this does not have to be true.

In my own testing experiences, I found that many black children who had just come North gave as response to the question, "Who discovered America?" the answer, "Abraham Lincoln." The response is obviously wrong and adds no points to the IQ score. But does this response mean that this child has no ability to learn or does it merely reflect the child's background? In certain ways, the answer could be considered a meaningful and pertinent response.

For items to which no one has been exposed and which therefore demand "on the spot" learning, similar problems arise. Usually, tests try to utilize nonverbal materials like blocks and puzzles as a way of minimizing factors like education and experience. But these are not equally novel experiences for all children. Many youngsters are familiar with educational toys long before they enter school. (Even more important, and less easy to identify, are factors related to "learning to learn" and test-taking abilities.)

Another assumption is that the mental test is a sampling of behaviors which directly reflect the general capacity for learning. Actually, all available intelligence tests are direct measures only of achievement in learning. We wrongly equate the inferences from scores on IQ tests to some native inherent trait. Many persons think of intelligence as a discrete dimension existing within the individual and believe that different people have different amounts of it. In a certain sense this is true, but one's intelligence is not a characteristic of a person so much as it is a characteristic of the person's behavior. We can only hope to measure or observe manifestations of it.

It is also not possible to add up the elements of someone's intelligence in the same way that you can count the number of fingers on his hand. Although two people can have the same IQ score, they may demonstrate quite different abilities by virtue of the fact that they succeeded on different parts of the test. All too often, undue weight is given to an IQ score, although numerical assignment of a child to a man-made concept, untied to real characteristics of the child, tells us very little. Even more unfortunate, parents and some teachers are led to believe that the IQ concept has deeper significance than its meaning as a score.

Unquestioning faith in descriptive concepts reaches the height of absurdity in the notion of overachievers—a word used to describe children whose classroom performance is higher than their IQ scores would predict. The concept makes no sense at all because it says, in effect, that although these children are achieving, they do not have the ability to do so. Their success is laid to other factors, such as motivation. It's like telling the child who had the highest batting average in the Little League that, on the basis of batting practice, he's really a very poor hitter. He only did it because he wanted to.

The danger in a meaningless concept like overachieving is that childern so designated may not receive as positive a recommendation for college as other children with the same grades but higher IQ scores. Few stop to consider that the methods used to judge ability must have been inadequate and that terms like IQ, MA, and overachievement are man-made.

In view of all the drawbacks, one might reasonably ask, then, why do we continue using mental tests? Even though many have argued for abandoning them, most psychologists still feel that they have value. In most cases, we can describe, evaluate, and even predict certain kinds of behavior much better with tests than without them. The paradox exists that most psychologists, who were responsible for the tests, have never given them as much weight as those in schools and industries who use and misuse them.

While various practical problems were being confronted, the academic world of psychology was still trying to resolve many basic issues about intelligence testing. One of these, the focus of several decades of research, concerned the whole heredity-environment controversy—the battle over nature versus nurture.

Not all psychologists in America were convinced that the IQ was the highly predictive, hereditarily determined measure it was held to be by Goddard and his followers. It wasn't long before studies were reported which demonstrated that not only was the IQ not fixed but that it could be altered with training, experience, and changes in adjustment patterns.

Although research was reported from all over the nation to support one or the other position, two distinct battle camps could be located. One group, at the University of Iowa, came to be known as the environmentalists. The other, at Stanford University, supported the significance of heredity. After a while, it seemed as if the heredity-environment controversy had settled down into a comfortable compromise: Most people were content to accept the notion that the IQ is the result of the interaction between the gene structure and the environment.

Everyone knew that the argument was not settled, however, probably because people were asking the wrong kinds of questions. Instead of asking how *much* is contributed by heredity and environment respectively, they should have been asking *how* each makes its particular contributions.

For example, in our present state of knowledge, nothing will enable a child who is born deaf to hear. How differences in environment can affect his future development, however, is a terribly significant factor: With appropriate educational procedures he can develop into a literate, communicating adult; without them, he can remain illiterate and uncommunicative. Concentrating on heredity versus environment obscures the more important problem of determining how education can help each child best use what he has at his disposal.

In recent years, the black community has become more and more vociferous in its objections to the mental test as being biased against them. The outcry has been especially strong against group testing because these tests depend almost entirely on the child's ability to read. Since the child has to read the questions in order to answer them, blacks question whether the test measures capacity to learn or ability to read. They also argue that IQ tests are self-fulfilling predictions. A child with a low IQ score is placed in slow learning classes, where he learns less, thereby supporting the original score. Prompted by such arguments, many major school systems abandoned group intelligence testing. Individual tests like the Stanford-Binet and the Wechsler Scales are less subject to criticism, since, hopefully, the trained psychologist ensures that the test is administered properly under an optimum testing climate, and is able to evaluate better to what extent a given child's performance is influenced by emotional, motivational, educational, and socioeconomic factors.

Some people have suggested that we discard the IQ test entirely and substitute for it a battery of achievement tests. The problem is that since the achievement test is a sampling of what a child has learned, usually in specific academic subjects, the achievement battery does not provide much information about general learning skills. Others have looked to new methods of measurement which could meet the limitations and criticisms posed by our current models.

One such method has been developed by John Ertl at the University of Ottawa. Dr. Ertl records the brain response to a flashing light by placing electrodes on the motor cortex. By averaging the responses, which are recorded on a computer so as to eliminate noise, he arrives at a score, known as the *evoked potential,* which he claims is a culture-free index of intellectual functioning.

Several drawbacks can be cited to Ertl's approach. For one thing, he has no strong theoretical rationale to support his hypothesis that more intelligent people respond faster to stimulation than do less intelligent ones. The results he reports may be explained, not by the greater (or lesser) strength of the brain, but by the fact that some people are better able to pay attention and to fixate on the light source. In addition, correlations with IQ, although significant, are low—as are correlations on retesting with the same subject. In view of all this, in my opinion, it is doubtful that Ertl's method can be of real use to the teacher, at least at this time.

Previous attempts had been made at developing culture-free scales. For example, an effort was made to remove the middle-class bias of IQ tests by changing the wording of questions and by introducing content more relevant to the lower-class child's background and life experiences.

The results were unsuccessful, and since the task of developing culture-free tests poses difficult problems, it seemed to make better sense to concentrate on improving the environment of the culturally deprived rather than on changing our tests.

As a result, many special programs were started that were designed to educate children from the lower socioeconomic strata. In too many cases, these programs were established in an atmosphere of emergency, with little planning and with limited knowledge of what should constitute suitable curriculums for such classes. Professional educators were not too surprised, therefore, when these programs failed to raise the IQ of black children.

Using the failure of these programs and an impressive array of statistical data, Dr. Jensen shocked many educators when he proposed that the reason these programs failed can be traced to an hereditary inferiority in black children. The great fear this aroused in the minds of socially oriented psychologists and educators is that it might be possible, by misinterpretation, to obtain "proof" that no matter what compensatory education the black child receives, he remains inferior in intellect. Another possible interpretation is that the schools are not to blame if black children fail to achieve academically.

The IQ Argument: Race, Intelligence, and Education (Library Press. 1971), a recent publication by Hans J. Eysenck, a British psychologist, lends support to Jensen's position. Actually, there was nothing so new about Dr. Jensen's position; it's the old nature-nurture controversy in new clothes. It is a fact that blacks as a group score lower than whites as a group on intelligence tests. It is also a fact, however, as Jensen notes, that many blacks score higher than a very large number of whites. People concentrating on the main conclusions in the article tend to forget this.

I recently received a rather touching letter from a young black boy attending an Ivy League college. He wrote: "I was interested that the specific areas in which Jensen indicated blacks were inherently inferior are precisely those areas in which I scored highest in my class. Maybe it was luck." Even he had lost sight of the fact that the Jensen data refer to averages and not to individuals.

It is unfortunate that Jensen presented his material within the context of a racial issue, since the emotional impact of this tends to negate all of what he has to say. Despite its incendiary qualities, the Jensen paper has the major merit of reminding us that we are dealing with a biological organism and that the educational environment is only one of the many influences affecting the growth and development of a given individual.

Black people as a group in America are poor, and poor people are subject to all kinds of health risks deriving from prenatal conditions and malnutrition. The relationship between poverty, health, and learning failure is now receiving the attention it deserves. It is becoming clear that not only does malnutrition play a role in retarded intellectual development but that more than one generation may have to be well-fed before all the effects of dietary deficiency are overcome.

Jensen was premature in evaluating just what portion of the black child's biological structure actually resides in the genes. It is difficult to evaluate the amount of damage caused by health hazards resulting from poverty, or to say how even slight changes in environment can produce large changes in behaviors, even where those behaviors are linked to genetics and biology.

Another criticism of the Jensen material is that the public does not have a clear appreciation of just what kinds of information can be validly drawn from hereditability data. The method used by Jensen and Eysenck can only tell what proportion heredity contributes to the variance of a specified trait in a given population under existing conditions. The data cannot tell us the reason for a given child's low intelligence, the origin of ethnic differences in test performance, or what educational intervention programs can accomplish.

Jensen's article should be credited with helping us recognize that compensatory programs of education in their beginning phases were inadequately structured. That he used these poorly planned programs as a basis for postulating hereditary inferiority in blacks is a major weakness. His reasoning could have proceeded the other way. If the programs failed to raise IQ scores, why place the onus on the black child's shoulders? Why not look at what's wrong with the programs.

A peculiar characteristic of American education is that, although we give lip service to meeting the needs of individual children, we seldom follow through with concrete actions. We meet the needs of individual children as long as they respond to the existing curriculum, but when a child fails to learn under the existing structure, we assume there is something wrong with him. If "meeting the needs of individual children" is to become meaningful, we should consider the possibility that perhaps a particular teaching method is all wrong for a particular child.

Certainly, we can't make wholesale prescriptions for black children as if they were all alike. A black child who is not doing well in school may be more like a white child who is similarly unsuccessful than he is like an achieving black child. The problem of understanding learning deficiencies and of locating appropriate pedagogy for overcoming them is not something we know too much about. The storm over the Jensen article may provide the impetus toward working for a true understanding of education and individual differences.

A first step might well be to define our aims and come to grips with why we test. Are we concerned with measuring the amount of cognitive ability an individual is born with, or do we wish to appraise, by sampling performance, the level of adaptive capacities at his disposal?

Do we seek to predict, by way of one or several tests, what an individual will do 20 years from now? Or do we seek to know how and at what stage educational circumstances might be arranged for the individual to achieve his highest level of intellectual functioning ability? Piaget, among others, has never been impressed with standard IQ tests because they do not lead to an understanding of how intelligence functions. His work is not based on predictions, but rather on assessments of the presence or absence of the essential abilities related to intellectual functioning.

Schools must decide what is the purpose of testing. If all we wish is to separate the bright child from the dull child, the brain-damaged from the neurologically intact, the retarded learner from the gifted, and to attach labels to the children in our schools, we can go on using tests the way we always have, and the argument over genes will continue. But if we mean what we say about meeting individual needs, we can put tests to better use.

The intelligence test, not the IQ score, can tell us the level of the child's functioning in a variety of tasks which measure general intelligence and which are intimately correlated with classroom learning. The goal of testing then becomes to describe the developmental level the child has attained. The next step requires that educators and psychologists together formulate the educational environment necessary to raise the child to the next developmental level.

1. According to Binet and Stern, what does the Binet test measure? After World War I, what else was the IQ test used to measure? Summarize the related dilemma cited by Zach.

2. Describe in your own words the three assumptions Zach says are implied in a standardized test.

3. How does the phenomenon of "overachievers" indicate a defect in the IQ test?

4. What is Jensen's position on racial IQ differences? Cite the major argument for his position and several criticisms made against it. What's wrong with using Head Start as the basis for a racial argument?

5. What does Jensen's position say about the individual black student?

6. What does Zach suggest is the most justifiable use of the IQ test?

Preparing Traditional Achievement Tests

OBJECTIVES

When you complete unit 33, you should be able to:

* construct original completion-type and selection-type test items appropriate to selected objectives, and identify specific flaws in sample items;
* list, with original illustrations, several technical errors to be avoided in constructing multiple-choice questions.

As we have seen, a good test is both valid and reliable. This means, among other things, that the test actually measures achievement of the objectives of the instruction. As you know, the basic question you must ask about a test item is: will the student answer this question correctly if and only if he has mastered the skill/knowledge specified in the objective?

Even if a test item is directly related to the material of the objectives, it can still be a poor test item because of its format. If the item is poorly written, it will not give a clear measure of the student's achievement.

The author is indebted to Dr. Jon C. Marshall, Unitersity of Missouri, who wrote the original version of this unit specifically for use in this text. The author, however, assumes responsibility for its revisions. Used by permission.

403

Just as there are a variety of ways to formulate a test item, so there are a variety of ways in which that formulation can lack validity or reliability. In this unit you will learn how to avoid format errors in writing supply, essay, selection, and multiple-choice types of test items.

Supply Type Items

Supply type items are those test questions in which the examinee is required to construct an answer. This constructed answer may be as short as one word or as long as several pages. We will consider the following types: *completion,* a one or two word response; *essay–short-answer,* a one phrase up to a several sentence response; *essay–extended-answer,* a response of one or several paragraphs.

Completion Items

The completion item is usually the easiest to construct. However, care must be taken to assure that the item is *clear* and unambiguous, yet not so specific as to make the item extremely obvious or extremely detailed.

A completion item is usually either in the form of a complete question or in the form of an incomplete sentence calling for a fill-in. Compare these two completion items:

What is the answer to a multiplication problem called?
The _____ is the answer to a multiplication problem.

The incomplete sentence is probably the most common format for completion items and probably the least valid. They are very likely to be ambiguous, difficult to read, and/or contain misleading or undesirable prompts. And all too often, teachers simply lift such completion items directly from the text. For example, try to complete the following item:

The incomplete sentence format should be used ____(1)____ because items written in this format are often either ____(2)____ or ____(3)____.

If you responded (1) sparingly, (2) obvious, (3) ambiguous, you get a gold star; otherwise ten lashes. The horrible part of this absurdity is that it is what some teachers typically do, and they call it testing. The item is taken out of context and thus is difficult to answer. Even though the idea is important, the particular words chosen have little importance. Furthermore, the lifting of textual material reinforces the poor study habit of memorizing isolated bits of information.

The better alternative to the incomplete sentence format is the direct question. Direct questions are less likely to be ambiguous, contain extraneous clues, and other such item faults. The reading difficulty will be lower. When key words are omitted from sentences they become more difficult to read. The item may measure reading comprehension rather than the content intended.

The following few pages contain a set of programmed frames designed to help you identify good completion items. Begin with Frame 1 and follow the directions in each frame.

Frame 1

Which of the following is the best completion item?

Who was one of the earliest developers of the automobile? . . . *turn to p. 407, Frame 2.*

How did Lyndon Johnson become President of the United States: . . . *turn to p. 408, Frame 3.*

Japan is a highly ——(1)—— nation. . . . *turn to p. 409, Frame 4.*

In what year was the Wankel engine first developed? . . . *turn to p. 410, Frame 5.*

You selected one of the poorest items: "Who was one of the earliest developers of the automobile?" This item does present a complete question rather than an incomplete statement. But when we ask "who," do we want the name of an individual or a company? The term "developers" does not help. Is the examiner after the initial inventor or the first group to put automobiles into production? The term "earliest" would leave the answer to the question open to almost any individual or group significant in the development of the automobile industry. The location of the developer was not specified. The examiner probably meant the United States, but similar research and development was also being conducted in several other countries.

This type of item is usually defended on the grounds that if the student knows the material taught in class then he will know the intended answer. Nonsense! It is unfair to ask students to answer the question intended. Moreover, it assumes that the only relevant information is that learned in class and consequently it discourages independent study.

Turn back to Frame 1 and make another selection.

Which of the following is the best completion item?

What is the simplest living organism? . . . *turn to p. 408, Frame 7.*

What is a cell? . . . *turn to p. 409, Frame 8.*

____(1)____ developed the first piston-and-cylinder steam engine. . . . *turn to p. 410, Frame 9.*

Frame 3

This item is a poor completion question. By definition a completion item should be answered with one or two words. It might be possible, but highly unlikely, with this item.

"How did Lyndon Johnson become President of the United States?"

Probably the word "assassination" was the intended answer. However, the question is poorly worded to elicit this response. This item could be revised to ask either of the following questions:

"How did President Kennedy die?"

or

"What happened to the President of the United States that allowed Lyndon Johnson to succeed to the presidency?"

Both of these questions are precise enough to elicit a specific response. The original item asked a general question that would take considerable time and space to answer. Even as an essay question it inadequately specified or limited the response.

Turn back to Frame 1 on p. 406 and make another selection.

Frame 7

This is the best of the three items because it is a direct, clearly stated question.

You should note that all the completion items have measured at the knowledge level. When measuring higher order skills, the item responses tend to be of the longer essay type.

Turn to page 411.

Frame 4

You chose an incomplete sentence over a complete question: "Japan is a highly ____ (1)____ nation."

How would you respond? In what context was the item written? The word "industrialized" would complete the statement and might well be the intended response. However, other terms such as "populated" would also complete the statement. Any term that correctly completes the statement would have to be marked as a right answer, even if radically different from that intended by the examiner.

The item should be revised to ask a specific question. The intent of the item to ask about population, industrialization, or the like would then be clarified.

Turn back to Frame 1 on p. 406 and make another selection.

Frame 8

This is not the best item. Even though the item is simply stated, the intended answer is not clear.

"What is a cell?"

A possible correct response to the item would be protoplasm, but other quite different responses could be made, such as receptacle or small room. Some students would try to explain the structure of a cell rather than answering it as a completion item.

Any correct response should be given credit, even if unrelated to the material that had been studied. Otherwise the student is put into the situation of having to second-guess the teacher.

Turn back to Frame 6 on p. 407 and make another selection.

Frame 5

Correct! You chose the best item. It was the only one that asked a specific, unambiguous question.
Turn to Frame 6 on p. 407.

Frame 9

The format is wrong, and it is written as an incomplete sentence rather than a question. It could be easily revised as follows:
"Who developed the first piston-and-cylinder steam engine?"
Now is not this a better reading item? There are a few instances when incomplete sentences would make better items, but they are very few.
Turn back to page 404 and go through the material.

Essay Items

Essay test items are most commonly used at the college level, because of the sophistication of language skills needed to write responses.

The writing of essay items often seems deceivingly simple. It is not uncommon for an instructor to think up items on the way to class or as he is writing them on the board. This same instructor will then defend his test items as clear and valid. If he is trapped by a student arguing the merits of an item, he will say "but you should have known what I intended" or "the good students know what I wanted." These are poor arguments for poor measurement.

A good essay test item has two technical qualities—*specificity* and *limits.* It asks a very specific question and limits the response to clearly specified points of comparison.

Poorly written essay tests are notorious for their low reliability. It is quite common to have two equally qualified readers disagree markedly when grading an essay response. Five recommendations are made here to maximize reliability.

1. Take extreme care in writing the test items; make sure that the question states a problem which is limited and explicitly *defined.*
2. Prepare detailed directions that explain precisely what is *expected* and give time or length limits to responses; the setting of length limits, particularly with short-answer questions, will help to stop the bluffing that often takes place;
3. Use *short answer* rather than extended-answer questions; the short-answer questions require less testing time per item, are marked more easily, and are less apt to invite bluffing.
4. Prepare a detailed *key;* this can be used for scoring, but it can also aid in spotting difficulties and thus making revisions.
5. *Carefully* mark the papers.

Three basic procedures are used for marking. One method is to compare the papers to prepared standards. Another method is to assign specific points for specific ideas or facts in the paper. The third is to sort the papers into predetermined piles.

One final point: do not use optional test items. This allows and often encourages students to study part of the material. Research studies indicate that readers do not mark different questions equally and that students are poor estimators of how well they can respond to specific test items.

Begin with Frame 10 and follow the directions.

Frame 10

Which of the following is the best essay item?

Should America have gotten involved in the Vietnam conflict?

. . . turn to p. 413, Frame 11.

Discuss the factors that led to the 1971 wage-price freeze.

. . . turn to p. 414, Frame 12.

Compare a contemporary V-8 engine with an equivalent powered Wankel according to size, number of parts, and basic operating procedure.

. . . turn to p. 413, Frame 13.

Compare and contrast the policies of President Nixon with those of President Johnson.

. . . turn to p. 414, Frame 14.

Frame 11

"Should America have gotten involved in the Vietnam conflict?"

Even though a yes or no is all that is asked for, most instructors would not give a student credit for such an answer. They would insist that the examinee explain his answer, since that is what was intended, though not asked. The essay question should *explicitly specify* what the instructor expects in an answer and limit the problem so that it is a reasonable task.

"Should America have gotten involved in the Vietnam conflict? Defend your position." This revised form of the question is a definite improvement over the original. However, the question is basically unlimited. Volumes can be written on this question. It is unrealistic to expect students to do justice to the question on an examination.

The question should be qualified. For example: "There has been considerable debate as to whether or not America should have gotten involved in the Vietnam conflict. Defend their involvement according to several relevant political and social events immediately preceding American involvement."

Turn back to Frame 10 on p. 412 and make another selection.

Frame 13

You made a good selection. The item asks a specific question and limits the response to three specific points of comparison. Remember that these two qualities—*specificity* and *limits*—are basic technical criteria for judging any essay item.

Turn to page 415.

Frame 12

"Discuss the factors that led to the 1971 wage-price freeze."

This essay item has two major faults. First, the behavior expected of the student is not specified. The term "discuss" does not indicate how the student is to deal with the problem. The second fault is that the problem is not realistically limited. The directions instruct the examinee to discuss the factors. How many? What depth? Is the examinee to discuss all factors or just the most important ones? These questions need to be answered as part of the essay item.

The item might be revised as follows: "State two political factors related to President Nixon declaring the 1971 wage-price freeze? Explain the probable effects of these factors on his decision."

The question is now *explicit* and *limited.* It does not ask the student to deal with all the factors, just two political ones.

Turn back to Frame 10 on p. 412 and make another selection.

Frame 14

"Compare and contrast the policies of President Nixon with those of President Johnson." This item has two major faults: (1) "compare and contrast" does not explicitly *define* the expected type of response, and (2) "policies" does not sufficiently *limit* the problem. Compare and contrast is a catch-all set of terms that can mean anything. It is often used when a person is not really sure what he wants.

Which policies are the students to deal with and at which points in time? Policies do not stay totally consistent throughout a man's term in office. Furthermore, a president recommends policy on foreign affairs, economic conditions, welfare, and so on. The specific areas of policy and time periods should be specified in the question.

Turn back to Frame 10 on p. 412 and make another selection.

Selection Type Items

Selection type items are those text questions that provide a set of possible answers from which the examinee is to choose the best or correct one. These items can be classified into three types: multiple-choice, matching, or true-false.

The generalized form is the *multiple-choice* question. It's structured as follows:

Stem: What is the largest city in the United States?

Alternatives: A. Chicago   } Foils
            B. Los Angeles
            C. New York   Keyed Response
            D. San Francisco } Foils
            E. Washington

The other two selection type items can be viewed as special forms of the multiple-choice item. The *matching* item is a set of interrelated multiple-choice questions with an introductory set of instructions to the items, a set of item stems called premises, and a common set of alternatives. The directions should specify the topic of the item set and whether or not the alternatives can be used more than once. Furthermore, the set should contain a homogeneous group of items; for example, all dates, places, names, or the like.

The *true-false* item can be considered a multiple-choice stem with only two alternatives to respond to the question, such as true-false, yes-no, or right-wrong. Usually the true-false test consists of a set of directions specifying the response mode followed by one-sentence test items.

Here are some hints toward improving test design with selection type items.

1. The stem should specify *exactly* what the examinee is to do. The stem should clarify the problem so well that a student who knows the answer doesn't have to refer to the alternatives to understand the question.
2. The stem should *not* include any *superfluous* words or phrases.
3. The stem should be a *complete statement* or question.
4. The test should have a cover page containing overall *directions*. These should include specifications as to the types of items in the test, method for responding, and sample items.
5. Two basic criteria for *item grouping* should be followed. First, items should be organized by *type* so that, for example, the multiple-choice items are together, true-false items together, and essay items together. Within these groupings, the items should be organized by *content* so

that items measuring similar things are together. The exception to this is when the grouping would provide undesirable clues to the correct answers.

6. The arrangement of items on a page, *item placement,* depends in part upon the age level of the examinees and the type and size of the item. In general, it is best to split the typed-page into two columns much like a newspaper. This will save space and make the test more readable. The exception to this would be with items requiring a large amount of space and when testing young children where oversized type is used. The complete test item should always be contained in the column on the page on which it was started. It should never be carried over to another page or column.

7. If at all possible, use a separate *answer sheet* for students to respond to the test items. The results of published research indicate that with instruction, separate answer sheets can be used as early as the third grade.

Begin with Frame 15 and follow the directions.

Frame 15

Which of the following is the best item *stem*?

Listed below are four possible functions of minor characters in a story. Rank these from the most to least important in the story *Red Badge of Courage.... turn to p. 418, Frame 16*

Why did the people on board the Mayflower rush up on deck when they heard the lookout shout, "Land ho"?... *turn to p. 419, Frame 17*

The author of your textbook recommended:... *turn to p. 419, Frame 20*

Frame 16

Good choice! Note that this stem *specifies exactly* what the examinee is expected to do. Given the list of functions as the criteria, the examinee could apply them to the given book and supply an answer. The alternatives would serve only to save administration and scoring time. Note that it is not necessary in this item to go to the alternatives to clarify the problem. Whether or not this is necessary is a good criterion against which to judge the adequacy of an item stem.

Turn to page 421.

Frame 19

This stem is poor since it does not *define* and *limit* the problem. In it should be specified the particular concern on appointments with which the item is to deal.

Turn to page 421.

Frame 17

Not a bad choice. Technically speaking, this stem is fairly good. However, what justification do we have for asking this type of test item? If education is the memorization of trivia, then this type of item is justified.

Of final note, this item is faulty in that nobody really knows why the people rushed up on deck, and there were perhaps as many reasons as there were individuals. This type of ambiguity should be avoided.

In 1964, President Johnson appointed:
Is this a good or a poor stem for a multiple-choice item?
Good ... *turn to p. 420, Frame 18*
Bad ... *turn to p. 418, Frame 19*

Frame 20

This is the poorest choice you could have made. Items of this type are quite common, but this does not justify their existence.

"The author of your textbook recommended:"
What is the problem presented in this item? All you can tell is that the question deals with recommendations that may or may not have been made in your textbook. The *specific* problem should be stated in the stem.

If this question as stated is really important, then you could set it up as a set of true-false items with each statement being a recommendation.

Turn back to Frame 15 on p. 417 and make another selection.

Frame 18

You really missed the point! This item is poorly constructed. Without examining the alternatives it is impossible to determine the problem of concern. This type of stem often leads to a set of heterogeneous alternatives. This problem is often avoided when using a complete statement or question as a stem.

Turn back to Frame 15 on p. 417 and make a new selection.

A multiple-choice item consists of the stem and alternatives. We have already noted that the stem is to state the problem and set the frame of reference for the item. The alternatives further delineate the problem so that there is one and only one correct answer which will be chosen by the well-informed student.

The alternatives are made up of the distractors and the correct response. The function of the distractors is to attract students who do not really know the correct answer. Therefore they should consist of *common* misconceptions of and faults made by students. The idea is not to trick a knowing student into selecting the wrong response, but to attract the unknowing student.

Here are some guidelines for constructing good alternatives:

1. Alternatives should be *grammatically* consistent with the stem;
2. Each alternative should be a *plausible* answer;
3. Alternatives should not contain irrelevant verbal *clues;*
4. Avoid overusing locations *"B"* and *"C"* for the correct response;
5. Avoid including two *opposites,* with one of them the correct response;
6. Avoid making the correct response *longer* and more complete than the other alternatives.

Begin with Frame 21 and follow the directions.

Frame 21

Which of the following is the best constructed test item?

B. F. Skinner is a:

  A. Economist.
  B. Engineer.
  C. Orthopedist.
 **D. Psychologist.

. . . turn to p. 423, Frame 22

The reliability of an achievement test is determined using a fourth grade group. If the reliability is reestimated using a sample of third, fourth, and fifth graders, how would the second estimate most likely compare with the first one?

 **A. Higher
  B. No difference
  C. Lower
  D. None of the above

. . . turn to p. 425, Frame 23

On Saturday, Tommy went to the ballgame. He had $2.50 with him. While at the game he spent 45¢ on a hot dog, 25¢ for a soda, 25¢ for chips, and 20¢ for ice cream. His trip home cost him 15¢ for the bus. These were his total expenses. How much money should he have left?

  A. $1.00
  B. $1.10
  C. $1.15
 **D. $1.20
  E. $1.45

. . . turn to p. 426, Frame 24

When was World War II fought?

  A. Early 1900s
  B. Pre-1940
 **C. Before 1950
  D. During 1950s
  E. After 1960

. . . turn to p. 423, Frame 25

The War of 1812 was:

 **A. short
  B. long
  C. horrible
  D. with Russia

. . . turn to p. 425, Frame 26

Frame 22

You stated that the following item is the best one:

B. F. Skinner is a:

    A. economist
    B. engineer
    C. orthopedist
**D. psychologist

As with many items of this type, there is a *verbal clue* that allows you to determine that response D is the correct answer. That is, the article "a" is grammatically inconsistent with the first three alternatives.

This item could easily be revised as follows:

Who is B. F. Skinner?

    A. An economist
    B. An engineer
    C. An orthopedist
    D. A psychologist

Remember that the alternatives of an item act as a team. Each member must be grammatically consistent with the stem and the foils must be plausible to those persons who do not know the right answer.

Turn back to Frame 21 on p. 422 and make another selection.

Frame 25

You chose the following item:

When was World War II fought?

    A. early 1900s
    B. pre-1940
**C. before 1950
    D. during 1950s
    E. after 1960

This item contains a very common fault: *overlapping* alternatives. You can quickly eliminate alternatives A and B because if A is correct, so are B and C and if B is correct, so is C. This reduces the item to three alternatives instead of the original five. The item could be revised as follows:

In which of the following time periods was World War II fought?

     A. 1898–1905
     B. 1914–1917
     C. 1928–1936
  **D. 1939–1945

Now the time periods are more specifically stated and nonoverlapping.

Turn back to Frame 21 on p. 422 and make another selection.

Frame 23

You state that the following was the best item:

The reliability of an achievement test is determined using a fourth grade group. If the reliability is re-estimated using a sample of third, fourth, and fifth graders, how would the second estimate most likely compare with the first one?

  **A. higher
    B. no difference
    C. lower
    D. none of the above

The problem encountered in this item is common to those persons who seem to feel that there is something holy in using four or five alternatives. In this case, it is ridiculous. The first three alternatives are all inclusive. The result can be either higher, same as, or lower. There is no other choice. Thus response D is not *plausible*. Research indicates that poor foils detract from the item as a whole. It is better to have few good foils than more foils when some of them do not work well.

Turn back to Frame 21 on p. 422 and make another selection.

Frame 26

The War of 1812 was:

  **A. short
    B. long
    C. horrible
    D. with Russia . . .

The most obvious error is the lack of a *specific* problem stated in the stem. What about the War of 1812? Examination of the responses indicates concern for its relative length, general characteristic, and who the war was fought against. Alternatives A and B are opposites, in which case one of the pair is usually the keyed response, as is response A in this case. Response C is a correct answer in that all wars are horrible. Of final note, the term 1812 in the stem indicates a relatively short period of time and thus may serve as an additional clue to the correct response. The item might be revised as follows:

Against whom did the United States declare war in the War of 1812?

    A. Cuba
  **B. England
    C. France
    D. Russia

Turn back to Frame 21 on p. 422 and make another selection.

Frame 24

You made a good choice! This item does not contain any of the common faults found in the other items, such as verbal clues, opposites as alternatives, overlapping alternatives, implausible foils, or indeterminant questions. Move on to the next page.

Five supply items are given below. Indicate whether each is a technically good item (G) or poor item (P) in the blank provided.

_____1. Compare current economic conditions with those of the past.

_____2. What is the tallest mountain in the United States?

_____3. Explain the major reason why Filipinos feared the Hawes-Cutting Act for Philippine independence.

_____4. Do you feel that the United States should be a member of the United Nations?

_____5. There are many differences among the states in their divorce laws. However, there would be many dangers in any attempt to achieve uniformity among the states. What would be the best way to achieve more uniformity of divorce laws and yet most likely to avoid the greatest of these dangers?

1. P
2. G
3. G
4. P
5. G

1. Cite two specific reasons why the complete question form is superior to the incomplete statement.

2. Describe two bases for grouping test items on the quiz sheet.

3. How much information should the stem of a multiple-choice question contain?

4. List and cite original examples illustrating three technical errors to avoid when designing alternatives in a multiple-choice question.

5. State and briefly describe the two basic technical criteria for a good essay test item. Give several original examples.

6. Be able to identify the flaws in poorly constructed supply type and selection type items.

7. Construct an original behavioral objective and a completion type test item to measure mastery of that objective.

8. Construct an original behavioral objective and a selection type test item to measure mastery of that objective.

Evaluation of Instruction

OBJECTIVES

When you complete unit 34, you should be able to:

* define and differentiate measurement and evaluation, validity and reliability, criterion referencing and norm referencing, evaluation for mastery and evaluation for selection;
* define and differentiate summative and formative evaluation on the bases of purpose, position in instruction, and degree of specificity;
* outline several uses and misuses of the results of standardized achievement tests, diagnostic tests, formative tests, summative tests, and unit pretests;
* construct original behavioral objectives and appropriate test items using each of the following test formats: paper-pencil, demonstration, checklist rating, application or synthesis project, simulation.

Everyone who has the responsibility of teaching also has the responsibility of measuring and evaluating. Without measurement and evaluation, teaching is bound to be hit-and-miss at best.

Evaluation and Measurement

A teacher must make frequent daily decisions about instruction: what *unit* of instruction to teach next, which students are *ready* for which units, how to give each student the *time* he needs to master the unit, what test items really test *mastery* of certain objectives, what *remediation* is best for a student who needs some, what *curriculum* is best for certain objectives, how to *improve* a unit of instruction, etc. When a teacher makes these decisions, he is evaluating various aspects of instruction.

Hopefully the teacher will make these decisions not on the basis of informal and casual observation or hunch, but on the basis of student performance *data* which have been carefully collected. In other words, to make proper evaluations the teacher needs carefully collected measures.

There is a basic assumption here (with which some will disagree): *whatever we attempt to teach we should attempt to measure.* Of course some objectives are more difficult to measure than others. But if we are taking the trouble to teach a student something, then we probably consider that thing as being worth knowing, and we need a way of finding out if and when the.student has learned it. Furthermore, if it is worth knowing, then we probably want every student in the class to end up actually knowing it; 30 percent or even 60 percent of the students won't do.

A lesson plan is not worth much without the kind of measures that enable the teacher to make moment-to-moment decisions about what to teach next. A beautiful set of behavioral objectives without careful measures of the mastery of each objective is like a teacher without students.

To begin, we need to consider some terms that will be used later on.

Reliability and Validity

A good test is both reliable and valid. Reliability refers to the *consistency* and stability of test scores over repeated use of the test. If you give a certain test to the same students on several occasions and the scores of each student fall in about the same position relative to the others, then the test is reliable (presuming none of the students received special instruction between testing).

Reliability only tells you whether you are measuring *something* consistently. It does not tell you whether or not the something you are measuring is what you *want* to measure. Validity indicates whether the test really measures what it was intended to measure.

You can see, then, that a test can't be valid unless it is also reliable. Validity can be thought of as reliability plus relevance to the objectives being tested.

A teacher's main interest is in determining whether or not students have mastered the objectives for instruction. A posttest for these objectives is valid, then, when a student passes the test *if and only if* he has mastered the objectives being tested.

The best way to construct a valid test is by going to your *objectives* for the unit. If your objectives are clear and behavioral, then it should be fairly straightforward to tell whether the test items are valid. Without objectives, a test is likely to consist of items that you remembered the night before (including a lot of trivia) and items that were easy to write and quick to grade. In addition, items that include heavy prompts or other give-away cues, that allow the student to pass by lucky guessing (e.g., multiple-choice or true-false), or that require a skill that the student has not been taught, all make a test less than valid.

The reliability of a test can be increased by using the methods indicated above to make the test valid. In addition, reliability is increased by increasing the number of items which test mastery of each objective. If a student makes a lucky guess on an item and that's the only item in the test which deals with a particular objective, the results are misleading and unstable. Several items for each objective will give more reliable information about a student's learning.

Measurement specialists frequently recommend choosing items so that about half of the students will get them right after instruction. In this way, they argue, you can separate the good students from the poor students. To do this, you must eliminate all the very difficult items and all the very easy items (because you can't discriminate among students if most of them respond incorrectly or correctly). This makes sense if your main purpose in testing is to be able to rank your students in order to give someone a prize or a dunce cap, but it makes no sense at all if your purpose is to teach well. If your instruction has been effective, most of the items will be "too easy" for your students; by definition, something is easy when it has been learned well. And you also want to know which items are difficult so that you can decide where remediation is needed and where your instruction needs revision. If you want to know how well your students have learned what you taught, it doesn't make sense to rig in advance the percentage of successes and failures.

1. What's the difference between measurement and evaluation?

2. How can you determine that your tests are reliable? valid? Construct an original example of a testing situation resulting in unreliable scores and one resulting in invalid scores.

3. Why must a test be reliable in order to be valid?

4. Indicate several useful ways a teacher could increase testing reliability and validity.

Norm-Referenced and Criterion-Referenced Evaluation

There are two basic ways to evaluate a student's achievement and progress. You can evaluate him with respect to *other* students by comparing his performance to an average score (or other statistic) from all the other students. This is called *norm-referenced* evaluation because the student's performance is compared to a norm or standard established by the group.

You can also evaluate a student's performance by comparing it with an absolute standard or *objective*. This is called *criterion-referenced* evaluation because the student's performance is compared to minimum standards or against the objectives of the instruction.

For example, if you say "John was the last one standing in his class's spelling contest" you are making a norm-referenced evaluative statement. If you say "John spelled all twenty of the required words correctly" you are making a criterion-referenced evaluative statement. Perhaps you remember taking tests in which nobody scored higher than 50 percent correct, but some got A's because the grades were given on the curve (meaning the normal curve); this was norm-referenced evaluation. In other classes your grade depends solely on your performance relative to the present criteria, regardless of how many other students reach that criteria; that's criterion-referenced evaluation.

Practice Problems

Before continuing, see if you have the distinction clear. Do the following statements reflect norm-referenced or criterion-referenced evaluation?

A. "I found that 90 percent of my students scored above the sixtieth percentile in the standardized math achievement test."

B. "I want to find out how many of my students can use the slide rule for simple arithmetic calculations."

C. "I wonder how Steve is doing on this unit."

D. "Well, it's grading time again. I suppose I should give 15 percent A's this semester, as I did last semester. But I've sure got a bunch of losers this semester."

Answers to Practice Problems

A. This is clearly norm-referenced evaluation since the performance of the students is compared to that of many other students. In this case the norm was probably a national norm. Most standardized tests are norm-referenced, in that they tell you how a particular student does compared to a sample of students across the country.

B. This is a criterion-referenced statement. The teacher is not interested in who knows more about the slide rule than others, but simply in who can meet certain minimum criteria in the use of the slide rule. These criteria have nothing to do with the skills of other students.

C. This one is not clear. If the teacher is wondering how Steve is doing compared to how other students are doing, then it's norm-referenced. If the teacher wants to know how Steve is doing in relation to the objectives of the unit, then it's criterion-referenced.

D. It's clear that this teacher is accustomed to grading on the curve (the highest 15 percent get A's, etc., regardless of any absolute degree of learning). He seems tempted to skew the curve a little this semester but only because of a general group deficiency, not because fewer students mastered his objectives for the course. One thing is for sure, if only 15 percent get A's, either his criteria are very unreasonable or the instruction was poor.

Evaluation for Selection

Throughout the history of education, one of the schools' most important tasks has been that of *selection*. The assumption has been that about 5–10 percent of first grade students really have what it takes to go all the way through a full professional education. An important function of the schools was to *iden-*

tify those few highly qualified students and give them special treatment and advantages. For the other 90–95% of the students, the schools established lower and, for some, minimal objectives, tolerated a student's partial achievement of those objectives, and allowed these students to be dropped at various stages of the education system.

This view of evaluation's purpose as being primarily to predict and select is changing, though not drastically. Particularly in countries such as ours, most young people complete high school (with varying degrees of success) and many of them continue for at least a year or two in higher education. With most students going this far through the education system, prediction and selection procedures become less meaningful. Education is thus being forced to concern itself with the fullest development of *all* students, and this in turn forces a concern more for methods of *maximizing the learning of each student* than for methods of predicting and selecting talent.

But the "honor student syndrome" still dominates many aspects of schooling. Quality education is still thought of as a pyramid of learning tasks, each of which is presumed to be more difficult than the last as one moves through them; as students move up this ladder, fewer and fewer will have the native ability or motivation to make it in the higher regions of scholarship. Those who prove to be nonhonor students but still wish to "continue their education" (or who must be retained in school) are rerouted through lower "remedial" rungs of the ladder or counseled and encouraged into technical "career" training deemed appropriate to their abilities (as exemplified and supported, for example, by high school counseling and college admission procedures). The fact that this lower rung curriculum is sometimes more functional and valuable than what the honor student learns is a fortunate accident. Despite the rhetoric, educational policy is dominated more by a need to identify the exceptional potential of a few than by a need to be responsible for the success of all.[1]

This can perhaps be seen most clearly in the role that examinations and *grading* play in education. Generally the purpose of evaluation is to grade and classify students. Examinations are used primarily to decide who is to be permitted to go on to the next level; their results, along with teacher judgments, are turned into a grading system in which all students are classified several times a year. These grades are then used to make critical decisions about a student's worth and his educational future, on the basis of whether he succeeded (A or B), failed (D or F), or just got by (C). But rarely are the grades used to make change decisions in a student's instruction which might insure that *each* student did *learn* what the school regarded as important.

---

[1] Benjamin Bloom, "Individual Differences in School Achievement: A Vanishing Point," *Education at Chicago* (Winter 1971); R. Hutchins, "The Schools Must Stay," *The Center Magazine* (January 1973).

This system of categorizing students is generally designed to approximate a normal distribution, and the system is highly consistent from level to level. Some students are told several times a year that they are talented, good, desirable students (those getting A's and B's), and others are frequently reminded that they are slow, tolerated, untalented, and undesirable (those getting D's and F's). Rarely is the *instruction* itself rated in the same way on the basis of how many and how well students learn. But many students are physically and legally imprisoned for a decade or more in a system that frequently and consistently reminds them that they are going nowhere.

The *normal curve* is symptomatic of the basic problem. Teachers at all levels begin a new course or school year convinced that about 10 percent of the students will master all the objectives, about 10 percent will learn very little, and the other 80 percent will be normally distributed between the two extremes. And most grades at the end of the course are distributed in this "normal" manner. This evaluation is determined more by each student's rank order in the class than by his degree of achievement; the F's of one year might have achieved as much as the C's of the next year, and the A's of one school may have learned about as much as the F's of another school. The grades are relative to each other more than they are to the initial teaching objectives.

There is really nothing sacred about the normal curve (except perhaps anatomically), even though educators have used the normal curve in evaluating students for so long that some actually "believe" in it. A teacher whose marks are not distributed normally is sometimes thought of as too easy or too hard on the students. Yet the normal curve is the distribution you are most apt to get from *pure chance* or random activity. If you lectured to your science class on harp playing for a week and then gave them a test on the science unit you were supposed to teach them, you would get a fairly normal distribution of scores because chance factors (not factors related to your instruction) would lead to normal variability around the mean. If you threw in an occasional science item here and there throughout your discussion of harp playing, the distribution of test scores would also be fairly normal, though the mean might be a little higher.

Evaluation for Mastery

Teaching is supposed to be a *purposeful* activity, not a random one. To the extent that we get a normal curve, our teaching may have failed to achieve much more than random effects. When instruction aims for mastery by all, the distribution of scores is highly *skewed* to the left.

For example, think of a series of lessons or units or chapters in arithmetic or algebra or chemistry or a language. Assume that these units are highly sequential and interdependent, such that unit 1 must be learned well before units 2 and 3 can be handled. Assume also that if a student does not learn a unit well, he will not have much opportunity later on to relearn it. If 90 percent of the students learn unit 1 well, the other 10 percent will not learn the remaining units adequately. Of those students who did learn unit 1 well, a few will not learn unit 2 well, and they in turn will not learn the remaining units. Similarly for each succeeding unit, a small percentage of students will fall behind and drop out of the learning sequence, until by unit 10 there might be only 10 percent of the students who are able to master that final unit, while the other 90 percent have dropped out somewhere along the way. If you then give an evaluative test to all the students, the distribution of their achievement scores is likely to approximate a normal curve with a considerable range (See Figure 34-1).

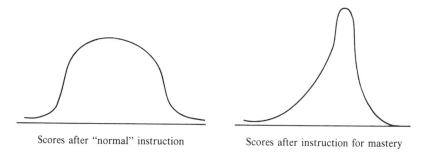

Scores after "normal" instruction   Scores after instruction for mastery

Figure 34-1

If, on the other hand, the teaching of these units is *individualized* so that the 10 percent who do not learn unit 1 are rerouted through remedial work in unit 1's material until they do master it, more students will be able to master unit 2. Even if only half (5 percent) of the 10 percent who do not master unit 1 the first time around finally succeed in mastering that unit and if this compromise criterion of having 95 percent of the students master each unit is repeated for each unit, the final test will show that as many as 90 percent of the students learned as much as the top 10 percent learned in the traditional "normal" approach. This increased effectiveness is partly due to the fact that students who require considerably more time and help in mastering the first unit or two require less and less extra time as they "*learn how to learn,*" so that by the tenth unit the difference in time between the slowest and the fastest students is cut to 1/5 or less.[2]

There is an important assumption underlying this concept; in a criterion-referenced learning system, *all students can be expected to master all the objectives.* In contrast, many teachers assume that their job is to find out which

---

[2] See B. Bloom, J. Hastings, and G. Madaus, *Handbook on Formative and Summative Evaluation of Student Learning* (New York: McGraw-Hill, Inc., 1971) for an excellent treatment of this mastery learning approach, as well as for aids to evaluation in many subject matter areas.

students really have the aptitude for their cognitive and affective objectives, require mastery of those students who are apt, and do "the best they can" with the others.

Yet we know, for example, that most children who fail to learn the basics of reading, numbers, and social compatibility in first grade do eventually learn these skills, even though their opportunities for relearning are often haphazard and painful. There is growing evidence to indicate that if the instructional materials at any level are at least adequate and if students are allowed to proceed at their own pace toward mastery of successive objectives, most students eventually master the skill—some faster than others. Perhaps *aptitude* is best viewed as the amount of *time* a student requires to master a specific task.

Of course, there are a few students (probably less than 5 percent) who have special disabilities (usually physically based) which make it extremely difficult for them to master certain specific skills. But, given a sufficient amount of time and feedback and a consistent mastery criterion, perhaps 95 percent of students can learn whatever we want to teach them—and learn it extremely well. They can earn a grade of "A," presuming that grades are used to evaluate individual degrees of mastery rather than relative achievement. This implies that when many students fail to master at this level, much of the fault lies with the instructional procedures.

5. Briefly describe two different classes of decisions that can be made about a student on the basis of his school grades.

6. Explain: "Any teacher can get a normal achievement curve; success is a skewed distribution."

7. Explain: "Aptitude differences among students are primarily rate differences."

8. Construct original examples of norm-referenced and criterion-referenced evaluation situations.

Formative and Summative Evaluation

The criterion-referenced approach to evaluation, with its emphasis on individual student mastery has led to the development of several new concepts and distinctions regarding the uses of evaluation. *Summative* evaluation is the kind we usually think of as being evaluation; it refers to evaluation which occurs *after* instruction has taken place and whose purpose is to evaluate the achievement of the students or the comparative effectiveness of several curricula. *Formative* evaluation takes place *during* the teaching and learning processes and attempts to identify areas of needed remediation while modification of instruction is still possible.

The distinction between the two is not clear-cut; if a unit of work is thought of as being composed of several subunits, then evaluation after the unit might be called summative, but if that unit is considered as one in a series of subunits, then evaluation could be thought of as formative. The difference between formative and summative evaluation is not primarily in the amount of content covered but rather in the *purpose* of the evaluation. If the evaluation is intended primarily to *grade* the student, then it is summative; if the purpose is to evaluate student mastery of a sequence of objectives in order to decide how best to *proceed* with the instruction of these students, then the evaluation is formative. In elementary math, for example, summative evaluation might test for the student's facility in translating word problems into quantitative solutions, whereas formative evaluation would try to identify whether a deficiency was due to vocabulary problems or arithmetic formulations.

Timing also tends to differentiate the two types of evaluation. Summative evaluation tends to come every four to six weeks or two to three times during a course. Formative evaluation tends to be given at much more frequent intervals and is concerned with more specific subskills within the overall course.

In this sense, level of *generalization* is a third distinguishing characteristic. Summative evaluation assesses the student's ability to put a number of skills and knowledges together, to synthesize, interpret, and apply them. Formative evaluation tends instead to look for more detailed and discrete capabilities which are prerequisites to the broader abilities.

Summative tests are composed of test items which *sample* from the specific objectives for the entire period of instruction being evaluated. If all the general areas covered in the instruction are considered equally important, then a sample of items from each area is included; otherwise the sample may be limited to some of the more complex end behaviors. The test results are then used to assign grades or certificates and to inform the students of their degree of achievement. The results are also used in some cases to predict student success in subsequent courses or to compare different groups or different procedures.

Formative tests are composed of items which deliberately test the student's skill or knowledge of *each* important objective in the unit. The size of the unit is important here. It should have enough unity to be recognizable as a legitimately separate segment of work. It's size should be small enough to be able to be handled by most students successfully without the need for intervening feedback and remediation. If some students can handle much more than the basic unit without needing evaluation, several basic units can be joined for them, but the basic unit must be small enough to be handled by the slower student. The items in the test for each unit should be based on behavioral statements of what the student is expected to learn, remember, or do with the subject matter of the unit. These may include definition of terms, memorization of facts, recall of principles and rules, ability to use procedures, ability to recognize synonyms, analogues, and translations or to formulate these translations himself, and the ability to use principles and rules and procedures in applied situations.

Each unit will probably not contain all of the possible kinds of objectives. Furthermore, some of the objectives in a given unit will be considered essential and important, while others may be only enrichment or background material. The evaluation need only include the items that are important in their own right or for future learning.

Analysis of the results of such a formative test on a given unit should produce several useful products. They indicate to the teacher and the student the level of mastery achieved for that segment of learning. If the test is a valid evaluation of each important objective for the unit, then a score of less than 100 percent indicates at least one important point of deficiency. The errors should provide a rather direct statement of the specific deficiency and therefore an equally clear statement of the content of future *remediation*. The procedure for conducting this remediation may not be as clearly indicated; perhaps a straightforward review of the same material would be sufficient, but in some cases other material or media or procedures might be called for to remedy the identified gaps in the student's learning of this unit.

The results of formative tests, when pooled over a group of students, can also be used effectively as a kind of *quality control* for the instructional materials and procedures. If a significant minority of students, perhaps as few as 25 percent, all err on the same item, this can be regarded as a strong indication of a deficiency in the materials or procedures themselves. The teaching segments related to each of these objectives should then be reviewed and revised, not only for the reteaching of these objectives to the students who failed them but also for the improvement of the unit in its future use with other students.

The above ideas imply that it is proper to "teach to the test." Many educators argue that it is not honest to say a student has mastered something when all he has done is learn what is on the test. The objection is correct when the test is simply a *small sample* of the total set of skills that the students were to learn. Because a student was taught to answer the small-sample questions does not mean that he has mastered the objectives of the instruction.

But teaching to the test is very appropriate when the test actually measures *all* of the objectives of the instruction and (as in the case of concepts) when the student is also expected to apply what he has learned to new situations.

Diagnostic Evaluation

Diagnostic evaluation, while similar in many respects to formative and summative evaluation, has two distinctive purposes:

1. When performed prior to instruction, diagnostic evaluation attempts to identify the proper *starting point* by determining whether the student has all the entry behaviors or skills required for achieving the objectives of the unit or whether he has already mastered some or all of the objectives of the unit.
2. When performed during the course of instruction, diagnostic evaluation tries to determine the basic *causes* for a student's repeated failures even when regular remediation procedures were used.

Diagnostic tests are used frequently to classify students into teachability groups, college bound versus technical school type, or bright versus slow, etc. This use usually assumes that this grouping, streaming, or tracking classification is largely determined by native ability. As we saw before, this assumption is not supported empirically, and it leads to a normal distribution of school success rather than to maximizing the achievement of all students.

Diagnostic evaluation need not be used to classify and brand—it can be used to diagnose for individually tailored instruction. Although many teachers start a class assuming that all the students are generally at the same level, most students come to school with a wide variety of educational, social, and motivational characteristics. Despite this wide variance, instruction starts at the same point for all students. As a result, many of the students are placed in instructional sequences without having mastered basic skills or *prerequisite* objectives, and their chances of succeeding are slim indeed. A typical fourth grade will include some students who have only first grade level reading skills and others who are well above the norm for the fourth grade. If you think of the complex of reading skills as ranging from basic letter discrimination and sound formation skills through a long sequence of objectives leading to very complex reading and comprehension skills, it is doubtful that any two students in the fourth grade are at exactly the same rung on this instructional ladder. If instruction starts at the same point for all these students, those who have already mastered the immediate objectives will become bored and disinterested, while those who lack the prerequisites for that instruction will quickly become discouraged, frustrated, and resentful.

A major function of diagnostic evaluation is to determine as precisely as possible the *position* of the student on this imaginary continuum so that he can be placed at the proper level in the instructional sequence.

Recall that in a task analysis you subdivide the objectives into subskills until you reach the point of a student's current behavior; then you construct a series of lessons to fill in the skill gap between this current behavior and your terminal objective. The process is a shaping process, starting with the current behavior and moving step by step through closer and closer approximations to the terminal behavior.

You can determine a student's current behavior by taking a baseline measure. In this case taking a baseline means guessing what a student can already do and then testing the student to see if you are right. If you are not, then you must supply remedial instruction to bring him up to this entry level before he begins the planned lesson.

When you are serious about the use of such *baseline pretests* in your instruction, you will avoid many problems which cause dropout, frustration from underpreparation, and boredom from overlearning.

Standardized *achievement* tests can help the teacher in this diagnostic evaluation, but only to a point. Their results can alert the teacher to the fact that a student is weak in *general* areas such as word discrimination, spelling, or arithmetic computation (when compared with the normative group), but they cannot tell her the exact nature of the deficiency. Even if you use the item data supplied by some test publishers, you still cannot pinpoint the problem because the test did not include enough specific items to measure mastery, if the specific skill was measured at all by the test.

There is no easy remedy to this critical problem. Test construction is a difficult and time-consuming task. The teacher can use the general indicators from a standardized test profile along with the student's own performance on specific tasks to generate a hypothesis about the specific area of deficiency and then devise tests of her own to determine mastery of these specific objectives. The fortunate teacher who has individualized curricula available for use with the students will not need to extemporize in this way because most such curricula come with built-in evaluative instruments that diagnose the student's proper placement in the sequenced instructional units and also provide frequent formative tests and remediation strategies to be used at each small step in the self-paced instruction.

One of the most carefully worked out examples of evaluation for mastery is Individually Prescribed Instruction (IPI). The IPI project has specified hundreds of clear behavioral objectives in elementary math and reading and organized them into small sequential units. Each unit has its own pretest and posttest, with remedial material and a second posttest to be used when needed. Teachers prescribe parts or all of a unit for each student, and each prescription is tailored to the student's current entry skills as demonstrated by a placement test or by the student's performance on the last unit. Each student works through these units one by one, with at least two assessment points per unit. Even when IPI materials are used in a self-paced procedure, the teacher is the focal point of instruction; the teacher makes constant decisions about the most appropriate next step for each student and is available on an individual basis for each student as he works through a unit.

9. Distinguish between summative and formative evaluation on the bases of purpose, position in instruction, and level of specificity.

10. Describe the formative test (size, items) and the three ways in which its results can be useful. What's wrong with setting an 80 percent criterion for such a test?

11. If many students miss the same question on a test, what does this tell you?

12. Briefly describe two useful purposes of diagnostic tests and a third harmful use.

13. How can—and can't—standardized achievement tests help the teacher in diagnostic placement? What's the alternative?

14. How is a pretest like a baseline?

Which Test Format Is Best?

There are many types of evaluation formats. It is clear from the above discussion that a paper-and-pencil format is not always the most appropriate format for evaluating certain objectives. In some cases, the objective might require evaluation by means of demonstration or interview or checklist. For more advanced objectives, the best evaluation format might be a student-designed synthesis project or a role-playing exercise.

Whenever possible, a test of what a student has achieved should require the student to perform the behavior named in the *objective,* and under the conditions specified in that objective.

In some cases, your objective will focus on a *product* which the student can produce. If your objective is for the student to be able to build a bookcase or paint a picture, then you can judge his achievement of the objective by analyzing the product. It would also help you if you observed his work on the product, so that if the final product is deficient you will be able to tell precisely where your instruction failed. If the objective is for the student to be able to define, identify, construct original examples, list, and so on, then the intended product is a verbal one and a paper-pencil or oral quiz is the most appropriate format.

In other cases a student's performance does not result in a product that you can analyze after the performance. Athletic performances, the delivering of a speech, and playing a musical instrument are examples of performances which must be evaluated *while* they occur. In these cases a *checklist* is frequently the best format. The checklist must list each specific aspect of the performance that is included in the objective—specified clearly enough so that the average person could judge whether it was present or absent at any moment in time during the performance. The various classroom observation forms are examples of such a checklist, though not all of them have the necessary clarity and specificity.

When checklists are sufficiently clear and precise, students can be trained to use them in evaluating the performance of other students (anonymously, when possible, to avoid bias). Student participation in the evaluation of other students is a very effective method for teaching all students, partly because it requires concentrated discrimination of important attributes of the performance using a variety of examples and nonexamples of the established criterion.

A *rating scale* is usually not appropriate in a criterion-referenced instructional setting. For example, rating a musical performance on the basis of a five-point scale such as: very well played, well played, adequately played, poorly played, miserably played) is inadequate for several reasons. "Well played" is so vague that several raters are likely to come up with different ratings. It would be difficult to use this rating to diagnose problems and improve subsequent performance. In several ways, a rating system is likely to lack the validity and reliability required for effective instruction.

The most appropriate format for evaluating student performance is not always feasible, and the teacher must sometimes compromise with an *approximation*. In driving school, for example, the teacher may want to teach the student to react appropriately in a freeway blowout situation or when an oncoming car goes out of control. Using a driving simulator approximates the real situation in some ways but probably won't create the neurochemical reactions (e.g., fear and panic) that the real situation might. Similar feasibility problems occur in first aid and medical training. In such cases the teacher must choose the format that most closely approximates the actual performance situation.

In other cases, approximation is unnecessary. If your objective concerns a student's ability to discriminate parts of a living cell, it usually is not necessary to compromise by using a paper-pencil test. A student who correctly identifies the cell parts in a picture may become confused by new features he sees when viewing a live cell under a microscope. Similarly, a student who can list the characteristics of an acceptable task analysis may not be able to analyze a task.

The general rule is that the format of a test should be dictated by the objectives; if the objectives are stated clearly and completely, the most appropriate format for evaluation should be obvious.

---

15. For each of the following formats, construct an original behavioral objective and an original test item, making sure that the objective actually calls for the type of item and the format.
    a) paper-pencil or oral quiz;
    b) demonstration;
    c) checklist;
    d) synthesis project;
    e) role-playing or other simulation format.

Individualizing Instruction

OBJECTIVES

When you complete this unit, you should be able to:

* name and describe the three characteristics of individualized instruction;
* describe several characteristics of a curriculum that is amenable to individualized instruction;
* state the basis on which the size of a task should be decided;
* construct an original example in which contingency contracting is used to teach positive attitudes toward particular academic subjects;
* outline several dangers and potential values in the "open classroom" movement;
* summarize the performance-based approach to instruction.

In the two centuries since our government was proclaimed democratic, the word "democracy" has been used as a rallying point for reforming or maintaining the status quo, for beginning or ending wars, for electing or defeating politicians. Despite nearly unanimous approval of its worth, the word "democracy" has lost much of its communicative usefulness by being applied to just about every form of government short of unmitigated dictatorship.

In the last decade, something similar seems to be happening to the word "individualization." It is being applied to self-pacing and to group-pacing, to self-contained graded schools and to ungraded schools without walls, to learning-by-doing and to workbook sets, tapes, and transparencies. It is being used to describe both wide-open happenings in which each student does his own thing as well as heavily structured classes using new textbooks described by the publisher as "individualized."

As a result, the word is losing its meaning. What's worse, a good idea is being tarnished by verbal incontinence and greed.

Open Classroom

A similar kind of problem faces us in discussing structured learning and the idea involved in "informal education" and the "open classroom." Here also the problem is one of meaningless cliches and excess. A student in a progressive school of the 1930s is reported to have asked, "Do we have to do what we want to today, teacher?" The history of the progressive schools may be repeating itself in current efforts to free students from the inhibiting structure of formal education. Instead of prison walls, students in the 1980s (as in the 1930s) may face the tyranny of a boring and aimless wasteland.

Though many progressive schools of the '20s and '30s became first-rate educational centers, the movement itself failed because most reformers insisted that schools must be either child-centered or subject-centered and that academic or disciplinary structure was incompatible with freedom. Even Dewey criticized the new reformers for encouraging an "absence of intellectual control" in many classrooms, by which aimlessness passed for spontaneity and chaos for individuality.

In the 1950s and '60s, another set of reformers made the same kind of either/or mistake, except that adult-dictation was substituted for student-dictation. Reformers created "teacher-proof" curricula, arguing that a carefully designed and integrated curriculum would minimize or handle individual differences in teacher abilities, student needs, and school environments. Though the courses they created are far superior to the usual material many students still use, curriculum reform did not by itself guarantee excellent education.

In the '70's, the "new" education became the open school. This reform's emphasis on the individual student's needs, his motivation, and his involvement in the design of his own instruction was a highly desirable reaction to the previous reform. But there are strong indications of an overreaction—of a mindlessly student-centered movement not unlike the worst of the earlier progressive movement.

Some have insisted that planned progress must give way to natural adjustment, that precise measurement of instruction interferes with a student's spontaneous fulfillment. Administrators and teachers trumpet the success of their open schools apparently on the sole basis of the children's joyfulness: "They're free at last to do their own thing." We observe open classrooms in which all students are actively and eagerly engaged in a variety of activities, but with no planned sequence to the activities, little monitoring and feedback to the students, and no measurement of remediation.[1]

Of course, such excess is not true of all the theory and practice in the open school movement. And even if it were, there is much of value in the ideas, emphases, and strategies of "informal education"—a deliberate focus on each student's needs and capabilities, instructional and motivational procedures tailored to these individual needs, and student involvement in the design of his instruction. These are critical concerns which must be translated into workable classroom and school systems.

Individualization

The idea of tailoring instruction to an individual's specific needs is not new. Socrates used individualized instruction very effectively. Over fifty years ago in this country, Washburnes' Winnetka Plan described a procedure for allowing each student to progress at his own rate toward common basic skills. But giving each student his own Socrates is patently unfeasible, and there is more to individualized instruction than self-pacing.

First, let's look at one applied definition of individualization, chosen for its practical value to educators: *Individualization is a function of how frequently an individual student's performance causes a decision to change his instruction.*[2]

Notice several features of this approach to the idea of individualization:

1. Individualization, being a function, is *relative.* Even the teacher who pauses in her group lecture to answer one student's question is individualizing her instruction to a small degree, at least for that one student. As with democracy, there are greater and lesser degrees of individualization in instruction, and the trick is to engineer the greatest degree of individualization that is possible and feasible, considering the resources at hand.

---

[1] For examples of these extremes as well as of more reasonable alternatives, see: John C. Holt, *How Children Learn* (New York: Pitman Publishing Corporation, 1967); Charles E. Silberman, *Crisis in the Classroom* (New York: Random House, Inc., 1970); and Joseph Featherstone, *Schools Where Children Learn* (New York: Liveright, 1971).

[2] Suggested by Lloyd Homme and Donald Tosti, *Behavior Technology: Motivation and Contingency Management* (San Rafael, Calif.: Individual Learning Systems, 1971).

2. Individualization's sole basis is the *individual student's performance.* It's not really a question of whether twenty students are working on the same or different things. The key is the degree to which objectives and curricula, size of each task, pacing, feedback, contingencies, and consequences for each student are dictated by *that* student's past performance—his scores on criterion tests for specific skills, his rate of working, his error frequency, his preferences for certain activities over others.

3. With this basic data, the degree of individualization can be directly rated by the *frequency of change (or no-change) decisions* regarding each student's instruction. The real question to ask is: how often *can* the teacher change some aspect of this student's instruction to meet his changing needs as indicated by his incoming performance data?

1. Can you think of several different ways (preferably from your own experience) in which the words "individualized instruction" are used?

2. Briefly describe several dangers and potential values in the "open classroom" movement.

3. Summarize the three characteristics of individualization.

To make these change decisions and still maintain each student's involvement, a teacher needs special kinds of curricula, data, and procedures for managing the instructional system.

Curricula

The one thing we do know about students is that their learning is different, and one of the most important individual differences (perhaps the only critical one) is *rate* of achievement—how long it takes a given student to master a given objective.[3] All else being equal, each student has his own rate. It can be changed somewhat, of course, by many factors, especially motivational. But the important point here is that instruction must allow for this difference. In fact, there is strong evidence that most of our elementary and secondary students can achieve all of our academic objectives if simply given the time and opportunity. It's not news to anyone that our current results fall somewhat short of this.

In a group-paced classroom, some students are advanced to new tasks before they have mastered prerequisite skills; eventually they drop or are dropped. If each student's advancement rate had been determined by his own previous performance, there is every reason to suppose he could have mastered the complete sequence. If schools are to fulfill their responsibility to instruct all students, each student must be allowed the time and opportunity to master one skill before moving to another.

To allow for self-pacing, a teacher must have individualized curricular programs; that is, programs which are (or can easily be) broken down into very small *units* each of which is tied to precise, measurable *objectives* and accompanied by effective pretests and posttests for frequent *evaluation of mastery;* programs whose units are properly *sequenced* and interrelated so that no skill is required without having been taught; programs that are complete enough to require only *minimum intervention* (remedial, supplementary, or diagnostic).

Most recently developed curricula are called "individualized." Unfortunately, many of these come nowhere near the above criteria, but adequately individualized programs do exist for the basic subjects[4] and some for secondary and college instruction.[5]

Truly individualized curricular programs can, even by themselves, do much to open up the schools by decreasing the rigidity of the advancement system, the frustrations and failures of students, the helplessness of teachers, and the uneven quality of instruction.

Sequencing of Objectives

Instruction is mindless and pointless if there is no order at all imposed on the sequence of tasks and activities. There is little that Johnny can learn about electricity if he can't count and add; there is little he can learn about anything academic, as things stand now, if he can't read. Each specific area such as

---

[3] Benjamin S. Bloom, "Individual Differences in School Achievement: A Vanishing Point?" *Education at Chicago* (Winter 1971): 4–14.

[4] For example, IPI Math, IPI Reading, Evco Reading, AAAS Science, Skinner Handwriting.

[5] For example, Individual Learning Systems courses in History, Sociology, Composition, Psychology, Statistics, English, Spanish, Anthropology.

addition or elementary reading has its own sequence of specific subobjectives and interdependencies requiring that certain skills be mastered before the learning of others can begin.

Individualized curricula deliberately impose the necessary sequencing within each subject matter. Sometimes additional sequencing is necessary between subject areas, as for example, in the case where a student must first be able to read and understand simple instructions in a physics workbook or kit before he can realistically engage that activity.

But often there is no necessary sequence between subject area activities during a day or a week, especially after the basic skills have been mastered. One student might spend all of Monday experimenting with the laws of motion, then spend several days researching a report on the origins of pop art, leaving his study of algebra's notation until the end of the week; for another student the order of similar activities might be reversed, without jeopardizing the instructional outcome for him. But neither student would benefit from putting off his algebra indefinitely because this would block the possibility of his acquiring a whole set of science skills which depend on this prerequisite knowledge.

4. What are the characteristics of a curriculum that is (or can be) individualized?

5. Construct your own example of a short set of objectives in which some are prerequisite to others and list two optional sequences for these objectives.

Data

To the extent that decisions about a student's instruction are based on his continuous performance data, to that extent his instruction is individualized. Data are needed to indicate precisely where in the sequence of objectives the student should be placed. Age and years of schooling are, at best, only approximate bases for placement, and achievement tests usually indicate only general areas of achievement or deficiency. *Precise* data are needed to determine exactly what the child knows and can do in each of the subobjectives of the curriculum.

Individualization also requires *continuous* data on each student's progress, so that his criterion mastery of the successive units will be achieved as efficiently as possible. Given an adequate curriculum, appropriate motivation, and enough time, all students can master that skill/knowledge which public education is designed to teach. The teacher thus needs performance information (time to completion, errors, etc.) on each student in order to *pace* each student appropriately. Pacing a class according to the slowest student's needs is inefficient and boring for most students; pacing according to the fastest will lose many students; pacing according to the average student combines disadvantages of both methods. To individualize instruction, the teacher needs the kind of continuous student data that allow her to make frequent decisions about each student's sequence of tasks, size of each task, rate and quality of performance.

Student Involvement and Motivation

Allowing students to do whatever they want in an unstructured situation is one form of student involvement, but it doesn't guarantee learning or the motivation to progress. Nor will activity-instruction motivate all students by itself, though there are many advantages to the "do your own thing" instruction over the "learning by rote and lecture" method. Most infants are not born with a native desire to learn to read, and most preschoolers would rather "goof around" with someone or something else rather than work with sounds and words. In fact, all children begin their first year of school (and their second, and their tenth) with a hierarchy of *preferences* for certain activities over others. Sally's preferences are not the same as Pete's or Cheryl's, and each one's preferences change from year to year, if not more frequently.

Individualized instruction must take these preferences into account, not as trivial signs of immaturity which will be outgrown or purged by the rod or as absolute untouchables of the student's personality, for they can and frequently should be modified for the development and adjustment of the student. Even young students come to realize the aimlessness and inefficiency of always "having to do what I want to." Giving a student *freedom* means not only teaching him a wide range of prerequisite skills but also teaching him preferences for further learning and application in an even wider range of areas. Love of learning is itself learned; education must teach it deliberately and systematically.

Motivation is primarily a matter of carefully arranging a sequence of events based on each student's preferences. If a small amount of an activity that is low on a student's preference list is required (or contracted) before he engages in a small amount of the more preferred activity, two things will happen over time:

1. the student will do more of the low preference activity than he would otherwise, and
2. the low preference activity will gradually move up in his hierarchy of preferences.

Both of these outcomes can be very valuable for a student for whom certain important academic areas are not near the top of his preferences. Even students who seem to do very well without any structuring or sequencing will do better, i.e., will move through their activities and objectives faster and achieve more evenly in all areas.[6]

An Example

Here's how it might work for some subjects in an elementary classroom. A teacher, using individualized curricula, organizes her room into several subject areas. One section of the room contains math materials, another displays science materials and devices, a third section is reserved for reading and writing materials and guides, and one section of the room is arranged for arts and crafts. Once each student's skills and deficiencies have been determined in each subject area, the teacher defines a series of objectives for his future progress.

To determine each student's general preference for each of these areas, the teacher gives all students free access to all the areas for an hour, requiring only that each student spend a few minutes in each area. By recording how long each student spends in each area, alone or with a fellow student, the teacher obtains a ranking of a student's preferences.

Then the teacher arranges a contract for each student. The contract states that a small task in his least preferred area, completed to criterion, gives the student access to another small task in the next preferred area, and so on through all areas, after which the chain begins again. Evaluation and feedback are provided after each small task, and criterion performance is a requirement for moving to another area. The contract's size is also individualized, so that each student is required to do no more in a given area than he personally can handle without serious error or loss of interest.

The free-access procedure may show that a few students are not turned on by any of the areas or activities. For these students the teacher finds other activities, games, or events, even if not strictly academic, that in fact do interest

---

[6] For a thorough guide to the use of this procedure, see Lloyd Homme, *How to Use Contingency Contracting in the Classroom* (Champaign, Ill.: Research Press, 1969); L. E. Morreau and M. F. Daley, *Behaviorally Engineered Classrooms* (Minneapolis, Minn.: Upper Midwest Regional Educational Laboratory, 1970).

these students and makes them available in say, the arts and crafts area. This ensures that there is at least one area which constitutes a high probability choice for each student. The teacher can also establish a contingency relating disruption in any area to loss of access to the next preference areas or to a time out period.

A contract-chain of four activities (one in each area) will be too large a requirement for a student who has a clear preference for only one of the activities. Since only the last area in the chain is motivating, his interest will wane long before he gets there. To maintain the quality and rate of this student's work, start him off with short contracts; a small task in the math area gives him access to a small task in the arts and crafts area, then a task in the language arts area leads to one in the arts and crafts area, etc. After the student is performing steadily for some time in this way, lengthen the contract to three activities at a time, and later to four, keeping the arts and crafts task as the terminal event in the chain.

A student's preference for each of the areas will change after some experience with this procedure, and eventually all areas will have some degree of interest for each student. The free-access period should be repeated periodically to take advantage of these changes in each student's preferences.

The above example implies that the teacher decides on the size and type of the task and the sequence of areas for each student. But once the basic contract-chain is functioning smoothly and producing steady progress in all areas, the teacher can gradually increase each student's responsibility for determining his own contracts by giving him graduated degrees of involvement in decisions about the size, sequence, and even type of tasks. This kind of gradual procedure allows students to learn to control their own learning without risking disruption of their progress.

There are many ways to achieve a productive blend of individualized structure and openness in all phases of instruction. In our attempts to tailor the school experience to each student's developmental and instructional needs, there is no need to abandon the precision, purposefulness, and efficiency that structure can offer. If we insist on an either/or basis, as past reformers have done, students will again begin to embarrass us—and rightfully so—with the question, "Do we have to do what we want to today?"

But if the curriculum materials are adequately objectivized and sequenced and if performance and preference data are available for each student (as described in previous units), the teacher and the student can jointly arrange instruction that is effective and enjoyable.

6. What are two effects of making a less preferred activity lead to a more preferred activity?

7. Give a detailed example of your own of how one might teach a student to like a particular academic subject.

8. On what basis should a task size be decided?

Performance-Based Instruction

The above heading could have been titled Competency-Based Instruction or Mastery Learning (see unit 34) or Personalized Instruction or even Individualized Instruction. All of these labels, plus several others, have at times been used to identify an instructional method that approximates the definition of individualization given earlier in this unit. Unfortunately, these labels are at other times used to refer to just about any kind of instruction, so caution is necessary.

The essential components of a performance-based system have all been analyzed in some detail in previous units. They are outlined again here so that they can be seen together as an integrated instructional system.

1. Public and measurable *statements* of the specific skill/knowledge to be learned by the student, available to the student before instruction begins, and derived from an explicit analysis of the multilevel skill/knowledge needs of the student.
2. Public and measurable mastery *criteria,* directly derived from the objectives, and used to assess individual student mastery of each objective.
3. A logical and tested *sequence* of intermediate objectives, organized into small units, derived from a thorough task analysis and organized into small units.
4. *Self-pacing* procedures which allow each student to progress through units as quickly or slowly as he can or wishes, with his progress dependent on demonstration of mastery at each unit level.
5 *Criterion-referenced* evaluation of each student's achievement at each discrete decision point in the sequence of objectives.
6. Immediate *feedback* to the student regarding the adequacy of his performance at each assessment point, with repeatable, nonpenalized opportunities to remedy deficiencies at each decision point.
7. A *research* component in which student performance data provide a continuing base for decisions regarding revision of objectives and their sequencing of measures and criteria and of content and procedures.

9. For each of the basic components of performance-based instruction, cite a real-life example in which the component is missing, to the detriment of learning.

10. In one or two sentences, try to summarize the performance-based approach to instruction. To do this, you will have to decide which of the essential components are basic to which others.

Design Your Own
Instructional System

OBJECTIVES

In unit 36, you are to:

* construct a complete set of posttest items for your previous task analysis and design presentation strategies appropriate to each subskill or set of intermediate objectives, outlining the materials you will use, the types of student responding you will require, your prompting and fading methods, and your procedures for individualizing evaluation, feedback, remediation, and pacing.

This project is an extension of the task analysis project (unit 23). As you know, it's not enough to develop a precise set of objectives, properly analyzed and sequenced. The effective teaching of those objectives calls for a well-designed instructional system. This project gives you an opportunity to apply what you have learned about instructional design to a classroom situation appropriate to your area of emphasis.

You complete this project in two steps:

1. Construct a set of posttest items for your task analysis. Be sure this set tests not only the terminal objective but also several intermediate skills, so that if a student does not reach criterion on the posttest you

will have enough information to know precisely *which* intermediate skills must be retaught and which are already mastered. You will probably want to include one or several intermediate tests also; that is, you will probably need to break your project into several "units" at those points where an instructional decision must be made about whether to continue or to remediate. Without such intermediate tests, errors can snowball and teaching effort can be wasted for some students. Review unit 34 on this topic. Have your instructor approve your set of tests *before* continuing.

2. Now fill out your task analysis with presentation strategies appropriate to each subskill. In doing this, review units 28 and 35 for ideas. Your outline of these presentation methods should include:

   a) a description of the materials and demonstrations you will use, with illustrations or samples;

   b) the types of student responding you will require of each student, and the times they will occur in the teaching sequence, with illustrations or samples;

   c) the prompts you will use in the initial stages of teaching a subskill, and how you will fade these prompts.

   d) the procedures you will use to allow for at least some degree of self-pacing;

   e) the details of how you will individualize evaluation, feedback, and remediation procedures.

Design Your Own Management System

OBJECTIVES

In unit 37, you are to:

* design a contingency management system for a classroom of your choice, specifying the behaviors, the reinforcing and punishing events, and the specific contingencies and system you will use.

This unit gives you an opportunity to integrate what you have learned about learning and motivation, contingency management, and individualized instruction.

Imagine you are the teacher in a hypothetical elementary, secondary, or special self-contained classroom. Presume also that you have at your disposal sets of curricular materials that are individualizable (see unit 35) and that you have the full support of your principal.

First, review the different types of management systems (token, contingency contracting, etc.) that you have studied or seen (see units 11 and 12 for examples).

Then begin to specify the details of your own management system:

1. State the grade level and subject matter area(s).
2. List a small set of behaviors which you will reinforce and/or punish; use measurable terms and include your criterion for each behavior.

3. List the reinforcing and/or punishing events you will use (including praise and extinction); state how you will make sure that you have consequences that are effective for each student and what you will do if some students are not reinforced by certain consequences you wish to be reinforcing.
4. State the specific contingencies relating each behavior to one or more consequent events.
5. State when and by whom the contingencies will be delivered.
6. Check to see if you have violated any of the Rules for Managing Consequences (unit 3), especially regarding relevant criteria, immediacy, frequency, and small steps; does your system focus on the reinforcement of improvement?

Your final report should be clear and complete enough so that a fellow student would know exactly what to do in specific situations.

Presentation and Evaluation Project

OBJECTIVES

In this unit, you are to:

* teach your instructional unit, as you have designed it, to a group of students, analyze the effectiveness of your instruction in terms of individual student achievement of your objectives, and identify and incorporate needed revisions in the design.

This unit is an application project in which you take your approved task analysis and instructional design into a classroom, use it as a plan in teaching some students, and then analyze the results of this teaching.

1. Arrange for a period of time with a group of students. Check the notes in unit 5 for cautions about making these arrangements. Use your task analysis as a guide in determining how many periods and days you will need to complete your teaching episode.
2. Collect and arrange all the materials you will need.
3. Mentally rehearse your teaching episode, trying to predict and plan for all the possible events you can think of. Ask yourself questions like: What if this doesn't happen as planned? What might a student do or say at this point? What kinds of problems might a student have

at this point? How could I adjust on the spot to this unexpected event?

4. Teach the unit according to your task analysis and design.

5. Analyse the episode. This analysis should include:

   a) the number of students who reached and who missed criterion on each item of each of your tests;

   b) an analysis of precisely where and why your instruction failed for some students, and a detailed revision of your task analysis, test items, and/or presentation and evaluation methods—as suggested by the student performance data.

Be sure to include your raw test data when turning in your final report.

You-Name-It Project

You may earn credits by designing and carrying out a project (study, research, or other activity) tailored to your own educational interests or needs. The project may be on any topic that is in some direct way related to the basic objectives of this course.

For example, the project might involve in-depth study of a specific and well-defined topic or it might involve your own practice at applying some of the skill/knowledge of the course or an attempt to test some of the principles of the course or you might arrange to tutor another student in the material of this or another course. Whatever the topic, you may carry out the project via any medium that you think appropriate (paper, audio or video tape, demonstration, etc.).

Before you begin such a project, you must submit your *plan* to the instructor for approval. This plan should normally include:

1. a *precise statement* specifying the limits of the topic or activity;
2. a list of the *resources* you will use;
3. a complete statement of your *objectives* for the project;
4. a procedure for *measuring* your achievement of these objectives.

When your final plan is approved (probably with suggested revisions from your instructor), the extra credit appropriate for the project will be negotiated between you and the instructor. You will receive this credit automatically upon completion of the project according to the agreed criteria.

Review and Application II

In addition to reviewing all the study-guide questions for *all* of the previous units, you should attempt to relate their ideas to each other and apply them to practical situations. The following items are *examples* of questions you might practice asking yourself as you review the units.

As part of this review unit, you may be asked to participate in group discussion with three to six other students. Use the Review Discussion Sheet for this unit to record your discussion. Be sure to complete your own private review beforehand so that the discussion can be as profitable as possible for everyone.

A.

1. The outside world's reinforcers are not M & M's or stars or pats on the back, nor are they given on a continuous schedule. But learning won't take place for many students unless one starts with "artificial" reinforcers on a continuous schedule. Outline a procedure for resolving this dilemma.

2. Identify a behavior of your own you might want to change (or develop) and outline a procedure you could use to change it. What if that procedure didn't work?

3. Specify the step-by-step procedures you would use with a student who seems to be paying attention, following directions, and working consistently, but who never gets over 50 percent on a worksheet or exam.

4. As a teacher, you find yourself procrastinating with your between-class assignment/evaluation work. Outline a procedure for shaping yourself up. What if it didn't work?

5. Outline a procedure teaching a student to "like" a subject you will be teaching.

6. Cite a nonaggressive behavior of your own in which you have learned not only that it leads to reinforcement but that, if reinforcement is withheld, increasing the intensity or duration of the behavior will work.

7. Outline a token reinforcement system you will use in your class. Include information about the contingencies, the behaviors to be reinforced, the mediating and the back-up reinforcers, when and how tokens are delivered.

8. Describe *behaviorally* an attitude you've developed over the past few years (political, social, academic, or personal) and how it developed.

9. What reinforcers are already available to you in the typical classroom situation in which you will probably teach?

B.

10. Draw a normal curve, label its axes, and locate the three measures of central tendency. Transform that graph into a mastery-learning distribution. Which measure of central tendency would you use to describe the "average" students' achievement in each graph?

11. Write a behavioral objective for teaching a child who cannot walk to walk; be sure your condition, action, and measure/criterion are precise and clear.

12. Revise the following objectives: The student will demonstrate his thorough understanding of the Premack principle, achieving at least 95 percent criterion.

13. Cite an objective from this course at each of Bloom's and Gagné's levels.

14. Cite a series of related behavioral objectives you would use in your classroom (cognitive and affective) for a specific small unit you want to teach. Include several of Bloom's levels and be able to identify them.

15. You are teaching a primary student the basic entry skills for simple arithmetic. Use a few of Gagné's levels of learning to describe how to do it most effectively.

16. Which of the following men's theories do you think would be the most useful to you as a teacher: Piaget, Gagné, Bruner? Cite several *specific* ways in which you could use theories.

C.

17. Do a task analysis for teaching:
    a) a child to tie his shoes or ride a bicycle;
    b) a student to type or play an instrument;
    c) a child to say his ABCs;
    d) a student to count to ten in French;
    e) the concept of "language";
    f) the principle of the Golden Rule.

18. Choose a unit in this or another course and show how each of the components of a careful task analysis was or was not incorporated into its design.

19. You want to teach a child to dress himself. Analyze the *interdependencies* among the following subskills:

    tie shoes
    put feet in proper holes in pants
    pull shirt over head, with sleeves in proper place
    put each shoe on proper foot
    put on sock so heel and toe are properly placed

    Where there are no necessary interdependencies, state why you would teach one of these subskills before another.

20. Identify the entry, intermediate, and terminal objectives, and their interdependencies for the general skill of task analysis. In other words, do a task analysis on task analysis.

21. Choose a concept included in the content of this course and analyze it in terms of its essential and irrelevant attributes.

22. Analyze the concept of "teaching."

D.

23. Identify the formative, summative, and diagnostic evaluative devices used in this course, defending your choices. Are they norm-referenced or criterion-referenced? Why?

24. Outline several ways, other than assigning grades, in which you could use a posttest in your teaching.

25. Revise this essay test question: What are the causes of imperialism?

26. Cite one (nonmath) example in which an instructor tried to teach you a particular skill without teaching you the appropriate S^D.

27. Devise an errorless procedure for teaching a child with the appropriate motor skills and coordination to write the number 8.

28. For the kind of skills and people you plan to teach, outline a set of procedures that are or approximate performance-based instruction and which you think would be feasible for you to manage.

29. What does the following information suggest about the instruction that preceded it: On a posttest of 100 possible points, 10 students scored between 50–60; 4 students scored between 40–50; 8 students scored between 30–40; 6 students scored between 20–30; and 4 students scored less than 20.

30. Cite several specific ways in which this class is and/or is not an example of performance-based individualized instruction.

31. Cite several specific advantages and disadvantages of performance-based instruction.

Review Discussion: Unit 40

DATE: *TIME:*

STUDENTS (identify chairman, recorder)

Summary of Topics, Questions, and Situations Discussed (identify contributors):

For Further Study:
An Annotated
Bibliography

Analysis of Learning

Becker, W., ed. *An Empirical Basis for Change in Education.* Chicago: Science Research Associates, 1971. An excellent set of readings on applications of behavior modification to classroom settings.

Catania, C., ed. *Contemporary Research in Operant Behavior.* Glenview, Ill.: Scott, Foresman and Company, 1968. Excellent research articles on schedules of reinforcement, stimulus control, conditioned reinforcers, and aversive control.

Glaser, R., ed. *The Nature of Reinforcement.* New York: Academic Press, 1971. A broad collection of current theoretical articles (advanced level); note especially Premack on reinforcement relativity and reversibility, Bandura on self-reinforcement and imitation, and Catania's argument against the operant-respondent distinction.

Goldfried, M., and Merbaum, M. *Behavior Change Through Self-Control.* New York: Holt, Rinehart and Winston, Inc., 1973. Thirty-three articles on self-control methods related to such areas as addiction, tolerance, creativity, fear, autohypnosis, compulsion, anxiety.

Honig, W., ed. *Operant Behavior: Areas of Research and Application,* New York: Appleton-Century-Crofts, 1966. A classic collection of definitive survey articles; note especially the chapters by Azrin on punishment, Terrace on stimulus control, and Bijou on child development.

Journal of Applied Behavior Analysis. Devoted to research articles on the application of the experimental analysis of behavior to human settings.

Meier, H. *Three Theories of Child Development.* New York: Harper and Row, Publishers, 1969. Describes and compares psychoanalytic, cognitive, and learning theories.

Riley, D. *Discrimination Learning.* Boston: Allyn and Bacon, Inc., 1968. An excellent brief integration of experimental knowledge about the topic.

471

Skinner, B. F. *Science and Human Behavior.* New York: Macmillan, Inc., 1953. Classic application of behavioral analysis principles to practical human affairs.

Sulzer, B., and Mayer, R. *Behavior Modification Procedures for School Personnel.* Hindsale, Ill.: Dryden Press, 1972. A thorough and clear introduction, with good examples and practice exercises.

Ulrich, R.; Stachnik, T.; and Mabry, J., eds. *Control of Human Behavior.* Glenview, Ill.: Scott, Foresman and Company, 1966, 1970, and 1974. Three volumes of application articles; volume 3 deals exclusively with educational applications.

Whaley, D., and Malott, R. *Elementary Principles of Behavior.* New York: Appleton-Century-Crofts, 1971. A thorough and easy-to-read text.

Design of Instruction

Bruner, J. *Toward a Theory of Instruction.* New York: Norton and Co., 1968. A paperback description of Bruner's approach to instruction, with examples (e.g., Man: A Course of Study).

Davis, R.; Alexander, L.; and Yelon, S. *Learning System Design.* New York: McGraw-Hill, 1974. A partly self-instructional text on task analysis and lesson design.

Gagné, R., and Briggs, L. *Principles of Instructional Design.* New York: Holt, Rinehart and Winston, Inc., 1974. A clear integration of Gagné's instructional design principles.

Joyce, B., and Weil, M. *Models of Teaching.* Englewood Cliffs, N.J.: Prentice-Hall, Inc., 1972. Describes a dozen models of teaching (e.g., group discovery, laboratory concept attainment, inductive, advance organizer, developmental, synectics, non-directive).

Piaget, J. *Science of Education and the Psychology of the Child.* New York: Viking Press, 1971. An integration of Piaget's theory and research on development and instruction.

Plowman, P. *Behavioral Objectives.* Chicago: Science Research Associates, 1971. A how-to-do-it booklet with detailed applications to literature and grammar, social science, math, science, reading, art, music, and health.

Resnik, L.; Wang, M.; and Kaplan, J. "Task Analysis in Curriculum Design: A Hierarchically Sequenced Introductory Mathematics Curriculum." *Journal of Applied Behavior Analysis* 6(1973):679–710. An excellent behavioral description of task analysis, with a detailed, large-scale example.

Skinner, B. F. *The Technology of Teaching.* New York: Appleton-Century-Crofts, 1968. A classic collection of articles on teaching methods.

Measurement and Evaluation

Adkins, D. *Test Construction: Development and Interpretation of Achievement Tests,* 2d ed. Columbus, Ohio: Charles E. Merrill Publishing Co., 1974. Brief but thorough introduction to the topic, with examples.

Anderson, R. "How to Construct Achievement Tests to Assess Comprehension." *Review of Educational Research* 42(1972):145–70. An important new approach to evaluating mastery; even more useful than its title suggests.

Bloom, B.; Hastings, J.; and Madaus, G. *Handbook on Formative and Summative Evaluation of Student Learning.* New York: McGraw-Hill, 1971. A large resource book which presents Bloom's approach to mastery learning and evaluation and gives detailed suggestions on evaluation methods in many areas (e.g., preschool, language, social studies, art, science, math, writing, industrial arts).

Gronlund, N. *Preparing Criterion-Reference Tests for Classroom Instruction.* New York: Macmillan Publishing Co., 1973. A fifty page how-to-do-it booklet. The author also has several other similar booklets on *Determining Accountability for Classroom Instruction* (dealing with specification of objectives, evaluation of instruction, and assessment of a school accountability program) and on *Improving Marking and Reporting in Classroom Instruction* (applicable to both norm-referenced and criterion-referenced testing), both published in 1974 by the same publisher.

Hopkins, C. *Describing Data Statistically.* Columbus, Ohio: Charles E. Merrill Publishing Co., 1974. A brief and clear self-instructional booklet on basic descriptive statistical concepts and methods.

Marshall, J., and Hales, L. *Essentials of Testing.* Reading, Mass.: Addison-Wesley, 1972. A standard, readable, and thorough introduction to the topic.

Sidman, M. *Tactics of Scientific Research.* New York: Basic Books, 1960. A classic, but very contemporary; clear and thorough application of the scientific method to the analysis of behavior.

Tosti, D., et al. *Psychological Statistics.* San Rafael, Calif.: Individual Learning Systems, 1971. A series of self-instructional booklets which will actually teach you everything you want or need to know about introductory statistics.

Integrated Instructional Systems

Hewett, F. *The Emotionally Disturbed Child in the Classroom.* Boston: Allyn and Bacon, Inc., 1968. Describes a special classroom design, individualized and performance-based, with a system for managing consequences.

Homme, L. *How to Use Contingency Contracting in the Classroom.* Champaign, Ill.: Research Press, 1969. A how-to-do-it booklet for use in individualized classrooms.

Johnston, J., and Pennypacker, H. "A Behavioral Approach to College Teaching." *American Psychologist* 26(1971):219–44. A position paper on the application of the experimental analysis of behavior to college teaching, with an example and some data focusing on the verbal behavior of students.

Journal of Teacher Education. The total Fall 1973, issue is devoted to performance-based teacher education: procedures, problems, resources, and some current examples.

Morreau, L., and Daley, M. *Behavioral Management in the Classroom.* New York: Appleton-Century-Crofts, 1972. An excellent, succinct how-to-do-it workbook which teaches you the varous techniques you need to set up a workable behavioral management system for your elementary classroom.

Peter, L. *Individual Instruction.* New York: McGraw-Hill, 1972. A how-to-do-it text, complete with workbook and record-keeping packet: expensive, but thorough.

Sherman, J., ed. *PSI: Personalized System of Instruction.* Menlo Park, Calif.: W. A. Benjamin, Inc., 1974. A collection of articles on the "Keller Plan," the application of performance-based instruction and contingency management methods to secondary and higher instruction.

Worell, J., and Nelson, C. *Managing Instructional Problems: A Case Study Workbook.* New York: McGraw-Hill, 1974. A how-to-do-it workbook covering both behavior management and instructional design, with helpful case studies.

Index